SOCIAL STUDIES AND THE CHILD'S EXPANDING SELF

Teaching with a Psycho-Social Approach

ALAN J. HOFFMAN
Georgia State University

THOMAS F. RYAN
Child Development Associate Consortium, Inc.

Intext Educational Publishers   *New York and London*

The Intext Series in
ELEMENTARY EDUCATION
Consulting Editor
JOHN M. KEAN
University of Wisconsin, Madison

Library of Congress Cataloging in Publication Data

Hoffman, Alan J.
Social studies and the child's expanding self.
Bibliography: p.
1. Child study. 2. Social adjustment.
I. Ryan, Thomas Francis, 1939-   joint author.
II. Title.
LB1117.H58   372.8′3′044   73-1928
ISBN 0-7002-2388-6

Intext Educational Publishers
257 Park Avenue South
New York, New York 10010

Text design by Caliber

CONTENTS

PREFACE

This textbook is predicated upon the assumption that the "revolution" in social studies education today should deliberately place instructional emphasis on meeting the physical, psychological, social, and cultural needs of all of society's children. The exciting innovations in intellectual and citizenship education are reflected in this book *only* when the authors felt that these elements were congruent with need theory.

The title of Buckminster Fuller's recent book, *Utopia or Oblivion: The Prospects for Humanity,* presents a dichotomy for the future that socially conscientious youth readily comprehend. The blessings of technology in the United States have been somewhat offset by the inability to handle and control rapid change within socio-cultural institutions. Exploitation of our natural environment, the nuclear arms race, impersonalization of societal institutions, maldistribution of income and opportunity, and physical confrontation of people in riots and war are but some of the road signs that oblivion is an everpresent possibility.

Abraham Maslow argued that man was born basically a loving creature, seeking out nurturance in his world of those elements necessary to sustain himself, physically and psychologically. It is, he posited, deprivation of the means to fulfill such basic needs as those for food, water, love, and recognition that results in antisocial behavior and in physically and psychologically ill people. His need theory serves as a major element in the structural framework of this book.

While our theoretical departure from other social studies methods textbooks may be of interest to some, most readers are no doubt asking more directly "What's in this textbook for me?"

For the reader who simply wishes to give the text a brief commitment of time, we feel that this book offers a "bag of tricks," a collection of numerous lessons, games, simulations, learning packets, and the like which can make the reader's own teaching of social studies more exciting both for him and for his pupils.

For the reader who wishes to study the text because he feels sympathy with the authors' points of view, the book offers a frame of reference which a teacher today can feel comfortable with and can defend. Further commitment can result in sharper insight into the motivation of students and colleagues, leading to greater emotional security and positive feedback about one's own teaching.

Finally, the model of teaching presented here can be integrated into a teaching philosophy which would allow the reader the flexibility to pursue his own personal goals of teaching, provided these are compatible with a need-filling approach.

We would be remiss if we did not thank some of the people most responsible for the directions and development of this book. Deep thanks are extended to Lillian R. Russo, Director of Project S.E.A.R.C.H., Research for Better Schools, Inc., Philadelphia, for much of the wisdom that led to the psycho-social model of instruction applied in this book. We also wish to thank John M. Kean, Professor of Education, University of Wisconsin, for his insightful editing and encouragement. Special thanks are extended to the many students at Temple and Georgia State Universities for reactions to the model and the development of lessons. They collectively face the greatest challenge of history: putting man firmly on the path toward construction of a utopia, and away from his relentless path toward his own destruction.

This book is dedicated to our wives, Judy and Laura, whose patience and understanding allowed us to meet our own personal and professional needs.

PART ONE

A Design for the New Social Studies

CHAPTER 1

The Ideal and the Real: A Framework for the Psycho-Social Development of Children

NEW YORK A young woman is assaulted in broad daylight. Numerous citizens witness the attack but fail to intercede. Several are quoted as not wishing "to get involved."

DETROIT A city bus driver is attacked by an irate passenger. Other passengers witness the attack. Only one, a seventy-year-old woman, goes to the driver's assistance.

WASHINGTON A research scientist employed in arms development appears before a Senate committee. He disclaims responsibility for the effects of weapons that he helps develop.

These newspaper references are representative of the rapid impersonalization which is confronting and confounding those who reflect upon our time and our life-space. Social scientists are groping for definitive answers concerning the whys of growing alienation while philosophers and theologians are searching for ethical guidelines against which individuals can judge their behavior.

What roles should a teacher play in helping youngsters interpret the continuing interplay of the messages in their environment? What skills should be developed to assist youngsters in their search toward "what is" and "what ought to be"? What role should a teacher's beliefs and attitudes play in the selection of instructional objectives, vehicles, and strategies?

These questions suggest the direction that the reading of this textbook might take. They have provided direction for the authors during development of the text.

It is important to realize at the beginning that the examples used, the concepts they illustrate, and the assumptions which support their use do not represent the entire universe of social studies instruction. Choices were based on the authors' personal likes and dislikes, the need to show some diversity of style as well as content, and the constraints imposed by the model of instruction. This model provides the structure of Part II of the text.

In this first chapter certain assumptions about the "real" and the "ideal" world of the individual child will be set forth. In addition, certain assumptions related to the social, economic, political, and cultural institutional imperatives of the child's expanding community will be set out. From these assumptions will be derived a psycho-social model of instruction.

The purpose of this intellectual exercise is to provide readers, as teachers, with a frame of reference which they can apply first to the material here presented and second to their own classroom presentation. This frame is a simplified representation of a complex system—no system is more complex than the interaction between human beings in the process of education. The model presented here may be used to help us, as teachers, understand our students in terms of two vital characteristics: cognitive growth and psychological needs. The model can be used subsequently to structure learning experiences in elementary social studies.

This chapter embodies an attempt to reduce the amount of esoteric language, philosophical discussion, and debate so that the reader may quickly discern the elements of the model. Chapters 2 and 3 provide more depth concerning the complexity of the authors' decisions in choosing the theoreticians and theories to include in the model.

First, however, a little historical perspective may be useful to establish a perspective.

SOCIAL STUDIES DEFINED IN CURRENT PRACTICE

A great many variables interact to determine the degree of success a teacher experiences. One of the most significant influences is the teacher's understanding of the local ground rules in force. Definitions and descriptions of content and method ideally employed in the various components of the school curriculum learned in a methods course are useful only if they are relevant to local practice. Although each school district in the United States employs its own social studies curriculum, all of these generally represent variations on one theme—expanding horizons. Many teachers experienced it in their own social studies in elementary school.

Basing curriculum design on the prevailing theory of intellectual readiness and social needs, social studies programs were developed which took the child from the known to the unknown. Thus, children first studied their immediate environment (self, family, and school), then moved into ever widening concentric circles: city, state, nation, world. Subjects were selected for specific grade levels consonant with the estimate of the average child's readiness to master content. The total curriculum was designed to provide knowledge and skills deemed necessary for successful social living. The curriculum which evolved from these considerations is pictured in Figure 1. Most readers will recognize

FIGURE 1

The curriculum of expanding horizons in social studies. (1) Self and family. (2) School. (3) Neighborhood. (4) Local city or county. (5) State. (6) Region. (7) Nation.

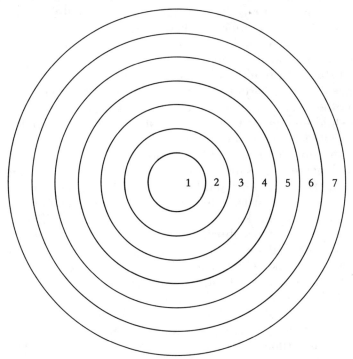

this curriculum as the pattern from which their own social studies program was constructed.

The curriculum pattern of Figure 1 was first mentioned in the report of the National Education Association's Committee on Social Studies in 1916. Despite new knowledge about how children learn, despite a vastly different and rapidly changing physical and social environment, and despite available new curricula designed to meet contemporary needs of children, our readers as teachers may well encounter this same 1916 curriculum. Expanding horizons constitutes the framework of social studies scope and sequence in the majority of United States school systems.

Originally the curriculum was designed to help a child understand his relationship to the world in which he lived. The particular topics and texts selected for each grade level were viewed as means to that end. However, over time this means-ends relationship was distorted. Topics (means) became ends in themselves; witness the classrooms where the school year is divided into segments each ending with an objective test that measures the child's recall of content contained between a set of textbook headings. *It should be stated that neither topics nor textbooks are inherently evil. They are merely tools. Topics and texts are as effective as the use we, the teachers, make of them.* Such a program reveals minimal relationship between segments of the social studies program and little regard for new knowledge about how children learn. Children begin, as a result of these programs, to think of countries in terms of location on the globe, of climate, of five major imports, or of other statistical attributes. Relationships between countries or people are reduced to comparisons of lists of characteristics. Too often we fail to exploit the understandings children bring to our classroom. No wonder that children repeatedly rank social studies at or close to the bottom of lists of subjects they enjoy and benefit from.

Yet the situation need not be considered hopeless. Educators have discovered that readiness for learning is not tied irrevocably to biological maturation. The individual child's experiential background is today recognized as having major influence in shaping his readiness to learn. In addition, we have acknowledged that the tests of intelligence traditionally relied upon to establish a child's I.Q. are inaccurate for a large segment of our population. These tests require ability to read and/or to recognize items, tasks which many children in our society have neither the ability or experience to accomplish. Some members of minority groups, particularly economically disadvantaged children, notably lack this readiness. Educators realize that they can no longer rely strictly on these tests to assess a child's potential for learning.

At the same time, numerous studies revealed that many traditional social studies programs were designed to teach skills and understandings that children already possess. For many of our students travel and television have broadened and deepened the base of skill and understanding which they bring to school. The evidence indicates that children are ready for much more than we give them. An in-depth treatment of the corner grocery store may have little relevance for an urban youngster accustomed to shopping only in a supermarket.

Suggestions have been made that readiness is specific for the task involved. Therefore, each task must be clearly defined to include the readiness dimension. If a particular child's readiness component is incomplete, a program must be designed to fill in his gaps. A logical extension of this notion of readiness reaffirms the belief that children differ in learning rate and learning style. Though educators constantly voice the opinion that learning is an individual trait and that we must consider these individual differences in planning for instruction, these same educators fail to implement their ideas because of the press of numbers or the lack of effective diagnostic instruments. This problem is compounded by uncertainty about what it is they are trying to teach. Consequently, they find it impossible to define readiness. In subsequent chapters we will illustrate an approach which provides for differences and describes diagnostic procedures.

We intend to inquire into techniques by which the traditional social studies curriculum can come alive. For some school districts, a transplant may be necessary but many will be able to rehabilitate the patient with a transfusion and extended therapy administered by enthusiastic new teachers and dedicated experienced professionals. Many schools have already begun the transformation. We will look to them for leadership in helping us shape the new social studies.

Lest the reader become pessimistic, note the contrast between the traditional goals and what the Wyoming State Department of Education describes as the goals of New Social Studies. (*Framework*, 1969)[1]

NEW

1. All facts related to the theory or structure of the discipline.
2. Built around multiple resources.
3. Concerned with concept development.
4. Student encouraged to formulate generalizations.
5. Student actively engaged in the process of proof.
6. Student activity aimed towards a logical process of inquiry.
7. Case studies used for understanding the present.
8. Concerned with learning strategies.
9. Interdisciplinary approach.
10. Strong emphasis on understanding human relationships.

[1] See the References, page 356.

11. Examination of values.
12. Activities provided at the level of understanding of individual students.
13. Planned concept development important at the earliest level of the education process.
14. Objectives stated in behavioral terms whenever possible.

TRADITIONAL

1. Facts taught for memorization.
2. Built around a single text.
3. Concerned with ground covering.
4. Student memorized generalizations.
5. Student given answers to learn.
6. Tendency to emphasize student acceptance of teacher-test statements.
7. Past blurred as background for present.
8. Concern with information built around content.
9. Single-discipline oriented.
10. Strong emphasis on factual learning.
11. Inculcation of values.
12. Activities often not adjusted to varying abilities of students.
13. Sequential planning often not emphasized.
14. Objectives often vague.

These characteristics were enumerated as part of a framework from which educators might develop programs designed specifically for their community. The Wyoming document, funded under Title IV of the Elementary and Secondary Education Act of 1965, is a prime example of the results of effective cooperation between federal and state agencies to influence curriculum development.

Similarly, the school systems of Contra Costa County, California, participated in a curriculum-development project under the sponsorship of the Department of Health Education and Welfare and the Joint Council on Economic Education. Under the direction of the late Hilda Taba, the notion of a concept-oriented spiral curriculum was implemented. The results constituted

> . . . a curriculum developed for teaching social studies in the first through eighth grades. Basic to this curriculum are certain key concepts which represent highly abstract generalizations selected from the social sciences for their power to organize and synthesize large numbers or relationships, specific facts, and ideas.
>
> These key concepts are treated again and again throughout the eight grades. Thus, as the student's own experience broadens and his intellectual capacities develop, the curriculum provides him with repeated opportunities in a variety of contexts to develop an increasingly sophisticated understanding of these concepts. (Durkin and colleagues, 1969 A)

The organizing concepts used are causality, conflict, cooperation, cultural change, differences, interdependence, modification, power, societal control, tradition, and values. In this manner social studies curriculum development has been stimulated by federal, state, and local governmental and educational agencies cooperating with school teachers and administrators. What individual teachers may do about these developments depends upon the decision of educators, politicians, parents, and a wide variety of interested citizens in the local school district.

ASSUMPTIONS ABOUT THE CHILD AND HIS WORLD

Any model of instruction is based upon a set of assumptions about the real and the ideal. Study carefully the assumptions which follow. They are the foundation of our model.

First assumption: There is, as Abraham Maslow described, a hierarchy of physical-psychological-social-cultural developmental needs. A hungry child is more concerned with satisfying his need for food than he is with doing some act of altruism. A child who has not eaten since yesterday morning will not be ready to discuss patriotism. Any psychosocial model must make provisions which allow children opportunities to move from highly self-centered responses to increasingly other-centered responses.

Second assumption: There are, as Jean Piaget has described, stages of intellectual development. Each individual moves through these stages at his own unique rate of growth. That is, while every person moves sequentially from psycho-motor through preoperational to concrete and finally abstract stages, we cannot say with certainty that "all seven-year-old children are operating in the concrete stage." Generally speaking, however, a five-year-old child is a very different problem solver from an eight-year-old child.

Third assumption: Children's personal-social and later cultural needs, as Erikson (1963) and Havighurst (1953) have described them, change with physical maturation. Content must be relevant to their lives. That means truthful and useful. For example, an activity in which a third-grade class learns how a voting machine works may fail the test of usefulness since such information cannot be readily employed in the children's near future. But if this third-grade class employs voting to decide whether money raised from their rummage sale should be used to have a Valentine's Day party or given to UNICEF, the activity may meet both truth and use tests.

Fourth assumption: Any psycho-social model must move away from a highly competitive system in which one student "wins" at the expense of many "failures." On the contrary, the effective model must move toward a system of greater cooperation, acceptance, and self-awareness. The model necessarily defines social studies as an area of applied learning distinct from the related intellectual disciplines which attempt to describe and/or predict human behavior. This is not to deny the intellectual aspect of goals related to understanding human behavior.

Fifth assumption: Children need to know. The natural curiosity of a child will not long exist unless it is fed. It will perish in a vacuum. The content of learning experiences is the "stuff" which feeds this need. The content selected throughout this text is drawn from the social and behavioral sciences.

ASSUMPTIONS ABOUT THE TEACHER AND HER WORLD

We will describe the social studies teacher as a director of learning and co-inquirer in the classroom. In social studies instruction, method includes all those actions and decisions by which the teacher influences the classroom environment. There is an ecology of the classroom analogous to the ecology of the natural environment. A change in any element results in changes in other elements. Thus, a sudden loss of heat on January 15 may result in the failure of a well-planned teaching activity. Professional teachers are aware of the myriad factors operating to influence the outcomes of instruction.

Time and again the teacher has been shown to be the single most important variable operating in the elementary-school classroom. If we accept this premise, it follows that a truly professional social studies teacher must:

1. Possess a concept structure grounded in key elements drawn from the social science disciplines.
2. Be able to select and/or define appropriate instructional objectives.
3. Have the capacity to conduct a wide variety of teaching activities.
4. Effectively evaluate his students' understandings of social science.

These are the elements of method. The formula by which each teacher blends these elements depends directly on his own knowledge about:

1. How and why children learn.
2. Levels of cognition.
3. Teaching methods designed to elicit varying levels of thinking.
4. The results of pertinent research.
5. The relationship among various elements of the school curriculum.

The all-ruling variable in the method mix is attitude. How social studies is pursued in a given classroom is finally a function of the practitioner—the teacher. When all the factors are weighed, the characteristics and effectiveness of method are directly related to the teacher's attitude. A teacher's attitude is a composite of how he feels about education, how he feels about social studies, how he feels about children, and —most importantly—how he feels about himself. A teacher's answers to these questions go a long way in defining his effectiveness as a person as well as teacher.

Method is the composite of these factors, revealed in teacher behavior. The effect of method is gauged in reference to the goals of the school and the objectives of classroom instruction.

SOCIAL STUDIES FOR CONTEMPORARY PRACTICE:
A MODEL FOR INSTRUCTION

We authors have found that our clearest thinking and most effective definition of the psycho-social model upon which the text is based occurs in classroom dialogue with our student-colleagues. They have helped us time and again to sharpen our focus. Thus, the most effective introduction to the model is actual participation in the discussion from which it evolves. Since a book reader cannot thus participate, a discussion of such classroom interaction follows. Those interactions from which the model evolved make it as much the product and possession of our students as it is of the authors. We have thanked them before individually and collectively and will do so again.

The dialogue usually begins with the question, "What kinds of things do children need?" (You might like to jot down your own answers!) While answers consist of a wide range of specifics, some of the most frequent are:

Appropriate sex model	Acceptance
Silence	Love
Restrictions	Positive self-concept
Freedom	Security
Discipline	Food
Activity	Clothes
Achievement	Attention
Success	Motivation
Praise	Guidance
Rewards	Clean air
Other people	To know

(How does your list compare? It is often interesting to note the similarities of ideas contained in different words.) As we examine the lists of children's needs we can begin to group them into categories. For example: food and clothes might be called biological needs. The items listed above may be categorized as follows:

Food, Clothes........................ Physical/biological needs
Love, Acceptance, Freedom .... Social needs
Security, Praise, Reward............... Emotional needs
Achievement, Success, Knowledge ...... Intellectual needs
Clean air .... Environmental needs

The question of children's needs is followed closely by the question of children's ability, "What can little children do?" Once again a list of abilities develops.

Children can:

Communicate	Move
Motivate	Construct
Match	Utilize tools
Think concretely	Perceive
Play	Pretend
Sleep	Love

The list is not exhaustive but it does represent a fair summary of the abilities which our students have attributed to young children.

Teachers find themselves faced with children who have these kinds of needs and abilities. The children vary both in terms of the relative importance of needs and individual ability "to do." We teachers are committed to helping them grow. We are expected to teach them something. How do we decide what? Or, having decided what we wish to teach, how do we decide the method by which we can approach the child with the highest probability of success in instruction? Perhaps answers can be found by looking at the kinds of things children need and the kinds of things they are able to do. Identifying the point where those two things come together may enable us to design instructional activities that focus right at the point of convergence. Fortunately, some people have already attempted this identification. If we talk about children's needs, we can look at some of the things that have been done by Eric Erikson, Carl Rogers, Arthur Combs, and Abraham Maslow. (References to specific work of these individuals will be found throughout the text.)

The choice of category systems to apply to children's needs in the process of instructional planning is arbitrary. We have selected the hierarchy proposed by Maslow because it seems to explain much about children in a relatively simple, straightforward manner. As we read Maslow, many of the things we had observed about children fell into place. His hierarchy thus became the foundation of our model for instruction.

Maslow suggests that human needs may be categorized as physiological requirements, safety, love, esteem, self-awareness, and self-actualization. Maslow's thesis is that people act to meet these needs. Therefore, each human action can be analyzed with reference to the hierarchy and subsequently categorized. For teachers the interesting characteristic of Maslow's approach is its entirely positive manner. He views individuals as basically good. We act to meet needs in a positive fashion. As teachers we find this a very useful way to approach children. Reexamine the categories which were used to group children's needs a few paragraphs earlier. We can now substitute Maslow's hierarchy with good effect. They then become:

Food, clothes..................... Physiological requirements
Security, praise, reward............ Safety
Love, acceptance, freedom......... Love
Achievement, success, knowledge .. Esteem, self-awareness, self-actualization

Clean air may be located in any one of the categories depending on the point of view of the person who locates.

Professor Maslow propounded his theory in both professional and cultural contexts. As to profession, the field of psychology was dominated by Sigmund Freud. The Judeo-Christian ethic provided prime influence in shaping the culture. The concepts of repression and drive constitute the keys of Freudian psychology. At the same time, Western thought was dominated by the vision of man overcoming the "sin of Adam." By contrast, Maslow started with the premise that man is good. The philosophy and the psychology may be argued at leisure. This book works from the argument that a positive view of the child is a beneficial view for a teacher. The argument accepted, the needs above set out can be categorized and translated according to Maslow's hierarchy.

Turn now to the question of ability. In examining the list of things children can do, keep in mind the reference to Maslow's hierarchy. Jean Piaget has posited the notion that from the time a child is born he moves through certain stages of cognitive development. His observation of children has produced data from which he has developed his categories: sensorimotor, preoperational, concrete, and abstract.

Piaget assigns certain age groupings to these levels of thinking, but we do not get hung up on the age groupings; the populations Piaget worked with tended to be different in many respects from the populations of boys and girls that teachers in North America are likely to encounter. Specifically, he was working with Swiss and French youngsters whose cultural background, dietary conditions, and other life would be distinctly different from those of children in the North American environment. The important thing to remember is that the sequence moves from psycho-motor to preoperational to concrete operation and finally to abstract reasoning. Piaget suggests that every child must, during his lifetime, move through these four stages of intellectual development.

For purposes of instruction, it would seem worthwhile to try to match up those two things—needs and cognitive development. This matching is appropriate when talking specifically about social studies instruction, but for that matter all instruction. It seemed to us authors that if we looked at the newborn child and consider the kinds of things that babies do, we could begin to identify some stages of what we could call psycho-social development. And we could. We started by observing the behavior of babies in hospital nurseries and when first brought home to be put in a crib or whatever.

Among the first things we noticed babies doing was a kind of random thrashing around in their environment. They keep stretching and moving their arms and legs, trying to figure out, we think, the limits of their world and how they can control these things that they seem to be waving in front of their faces. It seemed to us that this initial stage was in reality simply an exploration of their environment so we called it, with a lot of imagination, the *initial-exploratory stage* of psycho-social development.

The child is learning geographic principles—he reaches out; he rolls over; he hits the side of his crib; he bangs his head. He learns that his environment has a limit. That learning registers in the little computer that is his mind and perhaps next time he doesn't roll over so far, or rolls over slowly to avoid hitting the wall. Whatever his experience, we are talking about the initial-exploratory period, that period from birth to some point in time at which big people—usually parents or siblings—begin to change the environment, to structure it to meet needs (it happens very quickly, we think). Variously, they give the child a bottle or (to help develop him intellectually) put a mobile over the crib or bright-colored objects in front of him, or they wave hands or make faces. They structure the environment.

At that point, we said, the baby's environment becomes structured for some period by those people upon whom he is dependent—big people. This period of time, it seems to us, starts very early in the child's life; he is only days old. We called this the *structured-Dependent stage* of psycho-social development. During this period the child is totally dependent upon others; they provide the means or mechanism to meet his needs. The stage continues when he comes to the school and the teacher takes over the role of the big person in the child's life—structuring the environment, telling the child what he can and cannot do, making the decisions.

It seems to us that the initial-exploratory and structured-dependent stages interact. At least they can interact, depending upon the nature of the person controlling or manipulating the environment for the child, so both may be observed at a later stage of development.

As teachers we structure the child's environment; we take over for the parent. To illustrate the interplay between the first and second stages, consider this example. The child is out in the yard and sees the street, sees a child playing in a yard across the street, and starts to cross the street. His mother rushes out and grabs him by the ear or calls him back and tells him "no," that he can't go out into the street. If he tries it again, he probably gets punished. But later, as the child matures, the parent changes the structure by saying, "Yes, you can go across the street and play with Billie if you come and get Mommy and she walks you across the street"; or "if you look both ways" depending upon the level of the child's cognitive maturity. Teachers do the same kind of thing. But the teacher's job, every teacher's job, is to become unnecessary. Right? Isn't that our job: to become unnecessary; to take a group of youngsters and work with them until they don't need us any more? This is our real function as teachers.

We continue with the structure, but as quickly as possible, depending upon the differences in children, we try to make the structure an independent kind of thing; we start giving the child choices. We begin saying that we want him to learn this kind of thing in the classroom, and here are two activities that he can try—make a choice. Here is a free period during the day, and he can choose which of a variety of things he wants to do. Or to go further, we create a model like the British infant school; then we say, "During this period of the day the room is yours. You can choose whatever you want to do providing you accept the responsibility for your choice and follow up on it." As the number of choices provided increases, the child gains a measure of independence. But the number of choices is dictated by the teacher's assessment of the child's level of development. The independence is still limited by the teacher. Thus, the stage of development is labeled *structured-independent*.

We authors believe that the majority of boys and girls currently attending elementary schools operate in either the structured-dependent or the structured-independent level of psycho-social development.

What teachers seek, however, is a final stage of independence in which the child is exploring on his own: a stage we label *independent-exploratory*. We authors suspect that very few children have ever reached this stage in the elementary school. That very few reach it doesn't mean that very few are capable of independent learning. We suspect that the individuals who do reach it are the ones that we, the broad teaching community often considers the freaks, the weirdos, the kids who are doing the wild things. They don't seem motivated by what motivates us. Here is a cue to look deeply at those children and find out if they're in this stage of operation rather than an earlier stage.

We still haven't reached the instructional-problem level. We need to postpone that briefly and return to the concern-for-needs theory expressed earlier. When Maslow talks about needs, he suggests that as soon as a child's physiological needs are met he becomes free to start thinking about safety and love needs. There is some question as to the order in which these three operate—particularly safety and love—but that's another question to be discussed at leisure, not at this point. Let us accept them the way Maslow ordered them. When we said, "as soon as his physiological needs are met," we did not mean "sated" but rather "met to the person's particular need level." That measure may seem confusing at first; but levels plainly differ. Some individuals, needing and having little food, shelter, and clothing, move very rapidly to such other needs as safety and love. Consider the kind of people, usually young, wearing tattered clothing and carrying bed rolls around airports and bus stations. They certainly have few "things" to meet physiological needs. They manifest some other kind of needs that plainly have higher priority.

In other words, what one person might require to meet physiological needs is not necessarily what every person requires. And the same holds true at each of these other levels. For instance, an apparently little-loved child may have enough to sustain him in order to move on to be a self-actualizing person. The chances for self-actualization, however, are certainly directly related to success in meeting lower-level needs. We don't know how to explain it more thoroughly than that, but that is what we are talking about here.

People may act at the esteem level sometimes but occasionally go back to one of these other levels. Everyone needs a meal at intervals, hence may have to give up being self-actualizing long enough to go eat lunch.

CROSS-CURRENTS

We are now concerned with need stages and their relation to instructional strategies. Within each stage are a number of cross-currents. In each stage the first necessity for instruction is to make the child aware of what we are trying to do. *Awareness* therefore becomes the first cross-current in our model. If you are going to teach a particular concept in the structured-dependent stage, you might select initial kinds of experiences which are sometimes called motivational activities. You might seed the room with certain objects to help the youngsters become aware of the direction you are going to take in a plan of instruction. You might put out artifacts or posters or a big bulletin board, or you might start a dis-

cussion about what kids need, aiming thereby to develop some awareness. The second cross-current is *consequence.* The probable outcomes
of an instructional experience must be determined. They usually, but
not always, appear as objectives. Teachers don't always reach all the
instructional objectives specified for an experience. By the same token,
they often achieve results that had not been predicted. The effect of the
instructional experience as perceived by the child is the consequence.

Illustration: Bright-colored object on the table; the child perceives
it; "pretty"; reaches for it. What happens? First, "No no! That's a no no."
That is the first consequence he is aware of. That stimulus enters the
mind. But "no no" really doesn't mean much in the beginning. The child
may stop and look, but he probably will continue to reach if this is the
first time he's heard "no no." Then one of two or three different consequences will result: (1) the object will be removed; (2) the child may
be removed; (3) some kind of verbal or physical punishment may take
place. One of those three things will probably happen at this stage of
consequence. But sooner or later the child learns something about *cause
and effect* in relationship to that act. *Cause and effect* comprise the third
cross-current.

One need not believe that the child realized his reaching for the
bright object was going to result in his getting his hand slapped or in his
mother saying "no no." Moreover, "no no" may turn the child on. A little
baby will often play the "no no" game. He gets Mother's attention, assumes a devilish sort of look, and reaches for an ash tray—not touch; just
reach. Mother says "no no, no no" or comes and takes the child away.
One need not assign this game to cause and effect, or to consequence.
Either way, eventually, this behavior can become a very conscious
manipulation of the adult in the environment by the child's acting in a
manner that caused the adult to react in the past.

If we can move the child to the stage where he realizes this relationship, whether consequence or cause and effect, we are only one step
from *choice,* where the child can decide consciously what cause-and-
effect relationships he wants to establish, what consequences he's willing to tolerate. When he is aware of all these elements he can make the
choice and take whatever the consequences are, whether they are positive or negative. The fourth cross-current is *choice.*

For purposes of instruction in each stage of psycho-social development, teachers need to keep in mind these four cross-currents. In instructional activities a teacher might start with some activities that simply
create an awareness, move on to some notions of consequence from actions, introduce cause and effect, and finally provide opportunities for
choice. The build-up would be something like this example: I have feelings, *awareness:* sometimes I feel good and sometimes I feel bad. I perceive *consequence:* when I feel bad about something that my mother

did then I don't have much fun that day. If I feel good, then it seems that other people around me treat me nice. Other people and things cause me to have certain kinds of feelings: *cause and effect.* It is my interaction with people and things which eventually results in feelings. Further, I can act in a variety of ways based on my feelings. I have an option—a choice: If I'm aware of the fact that I am kind of blue, then I can act blue, or I can say, "To heck with it, I'm not going to be down today—I'm going to act the other way and maybe the people around me will act the way I act."

Some of our students employed this approach with preschool children, first at the level of "I have feelings; feelings are the consequence of interaction with people and things; they are caused by this interaction." Eventually they reached the conclusion, "I react in different ways to my feelings; I can choose the behavior that I exhibit as a result of feelings."

FUNCTIONS

One can say that in each one of these stages there are certain ways that children act, certain kinds of functioning behaviors that characterize a psycho-social stage of development. The whole purpose in psycho-social instruction is to move the child from feelings, essentially an "I" frame of reference, to choice, essentially a "we" frame of reference. In moving from the one to the other, he operates in certain ways.

For instance, the first stage was labeled *initial-exploratory.* This is the beginning; egoizing dominates this period as the child develops a self. *Awareness* is the primary cross-current in this period and stage. The child is egoizing—becoming aware of himself as a person. Instructional activities in this stage draw ideas from psychology, anthropology, geography, and history.

The second stage, *structured-dependent,* must then be involved primarily with *consequence.* At this stage the child's world is shaped, that is, structured by bigger people upon whom he is dependent. In a very real sense they govern his existence. During this stage, the teacher might introduce ideas drawn from political science, sociology, jurisprudence, or social psychology.

The third stage, *structured-independent,* focuses on *cause and effect.* Here the learning ideas are drawn from some of the sciences to create interdisciplinary studies; in the social study context, we suggest that the dominant function will be *exchanging.* The child and the people who structure his world begin to make trade-offs which increase his independence. We believe this is a good time to introduce more ideas from economics, political science, history, sociology, and their likes.

The experiences in this stage bring the child to the final stage —*independent-exploratory.*

Choice has to be the dominant cross-current in the *independent-exploratory* stage, and choice seems to bring in the emphasis on values. Most social and behavioral sciences would contribute. The cross-current of *choice* may be translated to the function of *valuing.* But to emphasize a "we" orientation, the function is named *ecologizing.* The use of this term is an attempt to focus on the notion that the ultimate success of psycho-social development resides in each person's understanding of his role in a complex set of personal, social, and physical relationships. His behavior in this role affects every other person who inhabits his life-space. It may ultimately affect every creature, every living thing that exists in present or future time.

As educators, we seek a person who is aware of the consequences of his behaviors, one who understands the causal relationship between himself and his environment and chooses rationally to act for the good of that environment and its inhabitants. This is the aim of the psycho-social approach. The model, which this presentation has been attempting to describe in words, is illustrated in a diagram on page 20.

ROOT DISCIPLINES AND DESIRED BEHAVIORS

What are the behaviors we desire as outcomes of a social studies program? The specific goals formulated for our model are necessarily derived not only from the social sciences of philosophy, sociology, anthropology, political science and economics and the temporal-spatial disciplines of history and geography, but also from social psychology, psychology, and the humanities.

The psycho-social needs of individuals in today's society are of primary concern in identifying the desired behaviors. The secondary concern is placed upon the societal needs as they complement or conflict with individual needs. Let us look at the place of the root disciplines related to social studies and delineate how each applies to our psycho-social framework for instruction.

Philosophy

Certainly the highest level of synergy in any psycho-social curriculum would be attained through building a highly consistent and deeply reflected value pattern, that is, a clear and rationally defensible pattern of personal or self behavior and of social or self-to-other behavior.

Piaget has described four states of psychological balance which need to be nurtured if youngsters are to emerge from adolescence with

A Model of the Psycho-Social Approach

Stages of Development	Age during Stage	Affective Needs	Intellectual Abilities	Instructional Strategies
Initial-Exploratory	Birth to adult intervention	Egoizing	Awareness	Providing concrete stimuli
Structured-Dependent	Adult intervention to approximately age ten	Governing	Consequence	Manipulating concrete objects and symbols
Structured-Independent	Approximately age ten to development of internalized self	Exchanging	Cause and effect	Labeling and classifying concrete objects and symbols. Making qualitative judgments about both
Independent-Exploratory	Point where child-adolescent can inquire and value independently and abstractly	Ecologizing	Choice	Labeling and classifying abstractions. Valuing and inquiring techniques

(↑ ↓ = interacting with)

a well integrated personality capable of continuing to build a well-reflected system of beliefs upon which to act. Ideally each adolescent reaches a state of psychic equilibrium where:

1. The social world becomes an organic unit which has its laws and regulations and its divisions of roles and social functions.
2. Egocentricity has been "dissolved" by a sense of "moral solidarity" which is consciously cultivated.
3. Personality development from this point onward depends upon an exchange of ideas by social intercommunication in place of simple mutual imitation.
4. A sense of equality supersedes submissiveness to adult authority. (Maier, 1969, 155)

To build such attitudes and accompanying understandings within early elementary and preadolescent children requires that teachers understand the affective (attitudinal) and the cognitive processes (knowledge and requisite thinking, intellectual and motor skills). Part II of this book is an attempt to provide such a framework to the prospective or practicing teacher. Chapter 2 includes an in-depth focus upon the problem of which values, if any, to promote in teaching psycho-social studies as well as a discussion about the merits of teaching techniques which attempt to help youngsters to be reflective in highly value-free situations. Later sections of the text provide lessons consistent with the conceptual framework set forth in the early chapters.

The philosophical considerations in our model are represented by the following goals:

Personal (Psychology) (I). The individual
Acts on the basis of existing personal abilities, interests, constraints.
Deals with success and failure in a constructive way.
Determines (gets) personal priorities in a useful way.
Accepts responsibility for his own acts.
Acts in terms of a personal system of values.
Achieves affectionate personal relations with others.
Expresses emotion (feelings) constructively.
Achieves status with (acceptance from) others.

Social (Sociology) (We). The individual
Accepts and works with abilities, interests, and constraints of others.
Extends to others the same needs satisfactions he desires for himself.
Reconciles personal desires, when necessary, with the interests of others, both individuals and groups.

Participates as a constructive group member.

Assumes a leadership role in appropriate situations.

Establishes (maintains) good relationships (family, school, or other).

Cultural (Anthropology) (Others). The individual

Accepts his own cultural background.

Accepts and reconciles differences between his own culture and the cultures of other groups: racial, religious, ethnic, social class.

Accepts and seeks to understand the cultural values and patterns of other countries. (Based upon Hoffman and Mickelson, 1970) for Research for Better Schools, Inc. project S.E.A.R.C.H. Lillian R. Russo, Director, 1970.

Economics

The theme of economics most prevalent in elementary social studies stresses that man is basically motivated by felt needs and wants. These needs and wants are seldom met completely, and when a particular want or need is satisfied it is replaced by others. Man is continually in conflict since his needs are greater than the existing resources he has to satisfy them. This notion of "scarcity," of conflict between unlimited wants and limited resources, can be used to support a number of key generalizations which can govern the selection of economic content for the psycho-social-needs model proposed earlier. We are concerned that youngsters see the vast interdependence institutions that produce things and render services. We are hopeful that youngsters will be placed in situations where conflicting "goods" exist, that is, where economic value decisions are needed.

Exchanging can also be seen as the key concept which illustrates the economic function in our society. It responded well to each of the generalizations cited by economists Senesh (1968), Lovell (1965), Brozen (1968), and Martin and Miller (1965), all of whom have been involved in the process of articulating the structure of economics.

Martin and Miller state, "The foundation of economic life in the United States is a vast network of exchanges or trade. The shrimp fisherman in Florida, the steelworker in Pittsburgh, and the studio extra in Hollywood are indirectly tied together and made dependent upon each other by this network of exchanges." (1965, 2)

Senesh has cited eight fundamental ideas which might be used in building an economics curriculum. Each of these eight ideas can be shown to be accounted for by the exchanging function.

Senesh begins with the generalization that ". . . conflict between unlimited wants and limited resources confronts every individual and nation." (1968, 2) Certainly, the notion of scarcity, which has been posited as the central construct of economics, must surely include the concept of exchanging. The exchange process of satisfaction of economic wants is then central to the field of economics.

Senesh further describes occupational, geographical, and technological specialization as ways in which men have tried to reduce the gap between unlimited wants and limited resources. The division-of-labor phenomenon is central to the exchanging functions. The related generalizations of the greater interdependence resulting from division of labor and the introduction of a money system to facilitate trade have obvious exchanging connotations. As specialization resulted in greater interdependence between consumers and producers, the need for more efficient means of trading resulted in more efficient mediums of exchange.

Senesh's fifth and sixth generalizations deal with the allocating mechanisms (the market in our society) which have been set up to make decisions regarding what and how much to produce, to set standards of quality, and to arrive at the price of certain commodities. (1968, 4) The exchange process in our economic system is central to these market divisions.

Generalizations seven and eight describe how the market can be modified or regulated by volunteer and political group decisions. Five societal goals which appear to reflect the value preferences of our society were then elaborated. They were:

1. Economic growth: a rising standard of living.
2. Economic stability: full employment without inflation.
3. Economic security: protection of income against the hazards of old age, death of the breadwinner, accident, disability, and unemployment.
4. Economic freedom: freedom of choice for each individual producer and consumer so long as it does not unduly abridge the freedom of others.
5. Economic justice: economic opportunities for all. (1968, 4-5)

This need to regulate the exchange process for the economic well-being of all groups of people, regardless of their ability to perform in the economic market, certainly has vast affective desirability from social determinants both within and outside of the domain of economics.

A person who understands the economic-exchange process:

1. Realizes that he has to make wise choices in selecting what to buy in the market.
2. Realizes that national economic priorities will require some modification of capitalism through state, federal, or international regulation.
3. Takes part in discussions which question the ways in which consumer-producer regulation operates.

4. Can apply principles of division of labor and diminishing returns in production situations.

5. Has knowledge of economic theories (socialism, capitalism, communism), as well as of their applications in some specific nations. (Hoffman and Mickelson, 1970)

The following economically related goals were established from the preceding:

Personal (Psychology) (I). The individual
Makes a wise vocational choice.
Manages his money wisely.
Achieves and maintains adequate work standards.
Purchases goods and services wisely.

Social (Sociology) (We). The individual
Acts to extend full economic opportunities to others.
Acts to influence the economic acts and decisions of business, labor, and government.
Actively supports programs to improve the status of the impoverished, the elderly, ill, the handicapped, the young.
Assures rights and responsibilities of workers.
Assures rights and responsibilities of business and industry.
Acts to provide essential financial support for governmental, educational, and social welfare activities.

Cultural (Anthropology) (Others). The individual
Acts to remove cultural, religious, and ethnic blocks against economic advancement.
Acts to aid different cultural religious, ethnic and social class groups, who participate in the economic life of the country.
Acts to foster the economic growth of underdeveloped countries. (Hoffman and Mickelson, 1970)

Political Science

What should be the role of political science in a functioning psycho-social curriculum? That is, what aspects of political behavior should teachers select to develop in youngsters?

Certainly youngsters should have experiences in which they can analyze the relative merits of differing political institutions. Their perspective, through simulated and/or real situations, should include experiences in a governing role as well as reflections about the numerous situations in which they are governed.

One needs only to check most curriculum guides to find that political responsibility and decision-making within our democratic framework is heavily stressed. Yet in most actual teaching situations the style of teaching and the political information portrayed appear to place emphasis upon attachment to certain objects, events, and people as well as on compliance with a set of unclear and often conflicting ideals. There are numerous situations in which the democratic principle of individual freedom to be heard and the right to participate in decision-making can be demonstrated in the classroom. Youngsters need to see, discuss, and participate; beyond these, they need to reflect upon the consequences of their collective and/or individual behavior.

The questions of who should govern, where certain decisions should be made, and many others are vital concerns of society and of the individual. Our model hopefully reflects these concerns in the following objectives:

Personal (Psychology) (I). The individual
Acts on the values expressed in the Constitution and the Declaration of Independence.
Participates responsibly in government at the citizen level.
Reconciles personal behavior with social and legal constraints.

Social (Sociology) (We). The individual
Acts to influence public opinion.
Seeks to influence the making and changing of laws.
Participates in the selection, nomination, and election of public officials.
Assures legal protection for himself and others, including the right to dissent.
Supports the development and maintenance of needed public services.
Actively supports the organization and maintenance of broad educational progress.
Participates in assuring provisions for local, national, and international welfare services.
Utilizes welfare services as needed.

Cultural (Anthropology) (Others). The individual
Acts to extend to other cultural groups, both within and outside the United States, the same rights, privileges, and responsibilities he covets for himself.
Supports the development and extension means for effective international cooperation. (Hoffman and Mickelson, 1970)

Geography

What role should the discipline of geography play in a functioning psycho-social curriculum?

Four key relationships appear to govern the field of geography. The first two deal with locational and mapping skills: skills related to distance, direction, and size, and skills related to map reading and construction, including use of scale and symbolization. Current research, by Jean Piaget and others, give curriculum builders clues relative to the sequential development of spatial and map-globe skills; these will be reflected in later chapters dealing directly with the varying developmental stages of elementary children.

The third and fourth relationships in geography are more complex and more vital to our curriculum. They deal with the concepts of distribution of human and nonhuman phenomena as well as the interdependences created by geographic proximity. It is here that ecology and geography come together closely in purpose and methodology. These four relationships are described in much greater detail in Broek (1965).

Stewart Udall (1968, 15) described the complexity of the situation as well as its vitalness to the survival of mankind when he wrote:

> It follows that people are interconnected to each other and to other faraway elements of the world in myriad of ways, many of which we neither recognize nor understand. It is this web of cause and effect interrelationships that makes up the "ecosystem." The concept is not an easy one to digest, but it is upon the success of getting across this somewhat tough idea to children that the future of the new conservation hinges.

The interrelatedness of the disciplines of geography and ecology can be inferred from the following quotations:

> The geographer must learn about the biophysical features of the earth; is deeply interested in the interrelations between society and habitat; needs to read the cultural landscape as the earth engraved expression of man's activity; inspects and compares distributional patterns; and formulates concepts and principles. All these means, each part of the whole, together serve the purpose of geography: to understand the earth as the world of man, with particular reference to the differentiation and integration of places. (Broek, 1965, 69)

This is to be compared to the definition of ecology in the *Dictionary of Social Sciences:*

> (1) The study of the reciprocal influences between humans and their physical, or geographic, environment; (2) the study of the spatial distribution and interrelations among human beings, and institutional functions, which are in competition with each other for the most advantageous locations in a community;

(3) the study of the effects of the spatial distributions of human beings on their social relations, and the influence of their social relations on their spatial distribution; (4) the study of the development and the composition of a community of people. (Zadrozny, 1959, 101)

Obviously the two passages coincide in meaning and even make use of similar terminology. Both submit that the geographer studies about ecology as it relates to man. A geographer is an ecologist and in particular makes interpretations of the environment.

The following competencies were selected, in these lights, to represent the discipline of geography:

Personal (Psychology) (I). The individual
Conserves natural resources.
Preserves the ecological balance of his community.
Orients himself to the environment through immediate surroundings as well as through abstract representations.

Social (Sociology) (We). The individual
Acts to secure appropriate use of natural resources in the community, nation, and world.
Works with others to maintain the ecological balance of the community, nation, and world.
Acts to improve the quality of community planning.

Cultural (Anthropology) (Others). The individual
Acts to preserve distinctive cultural patterns and lives of various religious, ethnic, and national groups.
Encourages the development of new cultural habits, patterns, and the like to replace the outmoded.
Acts to control and direct the impact of technology on humanity. (Hoffman and Mickelson, 1970)

History

The role of history[2] is seen as a process function in our curriculum. While historical goals are stated at the conclusion of this discussion, their realization can be measured only in relation to the psycho-social functions embodied in the preceding disciplines of philosophy, political science, economics, and geography.

[2] The question of including history among the social sciences has been debated for many years. The matter is of interest and importance to the academician. However, the authors feel that such an esoteric argument is of questionable relevance for the beginning teacher. Hence, we will speak of the social sciences as including history.

Edward Carr (1962, 22) characterizes the role of the historian in the following quotation:

> History consists essentially in seeing the past through eyes of the present and in light of its problems, and the main work of the historian is not to record, but to evaluate; for if he does not evaluate, how can he know what is worth knowing?

The authors view history as a reflective process. The reflective method or problem-solving method is elaborated in Chapter 3. Lessons presented in later chapters will further illustrate this process.

The true value of historical data resides in the perspective they provide. A date, movement, or individual accomplishment becomes significant through its relationship to events which precede or follow and through the perspective this relationship provides for contemporary questions. This exciting process through which children can draw from temporal data rational explanations and interpretations of events is seen as a core concern of a psycho-social curriculum.

The following historical-process goals were constructed in the perspective of the preceding views:

Personal (Psychology) (I). The individual

Accepts and accommodates to the inevitability of change.

Accepts the notion of the continuity of human experience.

Accepts and accommodates to the fact that past experiences influence his reactions to present issues, problems, and events.

Accepts the fact that projected change involves taking risks.

Solves those problems most pressing to his inner needs through rational inquiry.

Social (Sociology) (We). The individual

Accepts and acts upon the facts of the interrelatedness of man's experience—the increasing complexity of man's relationships.

Accepts the inevitability of change in man's relationships.

Acts in awareness that others interpret the present in the light of their past experiences.

Works to minimize the undesirable side effects of change.

Works to make social institutions responsive to human needs.

Uses rational inquiry to benefit those in his immediate environment.

Cultural (Anthropology) (Others). The individual

Works to make cultural patterns and values consistent with present needs.

Acts in awareness that changes in cultural patterns effect people differently.

Uses rational inquiry in dealing with problems of others outside his immediate world. (Hoffman and Mickelson, 1970)

Psychology, Sociology, Anthropology

The disciplines of psychology, sociology, and anthropology have been used to classify the experiential realms of man. Psychology is used to represent the intrapersonal dimensions of experience. Sociology refers to those experiences in which the student actually comes into the presence of another person. We realize that this is representative of only one area of sociology, the sociology of small groups, but find this use most functional for our elementary social studies framework. Anthropology refers to a student's experiences concerning people outside his personal time-space orientation.

Any curriculum must reflect decisions about what to make explicit in its framework and what to leave implicit. Terminology from the above disciplines will be used when it is functional. Introduction of an exhaustive list of concepts from these disciplines would cause much overlap of terms and would increase the complexity of the framework to the point where inclusion into an elementary school program would become nearly impossible.

SUMMARY

In this initial chapter the authors have sought to display the model of social studies instruction for which this book is written. We suggest that the reader carefully examine its contents and decide for himself whether this theory is both defensible and useful. Questions concerning the authors' assumptions should be raised. Goals cited at the conclusion of the chapter are illustrative; they do not define the universe. They may, however, prove useful in the selection and development of instructional objectives, materials, teaching-learning strategies, and assessment techniques.

The model itself is an attempt to draw attention to instructional needs in the affective as well as the cognitive domains of learning. Although we acknowledge the fact that these two areas cannot be separated in the real world, we ask the reader to focus in the next two chapters first on the affective and then on the cognitive domain. In this way we attempt to strengthen understanding of each area. The reader who thoroughly understands the distinctions and relationships of affect to cognition will be prepared for the application section: Part II, Plans for Action with the Developing Child.

CHAPTER 2

From Egoizing to Ecologizing: A Model for Affective Development

> . . . responsible freedom grows and develops from inside the person. The child must first learn self-respect and a sense of dignity that grows out of his increasing self-understanding before he can learn to respect the personalities and rights and differences of others. (Axline, 1964, 1)

This chapter is about the affective development of children through the early and elementary phase of their education. It expands on Axline's statement. "Affective" refers to the dimension of behavior which reflects a person's feelings, attitudes, and values. No human act is either totally cognitive or totally affective. Indeed, one does not really know a thing until he feels it. Therefore our focus on affect in this chapter is a matter of emphasis, not of distinction.

The precise meaning of each word printed on this page may be found in your dictionary. These words have been strung together to communicate some ideas the authors feel are important. That they can be read and defined does not guarantee that the communication will be effective. A reader may not feel that these words are important or may not perceive their meaning in the manner expected. (One suspects that communication may be enhanced by foul weather and deterred by beautiful sunny days.) This chapter deals with the question of feelings and how they affect a person's perception of himself, of others, and of the environment in which they live.

Our perception of the world is based on experience and feeling. As you look at the picture below what you see is shaped by your experience. You may perceive a poor, happy, lonely, adventurous, neglected, dirty, loved, . . . boy. What determines your perception?

This is the affective dimension of learning.

How Do You See It? Photo Courtesy of Addressograph-Multigraph Corporation.

GLASSES — TINTED

Each of us carries our personal set of glasses through which we view the world. Our view through these glasses, our perception, is our personal reality. The prescription to which our glasses are ground is made up of our life experiences, our perception of self and the resultant expectations we have for ourselves and others. Two contemporary news items reflect this notion.

During Halloween week of 1969, the following event occurred and was reported by the nation's wire services. An in-depth report (Engh, 1970) of the event that appeared in *Good Housekeeping* is reproduced below[1]:

> Falsely accused, Jack Thomas suffered jail and the scorn of his neighbors — but forgave them all.
>
> In the summer, Jack B. Thomas doles out ice cream and candy from a curbside truck to children along his route in Camden, N.J. His small customers call him, affectionately, "Uncle Jack." After the summer, when his seasonal job ends, Uncle Jack misses the playful banter of the youngsters and makes a special point of stocking up with candy, apples and boxes of raisins to give out on Halloween. His home is a favorite stop for the trick-or-treat bands that rove the housing project in Philadelphia where he lives.
>
> Last year at Halloween, his $7 worth of treats went quickly. It was barely dark when Uncle Jack closed the door on two young girls, having handed one of them the last of his applies. Satisfied that he had given some pleasure to the low-income neighborhood's youngsters, the stocky and good-natured 52-year-old puttered around until he was sure the trick-or-treat traffic was over, then he settled down to watch television until his wife returned from visiting relatives.
>
> He was barely settled in front of the set when he was roused by raps at the door. Expecting a couple of straggling, tiny goblins demanding candy, he opened the door with a smile on his face. Instead of youngsters two security guards from the project were at the door. They casually questioned him about the goodies he had given the children, and then left. Though slightly puzzled, Uncle Jack returned to his television program.
>
> Soon the guards returned, this time with police detectives, who told Uncle Jack he was accused of putting a single-edged razor blade into an apple he had given a 12-year-old girl when she and her sister had stopped at his house earlier that night. Protesting his innocence, Uncle Jack was taken to the police station for further questioning. The police also wanted to get him out of the neighborhood. Ugly threats were being made against him; one woman wanted to beat him with a chain, two youths threatened to burn down his house.

[1] Reprinted with permission of the author from *Good Housekeeping*, October 1970. © 1970 by the Hearst Corporation.

To have his neighbors and the children he was so fond of suddenly turn against him with threats and abuse was an experience Jack Thomas will never forget. Most families feel secure in their homes and might never dream that, suddenly, the police would be knocking on their doors; that they would be accused of trying to harm children. But it did happen to Jack Thomas, and he responded as anyone might — with indignant denial.

"I don't even own a single-edged blade," he protested to police.

The small, nervous girl who had made the charge was brought to the station house, where, through a one-way mirror, she identified Jack Thomas as the man who had given her the doctored apple. He was booked on charges of attempting to maim children, which carries a penalty of up to five years imprisonment.

Newspapers the next morning labeled him the "meanest man in town." A judge proclaimed from the bench that "they should have whipping posts for people like you!" And the story horrified mothers of all young children who are allowed to trick or treat on Halloween.

Not so quick to judge him guilty was one of the security guards, Mathew G. Glelocki. "Thomas didn't seem like the type of man who would do this," he said. Thomas had spent three nights in jail, when Glelocki had a day off and decided to find the answers to some questions which puzzled him. He asked the mother of the little girl who made the accusation to let him talk to the youngster alone. Because of the respect the residents of the project have for him, the mother agreed.

Glelocki had doubts about some of the answers the girl gave to his questions, but one especially convinced him she was not being truthful. She maintained that she, her sister and four other girls had gathered to examine the apple under a street-light after leaving the Thomas home. She described the exact spot where they all stood. But Glelocki knew that the streetlight in question had been out that night. It was his duty, as a guard, to report such a light failure. Why, he asked himself, would the girls make up this part of the story?

The girl's mother, convinced of her daughter's truthfulness, felt strongly that Jack Thomas had tried to harm the child. However, responding to Glelocki's doubts, she reluctantly agreed to take their daughter to the police station for further questioning by detectives. At the station house, the girl stuck so closely to her original story that the detectives saw no justification for believing that Jack Thomas should not stand trial as charged.

But Glelocki did not give up. He went back to the police station on Tuesday and insisted on talking with Captain Joseph Pearson, head of the detective squad. Even then, Glelocki's doubts were not accepted readily. "They really gave me the third degree," he said. But his persistence finally convinced Captain Pearson that a further investigation was needed.

Pearson then called in veteran policewoman Helen Agnew and sent for all six girls and their parents.

Lie-detector tests were arranged for the girls and the first was given the

12-year-old who claimed to have received the doctored apple. She failed the test. Captain Pearson then got ready agreement from Jack Thomas to submit to a lie-detector test in his jail cell. The results of his test indicated he was telling the truth. One by one the other girls were tested and each failed. Interviewed by Policewoman Agnew, the girls' stories became further confused and filled with crucial differences. At this point, the 12-year-old broke down and admitted she had lied; the other girls soon made similar admissions.

Just what Halloween hysteria had prompted the girls to make up a story, which jailed a man who had befriended them, may never be explained. But the excitement of Halloween had fired the imaginations of the group of girls when they met after the 12-year-old and her sister had left the Thomas house. They agreed on a story, rehearsed it and then told the 12-year-old's mother that they had been given an apple with a razor blade in it. They named Thomas as the man who had given it to them. At first, they said they had thrown the apple away. But—when pressed—the girls had decided they needed evidence. One girl produced a razor blade she had used the day before to clean a car windshield, another bit into an apple she had received and they inserted the blade into the bite.

Upon their own confessions of this cruel hoax (policewoman Agnew called the deed "the most cold-blooded thing I've ever seen"), the six girls were charged with filing false police reports and held overnight in a juvenile detention center. Later they were convicted and placed on probation for six months.

Jack Thomas was released from his cell following the girls' confessions, just four days from the fateful Friday night he had so warmly greeted the Halloween revelers with gifts of candy, raisins and apples. His first feelings of relief were coupled with gratitude to Glelocki, the project guard whose tenacity and belief in Thomas had paid off.

"Thank God for Matt," Thomas said. "Thank God for him."

The police had praise for both Glelocki and their own efforts. "We never worked so hard to put a man in jail," says Captain Pearson, "as we did to get this man out."

For Thomas, the experience was harrowing. Frightened both by jail and the serious charges against him, he was also fearful about his wife, who suffers from a chronic illness. He could see his house across the field from his barred jail window and, standing in his cell, he kept worrying about how his arrest would affect his wife's health, and about the threats the neighbors had made against him.

Yet when he was released and reunited with his wife, daughter and teen-aged son, Thomas was surprisingly tolerant of the girls' hoax.

"They're just some goofy kids who got a tiger by the tail and couldn't let go of it," he says.

The neighborhood's attitude toward Thomas changed overnight. From the threats and anger that had been leveled at him, the feeling turned to indignation that he had been wrongly jailed. Perhaps some of his neighbors, those who had so strongly reacted to the girls' story, felt guilty or contrite and wished to make amends.

Jack Thomas was welcomed back with fanfare. He was pointed out as a celebrity, because of newspaper stories and television appearances which related the fateful events which led to his jailing, and the slow unwinding of a fanciful tale concocted by a group of girls. Mail poured in from across the country praising his release and the forgiving attitude he took toward the girls.

Perhaps one of the most rewarding responses was from the girls themselves. They came in a group to his house to apologize. Uncle Jack hugged them all and assured them they were forgiven. He invited them to join his family for Thanksgiving dinner, but the girls were so embarrassed that none would accept.

Although he most likely could make a court case against the parents and the girls, Thomas had no thoughts about legal action.

"Who can you get mad at?" he says. "You can't really blame the parents. I'd probably do the same thing if a child of mine said he had been given an apple with a razor blade in it."

Jack Thomas was back on his ice-cream-truck route this summer, smilingly serving the youngsters who still call him Uncle Jack. The Halloween hoax is remembered mainly in his neighborhood. But as the night for "trick or treat" approaches, he must be harking back to last year's ordeal and wondering if others might be the victims of the fanciful but devastating pranks of youngsters.

He might wonder, too, about the quick rise to anger and threats that a false report can stir in a once-friendly neighborhood. Vindication certainly took some of the sting out of having been falsely accused. But for Jack Thomas the lesson he learned — and the message he has for others:

"I guess maybe people shouldn't be so hasty."

It may prove interesting to consider first the view of reality demonstrated by the behavior of the young girls and second that of Mr. Thomas. Reflect on the expectations which the individuals had of themselves and of others. How did the individuals' perceptions of self differ?

The second news item originated at the time of the death of Egyptian President Gamal Abdel Nasser in 1970. Miles Copeland, writing in *Life*, noted:

To understand a statement by any official spokesman — whether British, Soviet, Egyptian or Israeli — remember that it was made not merely to inform but to achieve a purpose. Don't ask yourself what it means: ask why it was made. Look for motive, not meaning.

President Gamal Abdel Nasser of Egypt had his own version of those words of wisdom, which are taken from a CIA textbook. He used to say, "I must put on different glasses before I consider that." We in the West who were trying to figure out what he was up to at the time of his death, and who are now speculating about what new horrors are in store for us now that he has been removed from the "game," would do well to consider his words. Horrors there may be, but almost certainly not the ones predicted by those columnists and diplomats who take at face value the threats and promises of Middle Eastern leaders. The potential horrors can be seen only through those very special lenses which are available to veteran Nasser-watchers. (Copeland, 1970)

Each of the two news items noted reflects the dual nature of reality. Personal reality is that which is perceived as real. Objective reality is that which is accepted by most people as real. Education must help minimize discrepancies between personal and objective reality.

OUR FRAME OF REFERENCE

The children in the Halloween incident had distinctly different perceptions of the situation as compared to the adults involved. Note, for instance, the egocentric nature of the girls' behavior as opposed to the other-centered position of Mr. Thomas. This difference is not an accident. The story illustrates some of the assumptions on which this book's approach to social studies education is based. While the focus here is on affective learning, the following three assumptions are equally valid in the cognitive domain, as will be illustrated in subsequent chapters. These three assumptions and the supporting material constitute our frame of reference.

Assumption 1. Intellectual Development through Stages

Children's intellectual ability develops over time through a series of stages of psycho-social learning. This is the first assumption.

These stages are based on the writings of Piaget. The girls' rather unsophisticated view of the Halloween incident demonstrates one stage, in contrast to Mr. Thomas's rather high-level abstract perception of the event. We set out earlier these four stages through which the child passes in his early or elementary education: initial-exploratory; structured-dependent; structured-independent; independent-exploratory.

The *initial-exploratory* phase may be characterized by a new baby playing in his crib. Initially, lacking power over his own musculature, he thrashes about indiscriminately. As he gains control of his extremities he reaches out to explore objects in his environment. Chapter 4 will describe learning environments which have been constructed to maximize the child's highly unstructured exploration.

During the *structured-dependent* stage of development, which we believe generally lasts until he is eight to ten years of age, the child depends largely on others, chiefly adults, to stimulate his activities. This period of a child's life is characterized by educational toys, trips, and sponsored experiences. Adults read to him and take him to the zoo. The boy becomes an Indian Guide, plays Little League Baseball, Buddy Young football, or the like. The girl is a Campfire Girl or a Brownie. Both belong to church youth groups. In each case the structure of activities is imposed by others (parameters), but the youngster then freely selects from those alternatives presented. Chapter 5 places emphasis on such structured-dependent activities.

The structure of group activities gradually gives way to the *structured-independent* stage in which activities come to be dominated by the peer group. Most upper-grade children are in the midst of this experience. During this stage of development gangs or cliques may emerge. These groups, while generally viewed as informal and certainly independent, create and preserve their own structure. They provide opportunities for the individual to act independent of the "establishment." He is able to display his powers and expand the limits of his "turf." During this stage boy-girl attractions develop and dating begins. Chapter 6 focuses upon teaching strategies believed to be most congruent with the psycho-social needs and intellectual abilities of children at this stage of development.

By the end of the elementary phase of education a number of individuals may be operating at the fourth level of development, *independent-exploratory.* This stage may be summed up in the oft-quoted exchange between parent and child: "Where did you go? Out? What did you do? Nothing!" Children operating at this level are often perceived as "different" by teachers and peers. These are the children who, while interested in exploring the nature of man and society, are often labeled as uninterested or unmotivated in the classroom. Chapter 7 expands the view of children operating in the independent-exploratory stage of development and provides directions for instruction.

Implications for Instruction

While most children must sooner or later pass through each stage of development, they need not proceed at the same pace. Thus it is highly probable that each elementary teacher will have some children operating at one level, some at another, some at still a third. Each teacher must be aware of this probability in order to diagnose each learner's level of operation, then provide activities designed for each level. Real-world examples of such activities may be found in each of the chapters that follow.

Assumption 2. Cross-Currents

Four cross-currents are present in each stage of development. This is the second assumption.

These four cross-currents are: awareness; consequence; cause and effect; choice.

During each stage of psycho-social development there is an initial need to establish just where the child is operating. Both the child and his adult associates must be aware of the child's position. It is quite impossible for an individual to move toward a goal unless he knows his starting point. *Awareness* constitutes the first element in the child's frame of reference. A friend arrives in town by automobile to visit you. He has followed a road map in order to arrive at your city. Now he needs specific directions to reach your residence. He phones for directions. What is the first question you ask? *The psycho-social function which we will use to discuss the awareness dimension is egoizing.* (Egoizing will be considered in detail later in this chapter.)

The second cross-current which we have identified is *consequence*. Almost as soon as the child becomes aware of objects in his environment he begins to explore. He soon confronts the concept of consequence. Certain objects in his environment are declared off limits — no no's. He becomes aware that handling these objects may result in (a) removal of the object, (b) removal of the child from proximity with the object, or (c) verbal or physical punishment. We will attempt to show in Chapter 4 the relative merits of these responses.

As the child grows he is confronted by a myriad of situations in which an extrapersonal agency identifies consequences for his acts. He is repeatedly informed that, for example, he can't cross the street, can't stay out after dark, can't . . . . Each restriction is reinforced by a statement of consequence by which the emerging person is controlled. *The psycho-social function which we will use to discuss the consequence dimension is governing.* Governing is the dominant function in the structured-dependent stage of development. Chapter 5 will present a detailed consideration of the structured-dependent stage of development with special emphasis on governing.

Cause-and-effect relationships constitute the third cross-current. The young child gradually develops control over his own body functions as well as his musculature. He soon learns the "if . . . then" relationship. Initially, evidence is found in the child's selection of objects which he particularly desires. Observers note the particular attraction of brightly colored, textured, taste-appealing objects in the child's environment. He discovers that particular behaviors such as crying may cause another person to help effect satisfaction.

As the child pushes out the boundaries of his environment, he becomes increasingly aware of cause-and-effect relationships. He learns the formal and informal rules which permit his society to exist. His most significant early learnings center on the effect of his behavior on members of groups which he belongs to or associates with. The child is reminded that, "if you're good . . . ," "if you get your dress dirty . . . ," and so on.

Cause-and-effect relationships dominate the structured-independent stage of psycho-social development. *These relationships are defined by the psycho-social function of exchanging.* Exchanging will be the major psycho-social function considered in Chapter 6 which deals with the structured-independent stage.

The fourth and final cross-current we shall consider is *choice.* Choice represents the highest level of operation. It presumes that the individual is aware of himself and his environment, of the consequence of his behavior, and of the means (cause-effect) to achieve a variety of ends. He must now face the necessity of making choices.

A number of skills are necessary to making rational choices. Initially, choices reflect the individual's concern with his own needs. Ultimately, his choices affect those who share his environment. This effect brings us to the question of values. *The psycho-social function of ecologizing describes the premise and process of making choices,* with concern for the total benefit of all people. Ecologizing is the dominant function in the independent-exploratory stage of psycho-social development. Ecologizing will be considered in a subsequent section of this chapter as well as in Chapter 7.

Implications for Instruction

In order to provide opportunities for optimal growth individuals interested in the education of children and of themselves must be aware of the particular stage of development. They must then provide learning experiences which require the learner to function at the highest level of operation of which he is capable.

Assumption 3. Responses-to-Needs Motivation

Individuals act to meet psycho-social needs. This is the third assumption.

The ideas discussed under this assumption have been drawn from the work of Abraham Maslow and Erik Erikson and correlated with the developmental ideas of Piaget.

It is generally accepted that most of an infant's initial behavior is directed toward satisfying physiological needs for food and warmth. Similarly, it is recognized that each infant requires psychological nourishment, whence the attempt of adults to provide love, security, success, acceptance, and outlets for aggression. One quickly detects in the interaction of infant and other the emergence of a pattern of social nourishment. These behaviors display in a shorthand fashion the psycho-social needs of the individual.

Maslow in 1943 proposed a taxonomy of five human needs beginning with physiological needs and proceeding through safety needs, love needs, esteem needs, to arrive finally at the need for self-actualization. Each of these needs is described below. It is important to remember that no need is ever completely satisfied. Thus, the human being is continuingly motivated to attempt to gain satisfaction. His attempts result in behaviors. As educators we must be aware of the need level at which children are operating. If we accurately diagnose the child's need level we will be in a position to provide experiences designed to capitalize on this intrinsic motivation to act.

Physiological Needs. Basic physiological needs are potent instigators of behavior, as has been illustrated with many animal experiments. Yet the place of these needs in motivating human behavior is limited, Maslow believes, because emergency conditions of hunger, say, are rarely found in a society such as ours. Where there is a genuine, extreme hunger (or thirst, or other physiological drive), all behavior will be determined by its satisfaction. Most of us simply never experience this condition. Maslow makes the point that when one of us says, "I am hungry," this means that appetite is aroused, not genuine hunger. Since normally we consistently gratify our appetites, the physiological needs do not act as motivators of behavior.

Safety Needs. If physiological needs tend to be met consistently and more or less completely, the organism expresses the next level: safety needs. Since the organization of the society protects us from threats and dangers such as attack by animals, assault by other humans, and the like, safety needs seldom act as motivators for most of us. We experience safety needs only when there is a threat to our existence. However, it is possible to perceive psychological threat just as one may perceive physical threat. The result of such perceptions leads to clinical conditions of neuroticism. Additionally, persons from the lowest economic and social levels are closer to genuine threat to existence and thus express behaviorally a number of safety needs. Many current evidences of attempted social upheaval in this country may directly reflect safety needs: a desire for decent housing, adequate employment opportunities, adequate wages, etc. If Maslow is right, satisfaction of these needs will open the door for expression of the next level of needs.

Love Needs. Rather than being a restricted area, "love needs" encompass all desire for relations with people. They include acceptance by others and achievement of some status within groups by which the individual is accepted. Maslow states that lack of satisfaction in this area is the most common source of maladjustment and consequent psychopathological conditions.

Esteem Needs. Each of us, Maslow says, has a need for self-respect and a need for the respect of others. The former expresses itself as a desire for achievement, adequacy, confidence: the latter, for recognition, attention, regard from others. When satisfied, we feel confident and worthwhile. When thwarted, we feel inferior and helpless. Again, neurosis is an expression of a lack of satisfaction of esteem needs.

Self-Actualization Needs. Self-actualization goes beyond esteem because it emphasizes becoming whatever one must be. Esteem can be achieved without self-actualization. Self-actualization means fulfilling our potential. Since this never occurs, the need can never be satisfied. As progress is made, new possibilities are opened by one's potential — and thus further striving toward actualization. (Edwards and Scannell, 1948, 461)

There are apparently two fundamental concepts involved in the fulfillment of psycho-social needs: self-realization and self-actualization. Each of these dimensions will be discussed later in this chapter. For the time being, we might note that in the search for satisfaction the individual's self emerges.

We have already alluded to the observation that the child seems to grow integratedly into a physical and psychological unit. The young child becomes himself. He tests his forward-surging independence in relation to the many facets of the immediate and extended environment. The child can gradually gain some insight into the institutions, opportunities, and roles which will permit him prospective responsible participation as an adult. (Maier, 1969, 53)

It is in the definition of the child's self that an additional dimension is developed, the *value* dimension. One's perception of his "self" is directly dependent upon value assumptions which he makes or which are made by others whom he perceives as significant in his environment. The frame of reference upon which the child acts is grounded in his value structure. It is vital for the child to recognize the values upon which he acts. Without a clear perception of his "self" one cannot understand the full extent of his environment and its impact on him.

Although each dimension of the environment includes unique elements, there are numerous common features. For example, community may be discussed in both physical (the geography of a town) and social (the common purpose or character which unites a group) dimensions. Constructs, concepts, and generalizations (these terms are defined in Chapter 3) from many different social and behavioral sciences are illustrated in the child's environment. As he grows, interaction with specific dimensions of the environment varies in frequency and intensity. Therefore, knowledge gleaned from a particular discipline also varies in importance or relevance. There is a kind of ecological balance in the child's life-space whereby change in one portion is reflected through his total environment. Since we as teachers cannot predict the specific nature of the individual child's environment, let alone particulars regarding emphasis of the moment, we face the daily charge of irrelevance. We must face this charge. Very well — one premise of this text is that teachers who adopt a theoretical base for instruction and hold to it will operate at a much higher level of relevance than teachers who lack such a foundation.

As a child builds a more complete self he may gain the confidence necessary to explore further his physical and social environment, even when it changes. He may ride a bus to an unknown section of the city or attempt to make the team in a local playground basketball league. An expressway constructed through a community may force him to change schools. The new school environment places him in new social boundaries. This alteration of the social dimension may bring changes in the physical (a bus ride to a new school) and personal (redefining self in a new peer group) dimensions of the environment.

The child's understandings of his environment and the pattern of the skills he needs to expand and apply these understandings make up his personal frame of reference. He uses this frame of reference to analyze his environment and to support his actions. Each child depends directly on the adequacy of his frame of reference for his effectiveness as a citizen of the community in which he functions. As social studies teachers we are charged with the responsibility of helping children build an adequate frame of reference and thus preparing them to be effective people.

Effective people must possess a data bank from which to draw information and must also have the ability to extend the usefulness of this source of information through addition or reinterpretation. The skills needed to enhance the data bank include the abilities (1) to identify problems in the environment, (2) to seek out data necessary to solve the problem, (3) to analyze data with regard to the problem at hand, (4) to formulate logical conclusions based on data, and (5) to act on conclusions.

The individual who possesses these skills along with an accurate self-perception is prepared to strive toward maximizing his human potential through what has been termed self-actualization.

THE I—EGOIZING

The frame of reference having been set out, we now turn to the child as he begins his formal education and consider his affective development from egoizing to ecologizing.

> Identity has to do with everything Erikson described in "Childhood and Society." With luck, the infant is held and feels held, craves food and finds his appetite satisfied, looks and sees in return the mother's eyes. The child learns his name, and finds his way about the house and the street. He learns to dress

himself, to talk. He also learns how others regard him, address him, and respond to him — teachers and neighbors, playmates and classmates, store clerks and relatives. The child feels, and grows to recognize in himself, emotions like desire, anger, hate and envy. He wants people and things; he wants to do away with people and things. He learns what he can do, what he must do, what he wishes he might do, and he also learns what others do in response to his various deeds. He gains command of his body, begins to feel a certain authority over his immediate world. He can act, and, increasingly he can act with consequences in mind. (Coles, 1970, 59)

Robert Coles's analysis of Erikson provides a framework for social study. It establishes the general path along which a child moves from egoizing to ecologizing. It is in this first step that the child creates a self-concept, that is, a distinct individual identity, an "I."

Reviewing the work done in determining aspects related to educational motivation makes the importance of self-concept abundantly clear. For instance, the work of Karen Horney continuously points to the conclusion that the individual who feels loved and confident is set free to pursue his inborn urgings to become capable and to gain approval of others. The individual perceiving himself as a complete person is prepared to attempt satisfaction of higher needs.

Apparently the child's self-concept crystallizes around his successes and failures with the objects and people who surround him during his early years. Experience during this formative period from birth to approximately age seven contributes to the child's identity as a distinct individual. If he experiences success in terms of mastery and approval he develops what is termed a healthy self-concept. In addition he tends to gain incentive to strive toward further self-realization. In Maslow's hierarchy, the child moves from operations based on physiological, safety, and love needs to operation in terms of esteem needs.

Using this motivational model based on the satisfaction of an individual's need for self-realization, Bessell and Palomares (1967) have created a program designed to facilitate the psycho-social development of young children. The program stresses the processes of child development as it relates to awareness, self-confidence, and social interaction. Bessell and Palomares depict the development of a healthy self-concept as highly dependent upon a nurturing environment where a child can respond to instinctual urges to become masterful and gain approval.

He feels that he can be capable and get people to like him. These rewards fire his incentive to try for more gratification through further efforts to achieve mastery and to gain approval. This is the picture of the child who is developing a healthy self-concept and high motivation to achieve. Liking of self and achievement becomes a positive reciprocal feed-back system in which liking of self gives the courage to try and efforts towards success lead to achievement that makes a child like himself still more. The whole process spirals upward once it has been launched from a good nurturing base. (Bessell and Palomares, 1967, 4)

The goals of the Bessell and Palomares curriculum include (1) the cultivating of an awareness of self and others, (2) an acceptance of self and others, and (3) an appreciation of the differences as well as the similarities between self and others. Emphasis is placed upon recognizing the differences between feelings, thoughts, and actions. The program is based on the assumption that potentials for motivation are inborn and that stimulation of cognition must begin formally as soon as possible.

AWARENESS, CONSEQUENCE, CAUSE AND EFFECT, VALUING

Awareness is the composite of ideas and attitudes which take shape as the individual sets forth on his career as a living person. In terms of developing the I, of egoizing, the young child's adults are particularly concerned with the attitudes or feelings he experiences. Their initial goal must be to help the child by providing opportunities for experience which will create a specific awareness of his emotions. This is the basis of egoizing. Once the child's awareness is established, they can help him to see causal relationships by providing activities which will help him realize that behavior may be related to interaction with people or to interaction with things. This is the *exchanging* dimension. Finally we reach a point at which we are able to help the child realize that he has alternate choices of behavior in any situation. At that point we enter the *valuing* area.

As teachers our intention is to avoid boxing the child in. We want him simply to be aware of ways to handle his feelings; we want to interact with children on a nonthreatening basis and to avoid zeroing in on any one particular child; and we want to give the child room to discover his own ways of working out feelings.

Piaget posed the question of why the young child assimilates reality to the ego rather than to experimental and logical thought. (Inhelder and Piaget, 1958) His studies reveal the answer. Experimental and logical thought processes have not yet been constructed and during development they are inadequate to the needs of daily life for interpretation and action. Thus the young child's frame of reference is egocentric.

Millie Almy (1966) points out that both social collaboration with other children and activities with concrete objects have roles in developing logical thought. Almy states that this ego assimilation makes it difficult for a young child to conceive a viewpoint different from his own. The interacting give and take of spontaneous play provides the first situation in which the child is confronted with the need to accommodate other's ideas. In the early stages of spontaneous play an individual discovers that others have feelings.

A major factor in developing awareness is the Freudian concept of repression, that is, the unconscious inhibition of expression. Repression has been recognized as the root of certain personality problems and stands as a particularly ominous barrier to self-realization. The object of promoting awareness is to help youngsters recognize the internal restraints (repressions) which modify overt behavior. As a first step, awareness is enhanced as children are encouraged to act out impulses.

It is true that actual enactment of some impulses may not be a desirable outcome; excessive impulsive behavior cannot be tolerated if we are to avoid disruptive, antisocial behavior in the classroom or in larger constructions of society. But as Bessell and Palomares point out,

> Our objective is not to merely increase awareness. Rather our objective is to increase the responsible, that is the self-controlled, direction of those potentially antisocial impulses which inevitably arise in all children. To accomplish this important objective, our basic method will be to at all times during the lesson sessions encourage the natural, honest, verbal expressions of potentially socially disruptive impulses, but to simultaneously discourage their behavioral acting out. (1967, 10)

An overview of such a human-development curriculum is set out below. Lessons in this curriculum are designed around specific topics; each topic is dealt with for a one-week period. The human-development program is further discussed in Chapter 9.

A HUMAN DEVELOPMENT CURRICULUM: OVERVIEW FOR THE YEAR

FIRST SEMESTER

Unit 1: Six weeks on Communication: The Language of Pleasant Awareness and Expression **(Four- and Five-Year-Olds)**

1st week:	Pleasant Feelings
2nd week:	Pleasant Thoughts
3rd week:	Positive Behavior
4th week:	Pleasant Feelings
5th week:	Pleasant Thoughts
6th week:	Positive Behavior

Unit 2: Six Weeks on the Development of Mastery: Acquiring Self-Confidence **(Four-Year-Olds)**

7th week:	Mastery in Naming Things
8th week:	Mastery in Concepts Involving Categorizing, Understanding Space Relationships, and Beginning Quantitative Concepts

9th week: Mastery in Motor Coordination
10th week: Mastery in Performance Skills
11th week: Mastery in Dressing and Health
12th week: Mastery in Social Comprehension

Unit 2: (Five-Year-Olds)

7th week: Mastery in Language
8th week: Mastery in Quantitative Concepts
9th week: Mastery in Motor Coordination
10th week: Mastery in Performance Skills
11th week: Mastery in Personal Hygiene
12th week: Mastery in Social Comprehension

Unit 3: Six Weeks of Social Approval and Disapproval: Understanding Social Interaction **(Four- and Five-Year-Olds)**

13th week: Understanding Approval-Getting Behavior
14th week: Understanding Disapproval-Getting Behavior
15th week: Understanding Approval-Getting Behavior
16th week: Understanding Disapproval-Getting Behavior
17th week: Giving Approval for Kind Behavior
18th week: Earning Approval for Kind Behavior

SECOND SEMESTER

Unit 4: Six Weeks on Communication: The Language of Pleasant and Unpleasant Awareness and Expression

	Five-Year-Olds	**Four-Year-Olds**
19th week:	Pleasant Feelings	Pleasant Feelings
20th week:	Unpleasant Feelings	Pleasant Thoughts
21st week:	Pleasant Thoughts	Positive Behavior
22nd week:	Unpleasant Thoughts	Pleasant Feelings
23rd week:	Positive Behavior	Pleasant Thoughts
24th week:	Negative Behavior	Positive Behavior

Unit 5: Six Weeks on the Development of Mastery: Acquiring Self-Confidence (Advanced) **(Four-Year-Olds)**

25th week: Mastery in Naming Things
26th week: Mastery in Concepts Involving Categorizing, Understanding Space Relationships, and Beginning Quantitative Concepts
27th week: Mastery in Motor Coordination
28th week: Mastery in Performance Skills
29th week: Mastery in Dressing and Health
30th week: Mastery in Social Comprehension

Unit 5: (Five-Year-Olds)

    25th week: Mastery in Language

    26th week: Mastery in Quantitative Concepts

    27th week: Mastery in Motor Coordination

    28th week: Mastery in Performance Skills

    29th week: Mastery in Personal Hygiene

    30th week: Mastery in Social Comprehension

Unit 6: Six Weeks on Social Approval and Disapproval: Understanding Social Interaction **(Four- and Five-Year-Olds)**

    31st week: Understanding Approval-Getting Behavior

    32nd week: Understanding Disapproval-Getting Behavior

    33rd week: Understanding Approval-Getting Behavior

    34th week: Understanding Disapproval-Getting Behavior

    35th week: Giving Approval for Kind Behavior

    36th week: Earning Approval for Kind Behavior

The overview reveals again that cognitive concerns cannot be removed from affective development. Which of them is furthered remains a matter of focus or emphasis. The same holds true for the cross-currents operating during a particular activity or series of learning experiences. Thus, the flow from awareness to consequence to cause-and-effect ebbs and flows with a great deal of overlap. Throughout, the child experiences feelings, develops beliefs and opinions, and gradually formulates a values system which from that time on influences his actions. We can, however, highlight specific cross-currents for purposes of instruction.

Teachers approach these cross-currents as they establish specific objectives, diagnose each learner's level of operation, prescribe a plan of instructional activities, implement that plan, and evaluate the learner's progress, the teacher's effectiveness, and the appropriateness of the plan itself. Examine the following plan of instruction. Note particularly the way the teachers who prepared this plan handle each cross-current.

A PLAN OF INSTRUCTION DEALING WITH YOUNG CHILDREN'S FEELINGS
    Objectives

        To help the child use all of his past experiences and problem-solving capacities in order to become aware of emotions and to cope with these emotions by seeing that he

Awareness	Demonstrates understanding of terms for emotions by contributing to room chart of "feeling" words.
	Demonstrates ability to identify different feelings by pointing to appropriate pictorial representations of faces that show such feelings.

Consequence	Demonstrates ability to express specific emotions by responding with appropriate facial expressions in a mirror.
Cause and Effect	Exhibits awareness of alternate choices of behavior by demonstrating through role playing different ways of coping with specific emotions. Makes inferences as to causes of different behaviors.
Valuing	Expresses methods of coping with emotions by exhibiting accommodations in spontaneous play and in real life situations.

Understandings
I. 1st Understanding: I have feelings, and so do others

A. **Concrete**

   1. Responds to situations specifically created to elicit emotional responses and answers questions about his feeling.

      a. Easel with not enough paints or brushes
      b. One doll for three girls
      c. Two riding toys for three boys

   2. Role plays stories.

B. **Manipulative**

   1. Uses flannel board.

      a. Teacher-directed — Using specific materials, as "Winkie and His Friends," David C. Cook Co.
      b. Child-directed — Child uses felt cut-outs to create his own story

   2. Uses puppets. **Note:** Regardless of the type of puppet used, include a family to depict home emotions and problems. The teacher may give a situation for a group to work on or the children may work out their own situations.

C. **Visual**

   1. Identifies emotions expressed in pictures of facial expressions.
   2. Contributes magazine illustrations depicting different emotions. **Note:** Objects and situations as well as people may arouse feelings, so the child's pictures may include a kitten, a birthday present, or a storm.
   3. Uses mirror to show different emotions, such as sadness, anger, fright, happiness, pride.

      a. "How do you look when you're happy? Do you smile a lot?"

b. "Have you ever thought how many things you say each day and how many things are said to you? Let's play a game. I'll say something. You repeat what I say. Look in the mirror as you say it. Are you ready?"

    i.   Good morning.
    ii.   Shut up.
    iii.   How are you today?
    iv.   Quit that.
    v.   Please don't do that.
    vi.   I want the ball.
    vii.   Give me the ball.
    viii.   I'd like to go with you.
    ix.   I'm going with you.
    x.   May I have a cookie?
    xi.   I want one more cookie.
    xii.   I like to play with you.
    xiii.   I won't play with you.
    xiv.   I picked up all the blocks.
    xv.   Johnny teases me.
    xvi.   I'll give you a turn.

D. **Abstract**

1. Discusses (or role plays):

   a. "What is being happy? Sad? Tired? Afraid? Angry?"
   b. "What is liking somebody?"
   c. "What is being unselfish?"
   d. "What is being naughty?"
   e. "What is being sleepy?"
   f. "What is wishing for something?"
   g. "How would it feel being a puppy? A worm? A bluebird?" (Scott, 1968, 35)
   h. "If you were an animal, which would you like to be? **Why?**"

2. Contributes to chart of "feeling" words—happy, sad, angry, calm, quiet, nervous, awful, jittery, etc. (Lee and Allen, 1963, 114)

   a. Make a chart of "happy" words.

          i.   Learning to ride my two-wheel bike
          ii.   Christmas
          iii.   cool wind on a hot day
          iv.   hot water bottle in bed
          v.   babies smiling
          vi.   candles lit on a birthday cake

    b. Make a chart of "unhappy" words

        i.   bedtime
        ii. scary TV programs
        iii. growling dogs
        Note: Some children might think i and ii are "happy."

3. Listens to sounds and responds.

    a. Use discussion to bring out feelings, perhaps asking the children how they feel when they hear:

        i.   ambulance or fire siren
        ii.   children playing
        iii.   raindrops splashing
        iv.   thunder roaring
        v.   skates on concrete
        vi.   strange sounds in a dark room
        vii. baby crying
        viii. birds chirping
        ix.   chalk scratching
        x.   dogs growling
        xi.   Mother cooking

    b. Use the book and recording **Listening for Sounds** by Adelaide Holl (published by Golden Book Education Service) to bring out feeling responses to sound stimuli.

    c. Use the Scott, Foresman Company record and card game kit which includes four sets:

        i.   Sounds Around the School
        ii.   Sounds Near Houses
        iii. Sounds Near Neighborhoods
        iv. Sounds on the Farm or in the Zoo

4. Responds to color stimuli.

    a. "One can learn much about a child's feelings by holding up a swatch of color and asking, 'What does this red color make you think of?' Colors of yellow, orange, brown, green, blue, pink, or purple will remind individual children of happy or unhappy experiences." (Scott, 1968, 23)

    b. "How would you feel if everything in this room were blue?"

    c. "If you had the power to change the colors of the tree, the grass, and the sky, what colors would you choose and why?"

    d. Let the child finger paint with just one color, and express an emotion.

5. Responds to stories.

    a. Correctly name certain emotions which are basic themes of special readings.

    b. Finishes open-end stories (teacher begins a story, stops at a point, and allows children to finish the story.) Suggestion: **Hailstones and Halibut Bones**

    c. Discusses **Seven Stories for Growth** (Sugarman and Hochstein, 1962). These are basically stories of conflicts in feelings, of the resolution of these conflicts, and of the management of these feelings. Each story includes a background section for the teacher, the story, and excellent questions and follow-up activities.

6. Makes up "feeling" similes:

    a. As happy as ——
    b. As sad as ——
    c. As jealous as ——
    d. As angry as ——
    e. As frightened as ——
    f. As jittery as ——
    g. As calm as ——

7. Writes creatively.

    a. Composes short stories about

        i. "Why I'm Glad (**or** Not Glad) to Be Me"
        ii. "Why I Like (**or** Don't Like) My Name"
        iii. "My Biggest Worry Is . . ."

8. Draws pictures describing Sylvia Ashton-Warner's (1963) "organic" words, which she describes as those which arouse emotions. Here are some examples of "organic" words which will stimulate discussion and arouse the child's interest quickly, since many of the words are close to the child's experience.

love	warm	scream
tears	win	dream
fight	bad	mad
sacred	bath	lick
ugly	lazy	yell
hug	kiss	touch

II. 2nd Understanding: There are reasons for my feelings

A. Concrete

1. Relates personal experiences illustrating the different feelings listed on the "My 'Feeling' Words" chart (I.D. 2 above).

2. Responds in the following situations:

    a. Tries to reach something that the teacher has placed a little too high for him to reach. Articulates how he feels and what he thinks made him feel this way.

    b. Struggles with a stuck zipper. Articulates how he feels and what caused him to feel this way.

    c. Works a bubble-gum machine and gets out a piece of gum. Articulates feeling and cause.

    d. Listens to loud dissonant music and moves his body the way it makes him feel.

    e. Finds himself locked in a play yard with his ball outside the fence (teacher should stay close by in this situation so he won't panic). Articulates cause of feelings.

B. **Manipulative** **Note:** Because creating a situation which demonstrates why a specific emotion is experienced is more difficult for children than determining the feeling resulting from a situation given to them, we have chosen to sequence the manipulative activities in the following order.

1. Uses puppets in situations made up by the teacher to reinforce understanding that situations cause feelings.

    a. They are watching a funny show on TV.

    b. The barber has cut one puppet's hair too short.

    c. Dad announces that he is taking the week off to take the family to the beach.

    d. Two puppets are fighting over a toy.

    e. A child is left at home alone and thunder and lightning begin.

2. Creates situations to illustrate **why** the following specific emotions might be experienced.

    a. boxed-in

    b. lonely

    c. up-tight

    d. angry

C. **Visual**

1. Contributes magazine pictures to scrapbooks "Things that make me feel Happy (or Sad, or Surprised)"

2. Shows in a mirror how he would look if

    a. "—you have a stomach ache."

    b. "—you discover it is pouring rain on the day you are going with your friends to an amusement park."

c. "—today is the hottest day of summer and your mother has just bought you a double dip of your favorite flavor of ice cream."

d. "—you found a real live horse under your Christmas tree."

e. "—you see a mouse. —a snake. —three kittens in a basket. —someone teasing the kittens."

f. "—you are having lunch at your friend's home and are served something you don't like."

g. "—someone salts your ice cream."

Note: We suggest that the teacher use a tape recorder to program the above situations. An excellent procedure is to also tape the child's verbal response to each situation.

3. Makes inferences as to causes for feelings through medium of pictorial representations.

   a. Responds to situational pictures.

      i. Family situations—as picture of a mother holding the hands of two crying children; the child infers as to why she is holding their hands, what their trouble might be, and how they might feel as a result of their trouble.

      ii. Looks at picture of an angry father (two children on floor playing noisy game). "How do you suppose the father feels? What is happening? Is the father's anger a happy or unhappy feeling for him? For the children? **Why** do you suppose the father got angry? Do you think this angry father will stop loving his children now? Do you think the father will stay angry for long?" (Adapted from Meeks and Bagwell, 1969, 21.)

      iii. Looks at picture of child who is angry with mother who is holding baby. In **Families Live Together** (Meeks and Bagwell, 1969, 23), is a sequence of such pictures showing as the last picture the father holding the calmed child. The teacher suggests questions like "What feeling is the boy showing toward his mother? **Why** do you suppose he is so upset? Will he be angry long? Does he love his mother? How does he feel when his father is holding him? **Why?** Have you ever felt this way too? Do you suppose children in other parts of the world feel this way when their fathers hold them?" The child infers answers.

   b. Looks at pictures of facial expressions, identifies emotion expressed, and tells **why** he thinks person feels that way.

D. **Abstract**

   1. Makes inferences as to causes for feelings through medium of situational stories.

a. "Someone goes ahead of you in line when you are taking turns at jumping rope."

b. "You go 'trick-or-treating' with your sister and she says 'trick-or-treat' **first every time** when the door is opened."

c. "Joanne is seven years old. Her brother, Russell is five. Joanne's mother has told her over and over not to bounce on the beds. Russell does it and is not punished. How does Joanne feel? **Why?**"

d. "You are operating an elevator for the first time. It stops between floors and will not go either up or down."

e. "Jane and I are playing school. She wants to be the teacher. I want to be the teacher too."

f. "Bob and I are playing 'firemen,' and he wants to be the driver everytime."

g. "I go to a birthday party and spill chocolate ice cream all over my new party dress. A little boy at the party rubs his icing-covered hands over me, even in my hair."

2. Discusses the **why** for feelings in any story from **Seven Stories for Growth.** (Sugarman and Hochstein, 1962)

3. Draws picture to demonstrate jealousy, fear, box-in feeling, frustration, love, joy.

4. Creates stories about "What Makes Me Happy." **Note:** We suggest the "blank book" method — child is given book with title on cover. The pages are blank; he creates his own stories and illustrations.

III. 3rd Understanding: Behavior grows out of feelings

A. **Concrete**

1. Role plays how someone acts when he is

   a. sick.
   b. alone in a big house.
   c. lost in a department store.
   d. hit by a bigger child.
   e. frightened by a strange sound or person.
   f. hungry (haven't eaten for two days).
   g. praised for doing a good job.
   h. hugged just for being himself.

2. "Each of us has found ourself in these situations." Role plays "What do I do when—"

   a. "I skin my knee?"
   b. "Someone takes away something that I have?"
   c. "Something gets in my way?"
   d. "I get a present?"
   e. "I want something?"

B. **Manipulative**

1. Plays commercial game, "Happy Face." (Cost $1)
2. Plays homemade games

   a. Players take turns spinning dial of game board. Situations are drawn on board with persons in situations represented by stick figures having no facial expressions. The child chooses a card to match appropriate facial expression to situation. Situations might include a child falling down, two children fighting over a toy, and the like.
   b. Variation of above game. Use dice to progress to different situations on board. The child tells an appropriate response to the situation landed on.
   c. Plays similar game using wired board which lights up when a correct response is given. A self-correcting game of this kind may be played individually or with two or three.
   d. Correctly matches parts of faces cut into three pieces.

C. **Visual**

1. Identifies with personalities in pictures (the teacher uses, for young child, the "This is you" technique) and tells or role plays how he would act if he were

   a. angry like the child in the picture.
   b. happy like the child in the picture.
   c. hugged like the boy in the picture.
   d. sad like the girl in the picture.
   e. screamed at like the boy in the picture.

D. **Abstract**

1. Responds to the following questions by telling what he would do.

   a. If you were angry with your sister, what would you do?
   b. If you were frightened, what would you do?
   c. If you felt left out of a game your older sister was playing with her friend, what would you do?
   d. Your teacher praises you for a kindness you have shown. How might you behave the rest of the day?
   e. You have just moved to a new neighborhood, and a child who looks just about your age comes out of the house next door and waves and smiles in a most friendly way when she sees you. How might you feel? How would you act when you saw her again?
   f. The child comes out, sees you, and neither waves nor smiles but turns and goes back into her house. How might you feel? How might you act because you feel this way?

2. Participates in singing

    a. "Sometimes I'm Happy."

    b. "I have something in my pocket that I wear upon my face" — Brownie Scout song.

    c. "Whistle a Happy Tune."

    d. "If You're Happy and You Know It, Clap your hands (clap, clap)"
    Suggestion: Create additional verses, as "If you're angry and you know it stamp your feet (stamp, stamp)"

IV. *4th Understanding: I have choices as to how I can express feelings; others have choices too*

A. **Concrete**

1. Role plays possible alternatives in given situations.

    a. When Bob is furious at Jim for having taken his toy, he could

        i. hit Jim.

        ii. cry.

        iii. tattle.

        iv. yell at and threaten Jim.

        v. demand the toy be returned.

        vi. tell Jim he may borrow the toy for awhile.

B. **Manipulative**

1. Uses puppets or flannel board to act out certain problems and to think of as many different ways as possible to handle situations.

    a. Mother and Father are going out for supper. They promised Susie she could go. At the last minute Susie spilled water on her dress. Mother said she would have to stay home with the sitter. If you were Susie, what would you do? What else could you do?

    b. You have just built a tall tower out of wooden blocks and a friend comes by and knocks it over. What would you do?

C. **Visual**

1. Tells different alternatives to situations in open ended film strips.

2. Responds to roll movie. (Situations are programmed by drawing sequenced scenes on long piece of paper, attaching the two ends of the paper to dowels, and rolling the paper to show different scenes on cardboard-box "screen.") Scenes for roll movie:

    a. This is Tom.

    b. One day Tom was playing with his truck.

    c. Bob came by and grabbed Tom's truck.

  d.   The truck's wheels fell off.
  e.   Tom said, "Oh, no! Look what happened!"
  f.   Tom started to cry.

  Can you guess what happened?

  —Did Bob call Tom a cry baby?
  —Did Bob run away and hide?
  —Did Bob say, "I didn't do it?"
  —Did Bob say, "I'm sorry," and get the truck fixed?
  —What would you have done?

D. **Abstract**

  1. Names different ways of acting when he is

  a.   happy.
  b.   sad.
  c.   angry.
  d.   jealous.
  e.   frightened.

  Suggestion: Use a tape recorder to program the material and to record the child's responses

  2. Tells: "When I am mad, do I show it by

  a.   pouting?"
  b.   hiding?"
  c.   biting?"

  V. 5th Understanding: I can accommodate my expression of feeling among the alternatives

A. **Concrete**

  1. Role plays open-ended stories.
  2. Participates in making movie (Bell and Howell video tape is an excellent aid for this activity), role playing the different ways, with emphasis on the **best** way, to show anger when the class bully hits, punches, and teases class members.
  3. Uses finger plays which illustrate alternatives of behavior.
  4. Participates in singing song which illustrates accommodation of expression of feeling.

B. **Manipulative**

  1. Plays a match game, matching facial expressions portraying opposite emotions.

2. Places in sequence individual frames cut out from comic strips which parallel expression of feeling.

3. Pastes first few frames (see the preceding) on paper and draws a final or missing frame.

4. Draws pictures to illustrate "feeling" dialogue cut from comic strips.

5. Variation of preceding (this is perhaps more abstract than manipulative but is placed here because of its relationship to the preceding): Creates dialogue with feeling emphasis appropriate to comic strips from which dialogue has been cut.

C. **Visual**

1. Watches the movie made with children role playing (see V.A.2 above)

2. Participates in making and observing a roll movie.

For this activity you need a roll of unglazed shelf paper, a large corrugated-board carton from a grocery store, a broomstick or mop handle sawed in half, thumbtacks, a ruler, a pencil, and a sharp knife for cutting the carton.

Have a brief planning session with the children. Briefly describe the movie and ask the children if they have a picture story that they would like to show as a movie or on television. After the children suggest several possible stories, ask them to choose the one that they would like most to do. After they choose a story, tell them that several "scenes" will be needed. As the children talk about the scenes, particularly if they are "readers," list them on a blackboard or chart.

Clear a floor space and unroll as much shelf paper as you have room for. Have crayons ready. With pencil and ruler, mark off spaces on the shelf paper so that each has a place to work. The number and size of the pictures will be determined by the number of children who wish to contribute to this activity.

Have each child crayon a picture in the space that was given to him. If possible, the pictures should follow the story sequence decided during the planning time.

Cut a square or rectangular opening in one solid side of the carton. Make the width a little smaller than the width of the shelf paper, and the length equal to the length of each child's allotted drawing space. Cut two round holes in the top of the carton for the broomstick halves to go through.

When the story is completed, thumbtack one end of the shelf paper to one broomstick half. Roll all the shelf paper on that roller. Next, insert this stick **in one hole.** Next, insert the other (empty) broomstick half in the other hole, and thumbtack the free end of the picture roll to it. The movie is now ready to be shown. The children may roll the story from one stick to the other stick and tell the story.

Almost any situational story for the movie can be adapted to alternatives of behavior. Following is one story.

The Story of Playing Together

(1) Picture of toys — THESE ARE OUR TOYS
(2) Picture of children — HERE WE COME
(3) Picture of children coming to kindergarten — WE COME TO KINDERGARTEN
(4) Picture of kindergarten — OUR KINDERGARTEN
(5) Picture of one child with a toy — WE LIKE TO PLAY WITH TOYS
(6) Picture of another child grabbing the toy — PUSH AND GRAB
(7) Pictures of what might happen (several children might draw pictures showing ways to resolve the fight between the two children who grab the same toy).

D. **Abstract**

1. Responds to situations such as "Which is the best way to show my anger?"

    a. Beat clay
    b. Hit someone
    c. Hit a doll
    d. Throw and break something

2. Discusses various alternative behaviors to stiuations.
3. Volunteers alternate behaviors in response to words —

fear	mad	scream
love	yell	happy
anger	push	excited

4. Composes poem, simple song, or story related to any of the alternate expressions of feeling.

VI. 6th Understanding: I can cope with my emotions

A. **Concrete**

1. Given an unfamiliar, difficult problem to solve, first attempts to solve it without help and when finding it too difficult, asks for help.
2. Copes with emotions in classroom situations (either contrived or natural) where the teacher observes his behavior. Later the teacher and the child discuss his responses and other alternate choices of expression of his feelings. The child evaluates which response for that situation would have been best for him.
3. Asserts his own rights while respecting the rights of others during free play.

B. **Manipulative**

   1. Uses puppets or flannel board to role play given situations. (The teacher stresses the importance of learning to cope with problems— for example, coping with jealousy or hatred of family member.)

      Children may crayon and cut out simple outline figures of their families and paste small pieces of flannel or felt to the backs of the figures. They use these figures on the flannel board to dramatize situations at home. Hopefully, if jealousy, hatred, or anger is felt, ill feelings will be taken out through punching a punching bag, pounding clay or nails, on dolls, or through finger painting rather than on real person.

      Children may give puppets such names as "Boxer," "Loudmouth," "Pushy," or "Shovey" to cope with their emotions in situations which arise in the classroom.

C. **Visual**

   1. Tells what he might do if he were in the place of people pictured in emotional situations.
   2. Participates in making a roll movie (directions may be found in V.C.2) related to coping with emotions.
   3. Views the filmstrip, **Brothers and Sisters,** from "The Home Community," Encyclopaedia Britannica Educational Corporation, 425 North Michigan Avenue, Chicago, Ill., 60611. This teaches the fun of living together, getting along with brothers and sisters. Chief emotion shown—jealousy. Steve is jealous because he feels his brothers and sisters are receiving more attention than he.

D. **Abstract**

   1. Makes posters showing different ways of coping with specific emotions.
   2. Writes or talks about assigned titles:

      a. "The Boy Who Ran Away"
      b. "The Girl Who Learned How to Laugh"
      c. "The Class Bully"
      d. "The Name Caller"
      e. "What Made Hedda Happy (**or** Proud)"
      f. "The Shortest Boy in the Class"

   3. Creates captions for pictures illustrating coping with emotions

   Diagnostic Test

I. Demonstrates ability to name an emotion by pointing to an appropriate pictorial representation.

   Level a: Show me the picture of the boy who is (————).
   Level b: Show me the picture of the boy who is (crying) because he is **sad.**

Level c: Show me the picture of the boy who is (smiling) and feels (happy) because his mother bought him a new toy.

II.   Demonstrates ability to name emotion when presented a picture stimulus.

Level a: Tell me how this boy (you) feel(s).
Level b: What makes him (you) feel (————)?
Level c: How do you know he (you) feels (————)?
(Same faces as above but on separate cards)

III.   Relates a facial expression to a given pictorial situation (add-a-face game). Example:

IV.   Demonstrates ability to role play a given emotion by making a facial expression in a mirror and acting out responses to the following questions.

A.   If someone gave you an ice-cream cone for no reason . . .

1.   How would you feel?
2.   What would you do?

B.   If you lost your favorite toy . . .

1.   How would you feel?
2.   What would you do?

C.   If you were lost in the woods and a big animal chased you . . .

1.   How would you feel?
2.   What would you do?

D.   If your mother gave your favorite toy to the child down the street . . .

1.   How would you feel?
2.   What would you do?

E. If you were playing with a jack-in-the-box and something jumped out at
you . . .

1. How would you feel?
2. What would you do?

THE CHILD AT AGE SIX: TRANSITION

A child whose background includes experiences such as those described in the preceeding plan of instruction by the time he is four or
five years of age may be expected to possess both a high degree of awareness regarding his feelings and attitudes and a positive self-concept at
age six when he enters the elementary school. Many children gain these
experiences informally at home or, more formally, in nursery schools,
kindergartens, or day-care centers. Diagnosis should determine the
degree of development and the required instructional activities. For
the purpose of discussion it is assumed that each child is given the opportunities described or alternate activities designed to meet similar
objectives.

As he enters first grade, the six-year-old child perceives the rapid
expansion of his environment. He stands now at the end of childhood
and the beginning of the process which leads to adulthood. New adult
figures, peers, and physical surroundings appear both exciting and
frightening. Pleasant and healthy growth experiences during early childhood will facilitate the processes of assimilation and accommodation
which are part of each new experience. The child leaves a world focused
on his family and his play group; he enters a world of adults and strange
new peers. This world requires increased socialization. A child's peers
become a prime factor in the process of psycho-social development. It
is through peer relations that much growth is manifested.

There is a noticeable reduction in egocentricity at this age. For
example, a child's speech pattern contains less monologue and more
adapted information. Adapted information occurs when one adopts the
point of view of his hearer and exchanges his thoughts; for example:
Child A, "I don't care for Johnny." Child B, "I really like Johnny!"
Child A, "I really do like Johnny." At six, social games with rules — such
as tag — predominate over solitary play. Make-believe games (games in
which the child thinks in terms of others) gain in popularity. The child's
association with his peers, then, influences his thinking in terms of
"others" rather than terms of "self."

A six-year-old child's thought processes are undergoing a gradual
yet continuous growth. He can now utilize speech to express his
thoughts, rather than rely on manual manipulation. However, there are

very definite limitations in a six-year-old child's thinking. He can ordinarily concentrate on only one idea at a time. Emphasis on the parts hampers his conception of the whole. He often uses language without full meaning, such as the concepts of "left" and "right." He can recognize multiple properties such as height and depth, yet his understanding of these properties is still weak. The six-year-old has the foundations that time and experience can fully develop.

At this age, children begin to behave more like adults, to show some consistency in their behavior. Yet the child is neither able nor invited to take equal part in the realm of adults. Consequently he works on mastering those tasks of which he is capable. He possesses a strong sense of competition. His peers are frequently used as measures for his own success.

As the child gains more independence, paradoxically he encounters more control. He has been exposed to the rules and regulations exercised in his own family circle. Now he is confronted with the codes of outside adults in his expanding world. This experience can prove confusing when a conflict in principles exist.

A six-year-old views an adult's judgment as right and fair. His disobedience does not represent a conflict in beliefs but rather an isolated rejection of authority—perhaps as a result of conforming to the crowd. The child expects to be punished for his wrongdoings and will reprimand himself in many cases. He has begun to develop a conscience. Moral values are cultivated at home and are nurtured by his interaction in the social environment.

THE WE—VALUING

The reader will have noted by now the subtle shift in the child: from an egocentric position in which satisfaction of immediate personal psycho-social needs was the primary value sought to the beginnings of a concern for the effect his behaviors may have on others. Needs, hence values, of others begin to play an important role in determining behavior as the child enters elementary education. Two specific types of phenomena bring value considerations to the surface. The first is conflict. We have implied the concept of conflict earlier when describing the characteristics of a six-year-old child. As spontaneous play gives way to organized games, individual conflicts arise. Have you ever heard conversations similar to those set out below. How do they end?

Boys playing football: *Sam,* "I want to be quarterback." *Willie,* "Joe should be quarterback." *Sam,* "———."

Girls gathering play group: *Cathy,* "Julie is my friend!" *Donna,* "No, Julie is my friend!" *Cathy,* "———."

Consider the ending you supplied. What values are illustrated by your statement? How was the conflict resolved? Of course, conflict is not limited to the play or peer group. It often extends to interaction with adults. Increased interaction multiplies the occasions for conflict as the child explores his powers and asserts his identity. Contradiction or inconsistency occurs in the area of conflict with adult requirements or expectations, the second yet overlapping value consideration. Simone de Beauvoir has summarized this dilemma beautifully.

> The fact is that it is very rare for the infantile world to maintain itself beyond adolescence. From childhood on, flaws begin to be revealed in it. With astonishment, revolt and disrespect the child little by little asks himself, "Why must I act that way? What good is it? And what will happen if I act in another way?" He discovers his subjectivity; he discovers that of others. And when he arrives at the age of adolescence he begins to vacillate because he notices the contradictions among adults as well as their hesitations and weaknesses. Men stop appearing as if they were gods, and at the same time, the adolescent discovers the human character of the reality about him. . . . The individual must at last assume his subjectivity. (Beauvoir, 1948; in Hellerick)

It is in the assumption of subjectivity that both the promise and the problem of psycho-social development reside. Up to this point, the child has reacted to the structure imposed upon him by others. His basis for action has been in large measure his perception of the consequences of acting to meet personal needs. He was *re*acting to the actions of parents and teachers, which furnished him a relatively clear-cut nonthreatening guide. In other words, his acceptance of an imposed structure effectively removed him from what might be called a *pro*active role.

As the child begins to discover that the people who structure his environment are human, his reactions are tempered by questions. He begins to ask whether the structure he encounters is valid. He asks the question, "Why?" In a deeper sense, his question reflects the need to know whether the structure that *is* is the structure that *ought to be*. Children facing the "is-ought" dilemma need the understanding and support of their teachers. The teachers need to understand that the question "Why?" does not simply indicate rebellion or disrespect. Rather, it indicates a significant development in the child's psycho-social growth.

THE IS-OUGHT DILEMMA

Charles Silberman in the landmark publication *Crisis in the Classroom* (1970) defines education as "the deliberate or purposeful creation, evocation, or transmission of knowledge, abilities, skills, and values." Silberman argues that the needs of the twenty-first century will be met only if there are masses of educated people, people who have developed both intellectual ability and the ability to feel. The educated person becomes at the very least a self-realizing person (awareness). But more than that, the educated person is a feeling, acting person, truly a self-actualizing person (valuing).

To develop such people requires the destruction of the artificial separation which has grown up between the cognitive and affective dimensions of learning. In order to accomplish this destruction we must reassert the importance of aesthetic and moral education. The arts — music, painting, dance, and others — must move from the periphery of the curriculum to its core. In addition, education must become an enterprise focused on moral purpose. We will discuss the meaning of the term moral and its place in the psycho-social studies in a later section. But lest confusion develop, let us state through Silberman (1970, 9) what moral education is not!

> This is not to say that education is or ever should be moralistic. There is a world of difference, as Dewey also pointed out, between "moral ideas" — ideas internalized so as to affect and improve conduct, to "make it better than it otherwise would be" — and "ideas about morality" — the pieties we acknowledge verbally and then proceed to ignore. Talking about morality, honesty, or kindness in no way insures that people will act morally, honestly, or kindly. The job of the educator is to teach in such a way as to convert "ideas about morality" into "moral ideas." In the words of a Talmudic axiom, "Let not thy learning exceed thy deeds. Mere knowledge is not the goal, but action."
>
> What educators must realize, moreover, is that how they teach and how they act may be more important than what they teach. The way we do things, that is to say, shapes values more directly and more effectively than the way we talk about them. Certainly administrative procedures like automatic promotion, homogeneous grouping, racial segregation, or selective admission to higher education affect "citizenship education," more profoundly than does the social studies curriculum. And children are taught a host of lessons about values, ethics, morality, character, and conduct every day of the week, less by the content of the curriculum than by the way schools are organized, the ways teachers and parents behave, the way they talk to children and to each other, the kinds of behavior they approve or reward and the kinds they disapprove or punish. These lessons are far more powerful than the verbalizations that accompany them and that they frequently controvert.

Moral Education

John Wilson defines a morally educated person as an individual exhibiting the following characteristics:

1. He acts for a reason

2. He has regard for other people's interest
3. He is logically consistent, knows the relevant facts and attends to the meaning of words.
4. He is good at identifying his own and other people's feelings.
5. He has and uses all these skills and translates them into action. (Wilson and others, 1967, 1)

The keys to moral education are reason and other-directedness. Each person passes through a number of identifiable stages on the way to becoming a moral person. These stages may be seen as roughly parallel to stages of intellectual development. Stages of moral development also coincide with the different psycho-social needs described earlier. Consider the relationship of the stages of moral development defined by Kohlberg (1964, 61) to Piaget's concepts of intellectual growth and Maslow's taxonomy of human needs:

1. Pre-moral — involves the relatively egocentric concepts of right and wrong as that which one can do without getting caught or as that which leads to the greatest personal satisfaction.
2. Conventional morality — during which good and evil are identified with the concepts of a "good boy" or "good girl," or with standards of the community and the concepts of law and order. In this stage morality is perceived as objective, as existing "out there."
3. Post-conventional — involves more abstract reasoning that may lead an individual into conflict with conventional morality.

This may need to be expanded. The first of two levels within the post-conventional stage basically involves the assumption that concepts of right and wrong result from a social contract, an implicit agreement among peers. The highest level is that in which the individual becomes devoted to personal principles that may transcend conventional morality and social contract. This is the stage exemplified by many of the youth rebellions of the late 1960's and early 1970's.

Questioning United States foreign policy in Southeast Asia brought many individuals to a direct confrontation with the traditional concept of "good citizen" or "patriot." These concepts have generally been defined in terms of characteristic behaviors. Thus, for example, a good citizen supports his country by obeying its laws. But one such law is the Selective Service Act which requires young men to serve in the nation's armed forces when called. The expected behavior upon notification of selection is to present oneself for induction and to follow all orders issued by superiors during the time of service. Some individuals concluded that within their frame of reference their country's involvement in Vietnam was immoral. Assuming that this position was an honest statement of principle, we must evaluate their behaviors — such as emigrating to Canada, serving in the armed forces but refusing to obey orders which involved killing, and so on—as examples of a post-conventional morality.

Similarly, but on a less emotional level, large numbers of individuals have become vitally concerned with environmental problems. Environmentalists have come increasingly in conflict with long-established and accepted practice. For example, concern with air pollution resulting from automobile exhaust led individuals to lobby for cleaner engines or fuels or to give up the use of an automobile as a means of transportation. Other individuals have protested the development of a supersonic transport plane. These behaviors are in direct opposition to the accepted notion that a "good citizen" supports his nation's position by contributing to its preeminance in technology traditionally exemplified by the notion that "bigger is better."

Citizenship Education

A cursory examination of state and local curriculum guides will reveal that citizenship education is listed as a primary goal of social studies instruction. Most organizations generally classified as patriotic, such as the American Legion and Daughters of the American Revolution, have published statements on education in which they emphasize their support of education for "good citizenship." These statements have often appeared in response to a public outcry about the moral degeneracy of youth or some other group. The strength and frequency with which these statements appear implies that public schools have failed to reach the stated goals. In general, responses to these charges of failure have not gone far beyond the defensive or apology stages.

William Fielder summarized the situation:

> Most talkers do two things: describe the value wash-out and prescribe a remedy. More prudent speakers insert an intermediate question. That is, after describing what is gone but before prescribing how to get it back, the careful speaker considers whether or not the school is the relevant institution to administer the getting-back program he has in mind. (1967, 34)

Emphasis on a defensive position has resulted in lack of attention to the critical question: "Should the school act as the primary influence in developing a moral person?"

The appropriate role of the school, hence the teacher, is a crucial question. Research on the development of political and social attitudes among children tends to show that a child's value constellation is pretty well established by age seven or eight. The inevitable conclusion is that the primary influence in the development of children's value systems resides in the home environment. If we accept this conclusion, the school has made little difference in the formation of political and social attitudes.

Yet we have reason to believe that what we in the schools do does make a difference. In the discussion on concept development in Chapter 3, we will note the importance of discrimination between exemplars and nonexemplars of a concept. By increasing the proportion of nonexemplars in the universe, we create doubt as to the validity of a concept. Sufficient discrepant data may require a redefinition of the concept in question. Thus it is with moral education in the school. Teachers provide reinforcement for some ideas and dissonance for others. The minimum effect is the child's awareness that "Miss Rider agrees with me" or that "Mr. Haggard disagrees with me." These perceptions are often communicated to parents and peers in the forms: "She likes me." "He doesn't like me."

The degree of importance (value) which a given child places on acceptance by his teacher influences directly his overt behavior and probably his covert motives for acting. (Look back to the passage from Silberman.) The ways we teachers respond to a child — our intensity, our posture, our expression, no less than the words we select — communicate our evaluation of his worth as an individual.

If teachers and community accept the notion that the purpose of education is to help children attain awareness of who they are (egoizing) and to provide opportunities for them to examine their selves in terms of their personal needs as well as their relation to the environment in which they live (ecologizing), then we as teachers cannot avoid giving purposeful attention to moral education. Hence, value-directed and value-affecting teaching becomes not only appropriate but requisite for social studies instruction.

Some teachers shy away from value-directed or value-affecting teaching on the basis that it is not subject to empirical observation. Scriven answers this challenge as follows:

> Of course, value judgments do not spring full-fledged from the facts about the entity being evaluated, but that does not show they are not empirical. They require a careful combination of those facts with other facts about the needs, wants and ideals of the valuing agents. (1969, 67)

In the past decade we have painstakingly examined our environment. Data collected reveal the irreparable damage done to many of our natural resources. Stanley Cain has written that in evaluating the current condition of the environment,

> Slowly there is arising the realization that uncoordinated scientific, technological, fiscal, political, social, and other attempts at change are failing to accomplish the needed adjustment between human needs and their fulfillment. (1967, 13)

We now understand that our environment is one ecosystem which is not the sole property of man but belongs to all things which inhabit it. A fine balance exists in this ecosystem and changes in any element of the system effect all other elements. Therefore, it becomes imperative for each person to think in terms of these relationships, that is, in terms of the ecology of the system. Cain points out that,

> Among the conditions for satisfactory relationships between man and environment are knowledge of the physical environment, of man's living associates, and of the relationships among them. But this is not enough. Man is more than an animal. His ecology must encompass also what man himself creates. (1967, 13)

This imperative brings man face to face with a whole series of questions involving the ultimate good of his own creative genius. At the same time he realizes that his technology has created an urban society in which each individual is inextricably involved with other humans. Each man must then move from a personal awareness or self-realization to what, therefore, Brameld calls a social self-realization. Brameld (1969) reflects the position that humans are

> . . . integrally related socially to other human beings in collective arrangements that extend from the family all the way to the periphery of racial, religious and political institutions that are eventually planetary in scope.

The good of any man's action becomes relative to its affect on his total ecosystem both animate and inanimate. Decisions for action will reflect his evaluation of these relationships because of his value system.

It is the role of the educator to help each child he encounters prepare to make decisions in value-loaded situations and to act on these decisions. This preparation requires development of a reasoning person capable of rationally analyzing a situation with regard to the effect his actions may have on himself and others and then acting consistently. The reader may wish now to consult the definition of a morally educated person set out earlier.

VALUES

Before proceeding, complete the following activity.

What do you value?

1. Below is a list of 14 value terms arranged in alphabetical order. Study the list and then place a **1** next to the value term which you feel is most important to you. Place a **2** next to the value term which is second most important. And continue to rank the terms until all have been assigned a

relative position with the least important assigned number **14.** When you have completed ranking all of the values, go back and check over your list. Please take all the time you need to think about this so that the end result is as true representation of your value performance as possible.

_____ AUTHENTIC (real, truthful)
_____ BROADMINDED (openminded)
_____ CAPABLE (competent, effective)
_____ CAREFUL (cautious, prudent)
_____ CLEAN (neat, tidy)
_____ COOPERATIVE (working well with others)
_____ COURAGEOUS (standing up for your beliefs)
_____ INDUSTRIOUS (hard-working, ambitious)
_____ INTELLECTUAL (intelligent, rational)
_____ PATIENT (calm, willing to wait)
_____ POLITE (courteous, well-mannered)
_____ PRACTICAL (down-to-earth, realistic)
_____ TENDER (gentle, warm-hearted)
_____ TRUSTING (not suspicious, trustful of others)

2. Find someone in your class with a ranking differing from yours. Spend some time (10-15 minutes) discussing a few points of disagreement.
3. With this person, or alone if you prefer, build a values lesson in which children might choose from two or more "goods," a lesson in which children might be confronted with a decision where alternatives might be reflected in two or more of the value terms above. A child, for example, might easily feel the conflict between cooperativeness and authenticity in deciding whether to reveal a dishonest act by his friend to some authority.

It might be appropriate to consider at this time a definition of the term value. Raths and his colleagues in their most useful book *Values and Teaching*, state that

> Persons have experiences; they grow and learn. Out of experiences may come certain guides to behavior. These guides tend to give direction to life and may be called values. Our values show what we tend to do with our limited time and energy. (1966, 27)

They set out seven criteria against which something might be measured to determine whether it is indeed a value. Their criteria may be summarized as follows: A value must be chosen freely from among alternatives after consideration of consequences. Further, an individual must feel good about his choice, be willing to affirm the choice when challenged, and he must act on the bases of his choice. Finally, his actions must be repeated; that is, they must be consistent in similar situations over time.

The process by which an individual arrives at value decisions is called *valuing,* and the essence of valuing, simply stated, "is the discovery of self followed by careful examination of what one finds." (Fielder, 1967, 73) One may approach this valuing process from three distinguishable directions; describing, clarifying, and reconstructing. In each case the ultimate objective is a system of values to guide an individual's action. However, in a descriptive approach the criterion is a set of ideal or consensus values established by some extrapersonal source. The clarifying approach on the other hand seeks to help the individual become aware of his values and their consequences and to promote consideration of alternatives. A reconstructive approach attempts to provide a basis for changing value patterns in the light of some ultimate psychosocial need.

It has been suggested that schools ought to teach American values. Although no definitive statement of "American values" exists there have been numerous attempts to set out the values implied.

Kluckhohn writes,

> The pattern of the implicit American Creed seems to embrace the following recurrent elements: faith in the rational, a need for moralistic rationalization, an optimistic conviction that rational effort counts, romantic individualism and the cult of the common man, high valuation on change—which is ordinarily taken to mean "progress," the conscious quest for pleasure. (1965, 199)

The Educational Policies Commission of the National Education Association listed the following moral and spiritual values in the public schools:

1. Respect for human personality
2. Moral responsibility of the individual
3. Institutions are servants of men
4. Common consent (peaceful adjustments rather than violence)
5. Devotion to truth (freedom of expression)
6. Respect for excellence
7. Moral equality for all
8. Brotherhood (the Golden Rule)
9. The pursuit of happiness (happiness considered as the fullest expression of one's potentialities—not mere fun)
10. Spiritual enrichment (NEA, 1951)

The Committee on Concepts and Values of the National Council for the Social Studies stated these societal goals of American democracy:

1. The intelligent use of the forces of nature.
2. Recognition and understanding of world interdependence.
3. Recognition of the dignity and worth of the individual.

4. Use of intelligence to improve human living.
5. Vitalization of democracy through the intelligent use of our public educational facilities.
6. Intelligent acceptance, by individuals and groups, of responsibility for achieving democratic social action.
7. Increasing effectiveness of the family as a basic social institution.
8. Effective development of moral and spiritual values.
9. Intelligent and responsible sharing of power in order to attain justice.
10. Intelligent utilization of scarce resources to attain the widest general well-being.
11. Achievement of adequate horizons of loyalty.
12. Cooperation in the interest of peace and welfare.
13. Achieving balance between social stability and social change.
14. Widening and deepening the ability to live more richly. (NCSS, 1965)

But are these really the values by which citizens of the United States live and act? Are they "the American Values"? Research conducted at the University of Chicago under the direction of Jacob Getzels shows a distinct set of values operating. However, these values have changed over the past thirty years. Initially, Getzels differentiates between those "codified-secular-values" (such as equality and democracy) to which we pay homage and the "uncodified-secular-values" which control daily behavior. Getzels sacred values do not fit the Raths criterion quoted earlier. In effect Getzels agrees, observing that what really counts is the secular-value constellation. But what does the research show?

In the 1940's Getzels' students found that four major secular values could be identified. (Getzels, 1970) These were labeled *traditional*. They are listed below with appropriate illustrations added:

Traditional Secular Values

Work Success Ethic. "By the sweat of your brow you will earn your keep."
Future Time Orientation. "Keep your nose clean and in twenty years you'll receive a nice pension."
Independence or Separate Self. "God helps him who helps himself."
Puritan Morality. "Cleanliness is next to Godliness."

During the 1950's the Chicago researchers noted a switch to what they labeled *emerging or transitional values.*

Emerging or Transitional Secular Values

Sociability—Frictionless Interpersonal Relationship. "The Man in the Grey Flannel Suit."
Present Time Orientation. Kerouac, "On The Road."
Group Conformity. "The Organization Man."
Moral Relativism. Situational Ethics.

In 1969 additional data were collected which revealed movement to another set of secular values.

1969 Secular Values[2]

Social Consciousness. "All men are entitled to a fair share of worldly goods." Nader's Raiders.

Relevance (perhaps Reciprocity?). "I live in a world I didn't make." Black Studies programs.

Personal Authenticity. "Do your own thing." Sensitivity and encounter groups.

Idealistic Moral Commitment. "I have a dream . . ." (Martin Luther King, Jr.). Peace Corps; VISTA.

The dilemma of education is summarized by Getzels' citing Goethe's comment to the effect that the child is expected to formulate a system of values from among a fluid constellation but the child asks the prior question, "What values?"

Franklin Murphy (1970) identified the dominant value criteria of the seventeenth and eighteenth centuries as Descartes' dictum, "*Cogito ergo sum* — I think, therefore I am." The consequent of this was emphasis on the rational and the emergence of the Age of Reason. This was supplemented in the nineteenth century when the watchword of the Industrial Revolution became "*Facio ergo sum* — I make, therefore I am," thus adding the principle of production to that of knowing. Murphy words a new philosophical credo for the twentieth century, or perhaps the twenty-first century, "*Sentio ergo sum* — I feel therefore, I am." It is no longer sufficient to measure the worth of personal existence in terms of ability to think and to make. An individual must also operate in sensitivity to his own feelings and attitudes and to the feelings and attitudes of others. If we accept this three-dimensional measure of existence and acknowledge the school's responsibility to facilitate awareness and development of personal existence, we must change nearly totally the emphasis on cognitive development. The affective dimension of feelings, attitudes, and values must be given appropriate place in the curriculum, particularly in the psycho-social studies.

How to Change the Emphasis?

Return for a moment to Scriven:

Moral behavior requires moral motivation as well as moral insight, and the mainspring for that (for egalitarian morality) is identification with others, empathy, sympathy. . . . This, too can be taught, from the very earliest ages, but not by parroting the results of cognitive research. It can be taught by

[2] The quoted attributes for the 1969 Secular Values were provided by Dr. Charles Crosthwait, Social Studies Professor, Georgia State University, in conversation with one of the authors. They are not necessarily those that Getzels might have provided.

role-changing games, by tests of prediction skills about the behaviors of highly different others by the use of highly graphic audio-visual material and by direct field experience supplemented with appropriate interviews and discussions. (1969)

Walter Coppedge placed the emphasis on cognitive development in the following perspective:

Our system is overwhelmingly rational and cognitive and in the last few decades it has either ignored or sacrificed the intuitive or affective. That kind of teaching which advocates dispassion, disinterest, and detachment is disastrous to a generation calling for commitment. The analytical professor will not speak to the generation who are crying for professors who profess. (1970, 75)

Assessing the current state of the classroom art, Coppedge states,

We teach as if the only realities were those captured at two removes in those rivers of ink which are words. We ignore the psycho-physical relationship of mind and body, feeling and language. (1970, 75)

The general methods or techniques mentioned by Scriven will be illustrated in subsequent chapters in the course of considering the various stages of psycho-social development. However, we would like at this point to refer to a number of terminal behaviors which might serve as prime objectives for instruction. Hoffman and Mickelson (1970) set out the following behaviors for children in the early grades.

PERSONAL (Psychology)	SOCIAL (Sociology)	CULTURAL (Anthropology)
The Individual	*The Individual*	*The Individual*
Differentiates between tasks he can perform and those with which he needs help.	Shares family responsibilities.	Takes part in national and international holiday celebrations: Thanksgiving, Fourth of July, U.N. Day.
Accepts the fact that he outperforms others in some ways and vice versa. Works to overcome "weaknesses" and to refine "strengths."	Extends to others the same loving response he seeks from others. Compliments others at the appropriate times.	Plays and/or works with boys and girls of different racial, religious, and national groups.
Chooses among alternative courses of action on the basis of a personal value system.	Empathizes with others in appropriate ways. Shares responsibilities in work and play group.	

PERSONAL (Psychology)	SOCIAL (Sociology)	CULTURAL (Anthropology)
Discriminates between acts of which he is "proud" and those of which he is not.	Accepts group decisions.	
	Acts in accordance with masculine and feminine roles.	
Deals with "success" and "failure" in a mature way.		
Achieves loving personal relations with others.		
Expresses feelings constructively.		
Secures acceptance from others.		

These are the behaviors which exemplify the *awareness* dimension of the child's development. As the child moves beyond the awareness stage he is able to begin to apply inquiry techniques to resolve conflict situations which occur in his daily existence. Gradually a psychosocial curriculum guides youngsters to a set of more sophisticated (cognitively) and more other-centered (affectively), values as evidenced in these behaviors.

PERSONAL (Psychology)	SOCIAL (Sociology)	CULTURAL (Anthropology)
The Individual	*The Individual*	*The Individual*
Acts on the basis of existing personal abilities, interests, constraints.	Accepts and works with abilities, interests, and constraints of others.	Accepts his own cultural background.
Deals with success and failure in a constructive way.	Extends to others the same needs satisfactions as he desires for himself.	Accepts and reconciles cultural differences between his own and other groups: racial, religious, ethnic, social class.

PERSONAL (Psychology)	SOCIAL (Sociology)	CULTURAL (Anthropology)
Determines (sets) personal priorities in a useful way.	Reconciles personal desires with the interests of others, both individuals and groups, when necessary.	Accepts and seeks to understand the cultural values and patterns of other countries.
Accepts responsibility for his own acts.		
Acts in terms of a personal system of values.	Participates as a constructive group member.	
Achieves affectionate personal relations with others.	Assumes leadership role in appropriate situations.	
Expresses emotion (feelings) constructively.	Establishes (maintains) good (family, school, etc.) relationships.	
Achieves status with (acceptance from) others.		

Ultimately, the behaviors sought in a psycho-social curriculum exemplify more than acceptance of the elements of the person's world and functional participation in their interplay. The object is to nurture in the child an ecologizing disposition, that is, movement beyond mere compliance with the factors which influence his life and toward an attempt to shape those factors: not to settle for a "Make the best of it!" situation, but to seek the creative alternative which springs from the mind, gives the option of choice and the skills and knowledge to support choice. Some of the kinds of behaviors that might be sought are described below:

PERSONAL (Psychology)	SOCIAL (Sociology)	CULTURAL (Anthropology)
The Individual	*The Individual*	*The Individual*
Conserves natural resources	Acts to secure appropriate use of natural resources in the community, nation and world.	Acts to preserve distinctive cultural patterns and mores of various religious, ethnic, and national groups.
Preserves the ecological balance of his community.		

PERSONAL	SOCIAL	CULTURAL
(Psychology)	(Sociology)	(Anthropology)

| | Works with others to maintain the ecological balance of the community nation, world. | Encourages the development of new cultural habits, patterns, etc. to replace the outmoded. |
| | Acts to improve the quality of community planning. | Acts to control and direct the impact of technology on humanity. |

These are the ends sought in psycho-social studies. Each educator must select the specific form of these behaviors appropriate for his students as well as the particular type of activity most likely to facilitate achievement of the objective.

SUMMARY

While we authors personally subscribe to the tenets of the "valuing" process, namely applying methods of problem solving to individual perception and feelings regarding conflicting data and interpretations, we are concerned about programs which attempt to apply these techniques within the elementary-school curriculum to primary-age children and to children living in economically impoverished areas. These children are often not ready for the valuing process.

Raths and his colleagues, in their seminal work entitled *Values and Teaching* (1966), spoke to the first of our concerns when they warned teachers that children with low ego development would not profit from such instruction. In other words, intensive valuing can indeed cause further reduction of a child's self concept. However, with respect to this first concern, our experience and observation would indicate that children with low ego development seldom get burned here; rather, they simply refuse to play the valuing game.

Our second concern is undeniably related to the first. Research in cognitive development gives us a second admonition: Do not ask children to do something for which they do not possess the cognitive apparatus. Cause-and-affect relationships, taught with any degree of integrity, cannot be successfully induced with a large proportion of elementary-age children.

There was a time when we authors sincerely believed that "readiness" for causal thinking was an entirely feasible objective for the primary-age children and that what was needed were better media and materials to accomplish this. Such materials have begun to appear, but children continue to say little when confronted with personal and social controversies. Consider, for a moment, two objectives from the highly acclaimed elementary program on human relations offered by Dr. Ralph Ojeman. Dr. Ojeman cites this major objective, among others, for his Kindergarten-Grade One Series:

> When presented with common, everyday, meaningful situations, such as he might experience directly or indirectly, the child begins to use some of the methods for understanding and dealing with human behavior.
>
> . . . He recognizes a need for knowing more about how a situation developed and for knowing the different sides before making a judgment or reacting to a situation.
>
> . . . He begins to use this information to try to think of what might be some of the most probable causes or reasons of a behavior. (Ojeman, 1959)

We authors have seen practice teachers get disappointing results from investing a disproportionate amount of time trying to teach cause-and-effect relationships to children of limited intellectual and emotional development. While we are aware of the need for greater research in the area of development of causal thinking in young children, we advocate fewer lessons designed to meet Dr. Ojeman's objectives in early grades. The question which must be posed to prospective elementary teachers, then, is "Given children who are operating largely in either-or black-or-white patterns of thinking, many of whom manifest strong feelings of personal inadequacies, what experiences do you feel are desirable and feasible (teachers can't do everything) to prepare students to perform what has been labeled the valuing process?"

If affective development needs are to be raised to the valuing level, then what strategies might teachers find helpful? Our tentative resolution of this problem, largely based on personal interaction with pre-service, in-service, and inner-city teachers, results in two assumptions regarding method:

1. Conflicts related to "good" and "bad" in classrooms are most salient when the situations, real or simulated, deal directly with the prevailing physical, psychological, social, and cultural needs of those involved, namely the teachers and the children.

2. Choices made in "good" conflict situations may be made primarily to satisfy a personal need rather than to arrive at some "accepted" truth.

A teacher concerned with affective development must possess a finely tuned perceptual apparatus. Sensitivity to the conflicting needs of individual children will lead to instructional activities designed to help each child validate his own self. Growth beyond awareness requires knowledge of the conceptual process dealt with in Chapter 3. The "A Plan of Instruction Dealing with Young Children's Feelings" included in this chapter contains numerous examples of applications of the two assumptions cited above. Others are included throughout the text.

RECOMMENDATIONS FOR FURTHER READING

Brown, George Isaac. *Human Teaching for Human Learning: An Introduction to Confluent Education.* New York: Viking Press, 1971. Readers are introduced to the emerging theory of confluent education. After providing and defending the concept of confluence, Brown includes some chapters written by teachers of varying grade-subject levels who are attempting to use some strategies congruent with Brown's concept of confluent education.

Bruner, Jerome. *On Knowing: Essays on the Left Hand.* New York: Atheneum Publishers, 1969. The blend of knowledge and feeling which constitutes knowing is described in a series of essays. The focus is on the left hand — the aesthetic sensitivity of the human makeup. Bruner weaves the technical manipulative abilities of observing through analyzing, as characterized by the right hand, with the ability to synthesize and evaluate, identified with the left hand. An excellent perspective on the global characteristics of knowledge.

Epstein, Charlotte. *Affective Subjects In the Classroom: Exploring Race, Sex, and Drugs.* New York and London: Intext Educational Publishers, 1972. Epstein's book contains a number of well-reflected strategies for diagnosing and treating problems related to human relations. Her years of experience in dealing with intergroup education include working in human relations with policemen as well as with teachers in the inner city of Philadelphia. Her sound ideas have been adapted and applied by many of our former students at Temple and Georgia State Universities.

Maslow, Abraham H. *Toward a Psychology of Being,* 2nd edition. New York: Van Nostrand Reinhold Company, 1968. Writing in an easy communicative style, Maslow relates his theory of need gratification. His concept of "self-actualization" is particularly developed and illustrated.

Maslow, Abraham H. *Motivation and Personality,* 2nd edition. New York: Harper & Row, 1970. A more technical (research) treatment of Maslow's needs-gratification theory. The first two chapters deal with the nature of science and scientists. Later chapters get into what Maslow has referred to as the "unnoticed revolution," humanistic psychology. See particularly Chapters 4, 11, 12, 15, and 16.

Piaget, Jean, and Barbel Inhelder. *The Psychology of the Child.* New York: Basic Books, 1969. A thorough introduction to developmental psychology as defined by Piaget. A readable text provides ample examples to illustrate the approach.

Raths, Louis E., Merrill Harmin, and Sidney B. Simon. *Values and Teaching.* Columbus, Ohio: Charles E. Merrill Publishing Company, 1966. A particularly significant book for values instruction with intellectually and emotionally mature youngsters. Our students who teach children of upper elementary and junior high age in suburban schools have made wide application of this method of instruction. Chapters 6 and 7 contain illustrations of the valuing process that Raths, Harmin, and Simon propound.

CHAPTER 3

Conceptual Teaching: Theory and Practice

Teachers concerned with meeting certain psycho-social needs of children must not only be cognizant of the driving motivations of their children, but must also have certain skills and understandings which will help them to meet student needs. In Chapter 2, emphasis was placed on affective concerns, where the authors of this book felt too little attention had been placed in previous social studies methods texts. In this third chapter the teacher is exposed to cognitive concerns which he will hopefully select, modify, or expand as he builds his own philosophy of teaching. Since this chapter is the only one with a heavy "cognitive" emphasis, the authors have included some specific objectives as well as a brief annotated bibliography at the end of the chapter for further reading.

The following objectives, written with the preservice or inservice elementary-school teacher in mind, served as the basis of this chapter:

1. Students will demonstrate through related oral discussion that they understand the rationale posited in this chapter, which supports the need for concept-based instruction. Emphasis upon tracing the concern for

identifying and teaching only key understandings from Dewey and others through Bruner should be elicited. Problems related to the explosion of information and the broad nature of the term "social studies" should be included.

2. Students will be able through related oral discussion and/or materials construction to operationally define the terms "concept," "generalization," and "construct" as well as give illustrations of the role of each in the teaching of social studies.

3. Students will be able to recognize the application of conceptual teaching strategies in commercially prepared materials as well as to construct concept-based teaching strategies consistent with those described in this chapter.

4. Students will be able to construct conceptual lessons at various stages of the maturity of the elementary-school child. Students should have a rationale for their way of doing things.

5. Students should be able to identify and to construct conceptual elements which incorporate various teaching strategies; for example, inductive and deductive methods of concept and generalization development, use of varying levels of questioning in development of a problem, concept, or generalization; and other problem-solving strategies.

6. Students should give evidence of paying attention to the five considerations cited in this chapter in the development of some concept-based materials. Attainment of this objective could be evaluated through a critical analysis of some concept-based materials which the student cooperatively or independently developed.

One of the most perplexing problems educators grapple with is the selection of content to be taught. When knowledge was limited, the question of what to teach may have been simple. The rapid accumulation of new knowledge in the twentieth century, often making previous descriptive knowledge inaccurate, makes the problem of selection of content all the more perplexing.

This problem of what is really worth teaching is most difficult in social studies. Social studies draws its content primarily from the six social-science disciplines mentioned in Chapter 1. The social sciences are currently undergoing some radical changes. Social theories are highly tentative since they attempt description and prediction of human behavior. Yet here, more than anywhere else in the school curriculum, lies the potential source of the most important understandings children will need to have if they are to find meaning and personal satisfaction in their future. This chapter attempts to aid a teacher in answering questions related to what important ideas should serve as the focus of social studies teaching and what strategies can be used to develop these understandings.

WHAT IS CONCEPTUAL TEACHING?

Educational theorists have long recognized the need for organizing subject-matter content around the most fundamental ideas which could be identified. John Dewey (1916), more than fifty years ago, urged curriculum specialists to identify the major ideas within each subject-matter field which could then serve as the logical arrangements of each academic discipline.

Alfred North Whitehead voiced essentially the same concern when he stated, "Let the main ideas which are introduced into a child's education be few and important, and let them be thrown into every combination possible." (1929, 3)

That such outstanding ideals have not been put into operation is quite apparent. Most students of the social sciences are hard-pressed to recall even a few "big ideas" which they learned through their social studies experiences in the public schools. While some students have retained a considerable amount of information, some of which may be factual, a great many have been unable or unwilling to commit large masses of information to memory.

Why have the ideals of Whitehead, Dewey, and others not been realized? Part of the answer may reside in the differences between the goals of the teacher educators and the social scientists. Teacher educators, though they usually possess more understanding of child growth and development and are convinced of the need for building student social relationships, have themselves been ignorant of just how to make application of the expanding body of social-science knowledge. Social scientists, in turn, have been concerned with uncovering new knowledge but not with teacher education.

A return to a concern for teaching the truly big ideas was ignited by a book primarily concerned with this problem as it related to mathematics and the natural and physical sciences. In this book, entitled *The Process of Education*, Jerome Bruner applied the term "structural knowledge" to the really big, abstract ideas which would serve as the basis of instruction. His rationale for such knowledge was:

> Scholarly knowledge has reached the point where factual knowledge of any field has become an impossibility even for the advanced scholar. More than ever before in the history of education, we need to devise a method of analysis which will enable us to sort out the truly important and organize it in such a way that the relatively few things we are able to teach will have maximum educational effect. (Bruner, 1964, 84)

Following Bruner's observation, both social scientists and social studies educators have made a number of attempts to identify key ideas permeating one or more of the social-science disciplines having most relevance for social studies education. An initial attempt to identify important generalizations for the social sciences was undertaken by Hanna, Lee, and their associates at Stanford University. This team originally identified more than 3,000 generalizations. (Hanna and Lee, 1962) Later attempts (*Social Studies Framework*, 1962; *A Conceptual Framework*, 1965; Faucett and colleagues, 1968) moved in the direction of isolating these "big ideas," which have been labeled structural concepts or constructs. The later work has greatly reduced the number of such ideas.

Most of the new social studies projects have developed either single-medium or multimedia materials based upon one or more frameworks of key ideas emanating from the social sciences.

One way of viewing the relationship between facts, concepts, generalizations, and higher-order constructs is presented in the model of Chart 1.

CHART 1.

Levels of Knowledge. Read upward.

4. Constructs (or advance organizers)

↑

3. Generalizations — which can be selected or related to

↑

2. Concepts — which can be arranged as

↑

1. Facts (attributes) — are arranged to form

Concepts

In this model or representation of reality, the learner is seen to build concepts out of the information (facts) he takes in as experiential data. At each higher level of abstraction the total number of subsumers decreases. Thus, the single construct "power" subsumes many political science generalizations and concepts and a myriad of specific facts and attributes. A child forms a concept related to "flag," for example, through several processes of association, discrimination and classification. Thus he may attach meaning to a group of letters spelling "flag" through the sum total of his experiences related to it. He may discriminate and associate the term "flag" with "a piece of cloth waving from a stick" and "something important." Later he may discriminate and associate the flag with its purpose. The process is one of sorting out the attributes which make "flag" a unique phenomenon for the child and applying these attributes to some particular symbol.

Also, the learner places each conceptualized idea in some hierarchy. The concept of "flag," for example, may become one attribute of a larger concept such as "symbol of patriotism." This process of conceptualization — that is, the process of discrimination, categorization, and association — serves as a key to the methodology of aiding youngsters in forming concepts.

A concept has been defined as a classification of stimuli having common characteristics. (Tanck, 1969) Another definition follows: "A concept is the abstract body of meaning a person associates with the symbol for a class of things, events, or ideas. It is the awareness of the attributes of the class for which a symbol stands. . . . A concept is an internal mental awareness that affects outward behavior." (McDonald, 1965, 22) Perhaps the essential concept of a concept is its contrast with a verbalism. A verbalism is the use of some word without any understanding of its meaning.

Here is an important characteristic of the conceptual process; it is an internal process. Concepts cannot be given to children by any such simple process as saying, "Here are all the attributes that I have found related to the concept of 'flag.' Remember them." The learner forms his own concepts. The teacher operates out of hers or his in making the decisions as to what ought to be taught. These decisions will result in some notion as to which abstractions should serve as the basis of instruction and will influence the results of the youngsters' concept forming. Though some current programs attempt to have youngsters arrive at a predetermined set of concepts and generalizations, we authors are opposed to such a closed method. We will argue for techniques that allow increasing individuality in concept patterning as the learner increases in physical, emotional, and socio-cultural sophistication. Such individuality is inescapable in any event since even children seldom approach a new learning experience with their concept patterns blank; however slight, differences in language and experience contribute to each learner's forming concepts unique to himself. Furthermore, the fantastic number of defined social science concepts makes arbitrary selection of concepts or indeed even deliberate attempts to develop all defined concepts rather futile. It also is antithetical to the notion that conceptualization is largely a unique and *individual* experience.

Generalizations

The level of knowledge above concepts in Chart 1 is generalizations. McDonald (1965, 692) has defined a generalization as a statement of the relationship between two or more concepts. Tanck (1969) states that ". . . a generalization is an understanding of a relationship between or among concepts. It is a chaining or linking among concepts." A generalization related to the concept of "flag" might be that "political institutions often use symbols, such as flags, songs, pledges, to which their members can attach allegiance." In this example, concepts such as "political institutions," "symbols," and "flags" are interrelated. It should be readily apparent that again, without some high-level constructs to direct the writing of generalizations, the list of such generalizations would be practically inexhaustible.

Tanck lists six attributes of generalizations. They are abbreviated here:

1. A generalization involves relationship(s) among two or more concepts.
2. A generalization pertains to whole classes. It asserts that something is true of some or all members of a whole class.
3. A generalization is a higher-level abstraction than a concept. It involves meanings of the concepts included but has its own meaning which is not the same as and is greater than the meaning of the (included) concepts.
4. A generalization is based upon inference. It is derived from reasoning or suggestion rather than from observation alone.
5. A generalization involves an assertion which can be judged for truth and validity.
6. The generalization is not the verbalized statement or assertion but the body of understanding represented. (1969, 107)

Constructs

Tanck defines a construct as "an organization of interrelated generalizations and concepts. It is a complex idea or image consisting of a number of correlated lesser ideas." (1969, 109) Social scientists and social studies educators have begun the important and arduous task of identifying the most salient relationships in the social sciences. While such tasks can only produce a number of tentative relationships subject to change as new information is collected and synthesized in the social sciences, these efforts are extremely important as flexible goals to social studies instruction.

How have these tentative abstractions been selected? Essentially the process has involved sorting through numerous social-science concepts and generalizations to construct theories of "what is" and "what ought to be." Many are heavily value loaded. Others attempt to describe the methodology of one or more of the social-science disciplines. The constructs identified in this text are those which the authors feel represent the product of some of the best thinking in the social sciences. The prospective social studies teacher needs also to seek out for himself those relationships which he feels are most important to teach.

An illustration of a social-science structural idea or construct is offered here: The construct of "scarcity" (man's wants are unlimited while his resources are limited) has long been identified as the organizing principle of economics. Scarcity serves as the central idea from which all supporting ideas (concepts, generalizations, and factual attributes) are selected. One important generalization related to the notion of scarcity was identified by Womack (1966, 3): "Since natural resources are limited and human wants are unlimited, every society has developed a method for allocating its scarce resources." The term "market," then, becomes a concept related to the construct "scarcity." Specific attributes of the concept of "market" could include the various ways in which societies set up means of allocating various resources. A third-grade teacher, for example, might be using the local supermarket as a vehicle for developing ideas related to scarcity. A sixth-grade teacher might be developing slightly more sophisticated ideas related to scarcity through a cross-time comparison between methods used by the Maya Indians of pre-Conquest Mexico and those currently used by the child's parents.

Curriculum specialists in social studies have, then, attempted to take these constructs for each of the six social-science disciplines and write conceptual strands for each grade level. These strands are written on the basis of some suggested content for a particular grade level (often chosen on the basis of the expanding-horizons principle described in Chapter 1) and on the basis of the maturity level of the child. These constructs then reappear at each grade level, in slightly more sophisticated form and written around some other topical area.

Consider the following lesson which introduces a third- or fourth-grade class to the problem of scarcity as it relates to family purchasing power:

Construct: Scarcity.
Generalization: People must make wise choices in deciding which goods and services to buy with their limited resources.

Procedure:

1. On the board is a list of items and their approximate prices.

1. Game	$5.00		9. Record Album	$4.00
2. Gloves	$3.00		10. Gum	$1.00
3. Shoes	$6.00		11. Ink Pens	$1.00
4. Candy	$2.00		12. Bongos	$5.00
5. Doll	$5.00		13. Book	$2.00
6. Pants	$4.00		14. Steak	$3.00
7. Spinning Top	$1.00		15. Milk	$1.00
8. Hat	$3.00			

2. The children are asked to make up a list of six items that they would like to buy, from the list on the board.
3. The teacher goes over the list that some of the children have made.
4. Then the teacher has the students make another list; however, this time they are told that they have only $10.00 to spend: "If you have only $10.00 to spend, which items would you select from the list on the board to spend it on?"
5. Then the teacher discusses with the class the point that when they have limited funds, it is essential to first buy what is important and necessary and then buy nonessentials. This will be done by comparing the two lists that the students have made.

Evaluation:

1. The class will be asked to make up their own list of items consisting of things which they need and things which they want in order of preference.
2. Students will also be asked to list their resources. Students will then be asked to describe how they might use their limited resources most effectively.

TEACHING CONCEPTS, GENERALIZATIONS, AND CONSTRUCTS

In this section specific suggestions are made relative to the development of strategies to be used in teaching concept-based social studies lessons. The reader is strongly encouraged to carefully make note of these procedures and to internalize those aspects which are congruent with his or her philosophy of teaching. It is important that preservice and inservice teachers participate in the construction and implementation of concept-based materials. The following five considerations, adopted from Tanck (1969, 45) served as the basis for the authors' related comments.

First Consideration: What Elements of Structural Knowledge Do I Wish to Develop?

Since there is no definitive list of ideas which should be taught in social studies, the three following suggestions are offered to assist teachers in content selection.

1. The reader may well give serious consideration to the structural ideas presented in Chapter 1.
2. Study of school curriculum guides and social studies materials available may influence what structural ideas one chooses to teach. What is presently advocated as worthy of being taught in my school district?

3. The preservice or inservice teacher's own conceptions of what is important to teach should be a major consideration. Such conceptions should be defensible through logical, empirically tested consideration. Teachers should ask themselves what societal understandings will be most beneficial to their children. The teacher should be involved in community action groups that share his concerns for helping his children become critically aware of their place in an expanding world society.

Teachers are urged to work toward development of concept-based social studies curricula in their respective schools. Most present social studies curricula *are not* concept-based.

> One method of building conceptually oriented media/materials, then is to start at the higher levels and then identify the related lower levels, because fewer constructs and high level generalizations exist which offer greater curricular control in development consistent with the philosophy of teaching the most significant ideas possible. (Tanck, 1969, 115)

An excerpt from a conceptually based unit of instruction illustrates this principle. The constructs used were selected because they represented two of the most salient notions of political science and sociology-anthropology, namely the constructs of **culture** and **social organization.** Here they are related to the institution of the family specifically as follows:

High-order generalizations:

1. Family membership exerts a significant cultural force within our society. It is a vital factor in how man adopts and adapts to his environment.
2. The family is the basic social organization in nearly all societies. Families can be compared through such social science concepts as roles, norms, status, positive and negative sanctions, division of responsibilities and labor functions.

Subordinate generalizations, concepts, and facts generated from these initial major ideas:

1. Family organization differs widely from society to society with respect to specific purposes of that organization and to how responsibility is delegated to family members.
2. Status and role within family organizations are usually decided on the basis of age and sex.
3. Expectations within a family group are usually set by the older members of that society.
4. One function of families is to provide for the basic needs of their members.

5. Families differ in size and composition. (a) The composition of families differs greatly both within and across cultures. (b) The composition of families may change due to numerous circumstances.

6. While specific families are unique in some of the things they do, most of their activities are shared with other families within their more immediate societal settings.

7. Family relationships are, in part, a product of both the immediate and the distant past. Historical continuity of family existence can be traced through methods of historical research.

8. The wants of man are unlimited, whereas resources that man needs to fulfill his wants are scarce. Hence, societies and individuals have to make choices.

9. All societies have made policies, rules, laws about how groups of people shall live.

10. Social classes have always existed in every society, although the basis of class distinction and the degree of rigidity of the class structure has varied.

11. The trend toward urbanization has accentuated problems of social disorganization, interpersonal relations, and group interaction.

12. Every society develops a system of roles, norms, values, and sanctions to guide the behavior of individuals and groups within that society.

13. The family is the basic social unit in most cultures.

14. Human beings live in groups.

15. Social systems have many problems which they must solve if they are to continue to exist. (Hoffman and Alleman, 1969)

Second Consideration: What Specific Cognitive Objectives Should I Have?

Most school systems have at some point in their history recorded a statement of objectives for social studies instruction. These statements are expected to guide teachers in organizing the learning environment. Since these objectives exist now, we would expect social studies to be a clearly defined curriculum area, accurately and efficiently evaluated. In fact, it is not! Social studies remains today a vaguely defined and in-efficiently evaluated dimension of the elementary school program.

Traditionally, social studies objectives tended to focus on three major themes: social science content, thinking skills, and citizenship education. Examples of objectives reveal statements which are incom-plete. Examine carefully the representative sample of objectives listed below.

Children should recognize the individual dignity and worth of every person.
Children should understand their country's history.
Children should understand the problem-solving process.

There can be no argument with the desirability of these goals. That is precisely what they are — goals. As goals, they resemble the goals for social studies stated in 1965 by the National Council for the Social Studies. Each of the 15 goals is stated below and may be identified by the head word.

1. INDIVIDUAL: Recognition of the dignity and worth of the individual.
2. INTELLIGENCE: The use of intelligence to improve human living.
3. INTERDEPENDENCE: Recognition and understanding of world interdependence.
4. CULTURE: The understanding of the major world cultures and culture areas.
5. CONSERVATION: The intelligent use of natural environment.
6. EDUCATION: The vitalization of our democracy through an intelligent use of our public educational facilities.
7. RESPONSIBILITY: The intelligent acceptance, by individuals and groups, of responsibility for achieving democratic social action.
8. FAMILY: Increasing the effectiveness of the family as a basic social institution.
9. MORALITY: The effective development of moral and spiritual values.
10. JUSTICE: The intelligent and responsible sharing of power in order to attain justice.
11. SCARCITY: The intelligent utilization of scarce resources to attain the widest general well-being.
12. LOYALTY: Achievement of adequate horizons of loyalty.
13. PEACE: Cooperation in the interest of peace and welfare.
14. PROGRESS: Achieving a balance between social stability and social change.
15. SELF REALIZATION: Widening and deepening the ability to live more richly. (NCSS, 1965)

Again, we note that there can be no argument with the desirability of these goals. Every social studies program must be based on a framework of goals which reflect the ultimate ends deemed appropriate by the community which it serves. Criticism of those goals centers on their lack of usefulness in the classroom. How does a teacher determine when or whether his students "use intelligence to improve human living" or "achieve adequate horizons of loyalty"?

New social studies objectives are needed which have more immediate application. Such objectives do not supersede or negate goals which remain the ends of education but rather define explicitly stages of development through which the child passes in pursuit of those goals. Social studies teachers realize that much of what they are trying to achieve will be demonstrated long after the child leaves the classroom.

Objectives of the new social studies developed by project staffs consist of two distinct parts: (1) a statement of the goal, and (2) a criterion measure by which to evaluate children's success in approaching the stated goal. Consider the following examples drawn from the *Framework for the Social Studies in Wyoming Schools*. (1969)

The pupil will be able:

when given a set of materials, to construct models which demonstrate the influence of forest vegetation on good and poor storage of ground water.

when given a map of the 48 contiguous states, to locate and define the six predominant forest regions of that area.

Each of these objectives is complete. It contains a goal which is the immediate end toward which the student is growing, for instance, understanding the relationship of forest vegetation and storage of ground water. In this respect it conforms to the traditional pattern. But in addition, each objective includes a description of behaviors by which the children may demonstrate their degree of growth toward the desired, in the first objective "construct models." The teacher is thus provided with a description of behaviors by which he can reasonably infer what the child has accomplished. This is a key notion. Children act in a way whereby that the professional educator may infer that the desired end has been achieved. Curriculum-development projects have demonstrated that objectives in any area of social studies may be phrased in behavioral terms.

An effective source for developing skill in designing behaviorally stated objectives is Robert Mager's *Preparing Instructional Objectives.* (1962) Mager supplies three key definitions which can aid in distinguishing "behavioral objective" from "objective."

Behavior . . . refers to any visible activity displayed by a learner (student)

Terminal behavior . . . refers to the behavior you would like your learner to be able to demonstrate at the time your influence over him ends.

Criterion . . . is the standard or test by which terminal behavior is evaluated.

Two major benefits flow from the movement toward stating objectives in behavioral terms. Initially, both the teacher and student are aware of the precise end toward which they are moving. Second, they are able to state with reasonable certainty the degree of success achieved. Teachers need not leave class wondering whether a plan of instruction had the desired effect or whether the grade awarded was appropriate. Evaluation becomes both efficient and educationally productive.

The use of behavioral objectives in a classroom will be facilitated by the teacher's taking the following considerations into account:

1. Efforts should be made to avoid the use of vague, jargonized language in writing objectives.
2. Objectives should be written in terms of observable *student* behavior *when possible.*
3. Objectives should be measurable *when possible.*

4. Efforts should be made to preassess the competencies that youngsters have prior to setting related instructional goals. Methods of preassessment will be elaborated in Chapter 8.
5. The conceptual problems related to mental maturity of youngsters should be considered. Children in the primary and early elementary grades can do only a limited amount of propositional thinking. Emphasis upon concept attainment and augmentation strategies described later under the Fourth Consideration may have greater growth potential.

Here is a behavioral objective related to the unit on the family in connection with the First Consideration, set forth earlier in this section.

Criterion measure: Given a series of flat pictures illustrating many types of family membership, . . .

Terminal behavior: . . . children will be able to list differences they see in the member make-up of various families.

Clearly, the criterion measure (the flat pictures) represents only one of many means of assessment a teacher might use in a given lesson. Attempts at listing all possible assessments — even at listing all assessments used during a lesson sequence — as advocated by strict adherents to the behavioral model of instruction, is not necessary or desirable, particularly in a diverse and changing curriculum area such as the social studies. Listing of all possible specific terminal behaviors can also be carried to extremes.

Third Consideration: What Vehicles — Parts of Knowledge — Would Be Most Appropriate to Use in Developing These Ideas?

The key question remains: *What do these youngsters need to know?* Related questions are:

1. What vehicle(s) would most readily facilitate those ideas?
2. Is the vehicle of interest and relevance to the lives of these youngsters?
3. Do I have access to the materials I feel I need? Do they exist?
4. What might be the positive and negative consequences of such a study?

The most visible development in the new social studies is the impressive array of materials (vehicles) currently available to support social studies instruction. Generally, materials for elementary social studies fall into four categories of emphasis. There is a great deal of overlapping coverage among the categories. The value of each set of materials is dependent upon the objectives of the particular social studies program and the skill of the teacher employing it. A more complete discussion and evaluation of materials may be found in Chapter 9.

The first group of materials consists mainly of those designed to reveal *the fundamental principles, generalizations, procedures, and concerns of a particular scholarly discipline.* The Lawrence Senesh *Our Working World* (1967) materials were early examples of this approach. Senesh used economics as the basis for instruction beginning in the primary grades. Ideas from other disciplines are considered as outgrowths of the economics ideas emphasized. Thus, while studying the concept of scarcity children may also consider the sociological concept of discrimination, the political-science concept of power, and the historical question of change.

Other materials have concentrated on anthropology, geography, history, jurisprudence, social psychology, sociology, and political science.

A second group of materials uses as the organizing focus *a topic which may be a social question* (What will the city of the future be like?) *or a geographic area* (Latin America). These materials are designed to permit students to apply ideas and procedures from many scholarly disciplines to develop an understanding of the topic. Thus, for example, the city may be studied from the perspective of the economist or the sociologist or the historian or all three, depending on the interests of the class and the objectives of the teacher. Prime examples of this multidiscipline approach are several of the new textbook series such as those of Allyn and Bacon, Follett, Laidlaw, and Scott Foresman. *The new texts do not attempt to fill the traditional function, that is, the textbook curriculum.* Texts are rather resources and spurs to further inquiry. Texts must be used in conjunction with a wide range of additional materials. There is no question that these materials have moved from the classification of supplement of a more vital role in instruction. The emphasis is on what the children learn not what the text says.

Another group of materials focuses on *the process by which the child explores social studies.* These materials provide continuous practice in the skills of problem rating and definition, data collection and analysis, as well as in the formulation and application of conclusions. In addition, most of these materials attempt to develop some skill in predicting the consequences of the child's actions. *The Social Science Laboratory Units* developed by Lippitt and Fox are excellent examples of materials focusing on process.

A fourth group of materials consists of *simulation, role playing, and games.* These are closely aligned with the process materials and are distinguished here because of their tendency to appear in each of the groups already mentioned.

Fourth Consideration: What Specific Teaching Strategies Are Most Conducive to Developing Structural Learnings?

The selection and application of specific teaching strategies is a most critical step in the teaching of concepts, generalizations, and constructs. Some specific aspects of concept and generalization development are therefore the subject matter of the remaining sections of this chapter.

Fifth Consideration: What Means Shall I Use in Determining Whether the Specified Knowledge Has Been Learned?

This concern, in reality, is dealt with when one sets his cognitive objectives. As was indicated under the Second Consideration, the ways of evaluating overt behavior are numerous. Chapter 8 is designed primarily to explore this important area of measurement.

This Fifth Consideration is stated here in order to display the five considerations compactly. The matter that follows, from here to the end of the chapter, is pertinent to the Fourth Consideration.

DEDUCTIVE VS. INDUCTIVE MODES OF INSTRUCTION

Methods traditionally used in teaching social studies have placed primary emphasis upon deductive modes of instruction; that is, youngsters have been exposed to selected concepts and generalizations and then have been provided examples to "prove" or "illustrate" the particular idea. Nearly all social studies textbooks are written in this expository fashion.

One of the subordinate generalizations related to the unit on the family was "One function of families is to provide for the basic needs of their members." When this generalization is introduced to children, it is often presented somewhat as follows (early primary class):

Teacher Boys and girls, today we are going to study how mothers and fathers work to take care of the things that we all need. All families and, indeed, all people have certain needs that must be satisfied. One of the needs is a need for food. How do your parents help to supply you with food?

Johnny My dad works and brings home money. My mother buys and cooks the food.

Other students (Give examples.)

Teacher (May introduce a second culture.)

(later Teacher concludes): So, boys and girls, what can we say about the
need for food?

Suzie   All people have to have food to live. Some members of families work to get food for others.

This presentation was highly deductive. The teacher started the lesson
by stating the generalization to be developed. Children then were asked
to deduce examples which supported the generalization.

How could a teacher allow children to discover this idea and test
its validity for themselves? Try to construct a small related lesson before
reading further.

One method might be to have children study two cultures (their
own and one other), make as many empirical observations related to
similarities and differences existing between these cultures as they can,
and record them. Later, the children could make inferences about how
these two cultures were alike. This process obviously consumes more
time. The children offer many generalizations, some superficial and
erroneous. Children can then check these generalizations against a third
culture which might need to be introduced. Thus, a highly inductive
approach might alternatively be employed to develop the generalization. This alternate method is generally referred to as an *inquiry mode of
instruction.*

Inquiry: What Are They Talking about?

Contemporary emphasis on inquiry as a method of learning and
teaching has produced a good deal of confusion among educators. Individual reactions tend to fall into two nonexclusive categories: (1) confusion regarding the precise meaning of the term "inquiry" and (2) apprehension regarding the effect of application in the classroom. The
purpose of this section is to attempt to clarify the confusion and in the
process to relieve some of the apprehension.

One aspect of the problem involves a lack of clear differentiation
between the terms "discovery" and "inquiry." It appears that discovery
is used to describe teaching/learning situations characterized by the
"aha!" phenomenon — that is, to situations in which there are no precon-
ceptions about what may be learned. Bruner (1961) likens discovery to
surprise. He suggests that in either surprise or discovery the well-prepared mind will capitalize on the situation.

But what does this well-prepared mind discover? Is the situation
the unique confrontation of the learner with data or relationships never
before encountered, which rolls back the frontier of knowledge? Or is it
limited, not unique, designed for the accomplishment of a specific instructional objective? In either case, the emphasis is on product — on that

which is discovered. The learner's reward, whether external or internal, is directly related to this product. One asks, "How is this different from problem solving?" A partial answer lies in the definition of the product. The end may be defined by the teacher or by the learner. If the end is defined at the outset by the teacher, a discovery lesson may result in the learner's failure. That is, the child may discover something other than what the teacher has set up as "the objective."

Problem solving emphasizes the reduction of anxiety. The learner —faced with uncertainty, conflict, contradiction, or threat to his physical, social, or psychological well being—seeks to relieve the state by applying known procedures that will lead reliably to a solution predetermined though not yet perceived. In the classroom, problems are most often defined by the teacher or by the textual materials. Hence we may accurately speak of threat to the child. Here again, emphasis is primarily on product, though secondary attention may be given to the faithful execution of the "scientific method." The essence of problem solving is the correct answer that removes the threat and thus produces the reward.

Problem solving requires attention to procedures designed to elicit the product. True discovery, in contrast, encourages the free and varied manipulation of concepts in order to form relationships meaningful to the learner.

Problem solving may be considered a form of directed discovery— the form that seeks a known end. For example, a child manipulating Cuisenaire rods is restricted by the form. He solves the problem by arranging the rods in the proper relationship which illustrates the quadratic equation. He may or may not discover the quadratic equation in the sense that he is able to generalize to other sets of data. Or consider a group of children producing some object for the explicit purpose of learning the principle of division of labor. They may find it beneficial to define roles and functions or to share responsibility. This strategy may in their view be solely related to the specific product involved. But if they are able to generalize the experience the learners have indeed made a uniquely personal discovery. The payoff is personal-internal.

"Process" is yet another dimension of the inquiry confusion. A number of curricula, particularly new science curricula, emphasize the sequential development of skills requisite to scientific inquiry. Such curricula are often billed as having a "process approach." The label is appropriate and descriptive, in that it puts emphasis on the means by which the learner studies a particular discipline or related disciplines.

Process is problem-oriented but differs from problem solving by its toleration of new or unexpected generalizations provided an acceptable process is employed.

Thus discovery, problem solving, and process are at once related and distinguishable. Each is a specific case of inquiry. Inquiry connotes an existing quantity to be examined, something to be inquired into or inquired about. The result of such activity may be the confirmation of a preconceived notion or the development of a new alternative interpretation. Each of the learning/teaching methods discussed above fits the genus "inquiry." The main goal of inquiry is the discovery of meaningful relationships. Relationships are the connections among variables and are sought to enable the inquirer to understand, explain, predict, and possibly control the world of reality.

A major misconception about inquiry is that inquiry is a totally inductive process. In recent years educators have been bombarded with materials promulgating an "inductive approach to −." In social studies education Edwin Fenton was one advocate of this approach. Later (1970), Fenton explicitly disclaimed the notion of an inductive approach, announcing, "I have not used the term in four years. I do not know what it means." He went on to clarify his continued advocacy of an inquiry approach.

Indeed, careful analysis of instructional materials fails to unearth any totally inductive programs. Critical examination reveals inductive elements in all inquiry-oriented materials. It is extremely important to emphasize the point: *There is no totally inductive social studies curriculum.*

Inductive procedures constitute specific elements of inquiry. An inquirer moves between the deductive mode and the inductive mode freely and often during the course of inquiry. The major roadblock to effective inquiry is the inquirer's allegiance to a single mode. Therefore, the major function of teachers who would enhance learners' inquiry skills is to provide opportunities for the learner to inquire often and freely.

This last requirement—free and frequent inquiry—has produced much anxiety among teachers and parents alike. A common concern is the preconceived notion of what a public-school classroom looks like and the traditional notion of what constitutes appropriate classroom procedure. Inquiry is often perceived as a kind of drift-and-fumble learning. Nothing is further from the truth.

The Discipline of Inquiry

Since inquiry is error-full learning it requires more instructional time than expository procedures. Effective inquiry requires careful planning in order to schedule appropriate experiences which may require that learners move beyond the classroom. Collaterally, teachers need to pursue a continuing inquiry into the availability of appropriate materials to feed the learner's need to know. The success of an inquiry is directly dependent on the teacher's knowledge of subject areas impinging on his student's environment. His knowledge must be broad and deep in order to recognize the potential of materials and activities for productive inquiry.

In addition, the teacher must possess great self-discipline. Teachers are in the main tellers and talkers. It is extremely difficult for most teachers to withstand the onslaught of silence in the classroom. Rushing in to fill the vacuum created as children silently consider a question or idea, teachers often stifle inquiry and trample the creative opportunity of the child. Extreme control is necessary to heed Piaget's dictum that every time we tell the child something we deprive him of the opportunity to learn it himself. The teacher who acts in concert with this view reduces the psycho-social distance between himself and the learner. The threat to the preeminent position of the teacher in the classroom setting is overcome when the teacher accepts the role of co-inquirer.

As co-inquirers all parties have the right to explore in search of logical generalization. Each party also has the right to be wrong. Thus we speak of learners, not of teachers and students. It is in the analysis of alternative relationships, some of which are more appropriate than others, that inquiry achieves desired educational benefits: the ability to understand, explain, predict, and possibly control the world of reality.

STRATEGIES FOR CONCEPT DEVELOPMENT

It may be necessary to spend some time developing a specific social science concept before involving youngsters in the generalizing process. Essentially, the process proceeds as follows:

1. Teacher decides which concept she wishes to develop as well as those attributes she feels are important for children to hold if they are to have functional use of this idea.
2. Teacher then selects some examples which illustrate the concept as well as some non-examples.
3. Children are then presented with negative and positive examples of the concept.
4. Children are asked to identify the concept and list its major attributes.
5. Teacher then gives further examples and non-examples of the concept. Children are asked to make proper identification.
6. Children are then asked to find their own positive and negative examples of the concept. (Tanck, 1969, 117)

The following lesson (adapted from Hoffman and Alleman, 1969) illustrates this strategy. An early-primary teacher is trying to have children expand their concept of family, to have them include the attribute that family composition differs greatly within our society. This attribute was selected because it was seen as necessary to further the child's understanding of the high-order construct that the family is the primary social organization.

A PLAN OF INSTRUCTION — FAMILY MEMBERSHIP

Behavioral Objective: Given a series of flat pictures illustrating many types of family membership, children will be able to list (either in writing or orally) differences they see in the member make-up of various families.

Activities:

Inductive lead-in

1. Have children draw pictures in which they are to include all the members of their family. Since some children might be reluctant to draw "people," one alternative might be to have the children cut out pictures of people from old catalogues to represent members of their family and to paste these figures on some large sheets of paper. Older children might wish to use some set of semiabstract figures as representations of various family members. If children ask questions regarding who should be included in their family, suggest to the class that only those members presently living at home or the immediate family should be included. It is important that older brothers and sisters who have left the family, either permanently (married, or working and living apart from the family) or temporarily (in service or at college), should **not be included** since these people will serve as discussion points in the following lesson.

2. An alternative might be to read to the children a book or case study depicting a family situation and then ask them to make distinctions between their family and that described in the story or case. Then lead the children to make comparisons between the different family types which exist in the class.

3. After all pictures are completed, choose three which illustrate the widest differences in family membership. Also select five pictures from textbooks or magazines showing identical or very similar family make-up. The following questions, which initially try to get children to note simple

The teacher is working to develop one attribute of the concept of family—that family membership differs greatly within our society (3, A to F)

similarities and differences and later require the child to do higher levels of thinking, are suggested.

A. Which family is largest? Which is smallest?

B. What types of members do we often find as part of families? (mothers, fathers, children)

C. What other relatives might be family members? (grandparents, aunts, uncles, cousins, others)

D. How do these three families differ? (Get the children to list size of family and types of members.)

E. Show pictures of identical family make-up. Ask if these pictures are realistic: If we checked five families in our neighborhood, would they all have the same number of members? (No)

F. Does a family need any one type of member to make it a family? (No—a family can be a family even if it has no father, or no mother, or no children.)

The idea that size is related to higher valuation is introduced in 4. Also that family organization type is not as critical a variable as how people relate to each other within respective families.

4. A teacher could now move to value questions. She could identify specific family functions (tasks, responsibilities, interests, other) and could then ask the children to describe the ideal family member who could best perform this function. Explore the reason for the choices the children make. Ask the children to role-play and, in so doing, to indicate which family member they consider to be ideal for the role portrayed. Pursue the "why." Lead the children to see (without directly telling them) that no one family type is best for all situations and that family make-up is only one variable. How representative members behave toward one another is a much more crucial variable.

Here the teacher introduces further non-examples.

5. Have the children make puppets to depict family members. Through the presentation of a puppet play, indicate family type, preferences, and rationale for choices given.

6. Some children might do a survey of family-situation television shows to determine if one or more types of families are repeatedly portrayed. Reading, language arts, and social studies textbooks in the school could be analyzed to note whether there is any prevalent type of family, with

respect to membership and size. These data could be saved for use in later discussions of social class as it relates to the organizational concept of family.

Here the teacher introduces further examples through pupil involvement.

7. Some children could do a survey[1] of family membership type and family composition in some neighborhood. (At this point, emphasis is to bring out distinctions only — this information could be collected from two neighborhoods where the teacher suspects that real general differences exist.) A telephone survey could also be used to collect this information. The teacher could select two surrounding areas where she suspects that differences might exist.

8. Plan a walk in and about the local neighborhood. Plan with the children to look for specified phenomena. For example: Are there any clues that teenagers live in a given house? Are there any clues that lead you to believe there is a father in the household? A grandfather? After the format has been developed, have one or more students record the clues and accompanying hypotheses. Map this information. Then schedule another walk through the same area and do a door-to-door survey to check the original hypotheses. Discuss your findings. This activity can provide and develop observation skills; it can develop skill in using the scientific method; it can be used to indicate that one needs to be careful about stereotyping and making broad and sweeping generalizations.

9. Construct a flannel board bearing the question, "Who is missing?" and family pictures that lack one member or more. Within reach, have flannel-backed pictures of missing members that a child can place where he thinks they belong. A

[1] Children will obviously need to be trained in manners and in methods before collecting data in surveys, either face-to-face or by telephone. Only very self-reliant and very trustworthy youngsters should be used. Language experiences can be integrated into this activity by having the children write down exactly what they plan to say.

Prepared forms for the interviews are needed. They need not, probably should not, have space for recording the name of the family; an identification number will serve all needs. With this there should be a checklist of family members who may or may not be at home, including spaces for check marks or numerical answers: Father, Mother, Boys, Girls, Uncles, Aunts, Cousins, Nephews, Nieces, Grandmothers, Grandfathers, Other Relatives; and Total Number of Members. The children can build this checklist, perhaps under guidance.

The families to be interviewed should be selected on some systematic basis; in small communities with their own telephone books, every twenty-fifth name might be taken. In residential areas of larger cities, one home in each block might be the basis. The object of any system is to avoid getting distorted results.

discussion will follow, and it will be pointed out
that not all families have fathers, for example.

10. Have the students make scrapbooks that depict
family members. Actual pictures of their family
members could be used or pictures drawn by the
children to represent the members.

11. Provide on audio tape short descriptions of family
members. Then have the youngsters role play in
order that they can express attitudes of family
members.

SPECIFIC STRATEGIES TO TEACH GENERALIZATIONS

Tanck lists the following elements which would seem to be useful
in teaching generalizations. The teacher should identify:

1. The key concepts involved in the relationship [among the concepts].
2. The relation, the abstract association among concepts, or the understanding
of how the concepts relate to each other. (Common relationships are
sameness, similarity, difference, inclusion, exclusion, size, if-then,
cause-effect.)
3. The assertion or statement of the relationship, claiming that a relationship
indeed exists among the concepts.
4. A problem, meaning a question or realized difficulty that in effect asks
what the relationship among the concepts is or whether it is as asserted.
5. Positive cases, situations in which the relationship among examples of the
concepts involved is as asserted. (Tanck, 1969, 123)

Some of these elements will be presented in the strategies described and illustrated here.

Teaching Generalizations through Verification

This method involves asserting a relationship and then presenting
or having youngsters look for positive or negative instances of the relationship. The strategy is highly deductive. Illustrations of this overused
method can be observed in any traditional social studies classroom or
textbook. While the process of verifying a generalization is one important stage within the process of inquiry, as the only process of teaching
it has adverse consequences for most learners.

Teaching Concepts and Generalizations through Problem Solving

Strong arguments can be built for development of concepts and
generalizations through problem solving. The search for tentative solu-

tions to social problems is particularly important in an open, democratic society.

Science can also be viewed as a method in which all data (physical, political, social, or other) are gathered, classified, and analyzed. This method applies to the discovery of new social-science knowledge. It is highly inductive, in that it moves from observations of discrete data to generalizations emerging from consistent patterns and eventually to the testing of generalized solutions on the basis of their underlying assumptions. The stages are somewhat as follows:

1. Data are gathered.
2. Data are organized and classified.
3. A hypothesis is formulated.
4. The hypothesis is tested.
5. A generalization or law results.
6. The generalization or law is then retested and/or restated for verification.

There are conflicting views regarding the utilization of social-science ideational concepts and generalizations in the problem-solving approach in social studies education. Some educators take the position that the problem search should result in children articulating the desired concept(s) or generalization(s) and/or applying their "findings" against those ideas drawn from the social sciences. The problem, then, might be deliberately selected because it originally evidenced, within the teacher's conceptual framework, one or more of the ideational relationships.

Those advocating some form of this position might list the following as strengths of this procedure:

1. It gives direction to the social studies. There are key ideas which should be taught in social studies.
2. Learnings are measurable; that is, people agree on some concepts and generalizations and the learning of these can be measured.

Their critics would probably list the following shortcomings of this procedure:

1. Such a procedure violates the tentative nature in which concepts and generalizations have been formulated. Youngsters need to question both the tentative hypotheses and the assumptions underlying these hypotheses.
2. Too much emphasis is put on the "product" of problem solving. Concern resides on knowledge of subject matter rather than on internalization of a rational way of dealing with social problems.

Bernice Goldmark (1968), for example, sees inquiry as a process of asking and searching for answers to social problems from certain frames of reference. Problems are not seen as having infinite possible solutions since they must be selected from real situations where alternatives are limited. Education is seen, then, as an inquiry process into the various human discourses. These discourses are, themselves, defined as methods of investigation of "what is." The process is then described as an inquiry into inquiries.

The pattern of inquiry begins when a question or concern is felt related to some societal problem, defined as a qualitative situation. This doubt can be stimulated through conflicting pieces of information. Goldmark (1968, 90) illustrates a number of problem situations which upper-elementary teachers can use. Later chapters concerned with youngsters in the formal-operations stage of development (Piaget) will illustrate this procedure more fully.

Studies in how people think have influenced the problem-solving tasks identified by Hilda Taba and her associates. Materials produced under her direction have as one objective the development of thinking. Because of the significance of these materials in the emergent social studies curriculum, a further elaboration of the procedures used to develop thinking is presented here. Teachers using these materials are involved in development of the following tasks and related thinking skills necessary to perform these tasks.

1. The first task is identified as concept formation. This task is consistent with the concept-development procedures described earlier in this chapter with one notable exception. Concepts here are seen as only of high-order magnitude, often closely approximating the construct level of abstraction. Students are involved in interrelating and organizing discrete bits of information to develop these abstractions.

2. The second task is related to the inductive development of generalizations or ways in which students interpret data and make inferences that go beyond what is given in the data.

3. The third and highest task involves having students make application of certain facts and generalizations to explain new phenomena, make predictions, and formulate alternate hypotheses. (Adapted from Taba, 1967, 8-9)

In the Taba curriculum (see Durkin, Duvall, and McMaster, 1969 B), the concept of interdependence is developed in the second grade through study of the roles of workers in a community. While the thinking processes are not easily separated and illustrated in a few paragraphs, since these materials are constructed in lengthy units, the following account is meant to be representative.

Main Idea: The nature of a particular community will influence the kinds of service it needs.

Organizing Idea: City, commuting, and farm communities each need some special services.

Note: Concepts related to the distinction between "goods" and "services" have been taught. The teacher initially moves to expand the children's concept of services to include certain attributes related to community size, purposes, and the like (concept augmentation).

Many activities are included. A few examples follow.

> Children are asked to list three or four services which they think are needed in their town. The children are then asked how many had the same item. The number who had the item is tallied. Each child's item is thus recognized. (Durkin and colleagues, 1969 B, 55)
>
> Then children are asked to group the items. Questions such as the following are asked: "Which of these do you think we might put together? Why do you put these together? What shall we name these groups? Which service might go in another group as well as the one it is in now? Does anyone see another one?" (Durkin and colleagues, 1969 B, 55)

After developmental activities are used to strengthen the child's understanding of community through expansion of his concept of neighborhood, children are further involved in collection of data regarding the actual services available in their community. Later the teacher moves to expand the child's concept of community services through other community types. If, for example, the school is located in a large urban center, some suburban and rural settings might be selected for comparison. Many suggested resources are included to aid the teacher in this endeavor. One activity includes taking a walk or bus ride through a commuting community and asking the children to observe such things as: (1) the number of gas stations on the main street; (2) the bus station that is a stop for commuter buses; (3) the train station.

Here the teacher might aid youngsters in *making inferences and generalizations*. The teacher could ask children why so many gas stations, buses, and trains are needed. Other data could be used as the basis of inferring or generalizing:

> Have some of the children whose fathers commute by car find out how often they fill their gas tanks. Let other children whose fathers work locally ask how often the gas tank is filled. Have the children contrast the figures. (Durkin and colleagues, 1969 B, 116)

The following series of hypothetical situations is written in an attempt to get youngsters to move from the descriptive level of reflection (what, how, when, where) to making application of previously learned information.

> Pretend all the main highways will be closed from now until (Christmas, Easter vacation). What difference will it make to the gas station man?

Pretend all the gas stations are closed. What difference will it make to our parents or (parents of a commuting community)?

Pretend all the families in a commuting community decide to move where the fathers work. What difference will it make to the community that they leave? (Durkin and colleagues, 1969 B, 120)

Questioning as a Strategy in Concept Development

A key element in the teaching/learning process is the use of questions. Research evidence indicates that teachers very seldom make use of questions which go beyond having youngsters recall information previously heard or read. (Durkin and colleagues, 1969 B, 119) The teacher's ability to ask high-level questions is particularly important for developing a child's ability to think critically. The importance of questioning in the use of the Taba Curriculum Materials has already been noted.

Strategies for development of high-level questions are usually derived from the work of Benjamin Bloom and his associates. Bloom (1956) formulated six levels of thinking which proceed in a hierarchy (from lowest level to highest):

1. Memory
2. Translation-Interpretation
3. Application
4. Analysis
5. Synthesis
6. Evaluation

The most notable work in applying these levels of thinking to questioning in the social studies has been done by Norris Sanders (1969). Each of the levels of questioning is briefly described and illustrated here.

Memory questions ask the respondent to recall or recognize information presented in a textbook, chart, film, lecture, or other material.

Conditions for this question: The students have read that Washington, D.C. is the capital of the United States.

Question: What is the name of the capital of the United States? (Sanders, 1969, 152)

Translation questions require the student to restate an idea in a different form.

Conditions for this question: The student has read a paragraph in the textbook.

Question: Now tell me in **your own words** what you read. (Sanders, 1969, 153)

In an *interpretation question,* a student is asked "to compare certain ideas or to use a functional idea that he studied previously to solve a problem new to him. The idea may be in the form of a skill, definition, theory, class, principle, axiom, law, rule, or generalization." (Sanders, 1969, 153)

Conditions for this question: After seeing a film on customs of marriage and bringing up a family in an African society, the students are asked:

Question: In what ways are the marriage and family customs in the movie similar to those in our society and in what ways different? (Sanders, 1969, 154)

Application questions go one step beyond interpretation questions. Here the respondent must use the idea in a new situation when not required or assisted to make this transfer.

Conditions for this question: In a primary school language arts class the teacher has taught students how to use an index and table of contents. Later in a social studies class the teacher asks this question:

Question: Find the page in our social studies book that tells about Booker T. Washington.

(Note: The question would have been interpretation if asked in this way: "Use the index to find the page in your social studies text which tells about Booker T. Washington.") (Sanders, 1969, 155)

Analysis questions, Sanders states, "are always preceded by instruction in one or more of the following often neglected logical processes: classification, induction, deduction, cause and effect, informal fallacies, logical necessity, semantic principles, and psychological obstacles to thinking." (1969, 156) The respondent is asked to solve a problem with an awareness of the rules for good thinking called for by a particular problem.

Conditions for this question: A primary teacher explained to her class that some ideas don't go together (contradiction). For example, it is silly to believe a man is both tall and short.

Question: What is silly or funny in this story? "Johnny had one dime. He went to the grocery store and spent the dime to buy candy. Next he went to the drug store and spent the dime for a comic book. After this he was tired so he went home and put the dime in his piggy bank." (Sanders, 1969, 157)

To respond to a *synthesis question,* the student must create a unique object, communication, model, or other appropriate item. No answer is considered as *the* correct response.

Conditions for this question: A box is to be inserted into the cornerstone of a new school. The students in the class are in charge of filling the box with things showing what it is like to go to school during that time.

Question: What do you think should go into the box? (Sanders, 1969, 159)

In an *evaluation question,* the respondent is asked to make a value judgment of some "product, communication, event, or situation. A value judgment is a rating of something as being good or bad; right or wrong; or perhaps beautiful or ugly. Part of the answer always requires the student to tell what considerations led him to make the judgment." (Sanders, 1969, 159)

Conditions for this question: The students have studied the colonial period of United States history.

Question: Did the colonists do right in throwing the tea overboard at the Boston Tea Party? Tell why. (Sanders, 1969, 160)

Suggested Techniques for Improving a Teacher's Questioning Ability

People speak of the *art* of questioning. The ability to ask appropriate questions, shifting from descriptive to analytical to evaluative levels based upon children's responses, some people argue, is largely related to a teacher's innate ability to reason and conceptualize. We authors have observed a wide range in performance among preservice and inservice teachers. What is equally clear, however, is that all teachers need work in methods of applying questioning to specific teaching/learning episodes. A few techniques are cited here.

1. Classes in social studies methods can take parts of some descriptive social studies units (some from this textbook, for example) and classify questions already in the materials as well as construct other questions (particularly high-level questions) which might be incorporated in this sequence.
2. Student teachers could construct some questions to accompany a commercially prepared concept-based lesson or unit.
3. Methods classes might cooperatively work up some concept-based lesson using a model described in this chapter. Questions could then be written which conform to the pattern stated or implied in the model.
4. Another way to apply appropriate levels of questioning to the teaching situation is to relate levels of thinking to the descriptions of how youngsters learn to conceptualize (the processes of concept attainment, concept augmentation, and generalizing). A chart of procedures and illustrative questions for these tasks is presented on p. 112. It is excerpted and adapted from some of the work prepared at the University of Washington as part of the Tri-University Project (Jarolimek and Bacon, 1968).

Using Questioning Strategies to Develop Concepts and Generalizations

Task	Procedures	Illustrative Questions
Concept Attainment and Augmentation	Teachers can help children learn to form or augment concepts through asking questions which required children to (a) summarize their observations; (b) help identify common properties (attributes) for grouping; and (c) label or define the grouping.	(a) *Observation* 1. What did you see? Note? Find? (b) *Grouping or Classifying* 1. What belongs together? On what criterion? (c) *Labeling or Defining* 1. What would you call these groups? 2. What belongs under what? 3. How would you name or label this?
Generalizing and Making Inferences from Data	Teachers can help children in forming generalizations and making inferences by asking questions which require children to (a) compare and contrast data from different samples (differentiation) (b) interpret the meaning of certain data (c) make reasonable inferences based on the data itself and (d) develop a generalization	(a) *Comparing and Contrasting (Differentiating)* 1. What did you note? See? Find? 2. What things are the same? Different? 3. How can you distinguish among things partly the same and partly different? (b) *Interpreting Data* 1. What does this mean? 2. How does it relate to other things? (c) *Making Inferences* 1. What can you infer? Imply? 2. What does the data suggest? (d) *Developing Generalizations* 1. What can you conclude?

Source: Adapted from Jarolimek and Bacon (1968).

DEVELOPMENT OF LOGICAL THINKING IN CHILDREN

Another concern in the selection of teaching strategies is the relationship of logical thinking ability in children to the conceptual process of teaching social studies. Definitive research studies in the area of logical thinking as it relates to social studies instruction of elementary youngsters has been fragmentary and conflicting. A few tentative comments based primarily on the writings of Piaget and his associates are made here.

Preschool and Kindergarten

Preschool and kindergarten children, and to some extent children in first and even second grades, may have serious developmental limitations related to the ability to conceptualize. Initially, preschool and kindergarten teachers are advised to place primary emphasis upon exercises geared to expose the elementary child to many varied readiness experiences rather than attempting to develop specific social science concepts and generalizations. Emphasis upon affective learnings (as discussed in Chapter 2) is also highly desirable. Research indicates that many prejudices which should receive attention in the school curriculum have been formed long before children receive any formal school experiences. We authors, then, advocate building a social studies program upon the psychological and social need structure of young children. Chapters 4 and 5 give primary attention to this goal.

First Grade through Fifth Grade

Piaget indicates that around age seven children enter what he calls the concrete stage of development. Two particular operations that characterize this stage are here briefly presented.

Class Inclusions Operations

The child can, on the concrete scale, manipulate part-whole relationships; that is, he can reason through use of addition, subtraction, and multiplication in concept formation. Anne Parsons, in the introduction to Inhelder and Piaget's book entitled *The Growth of Logical Thinking from Childhood to Adolescence*, states,

> Two classes can be added up so that they are included in a larger one: boys + girls = children; children + adults = people — i.e., A + A = B. By the same token, a part can be subtracted from the whole: people — adults = children. (Inhelder and Piaget, 1958, 15)

Children younger than age seven usually have great difficulty handling a task that requires solution of a problem in which four sub-classes intersect. For example,

> . . . children, given a box containing about eighteen brown and two white beads, all wooden, and asked whether there are more brown or wooden beads, reply that there are more brown ones because only two are white. That the categories are available and observations correct is shown by the fact that the younger children, when asked two questions separately, give correct answers as to the relative proportions of brown, white, and wooden beads. However, without class inclusions operations they cannot deal with the parts and the whole at the same time, and thus they make a false generalization. (Inhelder and Piaget, 1958, 16)

Primary and intermediate teachers, then, should carefully develop low-order concepts as prerequisites to higher-order classifications. Restricting concept development primarily to concepts requiring the grouping and labeling of attributes largely shared by many people will be the more fruitful strategy, in contrast to dealing with disjunctive concepts — those embracing many divergent attributes.

Serial Ordering Operations

Serial ordering operations ask the child to relate objects along a linear dimension rather than to classify. The child in the concrete stage of development, in reasoning questions related to ranking objects on the basis of length, will begin with one extreme (the smallest, for example) and then continue to choose the next smallest of those which remain and so on, rather than beginning at random and making corrections when necessary.

> Mentally he is able to conclude, from $A > B$ and $B > C$, that $A > C$. Other empirical factors are ordered in the same way at different points during the concrete stage, e.g., weights are ordered later than lengths, at about nine to ten years. (Inhelder and Piaget, 1958, 17)

A child at this stage can also learn to find correspondences between two independent series: "As opposed to the preoperational child, he comes to know which means goes with which ends." (Inhelder and Piaget, 1958, 17)

One would hypothesize on this information then that many children, as early as the first grade, could handle social-science relationships which provide concrete illustrations of the phenomena. To illustrate: One activity from *Our Working World* (Senesh, 1967) sets up a problem of making gingerbread men. Children are presented with a number of alternative ways of shaping, baking, decorating, and otherwise preparing gingerbread men. Hopefully, the children come to see the relationship between dividing up the labor (means) and increased production (end). We authors have seen many variations of the gingerbread-man lesson and have observed that most first-grade children can make this means-ends connection.

Shaver and his associates (1969, 958) have done some extensive research using the Senesh *Families at Work Series.* They found that first-grade children could handle, in some degree, all the concepts introduced in the materials. Anne Parsons concludes, "In sum, the concrete operations are based on the logic of classes and the logic of relations; they are means for constructing immediately present reality." (Inhelder and Piaget, 1958, 17)

Sixth Grade to Adult

At some time around age eleven or twelve, according to Piaget, children enter the propositional stage of development. Children are then capable of going beyond the empirical data given. They can isolate variables from a set of real or hypothetical data which they believe are possibly related. Later they can verify their hunches through experimentation.

Here children can explore cause-and-effect relationships. John Dewey's problem-solving model appears to be the more applicable at this stage of child development. (See Goldmark's descriptions, earlier in this chapter, apropos of teaching through problem solving.)

Piaget talks about two types of associative thinking, that is, of the ability to associate observed facts with cause and effect. These two thinking processes are implication and disjunction.

Implicative reasoning refers to connecting the observation of one variable with the occurrence of another variable. Here the child sees that if Z appears, then Y will occur. Such direct relationships are seldom present, if ever, in the social sciences.

Disjunctive reasoning occurs when a combination of two or more variables produces some result. Here the child is able to consider more than a single relationship at a time. He is then able to establish tentative causes and effects in studying some social phenomena. A teacher introducing problems related to air pollution, as one brief example, may expose children to multiple aspects of this problem (those related to industrial expansion, aspects related to legislation, aspects related to levels of governmental control, influence of corporate interests on governments, and other economic conflicts). Children will obviously need to use disjunctive reasoning in establishing tentative causes. Positions later formulated on what should be done in specific situations will be based in part on the child's ability to handle this complex data. Chapters 6 and 7 present several illustrations of disjunctive problem solving.

SUMMARY

Three concerns served as the basis of this chapter. Initially, we authors tried to confront our readers with the very perplexing problem of selecting what to teach in social studies. Second, a model of the structure of knowledge was presented as a basis for resolution of the problem of content selection. Finally, a series of procedures was set up to take the reader through five considerations in constructing conceptually based materials.

The explosion of knowledge, coupled with the wide and diverse nature of social studies, enforces teaching only the most salient relationships of the social sciences. Recent efforts to articulate the structure of the social sciences can serve as one basis for selecting of what to teach in social studies.

Constructs, the highest level of abstract knowledge, should serve as the original basis from which concepts, generalizations, and facts can be selected. Each level of thought is defined and illustrated in this chapter.

Particular strategies for the development of concepts and generalizations, whether taught directly through methods of inductive and deductive learning or developed incidentally through problem solving, were presented. The role of questioning as a strategy was then undertaken.

Finally, the relation of the development of logical thinking in children to the conceptual process of teaching social studies was described. Suggestions for the teaching of social studies at different developmental stages were given.

RECOMMENDATIONS FOR FURTHER READING

A Conceptual Framework for the Social Studies. Madison, Wisconsin: Department of Public Instruction, 1965. 36 pp. This document presents a framework interrelating key concepts and generalizations. These key concepts and generalizations drawn from six social-science disciplines serve as the basis of instruction from K to 12. Conceptual strands or "variants" have been written for various grade levels using the expanding horizons concepts as the basis of selection of the grade level vehicle.

Duvall, Alice, and colleagues. *Discovery-Oriented Instructional Technique.* San Anselmo, California: Search Models Unlimited, 1969. 97 pp. This manual provides specific techniques which can be used to further a teacher's understanding of (1) how concepts are formed, (2) how the generalizing process operates, and (3) how children can make application of social-science understandings. The manual is based upon the Taba Curriculum Materials described in this chapter.

Faucett, Verna S., and colleagues. *Social Science Concepts and the Classroom.* Syracuse: Syracuse University Press, 1968. 64 pp. Describes the conceptual process as it relates to the social sciences. Also describes how classroom activities can be used to develop concepts.

Fraser, Dorothy McClure, editor. *Social Studies Curriculum Development: Prospects and Problems.* 39th Yearbook of the National Council for the Social Studies. Washington: National Educational Association Publication, 1969. 335 pp. Chapters 4, 5, and 6 are pertinent. Martin Tanck's chapter, "Teaching Concepts, Generalizations, and Constructs" (pp. 99-138) served as the basis of the conceptual model elaborated in this chapter. Norris Sanders' chapter, "Changing Strategies of Instruction: Three Case Examples" (pp. 139-173) and John Gibson's chapter "Selecting and Developing Social Studies Instructional Materials" (pp. 174-205) could serve as valuable resources to the preservice and inservice teacher.

Goldmark, Bernice. *Social Studies: A Method of Inquiry.* Belmont, California: Wadsworth Publishing Co., 1968. 237 pp. (See specific references on pp. 107–108 of this chapter.)

Inhelder, Barbel, and Jean Piaget. *The Growth of Logical Thinking from Childhood to Adolescence.* New York: Basic Books: 1958. While much of the textbook provides specific studies with much mathematical elaboration, the introduction by Anne Parsons and the summary chapter by Inhelder and Piaget could prove profitable reading.

Mager, Robert F. *Preparing Instructional Objectives.* Palo Alto, California: Fearon Publishing Co., 1962. Specific techniques in construction of behaviorally based objectives are presented. Teachers wishing to sharpen their skills in objective construction can profit greatly from Mager's text.

Martorella, Peter. *Concept Learning in the Social Studies.* New York and London: Intext Educational Publishers, 1971. This book contains an in-depth look at the elusive word "concept," as well as its ramifications for social studies teaching. Later sections of the book provide some interesting lessons for concept building at a variety of instructional levels.

Sanders, Norris M. *Classroom Questions: What Kinds?* New York: Harper & Row, 1966. 176 pp. Sanders develops specific examples of questions at each of the levels of thinking defined by Benjamin S. Bloom. The book is addressed to the teaching of social studies at the secondary level, but his explanation of thinking levels would be worth reading for elementary teachers.

Taba, Hilda. *Teachers' Handbook for Elementary Social Studies.* Palo Alto, California: Addison-Wesley Publishing Co., 1967. 150 pp. Illustrations of the Taba Curriculum Project Materials are incorporated. Conceptual processes described within this chapter are also described here. Of particular interest is Taba's elaboration of the specific teaching strategies to be used for development of cognitive skills.

PART TWO

Plans for Action with the Developing Child

CHAPTER 4

From the Initial-Exploratory Stage to the Structured-Dependent Stage: Early Development

Chapter 2 noted the dual nature of reality: what the individual perceives as real and what most individuals perceive as real. A major objective of education is the reduction of any discrepancy between the two dimensions of reality.

Chapter 4 deals with the child's early exploration of his environment. The focus is on "orientation" to the world around him. Guiding questions are, "Who am I?" and "Where am I?"

THEME AND JUSTIFICATION

The frame of reference which supports each person's unique behavior is formed through interaction with the environment in which that person lives. A person's first awareness of life results from encounters with objects in his environment. The prenatal dimension of this idea is beyond the scope of our work. So let us consider the new born child reacting to his crib. His movements are restricted by the physical limits of the crib as well as by his lack of control over his muscles. Very early in his life the child reaches out to explore his environment. Over time his exploration becomes both more widespread and more sophisticated. As this happens, the nature of his environment is altered and his frame of reference becomes more complete. Similarly, his control (power is discussed in Chapter 5) over his environment increases.

The child's environment is physical, social, and personal. The *physical* environment is made up of those "things" which are encountered daily: clothing, home, city, and the like. To help the child understand his relationship to this physical environment, social studies teachers explore and use key elements of the social and behavioral sciences, particularly geography, economics, and anthropology. The *social* dimension of the environment is delimited by people and ideas. To build understanding in this dimension, teachers call upon social-science elements found in sociology, political science, and history. They supplement these ideas with others drawn from psychology and communications, which may also impinge on the *personal* dimension of environment. To help the child understand his "self," the personal dimension of his environment, teachers also employ key elements of anthropology, economics, geography, political science, sociology, and history.

Throughout his environment the child finds evidence of man's attempt to express himself and his time through literature, art, music, and architecture. The depth of children's perception of their environment is vastly increased as they inquire into the meanings and significance of the humanities.

Although each dimension of the environment includes unique elements, there are numerous common features. For example, community may be discussed in both physical dimensions (the geography of a town) and social dimensions (the common purpose or character which unites a group). Ideas from each discipline have relevance in all three dimensions of the child's environment. There is an ecological balance in which changes in one portion of the child's life-space are reflected throughout his total environment.

As a child builds a more complete self he may gain the confidence necessary to explore further his physical and social environment. As a result he may ride a bus to an unknown section of the city or attempt to "make the team" in a local playground basketball league. An expressway constructed through a community may effectively block a child's attendance in the school he went to last year. Thus, a physical change results in a new school environment and, hence, new social challenges. Similarly, a court decision may change school district boundaries. The result of this alteration of the social dimension may be changes in the physical dimension (a bus ride to a new school) and the personal dimension (redefining self in a new peer group) of the environment.

The child's understanding of his environment and the skills requisite to expanding and applying these understandings make up his personal frame of reference. He uses this frame of reference to analyze his environment and to support his actions. Each child depends directly on the adequacy of his frame of reference for his effectiveness as a citizen of the community in which he functions. As social studies teachers we are charged with the responsibility for helping children build an adequate frame of reference and thereby for preparing effective citizens.

Effective citizens must possess a data bank from which to draw information and the ability to expand the usefulness of this source of information through addition or reinterpretation. The skills needed to enhance the data bank include the abilities (1) to identify problems in the environment, (2) to seek out data necessary to solve the problem, (3) to analyze data with regard to the problem at hand, (4) to form logical conclusions based on data, and (5) to act on these conclusions.

Implications for Instruction

The instructional techniques illustrated in Chapters 4 through 7 are correlated with the stages which make up the model of psycho-social development described in Chapter 1. As we begin to explore these techniques, one point must be emphasized: Categorizing individuals is always a chancy business. We have suggested that all children proceed through each stage in sequence. However, the rate of progress is a purely individual characteristic.

Chapter 4 focuses on the child's rapid movement from initial awareness and consequent exploration to the first manipulation of his environment.

The child begins his active life reacting to stimuli both internal (like hunger) and external (like bright-colored objects). Development is fostered by the make-up of the environment.

Initial exploration is evidence of awareness. As the child encounters the consequences of his action, he begins to pass into the structured-dependent stage. But we know that he is constantly broadening his circle of awareness and consequently continuing to do initial-exploratory kinds of things.

SETTING AN AGE FOR TEACHING ORIENTATION

Clearly a child's initial-exploratory stage of psycho-social development begins with life. We have explored the concept of awareness with particular emphasis on feelings in Chapter 2. Techniques recommended to help a child develop understanding of his own feelings stressed freedom—freedom to accept his own feelings as worthwhile as well as freedom to explore the causes and consequences of his reactions. The reader will recall the relationship of feelings and this individual's environment. We recommend placement of units on "self" or "self-concept" early in the child's education. Our hope is that increasingly large numbers of children will have these experiences before their formal entry educa- tion in nursery school or kindergarten. We proceed here on the assump- tion that as children enter grade one they have had these experiences. However, we recognize that in the real world they probably will not have had them. In any case concepts and techniques explored in Chapter 4 constitute a continuation of those in Chapter 2.

Most children entering the first phase of formal education may be expected to be operating at one of two Piagetian stages of cognitive development, either the preoperational stage or the concrete stage. First-grade teachers may expect children to manifest at least five charac- teristic behaviors:

1. *Children judge physical characteristics such as size, weight, and height solely on the basis of appearance.* This behavior is exemplified by the child's confusion resulting from optical illusions or from questions such as "Which weighs more, a pound of steel or a pound of feathers?"

2. *When two or more changes occur simultaneously, children focus on one and ignore the others.* An example of this charac- teristic is seen when an adult blows out a lighted match. The child focuses on the disappearing flame not the change in heat.

3. *Children don't take into account spacing or gaps in the ar- rangement of objects but judge relationships on the basis of over-all appearance.* Four automobiles shown bumper to bumper are smaller or less than four identical cars spaced along a street.

4. *Children are egocentric, being dominated by their own point of view (perception) of a situation or object.* When shown a picture of a group of children in a playground situation the child is unable to alter his interpretation to reflect an alterna- tive perception which may be held by another.

5. *Children at this stage tend to be unable to perceive the whole as assembled parts.* We say they lack inclusion relationships. When a picture of a group is cut up to show individuals, the child fails to identify the individuals as part of the original group.

As children come to us in the first grade they are beginning to emerge from this stage of cognitive development. As teachers we must provide opportunities to facilitate this transition to the higher level of concrete operations. At the same time we must meet the individual child's needs for psycho-social development.

Each child needs the freedom to explore. But exploration cannot take place in a void. If the classroom, school, and neighborhood community are to constitute the environment to be explored they must each be richly stimulating. Too often, the classroom appears sterile in comparison to the world outside. To develop environments that are highly charged with materials which are both highly motivational and potent sources of learning is thus a need that requires creative professional teaching.

The development of the British infant school (see Silberman, 1970) provides an interesting illustration of an environment which facilitates the child's development through stages one and two. Infant schools are designed for children of ages four, five and six. Their classrooms are divided into learning centers or activity areas stocked with all manner of materials, including books, games, and crafts materials. Children are at first free to follow their interest, working individually or in groups in whichever activity area they choose. That is, initially they explore the environment.

But infant schools are not simply sophisticated playpens. Each item in the room is placed there because it has potential to assist learning. Very quickly the teacher who has structured the environment imposes one governing condition. Each child must identify the activity he chooses and participate in certain kinds of activities which show he accepts the responsibility that goes with his choice. The results of this approach, both in England and in numerous schools in the United States, indicate that it is potent for early formal education.

ORIENTING THE CHILD TO HIS ENVIRONMENT

In order to illustrate a variety of approaches to the concept of orientation, we have selected three plans of instruction. Each plan focuses on a major concept (space; family and culture; community) deemed significant in the child's psycho-social development. Although the concepts which bind the plans together are certainly of differing levels of abstraction, the activities included are designed to help the child move from simple to complex cognitive operations. They also strike at different need levels.

The plans were developed with the assistance of practicing classroom teachers who also tried the activities in their own classes. The plans follow differing formats, each of which is an adequate guide to instruction. Readers are encouraged to examine these organizational patterns to determine which meets their needs.

Exploring the Physical Environment

The first instruction plan focuses on *space* as the construct for an exploration of the physical dimension of the environment. Major concepts associated with space include position, location, and time. These concepts may be either absolute ("it is now one o'clock in the afternoon") or relative ("it's later than we thought").

Concepts that cross these major concepts are similarity and difference. These concepts are clearly essential and evident in the initial activities described in the plan of instruction focusing on *space*. Similarities and differences are discovered through the processes of classifying and discriminating. Children learn how phenomena in their environment are similar or different by classifying or discriminating among increasingly abstract objects and ideas. Chart 2 displays a number of phenomena listed in ascending order of abstractness as well as attributes with respect to which any specific phenomenon may be analyzed.

CHART 2

Phenomena in Ascending Levels of Abstraction, and Attributes

Phenomena	Similarities / Differences	Attributes
5. Communities		Ideas
4. Institutions		Possessions
3. Families		Relationships
2. Persons		Physical Qualities
1. Objects		

A PLAN OF INSTRUCTION — SPACE[1]

"From the moment he is born the child begins to explore his environment by seeing and hearing it, by moving around in it, and by touching and manipulating things. . . . Through his daily experience he acquires conceptions of size and shape and distance. When he goes to school he refines these conceptions by absorbing into his experiences some of the ideas about space created by inventive minds in the past." (Adler, 1965)

Concept: Perspective.

[1] The authors extend their thanks to the following graduate students, all of them classroom teachers, who assisted in the development of this plan of instruction: Judith Ables, Kay Beck, Suzanne Lindberg, Nancy Morley, Ann Parkman, Linda Poore, Betty Riley, and Sharon Wright.

Generalization: Helping the child develop different spatial relationships with and among people and other aspects of his environment.

General Objectives:

1. To exhibit awareness of the relationship of self, as a growing body, to the environment. (Environment includes peers, adults, objects, and the like.)
2. To show the awareness of the relationship of one object to another.
3. To actively demonstrate awareness of space through movement. (Establishing boundaries and other behavior)

Activities

Sensorimotor Stage

1. Placing the playpen or crib on the eye level of the adult, so that the child is not overwhelmed by the size of the adults and objects in his environment.

2. Changing the height and position of mobiles over a child's crib, so that the child can develop an awareness of change.

3. Presenting the child with objects of varying size and shape, so that the child will realize through manipulation that different objects occupy different amounts of space.

4. Playing peek-a-boo, so that the child begins to understand object permanence.

Preoperational Stage

1. Presenting the child with pictures and other environmental elements (such as furniture and pictures) on the eye level of the child, so that he may continue to associate with his environment.

2. (a) Using a peg board with different colored pegs in various patterns, so that a child continues to observe change. (b) Participating in a field activity, so that the child will be able to relate proximity with changes in size. (c) Experimenting with groups of objects of the same quantity, putting them close together, far apart, and in other arrangements, so that the child can observe conservation.

3. Providing opportunities for the child to play in, under, and around boxes and tubes of varying sizes, so that the child can experience his position in space.

4. (a) Guiding the child to observe his own image and other reflections in a mirror or in water, so that he continues to develop the idea of object permanence. (b) Manipulating a chain to disappear and reappear through a hole in a can, so that the child sees it and thus reinforces his understanding of object permanence.

5. Drawing a picture of the classroom, or any part of the classroom, so that the child begins to use symbols that will later serve as a foundation for map skills.

6. Providing experiences of discussing, viewing films, and role playing about outer space, so that the child begins to develop an awareness of extraterrestrial space.

Concrete Stage

1. (a) Measuring and recording on a large wall chart each child's height, so that he can see how he looks in relation to his peers and environment. (b) Making a graph of the height information of the class at different times during the school year, so that the child may see his relation to his peers and environment in still another way.

2. Using the Attribute Blocks, so that the child further develops ideas of the dimensions that make up space.

3. Guiding the child in swinging, hanging by the knees, sliding down the sliding board, standing on his head, climbing, and similar activities, so that the child may observe his environment from various positions.

4. (a) Using solids (beans, marbles, sand), liquids (milk, water), and gases (air) to fill containers, so that the different properties of space may be explored. (b) Using pupils to see how many will occupy a certain space (such as under a table, in a box, in a small room, or in some other limited space) so that the child further experiences properties of space.

5. (a) Making a map of the classroom on the chalkboard using X's to symbolize different objects in the room, so that the child can extend his map skills. (b) Using the map again, shading portions (sometimes combining two or more) so that the child can compare their areas.

6. Discussing, viewing, and manipulating models of the solar system, so that the child continues to develop the idea of extraterrestrial space.

Abstract Stage

1. Discussing and drawing objects in proportion as we see them in our environment, so that the child further relates to the proportions in space.

2. Discussing and drawing the dimensions of objects, so that the child further relates to the dimensions of objects in space.

3. Discussing, role-playing, and drawing experiences of relative position, (such as viewing from a distance the top of a tall building, parachuting from an airplane, being in a subway or tunnel, walking on the moon), so that the child further experiences different positions in space. (**Note:** These activities may be based upon real or vicarious experiences.)

4. Estimating quantities and amount of space occupied by certain objects, so that the child expands his generalizations of properties of space. (**Note:** Refer to activity 4 in the Concrete Stage above for suggested materials.)

5. Making maps and graphs in abstract form to represent concrete ideas in space, so that the child further expands his map skills and generalizations concerning space.

6. Constructing maps, graphs, and models of relationships of bodies in

extraterrestrial space, so that the child continues to generalize concepts concerning out space.

Evaluating Sequential Competencies
Sensorimotor Stage

1. Observing the child's eye movements. Does he adjust his eye movements to those objects of varying heights and positions?

2. Manipulating a set of objects varying in size and shape. Does the child place the objects in the set in the proper sequence of size, shape, or attitude?

3. Hiding different objects from the immediate sight of the child. Does the child pursue the search for the missing object?

Preoperational Stage

1. Presenting the child with a choice of different-sized objects (like furniture, clothing) and instructing him to choose the one of appropriate size for him. Does he choose the appropriate one?

2. Rearranging objects in patterns and quantities. Does the child point out the change? Does he perform an operation leading to a solution to the pattern of change?

3. Directing the child to move under, in, around, between, or in other relation to three-dimensional objects. Does the child perform the directed activities correctly?

4. Placing an object in combination with another object (as inside, behind, under). Does the child point out both objects?

5. Presenting symbols to designate objects in his immediate environment. Does the child actively associate the symbols with the objects?

Concrete Stage

1. Displaying a life-sized height graph and using positioned objects around the room to compare size. Does the child point out the differences in height between himself and an object?

2. Playing the one-difference and two-difference games (see "Things to Do") with the Attribute Blocks. Does the child point out the differences?

3. Presenting measuring problems to the child using concrete objects. Does the child arrive at correct solutions to the problem?

4. Presenting proportioned symbols to the child with directions to draw a map. Does the child produce a map with the approximate proportions? (For example: In the child's drawing, is his desk smaller than the teacher's desk?)

Abstract Stage

1. Drawing a representation from a **scale model.** Does the child correctly represent proportions?

2. Presenting the child with written problems dealing with measurement. Does the child arrive at correct solutions without manipulation?

3. Assigning the child tasks of making models or drawings showing the relationships of home, community, city, state, country, continent, world, and space. Does the child adequately complete the assignment?

Things To Do

1. Use binoculars with the child.

2. Use a View Master with the child.

3. Use a kaleidoscope with the child.

4. Accompany the child on a field activity to a planetarium.

5. Stack proportional-sized objects with the child, such as the commercial games Billy Barrels, Mailbox Game, Barn Game.

6. Observe shadows with the child. (a) Have the child observe the different area he takes up at different times of the day and year. (b) Have the child make shadow pictures of animals or other things with his fingers and hands.

7. Play the one-difference and two-difference games with the child. (**Explanation:** Using the Attribute Blocks, begin with one child choosing a block and placing it in the center of the circle. The next child must find a block which is "one different" (differs in only one attribute) from the first. This continues around the circle of children as a train is formed. The two differences game is played in the same way, but the block must be different in exactly two attributes, rather than one, from the block before it.)

Books for the Children to Read
The Very Little Boy, Phyllis Krasilovsky
The Very Little Girl, Phyllis Krasilovsky
The Sounds of Number, Bill Martin
"Little Jonathan" from **Shining Bridges,** Miriam E. Mason
"Sizes," a poem by John Ciardi
Let's Find Out What's Big and What's Small, Martha and Charles Shapp

Books for the Teacher to Read
Six books written by the Nuffield Math Project published by John Wiley and Sons:

Beginnings
Shape and Size 1, 2, 3
Environmental Geometry
Mathematics Begins

Arithmetic and Mathematics, Carl Bereiter
Laboratory Manual for Elementary Mathematics, Fitzgerald and colleagues

Exploring Our Cultural Environment

Kids are people! They cannot be divided into thinking animals and feeling animals. Similarly, their environment cannot be subdivided arbitrarily by adults. Do not do this to children — do not dichotomize!

This minor digression to preaching in no way alters this book's position that teachers must seek specific foci for the purpose of instruction. Specific ideas are selected to provide emphases and bases from which children can grow. Thus, for purposes of instruction teachers may select specific concepts which emphasize the physical dimension of a child's environment. However, we cannot ignore the concomitant growth of the personal and social dimensions of the child's environment.

We have probed the uniquely personal dimension of the child's world in the material on feelings presented in Chapter 2. Overlapping and evolving from exploration of personal feeling is the concept of FAMILY. Family is the most commonly studied social studies concept. It pervades the elementary curriculum, not only in the social studies but especially in reading and the language arts.

Traditionally, the family is accepted as the singly most important institution for the child and as the foundation of society. Serious questions have been raised in recent years about the approach to the family employed in our schools. Specific concerns relate to the definition of family and the apparent single-minded approach to the function it serves for the individual and for society.

We authors would offer an alternative to what has been termed the "Dick and Jane" approach. The plan of instruction set out below encompasses the traditional notion of family but attempts to provide opportunities to move beyond.

A PLAN OF INSTRUCTION—
THE CHILD AND HIS CULTURAL BACKGROUNDS[2]

Key Idea: The child's acceptance of his family and cultural background.

1. The composition of families can differ greatly within our society.
2. Families can reflect different cultural backgrounds.

Behavioral Objectives: The children will present description of their families and cultural backgrounds through oral discussion, written work, or both.

Motivational Setting: Set up a display table in the front of the classroom in view of all the children (visual stimulation). On this table arrange dolls of various sizes and sex to represent members of a family (father, mother, girl, boy, relative) as well as stuffed animals to represent pets. (To some children at this age, the family consists of all living things in the child's immediate

---

[2] The authors extend grateful thanks to four classroom teachers and graduate students who assisted in the writing of this plan of instruction: Ann Wendling, Joanne Smith, Sallie Rogers, and Martha Presley.

physical proximity and frequently includes the family pets.) Let the dolls and stuffed animals on the display table be furnished by children in the classroom.

Introduction

The teacher narrates a short story about her own family using the dolls and stuffed animals on the display table as visual aides to illustrate the family members. (Be realistic in presenting family composition — for example, if the father is dead or the parents divorced, say so.)

Encourage the children to come before the class and present their families, using the display table if they desire. Such an invitation can be extended through the use of leading questions such as: Are all families the same? Do all families have the same members? Does your family differ from my family?

Developmental Activities

1. **Research.** Have the children construct a booklet on the family.

Materials: Magazines and catalogues. Scissors. Construction paper. Paste. Crayons, pencils. Stapler.

Have the children cut pictures representing their family members from magazines or catalogues. (These magazines and catalogues may be supplied by the children and/or the teacher.) Some children may prefer to draw pictures of the members of their family. Have the children paste these pictures on sheets of construction paper to form a booklet entitled "My Family." Help the children label the pictures of each family member.

After the booklets are completed, questions may be introduced to reinforce the similarities and differences in family composition. The children use their booklets as a source of reference during the discussion.

What type of members do we often find as part of a family?

What other relatives might be family members?

Do families need any one type of member to make it a family? Lead children to see (without telling them) that no one member is necessary to make a family.

The children use their booklets to begin a bulletin board on the family.

Film strips may be used effectively to stimulate and enrich group discussions. A list of some available strips is given here, with some annotation.

A. Eye Gate Instructional Materials include the following:

202A — "Who Am I?" Material presented in this film strip helps the child take an objective look at himself and think about the kind of person he wishes to be.

78 — "Character Makes A Difference"

78A — "School Days"

78B — "Work and Play at School"

78D — "Getting Along with Yourself"

78F — "Getting Along with Friends"

The procedure used in this 78 set of film strips is to develop the basic ideas of character training indirectly through everyday situations in the home, in school, and in daily experiences.

ME 220 — "Patterns of Behavior"
ME 2204 — "All of Us Together"
ME 2205 — "Different May be Nice"

Various situations involving young children are presented in this ME set with constructive thoughts about conduct and manners.

48 — "The Story of Houses"
48B — "Strange Homes"
48G — "Homes Around the World"
48I — "Homes in the United States — New and Old"

This 48 series shows ways in which man has tried to improve his shelter, from cave dwellers, tree houses, tents and, long structures to stone manors, town houses, and apartment buildings.

B. Singer Education and Training Products include the following:

219 — "Living With Your Family"
219-1 — "What Is a Family?" illustrate the role of each family member and emphasizes the importance of cooperation, love, consideration of others and privacy.
219-2 — "The Family Has A New Baby" depicts a family preparing for the arrival of a new baby.
219-3 — "A Day With Your Family" shows how each family member has certain needs and responsibilities that are important to all the family members.
219-4 — "Family Fun" portrays recreational facilities and opportunities where families can have fun.

C102 — "Getting to Know Me"
C102-1 — "People Are Like Rainbows"
C102-2 — "A Boat Named George"
C102-3 — "Listen! Jimmy"
C102-4 — "Strike Three! You're In!"

A series of film strips that stimulate children to take a close look at themselves and each other.

208 — "Robert and His Family"
208-1 — "Robert's Family At Home"
208-2 — "Robert's Family and Their Neighbors"
208-3 — "Robert Goes Shopping"
208-4 — "Robert And Father Visit the Zoo"

Robert Anderson is a primary-grade Negro boy living in an urban area.

Full-color, on-the-site photography, with story-type narration portrays Robert and his family in their daily activities.

2. **Role Perception and Role Playing.** Dramatize a family activity.

Begin with an exercise in planning: (a) Consider the merits of the suggestion. (b) Agree on group decisions. (c) Organize ideas into workable scheme.

Proceed with an exercise in listening skills: If necessary, discuss good manners in listening to others. Divide the class into small groups. Let each group make up its own family. Let each group select a family activity and dramatize it before the class. At this point, introduce questioning related to values. **Examples:** Why did you choose this type of family to represent? Why did you choose this activity to portray? The teacher may take pictures of each family activity dramatized for the children to add to their bulletin board on the family.

3. **Reading.** Select books from the library displaying different types of families at work and play.

Be sure these books show all of the cultural backgrounds of the class members. Be sure they reflect the range of the class' reading abilities. Have the children read (or listen to stories read) about different families with varying cultural backgrounds.

Some books here described may be available.

Sam. (K-3) Ann H. Scott. 1967. McGraw-Hill. Each member of this Negro family is too pre-occupied to give Sam any attention until they notice his dejection and provide a satisfying job for him to do.

Evan's Corner. (1-3) Elizabeth Hill. 1967. Holt. Evan longs for a place of his own until his mother points out that there are eight corners in their two-room apartment—one for him and one for each other member of the family.

Peter's Chair. (K-1) Ezra Jack Keats. 1967. Harper. Peter learns to accept his new role of big brother and recovers from his jealousy of the new baby.

Grandmother and I. (K-1) Helen E. Buckley. Lothrop (D 61). A small girl explains the reasons Grandmother's lap is better than anyone else's.

What Mary Jo Shared. (1-2) Janice Udry. 1961. Whitman. A little Negro girl shares her father with her schoolmates during "Show and Tell" time.

Moy Moy. (K-3) Leo Politi. 1960. Scribner. A story of a little Chinese girl's life in a Los Angeles Chinese neighborhood.

The Fabulous Firework Family. (1-3) James Flora. 1955. Harcourt. A Mexican boy wants to be a master firework maker like his father and grandfather.

Kid Brother. (K-3) Jerrold Beam. Morrow. This story deals with the real problems in relations between older and younger children.

My Daddy Lost His Job. (1-2) Singer (Carousel Books Program). This story centers on how a family can help when Daddy loses a job. Very good for children of poor socio-economic situation.

Too Many Live In My House. (1-2) Singer (Carousel Book Program). A crowded family situation is the theme for this story. Very realistic and geared to ghetto-area children's problems.

4. **Family Identity.** Bring a camera to school and take a picture of the class.

Let this picture lead to a discussion of the concept "family." Lead children to see (without telling them) that the class can be considered a child's school family. Have the children place the picture of their "school family" on the bulletin board.

5. **Family Treasures.** The teacher brings a treasured object from her home to show and share with the class. (Motivating effect.)

Encourage each child to bring some object that has special meaning for his own family. This object could be a long-preserved Christmas ornament, an object handed down for generations, a baby or family picture, or many others. The teacher can initiate another values lesson. Question children about **why** these objects are important to them. Lead children to see (without telling them) that these objects are special because they belong to their **own** family—a very important institution in one's life.

The children may wish to set up a display table in the classroom for these objects.

6. **Family Play and Recreation.** The teacher brings a picture or souvenir from a family trip or vacation. (Motivating effect.)

Let the children bring in pictures and souvenirs of family trips and vacations. This activity can serve to illustrate different family likes and dislikes. For example, some families who like the ocean spend their vacations on the beach in Florida. Other families who enjoy the outdoors go camping at different sites across the country. Lead the children to see (without telling them) that the things they enjoy and value are influenced by their family's preferences.

The teacher may wish to use this activity as a geography lesson. The locations of family trips and vacations may be pointed out on a large-scale map of the United States or of the world—depending on the extent of the children's travels.

These family pictures and souvenirs may be an addition to the children's bulletin board.

7. **Family Origins.** Have a large-scale map of the United States and the world in view of the whole class.

The teacher places a marker at her birthplace, and another marker on the map at the area her ancestors originally came from. Through leading questions such as "Do you know where you were born?" and "Do you know where your grandparents [great grandparents, and so on] were born?" encourage the children to learn about their birthplace and their ancestral origins. The children will need to get help from their parents.

Help the children place markers on the maps at their birthplaces and at the areas their family originally came from. Perhaps the markers could have the children's names on them. Lead the children to see (without telling them) the number of different places of ancestral origin. Each different location represents a different type of culture. Thus the class represents many different cultural backgrounds.

The teacher may wish to incorporate a geography lesson with this activity. If desired, it can be enlarged to study of the customs of particular countries.

8. **Family Day.** Help the children plan a Family Day as a culminating event for the unit on the family and cultural background.

The children invite their families to visit the classroom.

Have the children draw a self-portrait to be placed on their desks on Family Day. Parents are challenged to locate their child's desk by his self-portrait.

Let the children introduce the members of their family to the class. Have the children explain their recent course of study to their families through the work shown on the bulletin board, maps, and display tables.

The children may wish to present all or several of the sketches of the family activities they created.

Let the children entertain by singing songs they learned during their study. These songs may include some from this list.

Making Music Your Own — Book One (Teacher's Edition). Silver Burdett Company.

"Don Juan Periquito" — page 98.
"The Porcupine" — page 106. (Israeli song).
"Nick-Nack, Paddy Whack" — page 111. (English folk song)

Book Two (Teacher's Edition).

"The Mill" — page 12. (German folk song)
"Grisette, The Squirrel" — page 32. (French folk song)
"Gogo" — page 38. (singing game from Kenya)
"A Gust of Fall Wind" — page 40. (Chinese-American folk song)
"On a Monday Morning" — page 114. (Polish folk song)
"Marching to Pretoria" — page 116. (Dutch folk song from South Africa)
"Shoes Squeak" — page 120. (Japanese song)
"The Bed" — page 120. (Puerto Rican folk song)
"A-tin-go-tin" — page 150. (African folk song)
"The Clever Monkey" — page 150. (African folk song)
"This Land Is Your Land" — page 160. (United States)

If the project is feasible and acceptable, refreshments could be furnished by the mothers. The food could reflect the different cultural backgrounds of the children's families. For example, food may be characteristic of a particular religious sect (Jewish unleavened bread) or of a certain geographical area (region of the United States, or foreign country).

Exploring Our Community Environment

The family is not the only institution through which the child is introduced to his culture and to the society in which he lives. Readers interested in exploring alternative means of introducing the child to his "self" and his social relationships may be interested in preparing a plan of instruction dealing with the kibbutz or commune.

The young person's environment may be summarized in a study of the concept of *community*. There is no single acceptable definition of community. However, a variety of descriptive definitions exist which are acceptable for our purposes. To some, *community* connotes the area contained within specific geographical or political boundaries; a city, town, or neighborhood might thus be perceived as a community. In another sense, a *community* may be defined more abstractly as a group of people sharing common interests or beliefs—the religious community or the community of scholars. For the young child, *community* generally refers to his neighborhood—that geographic area which he is permitted to explore by himself or in the company of parents or others responsible for him.

As the child explores his community, he encounters people and institutions as well as physical characteristics which help him to grow as a person. Below is a series of lessons designed to illustrate the notion the child's environment, specifically his community, changes as he grows. He may become a member of additional communities or withdraw from membership in others. At the same time the communities themselves may change. For instance, his neighborhood may change from residential to commercial.

The following plan of instruction requires the application of specific skills discussed earlier in this chapter. The reader will note both the reinforcement of these skills and concepts and an alternate system of presentation.

A PLAN OF INSTRUCTION—THE COMMUNITY[3]

Lesson One

Generalization: A community has many kinds of buildings and places with many kinds of uses.

Purpose: The purpose of this lesson is to have the students first note and

---

[3] The authors wish to acknowledge the contribution of the following graduate students, residents of Philadelphia, in the development of this plan of instruction: Susan Cross and Heather Ambacker.

then gather the information necessary for the construction of a three-dimensional model of their own community. The children will be able to gain much of their resources material from a primary source, their own neighborhood.

Behavioral Objectives: (1) By the information the children provide for the information cha.t, they will show their understanding of the need to note the number of buildings, the placement of buildings, the type of buildings, and the relative height of buildings, in gathering information for their scale drawings and legends. (2) By the sketches the children bring to school the following day, it will show whether they have been able to follow the information chart and gather data correctly for future use.

Procedure: As many parents as possible are invited to go along on a walking tour of the neighborhood, during which notes will be gathered for an information-experience chart. Each child is thereafter assigned to sketch one side of a city block. As much as possible, each child is assigned his own block or one that is very close to his own home. Then the children will be able to do some sketching on their own after school, if this is necessary. A convenient area is about ten blocks.

Before the walk commences, the teacher should hold a discussion that will help the children to understand exactly what they should be looking for. This will help to focus the students' attention on the relevant items. This discussion could be held in the morning; the walk could be held in the afternoon.

The measurements needed for the scale drawings of the various buildings and the information needed for the legends will be given by the teacher, in terms of the graphic scale. There are several reasons why we felt this was necessary. They are: (1) It would be, in our opinion, quite difficult for the children to measure their blocks and convert the dimensions to the graphic scale. (2) We felt it would be beyond the comprehension and state of readiness of second-graders to use the inches-to-miles scale or any other scale applicable to such work. (3) The purpose of our unit is not to teach measurement; rather the scale drawings are used as a means to an end. (4) More advanced mapping experiences will come in later grades, when the children are more ready for them. (5) Precise measurement by the children would take more time than the educational merit warrants.

Evaluation: The teacher will be able to judge the competency of her students by the quality, in terms of content, of their information chart and sketches. The idea of scale will be picked up in the next lesson so a lot of remedial help is not necessary at this point.

Lesson Two

Generalization: A community has many buildings and places we may not even think about.

Purpose: The purpose of this lesson is to help the children comprehend the idea of "community." The discussion involved in the writing of the information-experience chart will help to clarify what the children have seen, in terms of the types of buildings, public institutions, and houses that actually exist in the community. Another significant feature of this lesson is the formation of a direction chart, reviewing the important components of scale drawing.

Behavioral Objectives: (1) By the information the students state orally in the creation of the direction chart, they will demonstrate a clear understanding of the components of scale drawings. (2) By the students' oral statements and individual sketches, they will show a clear knowledge of the components of their community.

Procedure: The teacher and students will ask: "What did you see on your walk in the community yesterday?" The children should be quite eager to discuss all they have seen and should have much to say. Although they may have lived in the community since birth in most cases, they will quite likely be seeing things in a new light and really "seeing" some things for the first time. The information from this discussion will be recorded in an experience chart and should be displayed prominently in the classroom throughout the entire unit on the community. As the children compile the information-experience chart, the teacher should be showing them many pictures of the "present day" community. These pictures should also be displayed along with the experience chart. The experience chart and pictures should help to give the students an overview of the entire community. Working on their own block within the community, the children might tend to lose perspective of the whole community; this would be very unfortunate and should be avoided.

After this discussion, there will be a review of the components of scale drawings. This information will be recorded in a direction chart, which should be displayed in the classroom while the model of the community is being constructed.

Eventually the children will be divided into groups, approximately one group for each two-block area, hence approximately five groups with six children in each group. This will help co-ordinate the work on the community construction and help structure the work from individual small pieces into a single cohesive whole.

Evaluation: This lesson will be evaluated in terms of the clarity and awareness the children demonstrate in the discussion necessary for the formation of the experience chart about the community and its components. The relevance and completeness of the direction chart will show just how clearly the students understand scale drawings and legends and what information is necessary for their completion. If the children do not demonstrate adequate understanding of scale drawings and legends, this is the time for the teacher to provide any remedial work she feels is necessary. The teacher may need to work with only a few individual students at this time, rather than the class as a whole.

Lesson Three
Generalization: Our community has so many buildings and places that we have to do something special to think of all of them at once.

Purpose: The purposes of this lesson group are many. They are: to have the children make scale drawings for a real purpose, to have the children compile and coordinate all the individual students' work into a cohesive whole, to have the children actually construct a three-dimensional model of a community, and to have the children gain new insights and awarenesses into the components of their own community.

Behavioral Objectives: (1) The students will demonstrate their knowledge of scale drawings and legends by the accuracy and completeness of their work, as judged by the content of the direction chart. (2) The students will demonstrate an ability to do scale drawings suggesting three dimensions, shown in the correctness and content of their art work as judged by the content of the direction chart. (3) The students who coordinate all the individual scale drawings will demonstrate their understanding of the components of scale drawings and legends, as judged by the standards of the direction chart.

Procedure: This lesson marks the beginning of the group work and the beginning stage of the community construction in both a two-dimensional (buildings) and a three-dimensional (area) form. The children will all make scale drawings and legends for the block or blocks to which they have been assigned. They will be given the necessary measurements, paper, and measuring equipment. Sketches, pictures, the experience chart, and the direction chart will all be utilized. The teacher should have constructed a scale drawing of the entire area beforehand, so she can offer assistance to any child with inadequate resource materials. Certainly, the purpose of this community construction and scale drawing is not to penalize or frustrate any child who is usable to handle such work. Each child should have an opportunity to contribute to this project. Some may require more help than others, but that should not prevent them from making their own contribution.

The children who handle the skill of scale drawing best and enjoy it most will form a new group to coordinate the work of the five groups. The other children will start the construction of the art work of the buildings. This art work will give the effect of being three-dimensional, but the buildings will be two-dimensional with a piece attached to support them standing erect. This is necessary because of the children's somewhat limited motor abilities.

Thus, the children have first drawn scale maps and then have made from them scale buildings to be placed on the final large map. The group which coordinates the individual group maps will incorporate streets and sidewalks into the final large scale drawing, as well as a legend or key. The teacher will, as needed, provide necessary measurements and assist this group.

This group work and activity will last for approximately one week. At the end of this week, the community model will have been completed and will be displayed prominently in the classroom. With proper teacher guidance and the student enthusiasm and involvement which we feel this project will generate, the outcome of this work should be quite pleasing and gratifying to both teacher and students.

Evaluation: The teacher will be able to determine the effectiveness of this series of lessons by judging the quality of the individual scale drawings, the final scale drawing completed by the smaller group of students, and the work done on making the scale drawings into models. The teacher should judge this quality according to the components found in the direction chart the children have made.

Lesson Four
Generalization: There are many kinds of workers in the community. Each worker provides a service someone needs.

Purpose: The children should realize, through playing the game and through the discussion which follows it, their own and the larger community's dependence on various workers in the community and the services they provide.

Behavioral Objectives: (1) The students will demonstrate their ability to follow directions by playing the game correctly. (2) The students will show, by their oral statements during the discussion, their understanding of interdependence in a community. (3) The students will demonstrate, by their oral statements in the discussion, their ability to utilize information and to make inferences. The inferences will, of course, be drawn from the information gained by playing the game.

Procedure: The teacher will have prepared materials and rules for a game utilizing the model community. This game will be somewhat like **Candyland,** with relatively simple directions. The sidewalk squares will be used as the units of movement, with every fifth square colored in; when a child lands on a darkened square, he must select a card. The cards are of the following form: "You must go to the store right away. Your mother needs oranges." "A boy took your toy. Wait here two turns for the policeman to come." "You put the trash out well. This helped the trashmen. Move ahead 3 spaces." "The mailman has an important letter for you. He took it to your house. No one was there. Go to the post office and get it."

The object of the game is to get home first. The children should be realizing the great amount of importance people in the community play in their lives. When a worker in the community is not performing his job normally, it causes the child to wait or go out of his way, thereby hindering his progress in winning the game.

Each child will be assigned a specific time to play the game. We felt this was necessary for several reasons. First, this insures there will be an adequate number of students to play the game. Second, this will allow the teacher to hold the discussion only after she knows that everyone, having played the game, will be able to contribute intelligently and with understanding of what the discussion is about.

The teacher now holds the discussion to discover what the children have learned from playing the game. The teacher asks such leading questions as: "Why did the person who won the game win?" "If you lost the game, why did you lose?'' The children should, in their own manner of speaking, convey to the teacher their recognition of the idea of the dependence of people on others in the community for various life services.

Evaluation: The teacher will be able to judge from the students' comments during the discussion whether or not they understood the idea of interdependence in a community. If they have not, the teacher should ask additional questions similar to those presented previously.

Lesson Five

Generalization: Communities vary in the types of services provided according to the needs of the community. If there are not enough businesses in the community, people go outside the community to work.

Purpose: The purpose of this lesson is to have the students recognize those people and services needed for life to function in a community. They will also discover just which of these services and people are found in their own community and which are missing.

Behavioral Objectives: (1) The students will show their understanding of those people and services needed for life, by writing intelligent and complete individual lists. (2) The students will illustrate, by the completeness and correctness of the information they provide for a chart, their understanding of the people and services present in and missing from their community.

Procedure: The model of the community is in clear view for all the class to see. "What people do you see in our community every day? Please make a list of all the people you see in our community during the week." Having the children make their own individual lists will help to insure their thinking about the subject.

After the children have compiled them, the lists are discussed and the teacher puts them down on a large chart. The chart itself is divided in half: one half marked plus; the other minus. The plus signifies those kinds of people whose services are needed for modern-day living and who **are** found in the community. The minus signifies those kinds of people whose services are needed for modern living but who are **not** found in the community. While the children are helping the teacher to compile the list, the need for each individual mentioned (for example: policeman, mailman, milkman, store keeper) is discussed.

"What other people and services do you need to live?" These new items are written under the minus sign in the chart.

This lesson, thus, starts the children thinking about what people they need to live and what services they need to live. It also points out which of these people and services are found in their own community and which are not.

"Do your parents work? . . . What work do they do? . . . Do they work in the community? . . . They don't? Why not?" These questions again help the students to see what services are missing in their own community. It also helps them to realize that a community, especially today, may not be able to provide jobs for all its members.

Evaluation: This lesson will be evaluated in terms of the relevance and completeness of the information the students provide for the chart and show in their individual lists. There is not much need for remedial work at this time, since the ideas found in the chart will be picked up again, regarding the past.

Lesson Six

Generalization: Some communities change gradually with the passage of time.

Purpose: The purpose of this lesson is to introduce the idea of change on a broad scale. The children first hear about the whole city [Philadelphia is the example here] before their attention is focused on their own particular neighborhood. This progression, we feel, will help the children gain a better insight into both history and change.

Behavioral Objective: The children will begin to recognize change, as demonstrated in their oral statements during the discussion.

Procedure: The teacher shows a good film on the history of [Philadelphia]. The teacher must consider the quality and authenticity of the film and the age level of her students. This film should help bring the past alive for the children. This will give them an overview of what was happening in all of [Philadelphia] before they consider their own particular community.

The teacher can then hold a small discussion. In this discussion the children can tell what they felt and what was especially interesting or amusing to them in the film.

Evaluation: There is no major evaluation in this lesson as it is an introductory lesson. All that is hoped in this lesson is that the students begin to understand that communities change over time, and the ways of the changes.

Lesson Seven

Generalization: Our community changes when we get new neighbors and new kinds of buildings and services.

Purpose: The purpose of this lesson is for the children to gain insight into the change which has happened in their own particular community.

Behavioral Objectives: (1) The students will show the ability to interpret information and to record orally given information in drawings or in writing. (2) During the discussion of the pictures, the students will demonstrate, by their pictures and accompanying comments, their recognition of change in their own community.

Procedure: The teacher begins this lesson by reading from the book [**Philadelphia: A City of Many Neighborhoods,** compiled by the Board of Education in 1957]. This book describes the history of each section of [Philadelphia] and the teacher will read the section pertinent to her own class.

"Draw a picture of how you think our community looked then" (as described in the book). After these pictures are completed, the children will show them to the class. The teacher, at this time, should show as many photographs as she can find from books, magazines, newspapers, historical journals, or other sources. These photographs should be shown to the class as a whole and then passed around the classroom for each child to view closely. Thereby, each child will be able to study the pictures, compare the pictures to his own drawings, and gain a "feeling" for the history of their community.

Evaluation: This lesson will be evaluated by the teacher in terms of the sense of the past the students' pictures portray. The teacher will also utilize the content of the students' remarks to determine the extent of their understanding of change in their own community.

Lesson Eight

Generalization: Services change as communities change.

Purpose: The purpose of this lesson group, composed of many activities, is to help the students to see, by working with primary source materials, that services change as communities change. The students should gain this understanding not only by working on their own project but also through the presentation of other group projects.

Behavioral Objectives: (1) The students will demonstrate by the quality of the individual group projects their ability to utilize primary sources correctly and well. (2) The students will show, by the ideas that their group projects present and portray, their understanding of the generalization that services change as communities change. (3) The students will show, by their oral statements in the discussion following the presentation of the projects, their understanding of the generalization that services change as communities change.

Procedure: This lesson may take several days because several activities will be going on at the same time. These activities will all help to illustrate the generalization that services change as communities change.

The class will be divided into groups and each group will be working on a different activity. The class as a whole, in the end, will be able to benefit from the many different activities.

One of the major groups will be constructing a bulletin board. This group's only instructions are to make a bulletin board illustrating a few of the services available today that were unavailable or different in the past. The children are asked to bring in any materials they have available at home or can get from some public institution outside of the school. The teacher will make available many pictures and articles from old newspapers and historical journals. These articles can be read to the children in this group or rewritten on their level of understanding. This group will also be drawing many pictures of the students' creation, illustrating what they have read or have been read. Later, at the completion of the bulletin boards, they will tell the class what their bulletin boards have attempted to illustrate.

Another major group of children will be asked to write a small play illustrating an aspect of the present-day community, comparing it to a similar aspect of the past. Their concepts should, of course, be different than those being illustrated on the bulletin boards. They will present these plays, upon completion, to the class. The teacher should provide resource material for this group and utilize any materials they are able to supply on their own. If possible, the teacher should try to supply costumes for the plays of this group.

If the class is large enough to be divided into four groups, two groups can make bulletin boards and two groups write plays. By this arrangement, four different examples of services changing over time will be brought to the class's attention. The teacher must circulate around the room during these activities, providing aid to each group as it is needed.

Evaluation: To evaluate this lesson, the teacher will hold a discussion following the presentation of all the group "reports." During this discussion, the children should definitely be able to state the generalization, at their own level of understanding. If they are unable to do so, it is up to the teacher to lead them to this level of understanding. She can do so through questions like: "Has the number of grocery stores (for example) remained the same in our neighborhood?" She would, of course, mention a concept that one of the groups of students has utilized.

Lesson Nine

Generalization: When a community grows larger, more services such as stores, school, churches, and libraries are needed.

Purpose: The purpose of this lesson is to bring a primary resource, a speaker, into the classroom. The students are able to utilize the speaker to gain as much information as possible. The speaker should also help to make change alive, vibrant, and full of reality for the children.

Behavioral Objective: Through the quality of the questions the students ask the speaker, the students will show understanding of the need for services to change as communities change.

Procedure: The teacher should invite someone who has lived in the community for a long time to come in and speak to the class. This person, perhaps a druggist or a grocer, should speak about how the community has grown, how his services have changed, the larger number of people he must now serve, whether he is able to meet these new needs adequately, and if so, how he has done so. The speaker should, of course, gear his level of speaking to the children's own level of speaking and understanding. Although the children may realize what the general work of this speaker is, they probably do not realize the particular details of his job. (The children should be informed about the speaker before his or her arrival, so they can be formulating questions they would like to ask.)

Evaluation: The teacher will be able to judge her students' level and extent of understanding through the questions they ask and the comments they make. This idea will be reinforced in the next lesson, so the understanding the students demonstrate need not be full or complete at this point.

Lesson Ten

Generalization (similar to that for Lesson Nine): When a community grows larger, more services, such as schools, churches, libraries, fire protection, and police protection, are needed.

Purpose: The purpose of this lesson is to show the children, through primary source material, that through time the different services offered by institutions and people had to change. This change involved growth, increase in complexity, and technological advances.

Behavioral Objective: The students will demonstrate, by the insight and comprehension of their comments and questions during the discussion, their understanding of the generalization that when a community grows larger, more services such as schools, churches, and libraries are needed.

Procedure: The teacher will take her class out into the community to visit a fire station, library, post office, police station, or factory (all these are primary sources). Here they can see and be told how the institution has changed over time. The firemen, librarians, and others will be asked to discuss with the class, on their level, how the institution has changed over time, how it has grown to meet the larger number of people in the community, and whether it has been able to meet the greater needs of today. Since the class is actually visiting a neighborhood institution, they will be able to see, as well as hear, first hand, the changes which time has required of this institution.

Evaluation: After the class returns from this trip, perhaps the next day, the teacher should hold a discussion of both Lesson Nine and Lesson Ten. In this discussion, the idea of the need for change as communities grow should be brought out by the children. What they have learned from the primary sources should be brought into the discussion.

Lesson Eleven

Generalization: The changes that occur are not always desirable.

Purpose: The purpose of this lesson is to help the children to recognize that change is neither always positive nor always negative. Rather, at times change is positive and beneficial, but at other times it is negative and deleterious.

Behavioral Objectives: (1) The students will demonstrate, through their oral statements following the story, their comprehension of the fact that change is not always positive. (2) The students will show in their composition the realization that change can be both positive and negative.

Procedure: The teacher introduces this lesson by having each child read **The Little House,** geared to the first/second-grade level; the students should have no trouble reading it themselves. The story itself is about the movement of a house from the country, where it belongs and "fits in," to the city, where it is ill-suited. Eventually, the house is returned to the country where it always should have stayed. This story should get the students thinking seriously about the generalization that change is not always desirable. The teacher should hold a discussion to make sure her students are on the right line of thinking.

"I want you to write down why you would want to live in **our** neighborhood in the past. What was better then? . . . Now I want you to write down why you would want to live in **our** neighborhood today. What is better now?"

After the short compositions are completed, the students should share their ideas with the class. The compositions can be displayed around the classroom for the children to read at their leisure. These compositions start the children thinking seriously about some of the negative features of the present day which did **not** exist in the past.

Evaluation: This lesson will be evaluated, in terms of the content of the questions and comments during the discussion and in the compositions, on how extensive the children's understanding of change is. The students should be able to recognize that change can be both positive and negative. If the children do not demonstrate a sufficient understanding of this generalization, the teacher should present additional examples for them to consider.

Lesson Twelve

Generalization: Certain things remain constant over time in a community.

Purpose: The purpose of this lesson is for the students to recognize that while certain things change in a community, other things remain constant over time. Specifically, the students should realize that the interdependence of people in a community remains constant over time.

Behavioral Objectives: (1) The students will demonstrate by the preparation of a chart their understanding of the people and services necessary for life and their knowledge of those which were present and absent in their community in the past. (2) Through interpretation of two charts, students will demonstrate their understanding of the generalization that certain things remain constant over time in a community.

Procedure: The teacher brings out the chart from Lesson Five, which shows the people and services needed for life which exist in their neighborhood and those which do not exist.

"We are going to make another chart like this one. This time, however, we are going to be using the past for the information."

There is, of course, much discussion on the children's part in compiling this chart. If the students have any questions, the teacher can provide them with source materials for the answer, either reading to them or having them read the information themselves. Thus, the teacher should have a great deal of source material available at this time. The children will also be bringing their compositions into play here, as sources of information and opinion for the formation of this new chart.

"What things have changed in our neighborhood? . . . What things have remained the same in our neighborhood?" For these answers, the students will utilize the information illustrated on the two charts. "Does this make sense to you?"

Evaluation: "Have you enjoyed studying the community? . . . Do you

think you've learned a lot? . . . What things do you remember most?" These
questions will help tie the whole unit on the community together for both teacher
and student. It will also serve to point out to the teacher what activities and
methods of instruction have been most successful in reaching her students.
Things that have been missed or misunderstood by the students can be picked up
here and clarified.

SUMMARY

For the young child, parents are the source of freedom. Parents
establish the limits within which the young child operates. They define
his physical and social environment. Later the teacher, school, and
society in general assume this role. This chapter has emphasized the
importance of nurturing the child's self through activities which extend
his control over each dimension of his environment (personal, physical,
social).

It is not possible to stress too strongly the significance of freedom
during this initial-exploratory stage of psycho-social development. In
closing the study of this chapter, consider the freedoms outlined below
as emphasis for this major point. For convenience these comments are
sorted into (1) physical (Sensorimotor), (2) emotional (affective), and
(3) mental (cognitive) categories. Freedoms cited are to be considered
illustrative rather than definitive or exhaustive.

Up to 6 Months

1. The child needs freedom to interact with significant others at
   first, then expanding interaction. He also needs freedom from
   tight restricting clothes and covers, in order to have free movement.
2. He needs freedom to cry, to get angry, and to continue interaction with mother.
3. He needs freedom to experience stimuli (sound, visual,
   textural, smell, taste) from which he can make discriminations
   and begin to relate his environment to himself.

From 6 Months to 1 Year

1. The child needs freedom to increase his mobility from crawling to standing and taking steps with hands held. He is moving
   to the upright position of the human. He needs freedom to
   explore his ability to make sounds. His first words begin to ap-

pear. This capacity will increase his ability to communicate. He also needs patterning or modeling in order to copy.

2. He needs freedom to interact with others to explore his developing emotions. He expands his recognition to include his father and siblings as significant others. He begins to learn that his feelings interact with those of others and that such actions as kicking and beating are undesirable if they interfere with others.

3. He needs freedom to explore his ever increasing world, consistent with safety. He is crawling around the room and reaching for objects. He needs to learn some are satisfactory to play with but others are not. He not only needs experience but also needs to integrate it in a meaningful way (that is, to organize his relationship to the world around him and to man.)

From 1 Year to 2 Years

1. The child needs freedom of movement, which will include walking and climbing on furniture. More often than not he will not be happy to remain in a playpen; he needs more room. He will learn to use cup and spoon, crayon and paper.

2. He needs freedom to be himself yet must realize certain behaviors are expected of him. A critical experience is toilet training. It is best to seek his cooperation and not be too insistent or push him to the point of rebellion, saying "I won't."

3. He needs freedom to continue expanding his behavior, to recognize his own emotions and those of others. Often this is the first time he is introduced to peers and begins learning concepts of *mine, yours,* and *give and take,* although he is still very much self-centered. He needs freedom to learn concepts. He learns roundness of balls; squareness of blocks; colors. Toys often introduce many of these concepts.

From 3 to 5 Years

1. The child needs freedom to run, jump, and climb; he is becoming much more active. He learns to ride a tricycle, likes to push or pull toys, begins to sense his own power.

2. He needs freedom to be himself with his developing emotions, yet needs to learn certain controls. He should not be overexcited, particularly before meals, at bedtime, or when he is tired.

3. He needs freedom to operate within his abilities. He should not be requested or required to respond beyond his capacities.

His sense of timing is not developed so ample time should be allowed for any procedure such as dressing or eating. He needs freedom to explore his self and his environment. He will ask many questions generated by his curiosity; these should be dealt with patiently. He likes to take things apart to see how they work.

From 6 to 8 Years

1. The child needs freedom to determine his strength by rough-housing with peers. He learns fine manipulatory movements with his fingers (using a pencil). He needs more open spaces to explore his surroundings.
2. He needs freedom to explore his self with his peer group; his joys, sorrows, angers, and the like. School is a time of socializing with his own age group. He will put to use much of what he learned in his preschool years, trying it out in the new surroundings.
3. He needs freedom to learn in the school situation at his own pace and interest. For the first time, probably, he is faced with the formal situation, in many cases a learn-or-else attitude. He is exposed to systematized concept learning as well as to learning communication skills (reading and writing). For the most part this is a structured situation which could profitably be modified by more freedom in the interest of the individual child.

Structure

If we accept the need for freedom, we must equally accept the responsibility to provide an environment in which the child can exercise that freedom. It is important to realize that this does not result in a laissez-faire approach to instruction. An approach via "What shall we do today?" or "Do your own thing!" denies the child's need for structure.

The instructional activities described in this chapter were designed to provide opportunities to explore in order to gain personal competence. It is that competence—in the use of skills necessary to know our physical and social environment—which provides the confidence necessary to continued psycho-social as well as cognitive growth.

CHAPTER 5

The Structured-Dependent Stage of Psycho-Social Development

This chapter deals with the ideas and strategies associated with the governing-governed relationship—the necessary societal counterpart to the high degree of individual freedom described in the initial learning experiences of Chapter 4.

Any society, whether founded on largely rational or irrational outlooks—cultural norms, values, sanctions—requires for its maintenance institutions which develop some shared ideas and experiences. The school specifically serves these functions as intermediary between the child and his society.

THEME AND JUSTIFICATION

Early in life, children run up against a set of rules and expectations, all of which carry with them a set of positive and negative sanctions. Most children become *aware* of the controlling power used by significant elders before they are enrolled in any formal schooling.

When sufficient language development has occurred and when the child feels physically and psychologically "safe" from excessive elder harm, he begins to question decisions of authority figures. "Why?" becomes a useful word in his vocabulary. Such words give the appearance of a search for the reason the elder has made some decision. Instead, the message probably sent by the child deals more with such things as

1. Asking that something else be granted or given by the elder.
2. "Do you really mean what you say? . . . Do you intend to stick to that decision?"
3. Asking that he be given some power over himself, that is, asking to have some opportunity to make choices.

The exasperated mother who replies to the early "Why?" question with "Because I told you so" has, in most cases, correctly intuited the intent of the child's question: that the child is questioning the consequences or the authority of some decision rather than looking for some piece of adult logic upon which to accept or question a decision.

It is only after considerable maturation in language experience and the development of a healthy self concept that children can really begin to explore the "why" of certain decisions. We authors contend that most youngsters do not possess this cognitive and affective maturation during the early elementary years (ages 3-10).

While the sets of rules and expectations as well as the methods used to enforce them differ greatly, both across and within the ethnic, racial, and socioeconomic groups of our society, nearly all children can recite a set of "should do" and "should not do" actions before entering formal school programs. Further, while the rules and expectations may differ greatly between some hypothetical teacher and parent, we authors contend that nearly every parent sends his child to school with the admonition, "You do what the teacher tells you to do."

Why do so many youngsters flagrantly violate the norms and values expressed by parent and teacher alike? Why do teachers continue to talk about democratically controlled classrooms even while few are willing to allow "children" (defined as anyone still in school) a part in decision making? Such questions have evoked long philosophical discussions and a number of articles and books. The four statements that follow are partial answers, and they set out the assumptions upon which this entire chapter was built.

1. *Children (and adults) violate legal and/or normative codes partially or totally out of frustration with present conditions in their lives.* Battered continually by teacher and parent criticisms of low achievement, by humiliation on achievement tests, and the like, it is not surprising that youngsters refuse to value "formal education" highly. This is certainly not to conclude that these children necessarily do not value educative

experiences outside of schools; some grow and develop far beyond their associates within the classroom, including the teacher! Members of the Mafia may be deemed to have no values if values relate to the betterment of society; but within the organization the norms and sanctions reflect a value constellation not entirely different from that of the larger society. Honesty and loyalty toward associates, for example, are highly valued and the price extracted for failure to live up to the rules is extremely high.

Much of this chapter and the entire book has been written with suggestions for reducing unnecessary frustration for children. Certainly the value-valuing strategies that stress empathy and tolerance for the feelings and ideas of others are central to reducing some of the frustration with which youngsters meet.

2. *Teachers need to examine the maturity level of youngsters and to determine how much freedom/responsibility youngsters are capable of handling.* It is easy to point to extremes of decision making where parents or teachers obviously violate democracy. Some extremely authoritarian parents and teachers seldom, if ever, allow children any choices: "You'll have an ice cream cone and that's it." "The class will give all its money to UNICEF, and that's it." Conversely, some extreme democratic (maybe *laissez-faire*) parent and teacher types place choices before children which they are incapable of handling because of cognitive and affective immaturity, or for which children in fact really do not have a choice. Consider two examples: "Do you think that we should send you to nursery school?" (Parent asking three-year-old child). "Do you want to stay in school or stay home every day." (First-grade teacher to class.)

This chapter will attempt to put into focus certain types of decisions and the requisite student responsibilities attached to these decisions, which are representative of the maturity level of elementary students.

3. *Children sometimes violate certain rules to test the validity of them.* Before entering school, most children have begun to ask "Why?" concerning rules applied to their behavior by significant adults. Teachers who view the "Why?" question as threatening and undermining to their authority miss great opportunities for personal growth as well as opportunities to help youngsters grow. Appealing to the fact that one is *in* authority will not compensate for personal inadequacies which prevent an adult from occupying a leadership role in which he serves as *an* authority.

While true and deep exploration of the "why" concerning some "societal rules" awaits greater intellectual sophistication, certainly a number of conceptual and valuational lessons regarding the whys and the way of the governing-governed relationship can be explored very early with children.

4. *Children sometimes violate rules to gain peer-group acceptance.* Here again the needs of children must be considered. It is indeed a wise parent or teacher who can forbear uttering immediate and in some cases violent reprimand of a child because he or she has perceived and accepted some need response of the child. Some of the most vital lessons we authors have learned came in situations where a teacher did forbear making the expected and anticipated response. Such "failure" of the teacher to act "like teachers are supposed to" causes a child to do some real soul searching regarding the "why" of both personal and other behavior in that situation. Readers may recall some instances from their own schooling.

SETTING AN AGE FOR TEACHING POWER

Children in the primary and early intermediate grades are already beginning to think, to be reflective, to have an internal concept of self and of self-other. Piaget indicates that this last stage of concrete operations includes reflection of the governing-governed relationship formulated through the child's play with his peer group, and through his perceptions of the differences in the value systems operating from adult to adult. Maier (1969, 144), in his analysis of Piaget's work at the concrete operational level, states: "Collective games quickly accumulate representative rules. For instance, neighborhood children spontaneously playing ball are apt to form a highly structured game with some rules which are universal for the entire neighborhood." The extremely complex rules which spontaneously evolve and govern a street game of baseball, for example, further reveal a child's concern with rules. Such concern with rules is paralleled by the formation of the child's conscience.

Children gradually move from a largely unquestioning stage (about age five to six) regarding adults to a highly questioning and inquiring stage. Maier, in further relating Piaget's work, writes:

> . . . unilateral respect for adults slowly gives way due to an awareness of many adult authorities whose rules vary and to the inconsistencies even within one adult's rules. Simultaneously, the child slowly turns from his single authority, usually a parent, and tends to cooperate with other authorities, even without full awareness of the meaning of social cooperation. (Maier, 1969, 135)

Studies of the child's social behavior indicate that he is still largely egocentric at this stage of development, but that he is aware of the need for people outside his family. On the same page, Maier, in relating Erik Erikson's work with children at this level of development, writes:

> . . . his neighborhood and school become significant social determiners for him, and strangers become intriguing and important discoveries. Boys and girls search for other adults to identify with, because their parents can no longer entirely fulfill the child's requirements in this area.

As a result of insights drawn from both Piaget and Erikson, then, we can conclude that the child between the ages of eight and ten is becoming aware of his power in relation to others and aware of the power of others in relation to him. In the suggestions for teaching to follow, some attention has been given to all levels of development, but greatest emphasis and development will be with the eight-to-ten age group.

WHAT POLITICAL IDEAS SHOULD WE NURTURE?

It may be useful to recall or review the goals based in political science that were described in the first chapter. We authors offer these tentative constructs and generalizations as a basis for establishment of specific behavioral objectives for classrooms. The nature of such objectives will differ, we believe, on the basis of such matters as:

1. Legal normative community constraints which may influence what content is "appropriate" social studies content as well as how one is allowed to approach treatment of specific subjects.
2. The teacher's own personal "hang-ups"—or the converse, what he or she feels intellectually and emotionally prepared to handle.
3. Most importantly, what educators within some educational settings perceive to be the psycho-social needs of their youngsters.

The reader is asked to apply these criteria in the methods discourse to follow.

METHOD AND THE EMOTIONALLY-INTELLECTUALLY IMMATURE

While each child is born a uniquely different person and while each child's experience base is different from that of all other children, a few guidelines are tentatively set forth as generally desirable governing behaviors for teachers of children with low ego-intellectual development.

1. *Recognize the limits of the child's experience and then decide areas in which the child can choose.* Dr. Haim Ginot's book, *Between Parent and Child* (1969) contains numerous examples of how to develop this technique. When the teacher asks the child whether he would like to finger-paint at his desk or at the back table, he preserves a natural right the child feels, namely, "I must be allowed to make some decisions about me," but does not give complete autonomy to the child. To give such autonomy at this level of development could be devastating to a child not ready to assume this freedom-responsibility. It also might constitute professional irresponsibility in being an abandonment of the professional decision-making responsibility invested in a teacher by the people through granting the state teaching certificate. The people have not empowered children to make all decisions for themselves in the school.

2. *Be as consistent and equitable in enforcement of your decisions as possible.* Don't let things the teacher and/or the class has legislated be empty rules. If punishment is promised for breaking of some rule, it should be applied, assuming that both rule and punishment were decided rationally, and were then clearly and understandably conveyed to the children in class.

3. *Continually try to enlarge the realm of democratic decision making.* The teacher should gradually allow youngsters more voice in decision making as she sees that instructional efficiency is maintained or increased by such decision.

4. *Continually work to reduce the number of rules used to control deviant behavior.* As much as possible, move decisions about classroom management to the background. Children know the rules exist and usually conform to them, but they are seldom repeated; the children are not constantly trained or reminded to practice such rules.

THE DEVELOPMENT OF POWER THROUGH TIME

This section of this chapter attempts to introduce and develop the concept of being governed, and governing, through the various stages of cognitive development set forth by Piaget and already discussed in Chapters 2 and 3.

Development of the Power Concept in the Sensorimotor Stage

The child initially develops a sense of power through crying. When this crying produces the desired response the child grows in regard to his ability to control others.

As the child becomes aware of his ability to manipulate objects and parts of his body, he further grows in ability to control others.

Below are some suggestions for teachers who work with children at the sensorimotor stage. They contemplate *very early* childhood education; the teacher is inevitably a mother surrogate, often concerned with the child's learning toilet practices, dressing, bathing, and the like. These procedures can enhance a child's sense of power.

SUGGESTIONS FOR BUILDING THE CHILD'S SENSORIMOTOR POWERS[1]

A. Help the child learn to retrieve objects upon request.
  1. The teacher requests the child to bring an object to her. She rewards with attention and affection.
  2. The teacher requests the child to pick up and put away objects. Rewards follow.
B. When child uses babbling initially and later specific words and sentences to indicate needs and desires, the teacher can:
  1. Reinforce initial attempts at babbling to indicate what the child wants.
  2. Reinforce only those attempts at words which can be identified as meaningful.
  3. Reinforce attempts to use sentences.
C. Help the child develop the power to feed himself.
  1. Praise initial attempts to use fingers to eat.
  2. Provide food that can be eaten successfully with a spoon. Praise attempts.
  3. Withhold rewards when power is used to throw or spit out food.
  4. Provide opportunities to use a fork.
  5. Give the child opportunities to drink out of a cup independently.
D. Provide opportunities for child to use bathroom facilities and reinforce success.
E. Help the child learn to bathe himself independently.
  1. Provide a sponge toy for initial attempts at bathing.
  2. Switch to a towel and washcloth that can be called the child's own.
F. Help the child learn to brush his teeth independently.
  1. Initially provide a toothbrush and toothpaste for use. Praise all attempts at brushing.
  2. Reinforce only those attempts that indicate progress toward correct brushing.
G. Help the child develop skill in dressing himself and choosing appropriate clothes to wear.
  1. Provide practice in buttoning and zipping, using clothing or articles not being worn.

[1] The authors are grateful to the following Georgia State University students whose collective ideas contributed to these suggestions: Valerie Erickson, Cynthia Lewis, Mary Smith, Carolyn Wallace.

    2.   Provide clothing that the child can manipulate, and allow him to dress himself.

    3.   Help the child make choices of what to wear.

H. Help child develop physical power and coordination.

    1.   Provide rolling and tumbling activities.

    2.   Provide mobile toys, tricycles, pedal car, and playground equipment.

Development of the Power Concept in the Preoperational Stage

The following activities were constructed to aid youngsters in development of an understanding of power as related to such things as emotions, equality, truth, trust, responsibility, leadership, and expression through the fine arts.

ACTIVITIES FOR EXPERIENCING POWER IN THE PREOPERATIONAL STAGE[2]

A. **Emotions.** A child needs to learn to identify his feelings and emotions. This idea of power over emotions is an integral stage in childhood development which has its roots in the preoperational stage.

    1.   Use of expressions.

        a.   Game with moveable parts for felt-board faces.

        b.   Role playing — acting out certain expressions and feelings.

        c.   Crying (a very early stage).

        d.   Puppetry.

    2.   Verbalizing emotions.

        a.   Activity such as "I'm going to make you happy" (sad, mad, etc.). Example: You have on a pretty dress.

        b.   Have children complete this statement: "I'm afraid when . . ." This will help show the children that they share the same fears and hopefully help them control their fears.

        c.   Discussion of pictures — children, places, objects — using both color and black-and-white.

B. **Equality.** Children must learn to recognize equality before they can show leadership and power over others.

    1.   Sharing of objects.

        a.   This idea should involve pupil-pupil, teacher-pupil and teacher-class. Example: "Show and Tell," learning-center materials, and classroom materials.

    [2] The authors are grateful to the following Georgia State University students whose collective ideas contributed to these suggestions: Susan Chase, Gaylee Robertson, Gloria Shurbritt.

2. Fair play.
   a. Through games and various competitions children learn victory and defeat. Result: "good sportsmanship."
   b. This development of power to function in play is basic to coping with adult life with its competitive nature.

C. **Truth.** This may be used for developing power to show that unless one is truthful, he will be given no respect or power. It should be pointed out that many reach power by dishonest means, but they are not respected and their power is not truly effective.

1. Games.
   a. Play a child's version of "To Tell the Truth."
   b. Play a game of "Truth or Consequences," keeping the consequences mild but definite.
2. Select examples to role play in which telling the truth produces a positive result. Have children volunteer any exceptions to this rule if they wish.

D. **Trust.** This involves both the student and the teacher in many important ways. The teacher must take the lead and develop the trust of her students before they see that it really is important.

1. Books or records may be used such as **Peter and the Wolf.**
2. Discuss stories to help the children distinguish between fantasy and truth.
3. Let the children open a small bank and handle pennies for their classmates — a savings-type bank.
4. Have children tell another child one thing dear to them; the child told must tell no one else this private secret.

E. **Responsibility.**

1. Classroom tasks.
   a. (alone) Erasing blackboard.
   b. (pair) Dusting erasers.
   c. (group) Passing out papers, leading the line.
2. Carrying messages.
   a. Carrying message to the office for the teacher.
   b. Carrying message to mother at home from the teacher.
3. Responsibility for own actions and possessions.
   a. Decisions in play.
   b. Following through an activity. Example: Once the child has decided on an activity he must follow it through until completion.

    c. Bathroom responsibility.

    d. Decision in learning activity. Example: Activity and game center, child must report to the teacher before changing activity.

    e. Care of item brought from home.

    f. Use of library.

  4. Care of pets. Child has the responsibility for feeding pets daily and keeping the cage clean.

  5. Choosing friends and playmates.

F. **Leadership.**

  1. Individual leadership.
    a. Child of the day.
    b. Choosing teams.
    c. Leading lines.

  2. Small-group leadership.
    a. Caller for games.
    b. Helper in remedial group.

  3. Classroom leadership.
    a. Passing out papers or art materials.
    b. Leading songs.

G. **Fine Arts.**

  1. Rhythm instruments.
    a. Power over movement: keeping time to the music.
    b. Power with sound and tone: playing the instruments.
    c. Use of records such as **Elephant Walk, Train, Walk and Skip** (Children's Record Guild).

  2. Art work.
    a. Power over muscle coordination, as scribbling.
    b. Experimentation with large paper and dark crayons.
    c. Finger painting.
    d. Tearing paper and collage work.
    e. Group work.
      i. Music plays as children draw; when music stops, their drawing must stop; when the music starts, they continue to draw.
      ii. Mural and group work.

Development of the Power Concept in the Concrete Stage

Development of the child's power at the concrete level of experience is promoted largely on the assumption that it contributes to building the child's concept of self. Emphasis continues to be on the child's self as the reference for developing his concepts of power.

SUGGESTIONS FOR PROMOTING THE PERCEPTION AND USE OF POWER IN THE CONCRETE STAGE[3]

Activities: Rationale I—The Concept of Power Grows in the Development of the Self-Concept

A. **A sense of power is developed by having the responsibility for tasks.**

1. Children should have the responsibility of caring for self.
    a. Their own belongings.
        i. Coats, hats, etc.
        ii. Personal school supplies: notebooks, pencils, crayons, etc.
    b. Personal neatness.
        i. Face and hands clean.
        ii. Hair combed.
        iii. Shirts tucked in.
    c. Neatness of desks.
    d. Lunch money.
2. Children should have the responsibility of caring for the property of others.
    a. Textbooks (they should be covered).
    b. Borrowed materials (library books).
    c. School materials (Physical Education equipment, globes, etc.).
3. Children should have the responsibility of caring for the classroom.
    a. Watering plants.
    b. Keeping tables, window sills, bookshelves free from dust.
    c. Keeping paper picked up off the floor.
    d. Emptying wastebaskets.
    e. Feeding goldfish.
    f. Adjusting blinds and windows.
    g. Cleaning blackboard and erasers.
4. Children should have the responsibility for carrying messages.
    a. Lunch report.
    b. Attendance report.
    c. Notices to go home.
    d. Messages from home to school.
5. Children should have the responsibility for completing homework and bringing it to class.
6. Children should have the responsibility of bringing materials from home to use in class.
    a. Paper, pencils, scissors, glue and crayons.
    b. Scrap materials such as newspapers, yarn, buttons, magazines, glass jars, etc.

[3] The authors are grateful to the following Georgia State University students whose collective ideas contributed to these suggestions: Elizabeth Brown, John Foley, Jane Thacker.

B. **A sense of power is developed as a child increases his skills and begins to realize his potential.**

1. Children should have the opportunity to increase their skills in physical activities.
    a. P. E. skills, practice and testing.
        i. Sit-ups.
        ii. Pull-ups.
        iii. Broad jumps.
        iv. Fifty-yard dash.
        v. Throwing and catching a ball.
    b. Putting skills to use in games.
        i. Softball.
        ii. Kickball.
        iii. Dodgeball.
        iv. Relays.
2. Children should increase their power in academic skills.
    a. Reading activities (as a child learns to read, he becomes less dependent on others and is able to expand his world).
        i. Understanding written directions.
        ii. Reading for content.
        iii. Reading for pleasure (library books, stories, etc.).
        iv. Reading for enrichment (newspaper articles, using reference materials, children's magazines and newspapers.
    b. Language activities (as a child develops competence in the written and oral use of his language, he gains in the realization of power).
        i. Spelling correctly.
        ii. Thinking, speaking and writing in complete sentences.
        iii. Organizing materials (writing in paragraphs).
        iv. Preparing oral reports and talks.
        v. Creative power—writing original stories and poems to express his own creative ideas.
    c. Mathematics activities (as a child learns mathematics concepts, and practical uses of those concepts, he gains in independence and a sense of power).
        i. Activities using money: Learning to make change. Playing store. Figuring cost and profit (lemonade stand). Other.
        ii. Activities using measurement: Map activities (drawing to scale). Measuring distances for games. Building models (boys). Cooking (altering recipes—girls). Other.
        iii. Activities using four mathematical processes: Addition— numbers of stacks of paper. Subtraction—taking cost from price to get profit in playing store. Multiplication—computing number of pieces of yarn needed for art lesson if each child

in class has five. Division—sharing a number of candy bars so that each child in the class has an equal number.

Activities: Rationale II—The Concept of Power Grows as the Child's Interpersonal Relationships Are Developed

A. **A sense of power develops as the child is able to function among his peers.**

1. A child's self-concept grows as he sees himself as a worthwhile person in the group.
    a. Sharing family experiences with the class.
        i. Vacation trips.
        ii. Family outings, picnics, etc.
        iii. Other previous experiences at home and at school.
    b. Experiencing roles of different individuals in various group settings (role playing).
        i. Family: Father's role. Mother's role. Sibling's role. Family helpers (maid, baby sitter).
        ii. Community—skits involving roles of various community helpers, bringing out aspects of power in the relation of each one to the others and to the community as a whole: Postman. Truck driver. Storekeeper. Bus driver. Others.
2. Each child should have the opportunity to experience the power of leadership.
    a. Rotating responsibilities for leadership of routine activities.
        i. Row captains: Collecting papers. Checking to see if name is there and if work is completed. Reporting this information.
        ii. Playground team captains: Decides on game to play. Responsible for equipment. Assigns places in games.

B. **Seeing that each child has an opportunity to be a leader of a group activity.**

1. Producing skits as culminating activities.
    a. Writing a skit.
    b. Assigning parts.
    c. Scheduling rehearsals.
    d. Collecting props.
2. Producing a project for a science fair.
3. Organizing a debate team and planning a debate.
4. Producing a class newspaper.

Development of the Power Concept in the Abstract Stage

Some suggestions for teaching/learning methods for the development of the understanding of power at the abstract stage follow.

OBJECTIVES AND ACTIVITIES FOR THE ABSTRACT STAGE[4]

A. **Role-Playing.**

1. To help the student develop an understanding of the individual (or large group over small group) power.
   a. Activity—Have students enact the Salem witch trials by using a play with readings.
   b. Measurement—Observation of student involvement by teacher.
2. To demonstrate to the student, in a controlled experiment, group power and compromise.
   a. Activity—A reenactment of the Constitutional Convention.
   b. Measurement—Observation of student involvement by teacher.
3. To allow students to gain feelings of responsibility through dealing with a situation of qualified power or power by representation.
   a. Activity—Have the students set up and roleplay a summit meeting.
   b. Measurement—Observation of student involvement by teacher.

B. **Games.**

1. To give students an experience in power to show how an individual can have unrestricted or uncontrollable economic power and to help the student develop skills in investment.
   a. Activity—Students to play the game of Monopoly.
   b. Measurement—Observation of student skills and understanding by the teacher. Written exercise to determine skills and development of understanding.

C. **Readings.**

1. To guide the student in his ability to ascertain where power resides in different political systems: group (minority vs. majority), individual, etc.
   a. Activity—Selected readings by the student.
   b. Measurement—Testing. Reports, verbal and written.

D. **Mock Election.**

1. To provide students an experience in democracy; to reveal the power of the majority; to show persuasive power of the candidate.
   a. Activity—Allow students to hold mock elections over several days.
   b. Measurement—Comparison of survey vote preceding campaign with final results after a week of campaigning. Observation of student involvement and preparation.

E. **Community Survey.**

1. To reveal to the students the socio-economic structure of the power system of their community.
   a. Activity—Community survey done by the students.

---

[4] The authors are grateful to the following Georgia State University students whose collective ideas contributed to these suggestions: James Baum, Harry Gates, Bruce Rhyne, Pam Rhyne, Bill Willoughby.

      b.   Measurement — Observation of data sheet, and student activity.

F. **Advertising.**

    1.   To reveal to the student the power of persuasion, ideas, and gimmicks, and to help the student develop skills in research.

        a.   Activity — Fill in questionnaire (What do you see and why). Compile results of questionnaire. Observation of various advertising media.

        b.   Measurement — Did students return the questionnaire? Group reports — oral and written. Follow through to see what products are best by using **Consumer Reports.**

POWER, LAW, AND INSTITUTIONS IN TWO SETTINGS

The meat of this section is in two extensively presented plans of instruction. The one focuses on an inner-city situation of contemporary society, the other on the situation of settlers in a new country. In each, institutions for the creation and exercise of power are examined, the one outside existing law and antagonistic to it, the other in the absence of existing formal law and creating it.

Power and Law in an Urban Environment

The instruction unit that follows was developed for use in a fifth-grade inner-city classroom in Philadelphia by Miss Susan Shanzer while she was a preservice teacher at Temple University. Miss Shanzer gives clear evidence of the belief that youngsters will better learn such democratic ideals of freedom of speech and assembly, justice and equality through full democratic participation in the classroom. She advocates her unit on gangs for urban classrooms exclusively, since her approach presupposes certain knowledge and first-hand experience in the problem of gangs. The unit effectively uses the data (cognitive, attitudinal, valuative) which inner-city children possess before they start working in the unit.

A PLAN OF INSTRUCTION — GANGS
Lesson Group 1
Key Idea: There are definite reasons why people join gangs and there are certain conditions which promote the development of gangs.

Objective: At the end of this lesson the child will be able to state, and give dramatic expression of reasons boys join gangs, what gangs provide for their members, and what factors cause youths to join gangs.

Activity I
    Materials: Record player; album of **West Side Story.**

    1. Tell the class you are going to play a song for them about a group called the **Jets.** Then play the **Jet Song** from **West Side Story.** After it is

finished ask the class what kind of group they think the Jets could be. Discuss; establish that it is a gang.

2. Then play the song again, this time putting the words on the board.

> When you're a Jet, you're a Jet all the way.
> From your first cigarette to your last, dyin' day.
> When you're a Jet, let 'em do what they can
> You've got brothers around, you're a family man.
>
> You're never alone, you're never disconnected.
> You're home with your own, when company's expected.
> You're well protected.
> Then you are set, with a capital "J"
> Which you'll never forget 'till they cart you away.
> When you're a Jet — you — stay — a — Jet!!⁵

3. After this, ask the class if they could come up to the board and underline the reasons why boys joined this gang. (Example: "protected," "never alone," "brothers.")

a.   Are these things necessary?
b.   Are these things provided in any way or by any group other than a gang?
c.   Does a gang assure these things to its members? What is the responsibility of the individual?

Activity II
Materials: Picture of boy.

1. Show the students a picture of a boy about their age. Break the class into small groups of five or six students each. Tell the class you will tell them only two facts about this boy: (a) He is a member of a gang. (b) He lives in their general community.

2. Ask the class to figure out **why** the boy has joined a gang — **not** what the gang will offer him, but the causes, why he joined. (Example: tradition, revenge, poverty, bad home life, etc.). Each group should discuss the possibilities and be prepared to tell the class. Accept all responses, list them on the board, and discuss them. Let the class eliminate any they feel are inadequate. Let the rest remain. Look for similarities between these, and the reasons boys join gangs. Then let the class discuss the interrelatedness of these first two activities.

Activity III (Integrating the preceding two)
Materials: Pictures of various gang situations, props to go with them.

1. Role-playing activity: Using a set of pictures, have the class act out the situations illustrated. Have pictures not only on the situation, but of people

---

⁵ Leonard Bernstein and Stephen Sondheim, "Jet Song," **West Side Story.** Copyright 1957, 1959. Used by permission of G. Schirmer, Inc.

outside the situation. For instance, show a bunch of youths hanging out on a corner. They are members of a gang. In the center, have one boy approaching; identify him as not belonging to this gang, but to another one. What will happen? Also, have a picture of a neighbor who sees what goes on. Have someone role-play the neighbor and describe her feelings. In this way children will be bringing their own experience and feelings into play. You will be able to distinguish their feelings by the direction they give to the situation.

2. Role-play the preceding situation again, this time making the single boy not a member of any gang. Ask the class to pay attention to see if the roles change.

3. Try this with other pictures, always providing someone outside the situation with the opportunity to express a point of view. After each activity discuss the way the players acted — if they were believable, etc. If class desires, have different students act out the same picture, giving it a new interpretation. After each, comment on the motives of the characters and what caused them to act as they did. Tie this in with the two earlier activities.

Suggested Further Activities

1. Listen to more of **West Side Story.** It provides a novel approach to the gang situation. Have class react to the music of the **Rumble,** and the plight of the Jets in **Gee, Officer Krupke.**

Lesson Group 2

Key Idea: The neighborhood is an important consideration in a study of gang formation.

Objective: At the end of these lessons, the child will be able to discuss the role the neighborhood plays in the growth and perpetuation of gangs.

Rationale: To relate the subject of gangs to the child's own neighborhood. To teach him more about the gangs in his own neighborhood.

Activity I

1. Review the causes that give rise to gangs. Examine the particular neighborhood of the children in the class. Is there a gang problem in your community? Will a look at the neighborhood help us to answer the question? Does the neighborhood have a role in gang formation?

2. Take the class on a walk in the neighborhood. Have them note anything that would tie in with the earlier discussions, or help to answer the present questions. Examples: slum neighborhood, many young children, boarded-up houses.

3. Discuss the answers to the questions.

Activity II

1. Before this lesson, the teacher should go out and do some investigating on her own. From older boys, the police, and the community, she should find out the nature of the gang problem in that community.

2. Discuss the gang problem of the neighborhood. Establish:
a. Who the gangs are.
b. Their notoriety.
c. Personal experiences with them.
d. Approaches by them.
e. Members you know.
f. Seriousness.

Activity III
Materials: Film strip; projector.

1. Show the film strip **The Jungle.** It was made in the area right around Temple University, and is about two gangs of junior-high-school age. The "actors" in this film are the gang members themselves, but all the encounters of the film are staged. The film has a tape which describes what is happening. The film shows both the good and bad points of gangs and gang warfare. It shows both the protection offered by the gang, and the gang not helping when grossly outnumbered. It also talks with several of the boys in the gang. The teacher should be sure to stress that this is a film of an actual gang made right in the neighborhood.

2. After the film, the teacher should refrain from saying anything, but wait for the class to react. Then discuss the film. The film offers for discussion the inconsistency of gang protection. It shows the trouble the boys get into, but also the fun and excitement of gang life. Explore and discuss the possibilities the film suggests.

Suggested Further Activities

1. Bring in a member of a gang in the community. Let him tell the class about his gang. Encourage the class to ask questions. After his visit, discuss what he said.

2. Either as a follow-up activity to the above, or by itself, bring in a member of the police force and have him speak about gangs. Discuss his thoughts with the class. Compare the positions of the gang member and the policeman.

Lesson Group 3
Key Idea: The police have a certain role in gang warfare and gang control.
Objective: At the end of this lesson the child will be able to discuss the police-gang situation, and use his knowledge to make assumptions about a particular case.

Activity I
Materials: A "newspaper story" written by the teacher. Here is a sample story:

Police-Juveniles Clash — Hearing Set for April 24. New York (UPI) —

April 6. Violence erupted today between police and juveniles when police were called to the East Side to break up gang disturbances.

Just before police arrived, the fighting became worse and residents reported hearing pistol shots. When the police got there the juveniles turned on them and it took quite a while before police broke it up. When they did, seven had been injured, four seriously.

One boy, identified as Joey Williams, 14, who had been shot in the leg, charged that his wound had been inflicted by a policeman who he claimed was "very eager to use his gun." The patrolman, John Terry of the 21st precinct, denied this and said he had used his gun "only when it became absolutely necessary." A hearing for the case has been set for April 24th.

Residents had called police at about 8:30 p.m. after unsuccessfully trying to drive away the juveniles. "First there was two boys fighting, then four, and then it turned into a regular gang war," said one resident. "When we saw some of the boys had knives, we figured we'd better call the police."

1. The teacher will read to the class the article she has supposedly taken from the newspaper, but in reality written on her own. The article will be a fictitious police-juvenile encounter, comparable to the sample but adapted as necessary. The situation described will be purposely ambiguous. The children will react to the ambiguities in the way their past history and experience have directed them. It will be interesting to see in what direction this will go, and what biases, values, and deep feelings they will bring to the surface.

2. After reading, wait for a reaction from the class. Ask what happened and have the members reconstruct the events. Note where the children retain the ambiguities, and where they replace them with something definite. This will lead into a general discussion of police and gangs.

Activity II

Materials: Two "statements" from the persons involved. The teacher will have prepared these two statements, one by the gang member accusing the policeman of the shooting, one by the policeman describing what happened and declaring his innocence.

1. Discuss:
a. Could the gang member be telling the truth?
b. Could the policeman be lying?
c. What do you think might happen if this is brought to court?
2. Have the class make assumptions on what they think would happen. If a child brings up the question of race, explore the possibilities.

Suggested Further Activities

1. Have a mock trial of the above situation. Have lawyers, a judge, jury, and defendants. See who the class has found guilty.

2. Relate another police-gang encounter, this time using pictures to explain what happened. Have the gang be all Negro, the policeman White; Do

not point out this fact to the class. Discuss the situation. Note for later discussion the effect race has on the outcome. Repeat this with a White gang and a Negro policeman. Will the situation be different now? How about White-White? Black-Black? What kind of factor is race?

Lesson Group 4

Key Idea: People have various attitudes towards gangs, and you can often determine the sort of person someone is from his attitude.

Objective: At the end of these lessons the child will be able to compose various statements of attitudes of people towards gangs, and identify the type of person who would make that statement. Also the child will express attitudes he feels gang members would have, in reacting to a particular situation.

Activity I

Materials: A "newspaper quotation" to be read by the teacher to start a discussion.

1. Begin by announcing: "Here is something I found in the newspaper the other day that fits into our discussion about gangs." Then read the quotation: "The gangs are a terrible problem of our times. The police aren't strict enough with them. They don't want help. They should all be rounded up and thrown into jail. I have no sympathy for gang members."

2. Ask the class: "How do you feel about this statement?" "What kind of person would make a statement like that?" Discuss the possibilities, helping with more questions if needed: "Man or woman? Old? Young?" "Do you think she/he ever had any experience with gangs?" Include a brief explanation of **attitude.**

3. Break the class into groups of three. Instruct each group to compose a statement that will express an attitude or feeling about gangs. Each group will read the statement they have written and let the class discuss what kind of person would hold such an attitude. Example: "I've been beaten and robbed. Those kids steal me blind. They are liars and cheats and would steal from their own mothers." (The class could infer many things about the person who would have such an attitude. For example: could it be said by a shopowner who has had a negative personal experience with gangs?) "The kids are no worse today than when I was young. We did the same things." (Once a gang member?) "The kids are sick. They need help." (Sympathetic? A social worker?)

Activity II

Situation Setter: "Now that we've heard the attitudes of outsiders, let's hear some of the feelings of the gang members themselves. Tomorrow the whole class is to react as gang members."

1. Encourage class to do, wear, or say anything that will help to establish the mood. Try to create an informal class atmosphere.

2. Have class sit in a big circle. From now on they should react to whatever happens in the way they feel gang members would react.

3. The teacher first, and later other students, will then throw words out to the group and wait for a reaction. They should respond without raising their hands, whenever the word makes them feel like responding. Remind them of the role they are playing. **Sample words:** "cool," "tough," "boss," "protection," "trouble," "in," "dope," "rival."

4. The session should be permitted to last as long as possible.

5. The purpose of this is to give the class the flavor of gang attitudes towards various things in their existence. This is done in an indirect way—not through direct questioning, but through subtle, and often ambiguous words ("boss," "dope"). (The basis of this is the idea of free association.) In an exercise of this type, the students will be reacting not only as the gang members they are playing, but also as the individuals they are.

Note: Readers interested in additional rationale and example of this method of affective discussion are referred to Epstein's **Affective Subjects In the Classroom.** (See annotated reference in the bibliography at the end of Chapter 2.)

Lesson Group 5

Key Idea: Gangs are typically urban; gang formation is relatively uncommon in rural situations.

Objective: At the end of these lessons the child will be able to state differences between the city and the country, and to link, through discussion and example, the process of urbanization to problems of the cities. The child will also prepare a written list of generalizations about the relationships among gangs, urbanization, and other social problems.

Activity I

Materials: Two pictures, one typical of the city, one of the country.

1. Exhibit the two pictures to the class. Compare the two. Ask the class to make a list of generalizations about each. Write them on the board: Examples:

City	Country
busy	quiet
fast-moving	slow
many factories	fewer people
lots of people	fewer industries
noisy	less cars
air pollution	farmers
hurrying	take it easy

2. Ask the class, "In which area do we find gangs?" (The city.) "Why do

you think this is so?" Discuss. (This can lead into a big discussion that can be carried over several days.) The children may want to break into small groups to discuss this question.

3. Deeply interested children should be encouraged to work independently.

Activity II

Relate the discussion of urbanization and gangs back to the first topics covered in this unit: the causes of gangs and the reasons they form. Examine how related social problems fit into a discussion of urbanization, and discuss these as reasons for growth of gangs. Examples: Population, impersonal relations, identity crises, crime, slums, poverty, need and desire for social goods.

Activity III

Help the class to prepare a list of generalizations about the interrelatedness of gang problems, urbanization, and other social problems. Encourage independent work on these. If children express a desire for a class display on the unit, encourage them to try it on their own. Provide materials and guidance, but let the class do the planning and executing of the display.

Be sure to tie up all loose ends of the discussion. Tie in present ideas with the larger ideas of the unit.

Evaluation Lesson Group

Aim of Evaluation Lessons: To synthesize the knowledge of the child in role-playing activities that will call upon the child to utilize all the facts, principles, and generalizations he has learned about gangs in previous lessons, to effect a **realistic** portrayal of two gang situations.

Activity I. Gang-Gang Confrontation (Role-Playing)

1. Two ministers in two different "territories" have brought two hostile gangs together in the basement of one of the churches. The gangs have threatened each other numerous times with an upcoming rumble. Now representatives of both sides have agreed to meet to try to iron out their grievances and prevent the fight. The youths are bitter and hostile to one another. Their dispute includes: definition of territories and the beating of several of one gang's members by the other gang.

2. Present this scene to the class and explain what they will be doing. Assign roles. (That is, assign, for example, five to each side, but don't **you** determine who the leader or main spokesman will be.) Do this a few days before the "presentation" so the "cast" will have a chance to determine how it will run. Impress upon the class that they are to incorporate anything and everything they've learned about gangs—their beliefs, attitudes, morals, etc.— to make this as realistic as possible.

Activity II. Panel Confrontation (Role-Playing)

1. Various children in the room will be assigned parts for this second role-playing activity. They are to respond as the people they represent. They will be a community-based panel to discuss gangs. Examples: A schoolteacher, principal, policeman, gang member, minister, mother, member of a community council. The roles will be assigned, but they will not be as structured as they seem. The boy who is assigned the role of policeman, for example, must respond as a policeman, but it is up to him to decide the type of policeman he will be — punitive, or sympathetic to the gang problem, or of some other kind. Likewise the gang member may be the leader, a militant, or some other type. In this way the pupils have control over what their characters turn out to be. The only demand is that they remain consistent.

2. Props will be distributed for each role. Each child will have something to establish the identity of his character. (Example: policeman's badge.)

3. One child will act as moderator or leader and will direct the activity. The moderator will ask questions of the panel and they will respond **according to their roles.** Sample questions:

   a. What is the gang problem as **you** see it? What does it mean?
   b. Why has it happened? What conditions do **you** see as contributing to it?
   c. Why do kids join gangs in the first place?
   d. Do the gangs want our help?
   e. What can **we** — the school, parents, the community, the police — do about the problem?

4. Students in the room with questions will address the panel. The panel should continue as long as there are questions to ask.

5. At end, the moderator will ask for a summary statement from each of the panel members.

6. As added incentive, tape record the two previous evaluation activities. Replay them at a later date.

Activity III

1. As a third and final evaluation lesson, distribute a questionnaire to students which they are to fill out and return. This is not a test, but an evaluation technique. The results are for teacher evaluation of the unit. Sample questions:

   a. Did you want to join a gang before we began discussing and studying them?
   b. Do you want to now?
   c. Have you learned anything new about gangs?
   d. Have your attitudes towards gangs changed?
   e. Is the gang situation a "problem"? If so, is there a solution to this problem?
   f. Do you feel that these discussions of gangs were worthwhile?

After conducting a class through such a unit, a teacher can effectively make use of the context switch, for example, have the youngsters explore some of the value expressions in the Constitution and the Declaration of Independence to determine their relevancy and desirability within their lives. The teacher can further expand the "responsibility" aspect inherent in the structure of gangs to the larger and extremely important aspects of expanded citizenship: city, state, national, or international.

Power and Law in a Pioneer Environment

Teachers can employ content traditionally taught, rearranging it to instill political attitudes and values that better meet the psycho-social needs of their students. The plan of instruction that follows exemplifies this method. Note the interesting shift in content emphasis—first a present-day problem that students might encounter, then an inquiry into the experience of the Pilgrims in New England of the seventeenth century. This plan of instruction comprises selected portions of a unit developed by four inservice teachers.

A PLAN OF INSTRUCTION—PILGRIMS

Concept: Governing.

Main Idea: People, in the past and in the present, have banded together to accomplish a common goal, resulting in an organized governing structure.

Objectives

1. To demonstrate an awareness of living conditions aboard the **Mayflower** by depicting these conditions through role-playing.

2. To demonstrate a knowledge of the Pilgrims' feelings and emotions through the reaction of the individual diaries.

3. To form a governing structure, known as a compact, by employing governing principles developed through the classroom discussion of the Mayflower Compact.

4. To lead children into discovering characteristics of leadership by electing a boy and a girl to act as host and hostess for the class.

5. To be able to develop empathic understanding by listing, as a group, the fears and anxieties of the Pilgrims as they explored the new world.

6. To evaluate the first governing procedures and their relativity to today's situations by discussing the drawing of lots and the assignment of families.

7. To lead the children in a discussion of leadership qualities by elections through role-playing.

8. To lead the children in thinking about the necessity for caring for others by discussing the care for family and friends.

9. To demonstrate the necessity for cooperation between different societies by discussing the relationships between the Pilgrims and Indians.

Activities

1. Begin a discussion on the problems of families moving from one area to another. Ask: "What items would your family take with them if you were to move to Florida next week?" List all articles that the children suggest. The teacher may provide structure, if she wishes her charts to be grouped logically. For example, she may ask what the entire family would need, what the child would use, and similar questions.

2. Lead the children into thinking about the necessities of maintaining existence by asking: "Suppose your family had to move to Flower Island. You know nothing about the island except that you and your family will be the first people to live on it. What things would be best to take with you? Would you need the same things that you would need in Florida?" Write down their suggestions.

3. Prepare the children for the limiting factor of space that the Pilgrims faced by stating: "All of these articles would be useful on Flower Island. Would all of these things fit into a trunk? If your family could take only one trunk to Flower Island, what things would you pack?" List their ideas. Keep these on charts so that comparisons can be made with the articles that the Pilgrims actually took. Further discussion might revolve around asking other families to come along, why doing this would be good, and whether more goods could be brought later to Flower Island.

4. Introduce the Pilgrims: "Can you think of any people who really moved from one country to another and could only take a little with them?" If no one suggests the Pilgrims, give leading hints. After narrowing the discussion to the Pilgrims, ask why anyone would leave one country to go to another. Accept all answers. Then ask why the Pilgrims left their country and introduce the ideas of religious freedom and of leading one's own life in one's own way.

5. Since the idea of religious prejudice is probably new to most children in America, they may need to experience a form of prejudice in the classroom. Make certain every child has crayons and then appoint or elect one child "king of the classroom." The king will choose one color over all the others, and all work done for the next hour (or day) must be done in that color—no other. Explain that work or art done in any other color will be torn up and thrown in the wastebasket by the king. After the experience has been completed, ask the children:

"How did you feel?"
"Did you want to use another color?"
"How did it feel to be punished for using [for instance] red instead of green?"
"How did you feel toward the king?"
"How could they get around using just his color?"

Relate this experience to how the Pilgrims must have felt about being told what church they must attend.

6. Discuss how the Pilgrims got to America. About 120 people wanted to go, but only 102 went. "What did they go in?" "How did they secure the **Mayflower?**" Lead into the idea that they had to choose a group of men to make decisions for them like how they would go, who would back them financially, how they would repay their backers, what they could take, when they would leave. Bring out how it would be impossible for all people to take part in all decision making.

7. Let each child draw one family of Pilgrims. These could be combined to make a scrapbook of our first settlers.

8. Show the cut-away pictures of the **Mayflower.** Discuss its size (as big as the classroom), what each compartment was used for, what activities could be carried on in it (as, could they cook?) For some children, this concept of limited space may be hard to understand. To demonstrate it, move all of the children into about one-third of the classroom and involve the class in some role playing. Have them try to walk around, talk to one another, pretend to eat, try to take a nap. Ask and discuss:

"How did the Pilgrims cope with this lack of privacy?"
"What would happen if one child were angry with another?"
"What if you wanted to sleep and someone else wanted to sing?"
"How did the Pilgrims entertain themselves?"
"What did they do for nine weeks in this small space?"
"Would you have been willing to be a Pilgrim?"

9. Discuss why the Pilgrims could take so few things with them. "What did they probably take?" [Build a list.] How does this list compare with what you took to Flower Island?"

10. Have the class formulate a list of questions they would like answered about life on the **Mayflower.** (This will probably stem from their own role-playing.) Then show the film **Mayflower Story.** Check off those questions that can be answered. Ask: "Where might we go to find the answers to the other questions?"

11. An idea stressed in **The Mayflower Story** is the fact that the Pilgrims ate the same things every day while on ship. One little girl longs for cold fresh water. Many children will find this hard to empathize with. One way for the class to gain understanding might be to use only a picnic jug of water and paper cups for drinking during one day, not drinking milk or the water from the fountain. Another idea (with parental permission) might be to restrict one day's lunch to cold biscuits, cold sliced meat, cheese, and water. If the idea is impressed upon them that these were the only things the Pilgrims had to eat for nine weeks, the children might be more empathic.

12. Guide the class into seeing how the Pilgrims must have solved problems aboard ship. What kinds of problems might need to be worked on?

(Examples: bad behavior toward another, eating too much food.) How might these be solved? Would it be necessary to have all passengers meet at one time? Develop the idea that each family might have to send a representative to the meeting or that there might have been a group of Pilgrims who were in charge. Enact such a meeting. Divide the class into families of three or four and have them send a representative. Role-play problems and let the children devise solutions.

13. Make a mural about life on board the ship. Include such things as a drawing of the ship, the compartments of the ship, people working, people relaxing, taking care of the sick, watching the soldiers drill, a Pilgrim being washed overboard, and other known or probable events and activities.

14. Read the following value sheet to the children. Have the questions answered individually on paper and then discuss them.

The governor and his council issued laws ruling the lives of the people of Plymouth Colony. People who disobeyed these laws usually had to pay fines. Sometimes, however, judges sentenced a person to the stocks in order to make a public example of him. He would have to sit or stand for hours in the town square — with his ankles, his wrists, and even his neck locked in a wooden frame. The stocks were uncomfortable enough, but the stares and jeers of the people who passed by must have been even harder to bear for some of the offenders.

    a. If you had done something wrong, would you rather pay a fine or be put in the stocks for several hours?

    b. Tell why you make the choice you did.

    c. How might you feel if you were in the stocks and one of your friends came by and started laughing at you and calling you names?

    d. What would you do if this person were later in the stocks and you walked by? Remember some of the things he had said to you.

    e. Have you ever teased someone or laughed at someone? How did you feel about this later on?

    f. What if paying the fine meant going hungry for a few days? How might this influence your decision?

    g. Do you go along with the crowd when they are teasing someone even if you know they are wrong, or do you try to get the others to see your way?

15. Select a leader for a game. This leader must explain to his team how to play kickball. But the leader cannot speak because the team members cannot understand what he says; they speak other languages. Have the leader try to explain his game. After the rules are explained, talk about how the leader got his ideas across. Discuss how they used signs and gestures to make themselves understood by their team members. The Pilgrims also had a problem in that most of them could not talk to the Indians. They needed to make themselves understood. How did they do this?

16. Present these situations and questions:

You have just met an Indian child, who cannot talk to you because he cannot speak your language. You want him for a friend. What must you do so that you can play with him and both of you will be able to somehow understand each other?

How do you feel when you try to explain how to play your favorite game, but he cannot understand you?

Tell what you are trying to tell your Indian friend and then act out the situation.

You show the Indian a kettle with only a few blueberries in it. Then you pretend to hunt berries on bushes that have no berries. When you can't find any, you look at the Indian and shake your head; Then you point to the empty kettle again. (You want the Indian to help you find enough berries to fill the kettle.)

You take the Indian's arm and begin to walk. Suddenly you pretend to stumble and fall to the ground. You sit and hold your leg and pretend to cry because it hurts. Then you get up and point toward the woods. (Someone has fallen and hurt himself. You want the Indian to go with you to help.)

Remarks on the Instruction Plans

Our presentation of the instruction plans on Gangs and Pilgrims has three major purposes, among others. These are:

1. To focus much-needed attention on the question of what content vehicles are most appropriate in meeting the social and psychological needs of youngsters.
2. To illustrate some of the cognitive and affective considerations of methodology presented in Chapters 2 and 3.
3. To bring about greater thought/discussion concerning the disparity which exists between expressed democratic ideals and their application to student rights and responsibilities within elementary classrooms.

We strongly encourage exploration of these questions within teacher-education courses.

SUMMARY

This chapter has presented a theoretical position which argues that instruction with elementary-age children may well profit from consideration of political-science-oriented objectives applied with consideration to the existing needs and knowledge of the youngsters encountered. The governed-governing relationship as a focus for the structured-dependent stage of child development was elaborated. Teachers were admonished to consider personal and community constraints in selection of methods and content, but encouraged to use the personal, social, and cultural goals stated in the first chapter as a benchmark against which to measure constructed or selected behavioral objectives.

Suggested activities for all levels of cognitive development described by Piaget as well as the major portions of two extensive instruction plans were presented, not only to serve as exemplars for lesson construction but also to serve as catalysts in stimulating inquiry into certain unresolved curricular issues in social studies education.

While the emphasis of this chapter has been upon development of structured-dependent needs through political-science-oriented objectives, we do wish to point out that other social-science objectives could also be incorporated. Many of the social-science objectives mentioned at the end of the first chapter could be introduced and/or developed with the children of eight to ten years. Teachers preparing such lessons are reminded to keep in mind the guidelines regarding structured-dependent behavior cited earlier in the chapter.

CHAPTER 6

The Structured-Independent Stage of Psycho-Social Development

Give and take between individual children and adults — exchanging — provides the key to Chapter 6. Chapter 5 emphasized the rationale of constraints placed upon the individual. These constraints were at times imposed by external forces ("No, you can't go out after dinner."). At other times they were self-imposed ("My gang won't like it if I . . ."). The development of *power* became the focus.

In this chapter also we are concerned with constraint. The primary questions concerning children at this level of psycho-social development are: What are the reasonable forces that impinge upon us? Can we control their effect? When we wish to act, what trade-offs must we make or can we make? Cause and effect become central concerns. *Exchanging* becomes the focusing concept.

THEME AND JUSTIFICATION

Perhaps the single most obvious characteristic of elementary-school children correlated positively with success is awareness. The child who is "tuned-in"—aware of the ground rules—enjoys significant advantage over the naive youngster. Consider the maxim of the test-wise student: "When in doubt, mark C."

The child who knows the ropes enjoys the advantage of choice. He may opt to play it the teacher's way or he may choose to subvert the system. That is, he may consciously allow himself to be manipulated or he may become the manipulator.

Let any teacher ask herself or himself the question, "Is the brightest, most creative child in the class always one of the 'A' students?" Often the characteristics of neatness, attention to detail, following directions, and the like are missing from the creative individual. He never seems to learn to color inside the lines! Unfortunately, the sort of mindlessness which permeates much of institutional education soon forces him into the pattern created by the lines of the teacher's ditto sheet or the curriculum guide. How do we overcome this debilitating condition?

A partial remedy consists of developing the child's awareness of the system. Many of the ideas discussed in Chapter 5 as part of the governed-governing relationship were designed for just this purpose. They further highlighted the consequences of the child's acts. But a human person need not stand impassively before the onslaught of consequence. He may indeed act.

Action may take the form of rebellion, revolution, or withdrawal, to name a few options. We authors believe that none of these serve the needs of the individuals or institutions involved. A more rational approach would appear to be *exchanging:* the interaction of the child with individuals, groups, objects, and events, as he moves from limited experience and perception and low ego strength to expanding awareness and concern. Exchanging is a major function in psycho-social existence. Consider for a moment the myriad exchanges necessary each day to simply survive in a modern densely populated society:

What exchanges are made: (1) on the expressway? (2) to satisfy material wants? (3) to gain social status? (4) to soothe our social conscience? (5) to share living space? What effect does refusal to make an exchange have? What options does an individual have in each of the questions?

Traditionally, the concept of citizenship has served as the rather nebulous focus for socio-political exchanging. Citizenship is indeed an exchange. The responsibilities of service, constructive criticism, and participation are exchanged for such rights as belonging and protection (see the Declaration of Independence). We do not reject these traditional concepts but do strongly object to the means used to bring children to full understanding of and ability to act upon these rights and responsibilities.

The exchangings explored here are designed to provide opportunity for children to demonstrate responsibility by selecting from among options provided by the teacher to reach legitimate objectives. The burden is thus on the professional to provide those options — to facilitate the exchanging.

SETTING AN AGE FOR TEACHING EXCHANGING

At the structured-independent stage of cognitive-affective development, the child's life is characterized by an increasing capacity for abstractness; the child has less and less need of an immediate three-dimensional or pictorial referent for conceptualization and evaluation of experience. For example, in a discussion concerning some of the causes of sparse settlement of land in parts of his state, the child can attack this problem from several frames of reference such as political control of land use, climatic and/or geographic factors unfavorable to location, unfavorable industrial development factors, and still others. He can further explore some trends in urbanization and make some projections concerning further population growth in this area.

The child entering the structured-independent stage is also gaining a sense of awareness and concern regarding others in both his immediate and global environment. His ability to move cognitively to greater realms of awareness is coupled with an emerging sense of humanism. In role-playing situations, for example, his behavior can be characterized as an attempt at both authenticity and empathy.

Children who have reached this stage of development begin to see life as a process of social, economic, political, cultural, and historical exchanges. They are concerned, for example, with the maldistribution of wealth, and may recognize the need for raising the minimum standard of living throughout the world. The desired affective-value response will of course depend upon where the child and his family are in the socio-economic stratification. In the classroom, the decision of how to best spend the money raised for a Valentine Party could bring forth several alternatives, including decisions based on (1) personal needs such as candy and ice cream, (2) social needs ranging from sending Valentine cards to each other to giving the money to some local volunteer group, (3) cultural needs served by giving the money to some volunteer agency outside the local community. Certainly arguments used to support one alternative over another will be reflective of the exchanging need level upon which the child is operating. Hopefully children would make their selection based upon solution which would satisfy the physical and psychological needs of the greatest number of people. However, while the teacher could justifiably point to this goal as desirable, she must be aware of the competing needs of her youngsters and allow independence of choice (resolved through democratic processes in this instance.) She can, however, point out to the children why, as she sees it, they decided as they did.

Another characteristic of the structured-independent child is a readiness for further development of space-related skills (map and globe) and research-related skills (outlining, summarizing, note taking, reporting, and the like). Illustrative activities to facilitate this development are provided in the last section of this chapter. But since the readers of this text are assumed to have had some background in teaching reading in the content fields, this area will not be isolated for special emphasis.

We authors feel that the discipline of economics should furnish a major part of content to be taught at this level of development. This surely embraces the construct of "exchange," but exchanging has interpersonal, geographical, and historical-cultural components which also need attention at this level of development. Accordingly, various methods and materials drawn primarily from economics and secondarily from social psychology, geography, history, and anthropology will be presented and analyzed in this chapter.

STIMULATING PERSONALITY EXCHANGING IN THE CLASSROOM

One effective method of building greater personal acceptance of others within a classroom is for the teacher to stimulate discussion of individual differences which exist, and to instill the attitude that such differences are both necessary and good. Many books and articles can be read to gain skill in development of interpersonal relations.

The following lesson is illustrative of many such lessons.

A PSYCHO-SOCIAL LESSON — VALUING YOURSELF AS AN INDIVIDUAL[1]
Concepts
The main idea stressed in this lesson is the role of the individual in group process. Each child should learn to respond and react to each of his own socially accepted desires and needs.

Objectives
1. After having discussed how each person is an individual and that each individual has his own personality traits, everyone will participate in a game where each child will be able to accept and work with the abilities, interests, and limitations of the children in the group.
2. Before and after the reading of the child's book entitled **Just Me,** each

[1] The authors extend grateful thanks to Melanie Daniel, an undergraduate student at Georgia State University, for the development of this plan of instruction.

child should participate as a constructive group member when there is any discussion on individuality.

3. After the reading of the book **Just Me,** each child will act on the basis of existing personal abilities, interests, and constraints in the drawing of a picture of himself as a unique individual.

Materials
A child's library book entitled **Just Me,** by Marie Hall Ets.
Colored construction paper.
Crayons.
Mirrors (different sizes and shapes).
Writing tablets and pencils.

Procedure
1. Discuss individuality with the children, bringing out that each person is a unique individual: that he has his own physical appearance, his own personality, his own likes and dislikes, his own hobbies, and other qualities of his own.

2. Distribute a mirror to each child and let him look at himself for a few minutes. Then, going around the class, have each child in turn tell what items of physical appearance another person might see in him or that he might see in another person—things that could be seen in a mirror.

3. Then let the children tell about their personal qualities and feelings that can't be seen in the mirror. Each child tells as much as he chooses about his likes, his dislikes, and his hobbies.

4. Next, play a game of describing and guessing. Ask each child to write a description of another child. The description should give as many clues as possible that will enable other children to guess who is described; tell the class, however, to emphasize positive things about the child described. Each child in turn reads his composition aloud and the other children try to guess who he has described.

5. After the game is finished, read (or have a child read) to the class the book **Just Me.** It is about a little boy who can do a number of such different things as walk like the cat or take a nap like Pearl the Pig; but when Dad calls, he finds that the most fun of all is being "Just Me" as they go to sea together on the pond at the end of the cornfield.

6. When the story has been read, have each child draw a picture of himself or about himself. The picture need not be a body-figure drawing; it may depict some activity he likes doing or some hobby of his.

Evaluation
1. From the discussion held, and then passing the mirrors out, did the children seem to begin to realize just how much individuals are different?

2. Did the book **Just Me** seem effective for this lesson?

3. Did the children learn how to value themselves as individuals?

For the teacher's role as a problem solver and solution facilitator in interpersonal relations, one of the most exciting techniques which has emerged (from the fields of language arts and children's literature) is bibliotherapy. This term refers to the use of reading as a method for furthering personal adjustment. When a reader sees himself and his problem in what he is reading he experiences what Caroline Shrodes (1955) calls a "shock of recognition," borrowing Melville's expression. This shock may bring personal adjustment to the reader more easily than explicit discussion of real-life situations, since the mirror effect of the story enables him to escape direct attack upon his ego. A teacher can use children's books in this technique to facilitate psycho-social development of children. The following account describes how one teacher identified a particular social maladjustment in her class and then elaborates on the bibliotherapy techniques she used with the individual and the class.

A PERSONAL CASE STUDY—VALUING ANOTHER PERSON[2]
Background

My problem is found in my basic seventh-grade English class of fifteen boys and five girls. The children in this class are generally from the low socioeconomic level; the boys are very hyperactive and have, at many times, been discipline problems. The class has socially grouped itself. Aside from the normal everyday encounters, most of the children get along pretty well with each other—with one exception, Linda. Linda is a thirteen-year-old girl who is accepted neither by the boys nor the girls. She sits by herself at lunch, has her desk away from the other children by her own choice and theirs, and interacts with them in as few ways as possible. Linda's dress is very poor and her mannerisms are crude. She is not a "trouble maker," but she always fights back both physically and verbally when attacked. She has an older brother, a grade behind her in school, who seems to be her only friend. After talking with other teachers, I found that this situation has been prevalent as long as Linda has been in school.

Linda is not a bright child, but she is conscientious. When she speaks in class, the other children laugh and tease her.

I based my approach on John Goodlad's and Dorothy Fraser's ideas that social studies should meet the needs of the individual to identify with the rest of humanity; and that an individual needs to be able to accept differences among cultures and subcultures as normal if he is to deal effectively with life today.

I based the resolution of this problem on the fact that if this social studies program is humanistic in nature the children will naturally learn to accept and respect differences in others.

[2] Supplied by Nancy Prosser, teacher in Brockett Elementary School, Tucker, Georgia, and graduate student at Georgia State University, whom the authors thank.

Resolving the Problem

According to Fraser and others, the emphasis of the "new" social studies is on inquiry and discovery approaches. I tried to take steps in this manner to have the children realize, themselves, the basic concept of the importance of human relationships. Perhaps through this realization my students might be able to view Linda in a different way. They might not be able to accept her, but they might be able to understand her and themselves a little better. This was my goal.

The first step in my attempt to solve this problem was to give my class a sociogram. The results were as I expected. Linda was not chosen by any child for any item.

Step two was the administration of a self-concept test (Gordon, 1969). I marked Linda's inconspicuously so that I could study hers. It was interesting to note the responses that she gave. Either she felt very good about herself or she marked the sheet in the way she wanted to feel. I believe the latter was true. I also thought it was interesting to note the items that she erased and changed. For instance, in one item she first indicated a strong desire to be prettier, then erased it and placed her response midway between "My Face is pretty" and "I wish I were prettier." As compared to the other children in the class, Linda's answers tended to be more extreme. The others seemed to be more toward the middle on most questions.

After the self-concept test we discussed some of the things we liked and disliked about ourselves. We also talked about what made us like and dislike others. The class came up with some very good thoughts. They decided that they liked people who were courteous and nice. They disliked themselves when they got into trouble because they were mean. I really thought we were getting somewhere when, after Linda made a comment, Donnie said, "Oh! shut up, Linda." I thought all had been lost after that comment. I tried to salvage it and use it as a learning experience by asking if anyone had noticed something about that comment that might relate to what we had been discussing. Most agreed that Donnie's comment was unnecessary. One child even suggested that we might make people like us if we were "more willing to listen."

In my next step I employed bibliotherapy. I read Estes' **The Hundred Dresses** to the class. We discussed the implications made in the book. Then I had the children relate how they felt about certain incidents in the book. Many of the children felt sorry for the little girl. They said that it would be nice if we could "take back" cruelty to other people when we were sorry. I thought it interesting to note that some said that even "I'm sorry" doesn't help after someone's feelings have been hurt. I have included some of the children's papers.

Student #1. "How did the story make you feel?" When you hurt somebody feelings you all ways get payed back, in your on feelings to. You can say you are sorry and you didn't mean it but their feelings are always hurt. "Did you learn anything from the story?" Not to critizes people and not call them names becuase it alwyas hurts their feelings. And you can tell them you are sorry. And they will say its ok. but really its in their mind. And they will forget some of it. But it always troubles them in many ways.

Student #2. I felt bad a little. I thought about how Linda feels. When we call her names and when the boys call her names. And we don't like her sitting by us at lunch I have tried to be nice to her but she gets mad. What else is there to do. I will try hard and see if that works.

Linda's Reaction. "How did the story make you feel?" Pretty bad. Because a lot of people talk about me & I am like Wanda sort of. People don't like me Because the way they treat me, I don't like them. "Did you learn anything from the story?" Not to tease a person or people because it can hurt them like me.

Since February 12 was Lincoln's Birthday, I thought I might take advantage of this. I read the poem, "Born without a Chance" by Edmund Vance Cooke. This poem told the story of how people said that Abe Lincoln was born to poor white trash without a chance in the world to survive. I got some good reactions in discussion after this. Joe brought out that in many cases, we judge people by what they have rather than what they are. Linda said that just because people are poor, they are not bad. (There were no adverse reactions to Linda's statement.)

My next step was unplanned, but seemed to fit the project. We took the seventh-grade class to see "Gone With the Wind." I felt that after seeing the movie there would be a good opportunity to discuss the movie and hopefully have the children bring out the idea of persecution. We discussed slavery and why blacks were and are persecuted. I found it a little difficult to discuss this topic with these children because, as I mentioned before, they are from the low socioeconomic level and their ideas about blacks were still quite prejudiced. Parental influence was quite apparent. However, we did get to the idea that many people are unjustly persecuted. From there I went to the individualized learning package I developed on persecution [included below].

Because I felt that class interaction was better than individual written work with these children, I allowed them to work in groups on the package. Linda worked alone. I had very favorable reactions to this. They seemed to enjoy reading about the characters and seemed to begin to understand a little more about unjust persecution. We shared orally what each group discovered about their character. We then listed on the board some of the things that all the characters had in common.

We then discussed the word "persecution" again. This time some of the children brought up the terms "respect" and "understanding." I had the children answer [the question in objective 3.b of] the learning package. The results were very encouraging. The girls that had completely ignored Linda and had been so cruel to her were admitting their mistakes. For the first time during the project, I had some sign that what I was doing was "getting through" to some of them. Even some of the boys were discussing Linda before they began to write. I have included a few of the papers.

Individualized Learning Package—Persecution
Objective

This is a lesson about man's persecution of other men for no apparent reason other than difference among them. When you have completed this lesson, you should be able to do the [four] following things:

1. Choose one of the characters below:

The Ugly Duckling	Jim Thorpe
Satchel Paige	George Washington Carver
Thomas Edison	Bambi
Cinderella	Robert Fulton
Jackie Robinson	Eleanor Roosevelt

Write a character sketch of the character you choose. Be sure you include the following information:

   a. How he was persecuted.
   b. Why he was persecuted.
   c. How did the character react to this persecution?
   d. What was the future of this persecuted character?
   e. Were the reasons for persecution just? Why or why not?
   2. Be able to identify all of the above characters.
   3. Pretend you have taken a pill that has made you immortal. It is the year 3000.
   a. What is life like (relating to unjust persecution) in your world?
   b. What incident in your life during the year 1971 can you relate to your friends that would deal with unjust persecution?
   c. What can you tell them you learned from this incident?
   d. What has your new world learned from this incident?
   4. Be able to discuss all the points in the objective.

How to Complete the Objective

   1. Read about the lives of the characters I have mentioned. You will find each listed in the card catalog under his/her name.
   2. Find cards in the subject catalog that are entitled "Persecution."
   3. There are two film strips in the library that might aid you in your research. "Cinderella." "The Life of George Washington Carver."

Reactions to the Lesson on Persecution

Student #1. Feli how are you. Rember when we use to talk about people. Well I rember when I talked about Linda. I feel sorrry I wonder how she feels I know how I would feel but how could I be freind with her after every thing we've done. Oh I'm so sorry. I'll try harder Well by I'll see you later. The End.

Student #2. My Story. I am sorry, I've talked about Linda. And say hateful things and call her names. I was just saying things about my self. It was just going back into my face. It was all about me. I think I should treat her like. I would anyone else. I will treat her right. The End. And also treating teachers wrong: Such as: talking back to them. Doing things I shouldn't do to them.

Student #3. In 1971 I was mean to a girl in my class. I never talked to her and when she talked to me I didn't pay any attention to her.

That same day there was the second encouraging incident. Linda usually sat alone at lunch. That day two girls sat with her. They have been sitting with her for a week now. I'm not sure as to how long it will last, but it does seem encouraging to me to see them display even this small amount of affection toward Linda.

I had thought of personal counseling with Linda at the beginning of this project, but I decided against it for several reasons:
1. I felt it might make Linda self-conscious during the other activities.
2. I wanted to see what Linda's reaction to the project would be.
3. I was anxious to know if this would work with total inductive teaching.

I have not, as yet, told you about Linda's reaction to all this. She seemed very unresponsive. During many of the class discussions, Linda was drawing or doing something else. Perhaps she felt that things were directed toward her. She doesn't seem to mind sitting with the girls at lunch, yet she doesn't seem elated about it. I think that it's going to take quite a bit longer for Linda to accept others than for others to accept her. She has been alone so much and doesn't know how to handle this.

Evaluation

Evaluation of this project was in the form of my observation of the class's attitude toward Linda and each other. The girls are continuing to sit next to her during lunch. The reaction of the students to her in class has been pretty much the same. This was disappointing.

My last evaluative technique was another sociogram. I was hopeful that maybe one child might feel differently toward her. I was happy to see that on the fourth question on the sociogram "Who would you most like to help?" four girls put Linda's name. I realized the question was a leading one, but I felt that even if someone just felt a little compassion for Linda, it would be a step in the right direction. There were no other categories in which she was listed. I almost expected this.

I feel that it is difficult to evaluate this type of project, as it is difficult to evaluate feelings. I have certainly not succeeded in fully making Linda an accepted member of her peer group. But if I have made a few people take a better look at themselves and other people, I may have succeeded to an even greater extent than I had expected.

Note: Miss Nancy Prosser recently called the author to say that Linda, presently an eighth grader, has had a major security-love need stroke. She has a boyfriend! There apparently are some Hollywood endings in elementary classrooms.

TEACHING FOR SOCIAL-ECONOMIC EXCHANGING

Utilizing role-playing and simulation techniques (when possible) with young children can be a powerful stimulus to learning. The message of John Dewey and others that meaningful learning takes place when children are asked to reflect upon things in which they are actively involved is a viable principle to follow. In the following lesson, children learn economic concepts and generalizations through role-playing store owners and shoppers.

PERSONAL-SOCIAL EXCHANGING—A ROLE-PLAYING LESSON ABOUT BUYING AND SELLING[3]

Objectives

1. Children should be able to list several reasons why people may prefer to buy at one particular store rather than another: lower prices, better goods or services, convenient location, customer confidence.

2. Children should be able to tell why owners of stores earn an income from the sales of services and goods, and should be able to discuss what they must do with part of the income they make (must pay for the goods and materials to replace what they have sold, pay wages for workers, pay rents, and pay for utilities, repairs, and taxes).

3. Children should be able to discuss the meaning of the word "profit" (the income left over after the business owner has paid his expenses).

4. Children should be able to discuss the meaning of the word "competition," including the idea that owners compete to attract customers by having better goods or services or prices.

Content

1. Concept of profit.
2. Concept of competition.
3. Concept of choice of consumer to shop where he feels he is getting best goods, services, or prices.
4. Concept of expenses—what store owners must do with part of their profit.

Materials

1. Play money.

[3] Prepared Fall, 1970, by Donna Freedman, undergraduate at Georgia State University, whom the authors thank.

2. "Goods" to sell (pictures from magazines).

3. Cards (see Procedure).

Procedure

1. Children are divided into two groups, shoppers and store owners; about 11 shoppers for two stores; each store has two owners.

2. Each shopper receives an equal amount of play money, and all shoppers receive an identical shopping list of items to be obtained at the stores.

3. The stores are provided with play money, and goods for the shoppers to buy, but the quantity and prices vary among the stores.

4. The shoppers try to buy all the things on their shopping lists. The shopper who completes his list in the given time is the winner. If there is a tie, the shopper with the most money left over is the winner.

5. The store owners try to sell all their goods at the prices the teacher has set. The store with the most profit is the winner.

6. Rules:

a. All sales are final.

b. Shoppers cannot resell goods.

c. Store cannot trade.

d. Shoppers cannot trade.

e. When the teacher blows a whistle and draws a card, the store owners must do what the card says (such as "pay $5.00 wages," "pay $15.00 rent," "pay $25.00 to the wholesaler," and other).

7. Before playing the game, there should be a discussion involving following questions:

a. Have you ever gone shopping with your father or mother? If so, where did you shop, and why not at some other store?

b. Do you shop at stores near your house? If so, why do you shop there?

c. Does anyone know what the word "competition" means? Do you "compete" sometimes when you play ball, or some other games? How might store owners "compete" with one another?

d. Discuss the meaning of the word "profit," and ask what store owners might do with their profit.

Social-economic exchanging can be effectively developed through simulation and gaming. "A simulation game is a selected representation of a physical and/or social phenomenon incorporating a game technique. Players assume roles, interact with other players, and make decisions on those roles and interactions." (Rogers and Kysilka, 1970) "Simulation techniques involve learners. Learners enjoy simulation techniques. Simulation techniques teach." (Christine and Christine, 1970) The technique of simulation involves students in complex conceptual learning. It is discussed at greater length in Chapter 9.

The simulation game that follows attempts to develop some of the key ideas of economics through recreating conditions of a mining camp in the 1850's.[4]

A SIMULATION GAME FOR TEACHING SOCIAL-ECONOMIC EXCHANGING — THE GOLD-MINING CAMP

Objectives

A major organizing principle in the functional economy of any community is supply and demand. The similar applications of that principle in a California mining camp of the 1850's and communities of today are apparent. Students can readily transfer the notion of limited resources vs. unlimited wants from the 1850 historical setting to the contemporary world. Therefore, by simulating the economic functioning of an early mining camp, the students will attain the following objectives.

A. At the conclusion of the simulation the student will be able to state three consequences of the demand for a good surpassing its supply.

1. The price of a unit increases.
2. The availability of the desired unit decreases.
3. The production of units usually increases as demand continues to increase.

B. At the conclusion of the simulation the student will be able to state at least three consequences of a large amount of capital becoming available in a locale.

1. The demand for goods and services increases.
2. The demand for certain items surpasses the supply; new clothes and homes are examples.
3. The price for a unit of goods or service increases.
4. Speculation occurs in segments of the economy as people freely spend money.

C. At the conclusion of the simulation the student will be able to state two consequences of speculation investment.

1. Large amounts of capital are invested in activities or goods which may increase in value with time.
2. The value of certain goods is inflated because of increased investment attention to them.

D. At the conclusion of the simulation the student will be able to state two

[4] The authors are extremely grateful to Dr. Everett T. Keach of the University of Georgia for allowing them to include this game, which their students at Georgia State University have rated very highly.

conditions which result in economic cooperation and interdependence between individuals.

1. Cooperation occurs when the capital or labor of a number of individuals is necessary to attain a specific end product. Examples: large mine, partnership.
2. Interdependence occurs when two or more items are essential and the owners of each provide the respective components. Examples: pick and shovel.

The students are not expected to parrot the examples in the above objectives. It will be much more suitable if they can verbalize a situation in which the "price of a unit" will increase.

Key Concepts

supply	capital	interdependence
demand	goods	speculation
barter	services	

Lexicon of Economic Terms[5]

The teacher should use this lexicon to introduce economic terms and ideas to the students. It is important that students be aware of the terms as the simulation gets under way. The students are not expected to respond rotely the definition of any single term, but rather to be able to describe the process involved in respective economic activities. In addition, the teacher should not use advanced economic terminology which the students will probably not comprehend. Instead, for example, speculation can be described as follows: "A man buys a farm. He is not a farmer nor does he know how to farm. Instead, he keeps the farm until someone else wants to buy it. Then he sells it for a greater amount than he paid; the difference is his profit."

Supply—The amount or number of things ready for use or for sale. A supply of 10 shovels is not enough if 15 miners each need a shovel.

Demand—The number of supply items people want to buy or use. If 15 miners each need a shovel, the demand is for 15 shovels. If only 10 shovels are ready, the demand is greater than the supply.

Barter—When money is not used, people trade items of value. Trading a horse for a cow is barter. Trading a pick for a shovel is barter. Money does not change hands, but items of value to the people involved change hands.

Capital—(All things that have value can be capital.) In some countries bright stones are capital; they are used as money. In the United States money is capital. A house is capital because of its value. A car is capital. The school is capital. Capital can be converted to money.

---

[5] Definitions in this lexicon contain some compromises with economic-scholarly rigor that accommodate to young students' capacities. If an alert student questions them, there is opportunity to elaborate and refine—and to encourage the student.

Goods — Goods are tangible items that have value. Goods are produced to meet demands of people. All goods are capital. Goods are usually for sale. A dress is a good. Shoes are goods. A pick is a good. Food is goods.

Service — Service is work that helps other people. The salesman in a store helps people select what they want to buy. He is providing a service. Carpenters build things. They are providing a service.

Interdependence — The condition that occurs when two or more things depend upon each other in any way. City people depend upon farmers for food; farmers depend upon city people for cars and tractors. Miners depend upon store owners for goods, upon carpenters for services; in return the store owners and carpenters depend upon the miners for sales and jobs. Farms may depend on fertilizer factories; fertilizer factories depend on farms.

Speculation — Holding capital for a time in hopes that its value will increase. Someone may buy a farm, then keep it until someone else offers him more than what he paid for it. Then he sells and makes a profit.

Planning the Simulation

The simulation is planned to perpetuate itself after the initial activities. Therefore, the physical layout is essential.

The service/goods people should be located in one area that represents a settlement. The farmers will be the only service/goods people to locate away from the settlement. The miners will be able to locate wherever they want. However, 24 original gold strikes will be placed in various areas of the room/school grounds. These should be the small ones. As the miners work, the teacher can distribute or call out strikes to the various groups. Care should be taken to award one or two mine sites a far greater amount, so the students witness the survival/production aspect of functional economics.

Once the students have reached their mine site and staked a claim, they are free to go about solving the problems they face: namely, procurement of food, shelter, clothing, and equipment. The store owners should be awaiting them. It may be necessary to stop and assess the predicament of a student who fails to react. Peers may be able to offer suggestions regarding ways in which the individual can acquire the things he needs to live and mine.

All of the miners will have to journey to the settlement or farms to buy things. When the good or service desired is sold out, the individual miner is faced with a problem situation. The cards are stacked so some miners will run out of food and money. The teacher should anticipate those problems.

The length of the simulation activity will depend upon numerous variables, some being: the teacher, the class interest, the facilities available, the discussion, and the evaluation. The simulation should be organized to represent days in a typical sense that meals are eaten, jobs are performed, etc. The real time necessary to reconstruct 15 to 20 days of life in an early mining camp will provide ample opportunity for the activity to operate successfully. By trading role positions, the simulation can be started anew the second or third real day. This gives the students an opportunity to participate as two or three kinds of community members as well as to improve their ability to predict the types of situations which developed unexpectedly on a prior day. In nice weather the simulation can be held out-of-doors and the students can establish camp sites, mine sites, service sites, and routes of travel.

The students should be involved in much of the actual planning. Role positions in the camp can be drawn by using a deck of cards (each card denoting a position). Students may also trade positions with others if they desire. The students will thus become readied through planning involvement for expected roles in the simulation.

A few days prior to initiating the simulation game, the students should begin to construct the props and artifacts necessary. Much of the material can be prepared during art sessions, while some material can be acquired and prepared at home.

Materials

These lists contemplate about 48 students.

1. Money—950 pieces of drinking straws of four different colors about one inch in length: 450 yellow = $1 each; 200 green = $2 each; 150 silver = $5 each; 150 gold = $10 each.
2. 150 styrofoam cups labeled as canned food commodities.
3. 110 sacks stuffed with paper and labeled as: corn, flour, beans, feathers, salt, coffee.
4. Construction paper outlines to indicate: 20 shovels, 20 picks, 10 pans, 10 axes, 10 saws, 20 shirts, 20 trousers, 10 jackets, 10 pair of boots, 20 pair of gloves.
5. Service labels to indicate: blacksmith, carpenter, barber, restaurant.
6. Gold strikes, represented by sacks: 8 $5 sacks of gold, 12 $20 sacks, 16 $50 sacks, 5 $100 sacks. Each gold-strike sack has in it a list which guides the students/miners in disposing of their "gold" and money. For example, a gold strike of $100 might halve the following:

   a. You must exchange gold for money at the bank (the teacher).
   b. You must have a carpenter build you a sluice box or a rocker crib, and pay him.
   c. Follow these guidelines in spending the money: For groceries and supplies [about half the value of the gold strike], from farms, $20; from stores, $20. For clothing, $5. For the carpenter, $40. For miscellaneous items (restaurant, barber), $15.

Roles
Students' Roles (Assuming 48 students)
4 Storekeepers—They have approximately one-half of all the commodities available. They also buy items from the farmers for resale.

2 Blacksmiths—Each makes five shovels and five picks which are sold to the miners.

2 Barbers—Each cuts hair for whatever price feasible.

4 Restaurant Owners—Two are in business with general meals. Two specialize in high-priced meals. They buy supplies from the stores and farmers.

6 Carpenters—They build rocker cribs and sluices.

6 Farmers—They produce commodities on their farms for sale to miners and businesses. They begin with about one-half the commodities.

24 Miners—The miners arrive at the gold-mining town with none of the supplies they require for prospecting and mining. They have the following amounts of money: six have $20 each; six have $30 each; six have $50 each; six have $80 each.

Teacher's Role

The teacher's responsibility, in addition to directing the construction and collection of props, is to supervise and officiate the activity. Ground rules which the teacher must enforce are:

1. Anyone who wants to can be a miner. However, he must have a pick **and** a shovel, or be associated in a partnership that has them.
2. The teacher will act as judge in settling disputes between claims.
3. The teacher acts as the banker and exchanges money for gold strikes.
4. The teacher distributes the gold strikes to various mines as the simulation progresses.

Rules

The teacher will read to the students the following statement and read or post the rules.

The activity we are beginning today involves creating an early gold-mining camp. (We are going to be concerned with the problems of working and living in the camp.)

The rules of the game are:

1. Obtain the tools you need to mine. Each miner has to have a pick **and** a shovel. A mine may have more than one miner. To dig for gold a miner, or mining partners, must have a pick **and** a shovel.
2. Obtain the food that you need to live for three or four days. When you run out, return to the stores or farmers and buy more.
3. Store owners and farmers are going to charge as much as they can for the supplies they sell. As the demand increases, so will the price. If something costs more money than you have, you may need to put your money with someone else's to have enough.
4. The object in the end is to have the most money and live the best life. However, directions found in the gold strikes must be followed.

Steps in Starting

1. Have the necessary props on hand.

2. Read and explain the rules to the class.
3. Develop the simulation layout in accordance with facilities available.
4. Distribute gold strikes with directions.
5. Miners then begin obtaining the tools and supplies they need to initiate the mining process, opening gold strikes if they have them.

Simulation Game in Practice

The simulation activity was scheduled in the cafeteria of the school. The simulation was initiated at 12:30 p.m. and terminated at 2:30 p.m. All the props were prepared prior to the activity.

FIGURE 1

Set-up to represent the gold-mining camp with associated settlement and business area and nearby farms. Each × represents a mine site.

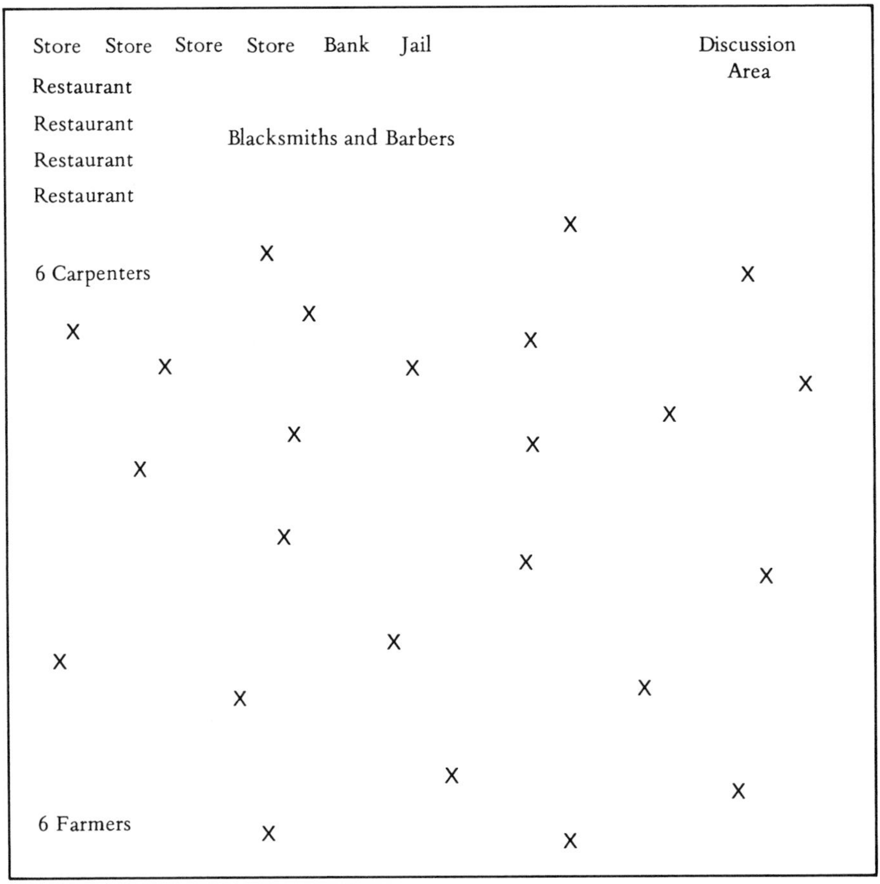

The tables in one part of the cafeteria were arranged to represent the central business district of the mining-camp (Figure 1). Store owners and other commercial establishments were located there. That section of the room became the focal point for the ensuing bartering and selling of goods and services. Ample space permitted numerous students to gather in the central business-district area at any time. The responses of the students to interaction activities centered in this area were recorded by tape recorder and on still film.

As set forth by the guidelines in the simulation activity, each student was assigned a gold-mine community role to play. After observing the simulation in operation for approximately thirty minutes, the teacher called the students together for a formative evaluation session. At that time the following conditions which had developed were discussed:

1. The circulation of money.
2. The perishability of goods.
3. The acquisition of essential services and their cost.
4. The matter of generally rising or inflated prices.

Up to that point in the simulation there had been no mention of social problems inherent in the operation of an early mining town. The matter was not to lie long dormant, even though social organization was not a major objective of the unit. The students raised the question of law and order and the presence of a sheriff. Upon realizing that no sheriff was present, a spontaneous "riot" situation developed in which students robbed the bank (to the surprise of the teacher in charge of banking) and freely robbed and stole from each other. The sequence of events in the "riot" situation was not planned, nor was it anticipated from eight-year-olds.

After calm was restored the students again gathered to discuss the notion of law and order and the application of social control. A sheriff was elected to enforce rules and maintain a jail. However, no rules were established by the students at that time. The resumption of the activity again resulted in a breakdown of law and order. The sheriff was at liberty to make arrests, but no guidelines for arrest and prosecution had been established. Although physical violence did not erupt, there were instances of confrontation between thief and intended victim, with the intended victim expecting protection from the law officer.

The students again formed a large discussion group to evaluate the situation. They agreed upon the series of actions that would be enforced by the group against those who violated mutually accepted laws. The activity of the simulation resumed with a quite different tone. Interaction, both social and economic, was carried out in a more structured fashion. A small number of law violators were reported to the sheriff who arrested them and detained them in the local jail. Because of time factors, the simulation was terminated before judicial action could be taken.

The high involvement by students in the simulation was indicative of the ability and interest of eight-year-olds to participate in this type of learning activity. Their ability to discuss and evaluate timely developments in the operation of the community is representative of their adaptation to a new dynamic learning situation.

Evaluation

A situational test was designed to measure the effects of the simulation activity. A two-week time lapse occurred between the activity and the administration of the test. The instrument was designed to measure the degree to which the children understood basic economic behavior as identified in the objectives of the activity. Situations to examine the spontaneous social aspects of the simulation were not designed. The general structure of the instrument was such that the children could relate aspects of the simulation to situations contemporary to their lives.

During a summative evaluation the students were asked the price of a specific good during the opening minutes of the simulation. The beginning base price was usually given as the response. They were then asked what the price was during the later periods of activity. Responses varied from "it cost much more" to "the price increased twenty dollars." They were then asked why the price had increased. Responses generally included the greater amount of money in circulation and the increased demand for certain goods. Most students selected tools and food as the first to increase in price, followed by nonessential items when more gold strikes occurred. The students were then presented a hypothetical situation in which farmland near an urban center was being sold. They were able to trace the same pattern of inflated prices due to the large amount of capital found in an urban area and the desire of people to live in suburban locations, as a result of which the cost of such land increases rapidly.

The teachers evaluated the performance both of individual students and of the group. They were especially impressed with the contributions made by "poor readers" and "behavior problems." The better students responded in the expected "academic fashion," while the less able students viewed the activity as a real-life situation where they were measured by economic success. The teachers were also impressed by the student-initiated follow-up questions and discussions, which lasted three days after the activity.

Independent observers were equally impressed with the simulation. High interest, involvement, and socioeconomic interdependence gave every student an opportunity to contribute to the community's functioning. In addition, during the activity the students were able to evaluate their economic success and failures, and the manner in which they made economic and social decisions. The simulation was judged by observers to represent a realistic and accurate experience for the children.

TEACHING FOR HISTORICAL AND CULTURAL EXCHANGING

Many social studies programs are still heavily oriented toward history. As we have stated earlier, the authors feel that the teaching of history must be viewed as process, as historiography.

There is a lag of good source materials, realia, and similar needs for the elementary grades. This void is slowly being filled. A number of companies are developing historical-artifacts kits. Unfortunately, purchase price and the cost of keeping the kit in good repair are usually high. One program which may get costs down in the future is operating out of the children's Youth Museum in Cobb County, Georgia, where women volunteers build and repair kits for use in the Cobb County schools.

Another strategy identified earlier is the individualized learning package. A teacher in DeKalb County, Georgia, uses this device to make the life of a Civil War soldier take on real meaning to her seventh-grade students.

AN INDIVIDUALIZED LEARNING PACKAGE — A SOLDIER'S LIFE IN THE CIVIL WAR[6]

Objective

This is an Individualized Learning Package (ILP), about the experiences of the men who fought during the War Between the States. There are many interesting things to learn about these men. Because times have changed and because most of us have never been exposed to a real war, it is hard for us to imagine just what these men did go through. When you have completed the ILP you should be able to do **two** of the following:

1. Pretend that you are a doctor in the Confederate Army and you are tending the wounded after the battle of Gettysburg. Describe your experiences as a doctor. Be sure to explain usual medical procedure in the army, medical kits or instruments (and availability of these), medical problems other than wounds. Give statistics if possible. You may also be interested in finding out what happened to the men who could not be saved.

2. Pretend that you are a Union prisoner at Andersonville in the summer of 1864. Describe your experiences. Be sure to include the set-up of the camp, provisions, food, shelter, sanitary complications, medical care, diseases, and other features of life. Be sure to use some statistics also.

3. Pretend you are a soldier in the Confederate Army. The war is almost over and before you go home, your commander has asked you to write some

[6] Written Winter, 1971, by Penny McNeely, graduate student, Georgia State University, whom the authors thank.

memoirs from the diary you have written in daily. Write what an average soldier's life was like. Feel free, however, to include unusual as well as typical experiences of a soldier; but don't let your imagination take the upper hand. Keep it in line with your readings and observation.

How to Complete This Project
Use the library at your convenience, but this cannot be your only source. You must use at least three of the following:

1. Museums around the Atlanta area. You can visit these, observe artifacts, take photos, draw pictures.
    a. Cyclorama and Museum—Grant Park.
    b. Confederate Museum—Stone Mountain.
    c. Kennesaw Mountain Museum.
    d. Andersonville—near Albany, Georgia.
    e. State Archives—Atlanta Museum.
    f. Atlanta Historical Society.
2. Historical societies. Write or call.
    a. Atlanta Historical Society
    b. Georgia Historical Society
    c. Daughters of the Confederacy
3. State Archives for old letters and documents.
4. Any source in the classroom.

A learning game developed by two Temple University students illustrates another way to have children discover how their community has changed, progressed, and yet remained somewhat stable in certain respects.

A LEARNING GAME—A KEY TO TWO CITIES[7]
Grade Level: Fourth and fifth grades.
Structural Concepts: Historical Continuity and Historical Change. (We feel these **two** concepts are equally represented here.)

Generalizations
1. Elements of human societies of the past influence those of the present.
2. Although aspects of the past are present in modern society, many modifications or changes have been instituted.

Behavioral Objectives
1. The children will perceive and announce that the two cities are Philadelphia past and Philadelphia present.

---

[7] Written Fall, 1969, by Helene Ansel and Terry Kleitman, whom the authors thank.

2. The children will explain their answer by telling that they reached their conclusion by noticing that one city was older than the other, but that certain attributes were the same.

Description

1. This simulation requires a game board in the shape of a key, and one die.

2. The game is entitled: "Key to Two Cities."

3. The path of the board consists of clues in a sequence ranging from least revealing to more obvious.

4. The types of clues include: information about City 1 alone, information about City 2 alone, information that applies to both cities, and comparative or correlated information about each city.

5. The game is played by four individuals or four groups, at the discretion of the teacher. If the class is divided into four playing groups, children may see the value in cooperative thinking and the general sharing of ideas. If the game is played on an individual basis, it may serve as a valuable enrichment activity.

6. The "winner" of the game will receive a replica of a key to represent the fact that (he/they) successfully "unlocked" the "key" or main ideas leading to the discovery of the names of the cities.

Rules

1. Each player, or a representative of each playing group, will throw a die and move accordingly.

2. Each player (group) will land on spaces which will contain clues or directions to follow.

3. Players may use any sources found in the classroom. These may include the encyclopedia, textbooks, or trade books about Philadelphia which may be inconspicuously left on the shelves with other classroom books.

4. Players must remain silent until they reach the end of the game, at which time they can make a guess as to the names of the cities.

5. After announcing the names of the cities, the player or group who has done so should explain how the conclusion was reached. A general discussion involving all players should follow to insure that everyone has an idea of the generalizations involved.

6. If a player reaches the end of the game without knowing the answer, or guesses incorrectly, he is out of the game. The game continues with the remaining players.

7. If the game ends without any players knowing the names of the cities, all players or groups of players will initiate a discussion and general sharing of clues. If this is unsuccessful, the teacher will lead a discussion with provocative, structured questions using the children's ideas as a basis.

Evaluation

This simulation game does not necessarily have to involve Philadelphia. We chose this topic because it is relevant to children in the Philadelphia Public Schools and for the chosen grade level. The game may be changed for use in other classrooms with other cities. The use of the simulation game may be extended by programming the game for a different topic.

Sequence of Clues

1. This city won an award three times for being the cleanest city in the country. (modern Philadelphia)

2. This city is called "The City of Homes." (old Philadelphia)

3. This city is the first to make ice-cream. (old Philadelphia)

4. The fourth United States Mint opened in this city. (modern Philadelphia)

5. The English, Germans, Swedes, Finns, Irish, and Dutch were early settlers in both of these cities. (both Philadelphias)

6. This city is a leading center in the Eastern United States of manufacturing, shipping, finance, and culture. (modern Philadelphia)

7. Both cities are located in states which make up the Middle Atlantic states. (both)

8. To raise money to have the streets in one city paved, chances are sold. (old Philadelphia) The Department of Streets takes care of all maintenance work in the other city. (modern Philadelphia)

9. This city has one of the largest seaports in the country, ranking second only to New York. (modern Philadelphia)

10. Both cities are located in the northeastern United States. (both)

11. This city and New York are the two largest cities in the United States. (old Philadelphia)

12. The population of this city is over 2,000,000. (modern Philadelphia)

13. The state in which this city is located has the third highest amount of electoral votes. (modern Philadelphia)

14. This city has a sheriff. (old Philadelphia)

15. High Street, a main street in this city, is 100 feet wide. (old Philadelphia)

16. Oil lamps are on street corners. (old Philadelphia)

17. Both cities are located near the Delaware River. (both)

18. A Quaker School is built in this city. (old Philadelphia)

19. Steam-driven cars are a means of transportation in this city. (old Philadelphia) Cars with seat belts and headrests are seen everywhere in this city. (modern Philadelphia)

20. The Area Code is 215. (modern Philadelphia)

21. There is a place of interest in this city where one may go and walk through a model of a human heart. (modern Philadelphia)

22. Gilbert Stuart, the famous painter, was born here. (old Philadelphia) Bill Cosby, the popular comedian, was born here. (modern Philadelphia)

23. There is a building in this city where patriots signed documents to free our country from England. (old Philadelphia) There is a building in this city which is surrounded by a mall and attracts many tourists. (modern Philadelphia)

24. Electric trolleys are used by many people to get to work. (old Philadelphia) Public transportation is supplied by SEPTA in this city. (modern Philadelphia)

25. A newspaper in this city is the "Cummings Telegraphic Evening Bulletin." (old Philadelphia) A newspaper in this city is the "Evening Bulletin." (modern Philadelphia)

STIMULATING INTERCULTURAL EXCHANGING

In the series of questions and content that follows, one student teacher has set forth some of the social-science-related questions that might be explored in a study of India, as well as some activities that she felt would stimulate thinking about a world far removed in space and culture from her Philadelphia classroom. The questions and content (answers) are arranged under social-science headings. They are presented in this book as a guide to the teacher in the selection and construction of concept-based activities, not as the direct basis for teaching. The children's bibliography and the lists of media materials for teachers are directly useful. An excellent further source, particularly for a list of Indian children's books, is *A Guide to Indian Books for Use in American Schools*, obtainable by writing to Dr. Henry Ferguson, Box 277, Thompson, Connecticut 06277. An outstanding artifact kit is also available through Inter-Culture Associates at the same address. Other items for artifact kits can be assembled through writing to the Indian Embassy, 2107 Massachusetts Avenue, N.W., Washington, D.C. 20008. Most major cities have shops which sell items from India.

Readers may recognize that the level of the questions raised and answered by the contributor-teacher is principally in the factual-translation range. Despite much research, her work has not achieved conceptualization of the diverse elements of Indian culture in a manner that offers high-level learning situations to her pupils. For most teachers, this kind of difficulty (limited acquaintance with societal conditions within a diverse and rapidly changing culture), coupled with the limited experiential base their children will no doubt possess, sets up a major dilemma: though attention to common sociological-anthropological understanding may be helpful, such studies, to be effective, must be supported by strongly motivating materials and equipment (like the artifact kits mentioned above).

The activities items that follow the questions and content generally focus on higher-level learning activities. Their use would quite likely increase the chances that youngsters would retain some of the factual information provided by the teacher.

QUESTIONS FOR AN INTERCULTURAL UNDERSTANDING — INDIA[8]

Geography Questions

1. What climatic problems do the people of India have?
2. What problems do Indian farmers have along with climatic problems?
3. How do rivers and summer monsoons fail the farmer?
4. What are some of India's natural-resource problems?

Content

1. In the plains, season rhythms dominate life of the people. Cold weather from November to February; hot from April to June. Near the end of June, monsoons transform dry, parched land to green.

2. Farmers have crop failure, poor equipment, and fluctuating markets.

3. Many rivers dry up during periods of little rainfall. Monsoons cause either too much rain or too little.

4. Most natural resources are not used. Fertile soil (the greatest resource), coal, and iron are the most important. India also has petroleum, bauxite, manganese, chromite, copper, gold, diamonds, forests, cattle, and buffalo. Livestock resources are not intensively used; most Indians are vegetarians. Despite need, India has developed only about 3 percent of its water power.

Economics Questions

1. How are cattle an economic drain?
2. How do religious taboos prevent help for the farmer?
3. Has abolition of **zamindars** (great landowners) helped?
4. How has unemployment been affected?
5. Has education helped? How has it failed?
6. What has industry done to meet these needs?
7. What has the Planning Commission been doing since 1951?

Content

1. Millions of rupees come from state funds for building and maintaining facilities to keep cattle for religious reasons.

2. Hindus oppose irrigation and do not desire great incomes. They share hostile attitudes toward progress.

3. It has not been effective. Many peasants have become landless. People are usually indebted to village moneylenders.

4. The Planning Commission still sees little hope of diminution of unemployment.

---

[8] Written 1969 by Selma Kemeny Lucca, Temple University undergraduate, whom the authors thank.

5. Negligibly. Millions who have attended college are still out of work. Standards are rising very slowly.

6. Industry has increased but India is still very much dependent upon foreign aid for achievement of its plan target.

7. It has set up five-year plans of economic improvements to balance development in all parts of the country.

Sociology Questions

1. What races and ethnic groups live in India?
2. How does the caste system affect the way of life?
3. What have been the reasons for poor general health?
4. How does the culture of the urban businessman differ from that of the villager?
5. What factors have been breaking down caste distinctions?
6. What has been the state of the "outcaste"?
7. How are medical care, unemployment insurance, and social security provided for?
8. What is the most immediate internal problem?

Content

1. **Races:** Caucasians, including Indo-Aryans, Dravidians. Also Bhils, Nagas, Santals, and Todas (these tribesmen make up 7 percent). There are small groups of Arabs, Jews, and Turks. **Religions:** Hinduism (Brahamaism), Sikhism, Christianity, Buddhism and Islam.

2. Religion is a way of life governing the whole scheme of living. It affects health, clothing, food, and occupation.

3. Famine, poor diet, unhealthful living conditions.

4. The villager lives with the customs of old; the city businessman dresses in western clothes, is breaking down many caste rules, lives in modern American-European style.

5. Universal enfranchisement, state-supported education, economic development, and increasing urbanization are breaking down caste.

6. An "outcaste" may make his way to a large city and possibly find work, but can never have a normal family life and has no cushion to support him when he is old.

7. This kind of care is provided by the Indian family and caste.

8. Securing sufficient food for the population is most pressing problem.

Political-Science Questions

1. What is the position of the Congress Party?
2. What are Indira Ghandi's attitudes towards equality?
3. How is Indian government similar to that of Britain and United States?
4. What is the government doing in regard to education today?

5. How is the Proclamation of Emergency a loophole in government?

6. What are the problems of equality for all?

Content

1. The Congress Party has been the political party with practically no opposition and has been running the government since 1950.

2. Indira Ghandi is following her father's (Jawaharlal Nehru) ideas in trying to promote equality for all and wants to make India a secular nation, but is not above illegal means in order to stay in power.

3. The Indian government structure shares features with the United States and Britain but has built-in loyalties to religion.

4. Free and compulsory education for all; a staggering task even if the economy were greatly developed. There is a lack of funds and there are many, many languages.

5. In case of emergency, the head of state has power over the Constitution for two months.

6. Equality is impossible with the present caste system, although in April, 1969, for the first time a Hindu priest was arrested for discrimination. This was done to set a precedent.

Developmental Activities

1. Locate India on a map and share known information or information on references.

2. Make a scrapbook on life and problems in India.

3. Set up a card file on facts of education, economics, population, government plans, etc.

4. Write letters for specific information on India.

5. See films, filmstrips, slides, TV programs, exhibits, or displays available.

6. Study maps, globes and atlases. These skills are not learned separately, but along with working out problems.

7. Interview community experts on poverty.

8. Collect news articles, pictures, maps, graphs, objects relating to Indian problems of people.

9. Learn songs, games, rhythmic expression, folk dances — only to create mood and feeling, not as an end in itself.

10. Record information on tapes, charts, graphs, maps, diagrams in relation to study going on.

11. Appraise information by checking one source against another.

12. Build a diorama on a living problem.

13. Conduct class panel discussions, debates, forums, and round tables.

14. Write descriptive statements, classroom newspaper articles, stories, and playlets that are meaningful, with respect to social problems.

15. Prepare charts on population, education progress, economic progress.

16. Make time lines, tables, and diagrams of development along same lines as in the preceding activity.

17. Discuss feelings and how poverty conditions can lead to aggression.

18. Role playing is very important. Act out various social-problem roles.

19. Arrange displays, bulletin boards, pictures in sequence, exhibits, or files of related materials.

20. Make up a chart on "How Are Indian Children Like Us?" or "How Are They Different?"

21. Draw cartoons, murals, or posters about feelings at election time, applying for jobs, school children from various areas, or other problems.

22. Model objects out of clay, papier-maché, or other material to be used in plays or other meaningful events.

23. Dramatize or pantomime events, activities, processes in government or education. (Example: a mock election)

24. Construct objects, models, puppets, if these relate to discussions.

25. Create original rhymes, stories, poems, songs, dances.

26. Interpret moods and feelings through dramatics, singing, or playing instruments, in order to help clarify values.

27. Make up crossword puzzle using terms in study such as:

communal	zamindars	prejudice
regional	poverty	discrimination
castes	republic	religion
sari	maharashtra	ostracism

28. Collect travel folders and give simulated guided tours.

29. Construct a model of village and a city in India so as to compare.

30. Have a panel of students interview a native (one of the children).

31. Present a fashion show of village dress and city dress.

32. Write a report on Ghandi, Nehru, Bhave, or some other historical or important figure.

33. Psychological activities are very important and make children aware of personal opinions and feelings as possible sources of error and bias influencing interpretations. These would be value-clarifying experiences. One example would be writing the characteristics of two or three important figures from different sections of the country and discussing how each might feel about a particular issue.

34. Play a game called "Look It Up." Each child uses a different source of information. Ask each child to report in class; compare and note differences. Discuss why there were differences.

35. Divide the class into two groups; one high caste and one outcaste or untouchable. List various experiences such as applying for a job and exploitation by businessmen. Elicit reactions from both groups.

Culminating Activities

1. A visitors' day could be planned during which the class could exhibit the things they have made (murals, cartoons, maps, charts, posters, models, other).

2. Prepare a simulated trip to India, including visits to schools, villages, and farms. Certain students can act as guides, others as tourists, and others as natives.

3. Take a field trip to see a museum exhibit on India, or an exhibit at an art museum which pertains to life in India.

4. Present a play on a social problem written, directed, and produced by the class, for the whole school.

5. Compile a file in which all the information is presented in capsule form on index cards, for further use by other classes.

6. With the cooperation of several sets of parents, the class could go out to dinner at an Indian restaurant and sample a typical Indian meal.

Children's Bibliography

Belgrave & Hart. **Children's Stories from Indian Legends.** London: Raphael Tuck & Sons, n.d.

Bethers, Ray. **Rivers of Adventure.** New York: Hastings House, 1960.

Bhattacharya, Bhabani. **Music for Mahini.** New York, Crown Publishers, 1960.

Bothwell, Jean. **Story of India.** New York: Harcourt, Brace and Co., 1952.

Bothwell, Jean. **Ring of Fate.** New York: Harcourt, Brace and Co., 1959.

Bothwell, Jean. **Omen for a Princess.** New York: Abelard-Schuman, 1963.

Bowles, Cynthia. **At Home in India.** New York: Harcourt, Brace and Co., 1956.

Caldwell, John C. **Let's Visit India.** New York: John Day Co., 1960.

Collins, Ruth F. **Krishna and the White Elephant.** New York: Henry Z. Walck, 1961.

Davis, Caroline. **Jungle Child.** New York: Viking Press, 1960.

Eaton, Jeanette. **Fighter without a Sword.** New York: William Morrow and Co., 1960.

Fairservis, Walter A., Jr. **India.** Cleveland: World Publishing Co., 1961.

Falkner, Edward. **Games, Ancient and Oriental and How to Play Them.** New York: Dover Publications, 1961.

Friess, Horace L. **Non-Christian Religions.** New York: Grosset and Dunlap, 1963.

Guthrie, Anne. **Madam Ambassador.** New York: Harcourt, Brace and World, 1962.

Hazeltine, Alice I. **Hero Tales from Many Lands.** New York: Abingdon Press, 1961.

Katz, Elizabeth. **India in Pictures.** New York: Sterling Publishing Co., 1962.

Keene, Frances W. **Fun Around the World.** New York: Seahorse Press, 1955.

Films
Available from Information Service of India, Film Section, 2107 Massachusetts Ave., N.W., Washington, D.C. 20008. Book four weeks in advance. All are shipped express collect.

Saga of Progress. 16mm, sound, 15 minutes. Shows achievements of the Five Year Plans of India. Shows major projects set up under the planned economic development of the country.

Public Schools of India. 16mm, sound, 10 minutes. Describes public schools of India and shows a number of schools in various parts of the country.

Man on the Land. 16 mm, sound, 30 minutes. Shows that backbone of India is its farmers (or peasants). Their way of life, their hardships and their expectations are seen in the everyday life of one cultivator, Shanker.

Seven Hundred Thousand Villages. 1.6 mm, sound, 30 minutes. Shows that centuries of customs and traditions, which held each of the Indian villages as isolated units, are slowly being broken down as the Indian people begin to look outward.

Silent Revolution. 16 mm, sound, 15 minutes. Gives a good picture of life in a village in the Punjab (India) and explains the role of community development plans to improve the lot of the villagers.

Saga of Service. 16 mm, sound, 11 minutes. Shows the life of a typical village teacher, his devotion to his work, and how he trains a truant boy to become a worthy citizen.

Songs of Bengal. 16 mm, sound, 11 minutes. This film captures the rhythm and pulse of life in a riverside village of Bengal.

This Is Our India. Full color, 16 mm, sound, 9 minutes. By means of animation and diagrams, presents some geographical and economic facts about India.

Vijyan Mandirs. 16 mm, sound, 17 minutes. Tells the story of Vijyan Mandirs set up by the Ministry of Scientific Research and Cultural Affairs in Indian villages to bring the benefits of science to the rural population.

Village and Women. 16 mm, sound, 25 minutes. Portrays the very important role women have been playing and continue to play in India's community projects.

Free Materials — Sources
1. Government of India Tourist Office, 19 E. Forty-ninth St., New York, N.Y. 10017.

2. Information Service of India, 2107 Massachusetts Ave., N.W., Washington, D.C. 20008. General information, booklets, films, tapes, photographs.

Inexpensive Materials — Sources
Basic Data on the Economy of India. Government Printing Office, 1961, 15 cents.

Economic Developments in India. Government Printing Office, 1961.
India Educational Data, 1960. U.S. Office of Education. Free for single copy.
India. Foreign Policy Association, 345 East 46th St., New York, 1961; 32 cents.
For grades 4-6.

SIMILARITIES AND DIFFERENCES AS EXCHANGING

An interesting approach to stimulating universal cultural exchange is presented in the following individualized learning package.

AN INDIVIDUAL LEARNING PACKAGE— DIFFERENCES AND COMMUNICATION[9]

This is an ILP about differences and similarities in people, their skin colors and clothing. Many times communication among people is interrupted because the members of society are prejudiced by a person's skin color or dress. When you have completed these activities, you should be able to do the following assignments.

Objectives
1. Describe what you see through colored goggles: how things change; in what ways they are the same.
2. Paint a mural of boys and girls of different skin color, wearing different kinds of clothing.
3. Write a story about yourself and a friend in the mural who appears to be different from you.
4. Describe who you would be if your skin color and clothes were different.
5. Pretend that you are a world leader. What would you say to people about skin color and appearance? How would you prevent misunderstandings among people of different races?

How to Complete the Objectives
All materials needed for completion of these activities will be assembled in a Goggles Kit. The children make the goggles using wire, pipe cleaners, glue, and several colors of cellophane. The construction will be most effectively completed by children working in small groups.
1. While wearing goggles of different colors, look at the people around you. Describe them as they appear through the goggles. How do you feel toward them as you look at them through the different colors?
2. Look at yourself through the goggles, using a large mirror. Describe how you appear and how you feel about what you see.

[9] Written Winter 1971 by Carole Dudley, graduate assistant, Georgia State University, whom the authors thank.

3. State some of the things that never change even though you are wearing the goggles. Describe what seemed to be different. What changes — the people, or the colors of the goggles?

4. Dress in different outfits. What changes as you wear different costumes? What appears to change?

5. Look through goggles at yourself and/or your friends wearing costumes. What changes — the people, the clothes, or the goggles? What appears to remain the same? What appears to be different? How do you feel about what you see?

6. Look up in an encyclopedia, text books, and especially in your library the following words: pigment, skin, carotene, light, color, color wheel, prism, clothing, costumes. Most of these words will be listed headings in the card catalog.

MAN AND HIS PHYSICAL ENVIRONMENT — GEOGRAPHIC-SKILL EXCHANGING

A few ideas regarding development of map and globe skills will be presented here. It is important to remember that such skills should be taught relationally, that is, as part of ongoing experiences. A teacher should ask himself, "What skills are needed to do the things in this unit?" *not* "I want to teach these and those skills, so we'll study the following unit and do the following things."

The key ideas of map- and globe-skill development involve the constructs of distance, scale, direction, and symbolization. Skills in these areas are directly related to ability to think abstractly. For example, a young child usually thinks in three-dimensional terms; a two-dimensional map confuses him. Symbols for him are learned through touching (see in Chapter 4 A Plan of Instruction — Space). Later he can move to concrete two-dimensional symbols, then to semiabstract symbols, and finally to symbols which do not remotely resemble that which they represent. (An example is the use of color on certain maps.)

Later elementary-school experiences in mapping should help the child to integrate and utilize the various types of maps available to him in his study of a particular location.

After a study of Mexico with his sixth-grade class, one of the authors of this text had his students view several different maps of countries in Central America and graphic charts of data concerning them. From these, the children made observations; they also formed hypotheses to explain or enlarge on the observations. Both were recorded. Then the children were asked to read books and other material about the countries in order to verify or revise their hypotheses.

NOTES ON A MAP STUDY — CENTRAL AMERICA

Directions to Students

Look at political, land-surface, rainfall, population, and occupation maps of (countries). Make observations, and then make hypotheses based on the observations.

Observations and Hypotheses of Students

British Honduras — Observations: "It receives over 80 inches of rainfall except for the top corner. Almost all of the land is forest. The population is about all under 10 per square mile. It is land that is not far above sea level. The products are furniture and paper." **Hypothesis:** "The problems might be labor and transportation."

Guatemala — Observations: "It has lots of agriculture, some livestock ranching, a little unused land, and fishing. Over half is 20,000 feet above sea level. Manufacturing center in the middle of the country. One-third (N.E.) receives 80 inches of rain; other two-thirds receives 40-80 inches. One-third (S.W.) has 125-250 people per square mile; one-third (N.E.) has under 2; one-third (S.W.) has 25 to 125." **Hypotheses:** "The northeast part is unused because of a jungle. Transportation is a problem."

El Salvador — Observations: "Occupations of livestock ranching, agriculture, forest and fishing. Most receives 40-80 inches of rain. Population is 25-125 people per square mile. Country contains a manufacturing center. Border of 25 miles is plain; rest is mountain." **Hypotheses:** "Mountains might prevent agriculture. Good fishing. Mountains might make the climate cool."

Honduras — Observations: "N.E. receives over 80 inches of rain. The remainder receives 40-80 inches. N.E. plateau (flat) or lowland. The remainder is mountainous. N.E. has under 2 people per square mile. Middle has 2-25. South has 25-125. Very little part. Eastern part is agriculture. Central unused land. West is livestock." **Hypotheses:** "N.E. is lowly populated because rainfall is heavy and it is a swampy land. Bananas grow there. One product is livestock."

Nicaragua — Observations: "One-half of it's plains (coastal parts). Middle is mountainous bordered by plateaus. Population 2-25 N.E. and central. Near the capital is 25-125. N.W. 20-40 inches of rain. Rest 40-80 inches of rainfall. Central unused. East agriculture. West livestock." **Hypotheses:** "Very similar to Honduras. West land is jungle area. Good fishing."

Costa Rica — Observations: "Border along the Pacific receives 40-80 inches. Rest receives over 80 inches of rain. N.E. part has much unused land. N.W. livestock. Mining (central) and agriculture. Population 2-25 in all areas except the central and south part along the Pacific. Mostly plateau area." **Hypotheses:** "Fishing on western coast is good. A poor country because of great amount of unused land."

Panama — Observations: "It has a mining center. Receives over 80 inches of rain. Population is 2-25 in most areas except peninsula in Pacific and near Canal Zone. Part nearest South America agriculture. Part nearest Costa Rica is unused land. Fishing is good. The land surface is mostly lowland except near Costa Rica." **Hypotheses:** "Can raise livestock because land is low. Mountainous land is unused land. Warm wind currents blow across onto the land. United States has some effect on Panama because of the canal."

Ideas for Further Activities
Compare to [state or locality in which you teach] with respect to rainfall, land surface, and population.

Do one country in class with students. Have them choose another country and use as many different kinds of maps as they can to find out something about the country.

Type up charts with columns for: Observations. Related Factors. Hypotheses.

Hoped-for Outcome
Careful observations.

Discovered need for accurate descriptions.

Discovered relationships among various factors (examples: land use and rainfall).

Use of information to make hypotheses about the country (making the hypotheses should create a desire to find whether it is correct or not).

Another technique, beautifully described in the textbook from which the following map exercise is adapted, is highly recommended. Here a teacher has the children construct a creative map in which certain mapping skills as well as knowledge of landform types must be utilized. It serves the teacher as both an excellent teaching and diagnostic tool.

CREATIVE MAP EXERCISE—UPPER ELEMENTARY[10]
Behavioral Objective
The child will demonstrate map skills related to direction, distance, and symbolization at some level of abstraction (pictorial, semipictorial, abstract) through construction and use of a map.

Materials
1. Crayons and drawing paper for each child.
2. Pictures, photos, three-dimensional models, atlases, dictionaries.

Procedures
1. Ask questions in which children relate to the type of map they are to make. "Have you ever traveled to [some place]? What did you like/dislike

[10] Based upon James and Carpe (1968), 115-120.

about this place? Have you ever tried to picture a land where everything was as you would like it to be? A place where you might find beautiful sunny beaches and rugged mountains? Where people would have lots of room to live?"

2. Tell the children to plan a country like this. This country will be an island. Develop the concept of "island." "We are going to have some fun making your island country. You may name your island anything you wish, and you may make it any shape. Let's see how much originality you have in working out a clever map." (Suggest name "Animal Isle," for example, and make the island in shape of an animal head; or "Flower Island," and give flower names to all of the surface features, water bodies, and the like.)

3. The children can make both physical-political and land-use maps. Have the children put the following (suggestive) items on their physical-political map:

a desert	a lake	a peninsula
five cities	mountains	a bay
a railroad	a direction indication	a swift river
a scale of miles	plains	a meandering river
a map key	a cape	a delta

4. After the map is constructed, ask the children questions like:
a. How far is city A from mountain X?
b. What direction am I going from bay Y to city B?
c. What does this symbol (on map) mean?
5. Children can try to read maps made by other children.

The Lesson could be extended to having the children write a brief description of their country for **The World Almanac** and also by making a travel folder of their country.

Grade Levels for Globe and Mapping Skills

The following list, based on Joyce (1964) will be helpful to teachers as a guide to the globe and mapping skills that children may have or may develop in grades 4, 5, and 6.

GRADE FOUR

Using a globe, discovers that east-west lines are parallel to the equator, to each other, and encircle the earth.

Orients street maps of his local community to aerial photographs of the same area.

When comparing different kinds of maps, understands that north is not always at the top of the map—it depends on the location of the north pole. (For example, north would lie at the top of a Mercator projection, but would lie at the center of a polar projection.)

Locates north, south, east, west, northeast, northwest, southeast, and southwest on maps and globes.

Understands that distance along the ground can be calculated in terms of feet, yards, miles, etc.

Measures and records distances in terms of inches, feet, yards, miles, etc.

Using a globe, locates the four hemispheres and the equator.

Studies simplified maps of his local community and makes such observations as: (1) Gas stations are generally located at busy intersections. (2) Schools are generally located in residential sections of town. (3) Shopping districts are generally located in main thoroughfares and are usually close to public transportation. (4) Many streets are laid out in north-south and east-west directions.

Using a map of the world, locates the equator, the poles, rivers, lakes, islands, peninsulas, the arctic and antarctic circles, and north-south and east-west lines.

Compiles a list of places visited during trips taken by his class and by his family and then, using a road map, locates these places with reference to each other and to such natural features as lakes, rivers, mountains, etc.

Describes the location of his home community in relation to natural and man-made features of the environment, to transportation routes and facilities, and to nearby communities.

Describes the location of communities and nations studied in class in relation to natural and man-made features of the environment, to transportation routes and facilities, and to other communities and nations.

Locates cities, countries, and continents studied in relation to the poles, equator, and arctic and antarctic circles; discovers interrelationships among location and climate, weather and terrain.

Using maps, locates important cities, countries, and continents studied in class; discovers interrelationships that exist among location and commerce, transportation routes, and the like.

Using maps, identifies the more complex semipictorial symbols which depict falls and rapids, deltas, dams, canals, deserts, swamps, and other features.

Draws a map of his local community, using either conventional semipictorial symbols or his own symbols to represent natural and man-made features.

Compares different kinds of maps with regard to the use of color; discovers that color may be used to designate elevations of land or the depth of water, to represent political boundaries, and to show rainfall, population, temperature, and other similar data.

Compares different kinds of maps with regard to keys or legends; recognizes that keys or legends indicate the meaning of symbols used on maps but that the same symbol may mean quite different things on different maps.

Compares text descriptions in social studies textbooks with accompanying maps.

Uses maps and globes to secure specific information; selects the best map for the purpose at hand.

Reads a map and infers the relationships suggested by the data shown. (For example, the factors determining the location of cities, manufacturing centers, crop and livestock production, political boundaries, recreation facilities.)

GRADE FIVE

Uses the terms **northeast, northwest, southeast, southwest,** in referring to directions in his classroom and around the neighborhood.

Reads a compass to find directions.

Uses the terms **upstream** and **downstream** to show that he knows that **upstream** means going toward the source of the stream and against the current, and that **downstream** means going toward the mouth of the stream and with the current.

Uses the north arrow on maps as a directional finder.

Estimates and then measures the dimensions of his classroom; draws a floor plan of the classroom to scale, with all measurements in inches and/or feet.

Estimates and then measures the dimensions of his school yard; draws a map of the school yard to scale, with all measurements in feet or yards.

Estimates and then computes ground distances between the same two points on maps of identical areas, but of different scale. Compares the results.

Estimates and then computes air distances between various places on the globe, using the great-circle routes.

Compares straight-line ground distances computed from a map with air distances computed from a globe.

Estimates and then computes the length of time needed in traveling between locations shown on a road map.

Estimates and then computes the amount of time needed in traveling between locations shown on a road map with regard to the mode of transportation used, such as walking, riding a bicycle, riding in a car, riding in an airplane.

Estimates and then computes the amount of time needed in traveling between various parts of the world with regard to the mode of transportation used, such as an airplane, a ship, a space capsule.

Using the equator as a point of reference, locates the low, high, and middle latitudes on a globe and world map.

Uses a number-and-letter grid for locating places on a road map.

Understands that the more north-south and east-west lines he has to work with, the more precisely he is able to locate places on maps and globes.

Locates time zones on maps and globes; explains how time at any given moment will vary from zone to zone.

Recognizes the differences between various map projections, and notes the distortion involved in any representation of the earth, other than that of a globe.

Using maps and globes, computes air and ground distances between important cities of the world; discovers interrelationships existing among distance and commerce, military strategy, etc.

Reads merged relief maps showing altitude and slope of terrain, as indicated by gradual shading or merging of colors.

GRADE SIX

Constructs maps of his local community by laying out directional lines with the aid of a compass.

Uses north-south and east-west lines in locating directions on maps and globes.

Estimates and then measures distances around his home neighborhood; draws a map of the neighborhood to scale, with all measurements in yards, blocks, or miles.

Estimates and then computes ground distances between the same two points on a globe, using latitude as a basis for measurement.

When given the latitude and longitude or a place, he can show its approximate location on a map or globe.

Reads distribution maps containing data relative to rainfall, crop production, population, transportation facilities, and the like; understands the use of dots, lines, and shading.

SUMMARY

This chapter has attempted to broadly outline a content-method approach in which the construct of "exchange" could be explored from interpersonal to intercultural dimensions. The content has been structured along the guidelines established in the model and foundations chapters (Chapters 1 through 3). Further examples of existing media materials available to the teacher working with youngsters in the structured-independent stage of development will be presented in Chapter 9.

CHAPTER 7

The Independent-Exploratory Stage of Psycho-Social Development

Action is the end product of social study. Instructional techniques and materials discussed to this point were designed to provide a sound base, a frame of reference, for personal and/or group action.

Each individual's frame of reference is influenced by his system of values and his competency in specific skill areas. Factors impinging on the formation of an individual's personal value system have been touched on, and the particular skills of inquiry have been alluded to in Chapters 4, 5, and 6. This chapter seeks to polish these concepts by focusing on movement from an "I" orientation to a "we" orientation.

THEME AND JUSTIFICATION

Social study assumes the existence of an aggregate of people sharing defined spaces for specific reasons. Ideally this association of people is voluntary; that is, they have come together to accomplish common objectives. Clearly, society is a means to an end. Again, ideally, each individual in a society submits himself and his personal goals to the

221

wishes of the majority—cooperation becomes the key concept. The conflict engendered by differing personal aspirations is submerged in a compromise-consensus goal orientation.

Conflict, however, does not disappear from the scene in the real world. It often moves from individual to a larger arena of societal conflict. International and civil wars are the most obvious examples of this transfer of conflict from the individual to larger groups. (It may be useful to consult your local telephone directory to identify "societies" located in your area. What is their purpose? What is the result of overlapping purpose? Are there other groups in your area which you might examine?) The annals of history are replete with evidence of conflict. Conflict as a key concept in social study underlies the material in Chapters 4, 5, and 6.

In pressing for the establishment of a unique personal frame of reference designed to support action, which implies as many frames as people, have we authors advocated the development of a situation designed to continue the violent conflict reflected in contemporary history? Or have we provided a strategy by which individuals can be prepared to confront conflict situations and to resolve them in a socially as well as personally satisfactory manner?

A set of personal priorities emerges as the child participates in the trade-offs associated with the exchanging function discussed in Chapter 6. Teachers as well as other persons offer alternative courses of action in exchange for a demonstration of interest, commitment, loyalty, responsibility, or some other desired quality. The opportunity for choice may be limited: "Would you like to eat squash for dinner or go to bed hungry?" It may be relatively more open, as in a classroom structured along the model of a British infant school: "You have two hours to do the activity which interests you." Each party to the exchange must both give and take.

Exchanging was a distinct departure from the emphasis on the governing function in Chapter 5. During the structured-dependent stage the major constraint on the person's choice resided in the individual or individuals who governed his actions. Typically they governed by defining consequences for actions. All that was required for action was awareness of consequence. Essentially, the child lived in a dichotomous life—to do or not to do.

Activities, materials, and teaching techniques described in this chapter form a potential basis in experience through which a person defines alternatives and chooses a course of action. Choice reflected in behavior indicates a system of priorities. Priorities in turn may be directly tied to the individual's values. Thus, our focus will be the process of *valuing*. We will structure our presentation to show the individual as one element in a system which includes other men as well as man-made societies, institutions, and other intangible artifacts. The presence, ideas, and actions of each element may effect all other elements in the system. Thus, the emphasis on the function of ecologizing.

SETTING AN AGE FOR ACTION

The model of psycho-social development presented here represents a marriage of a need theory and a theory of cognitive development presented in the social realm.

We have argued that children entering the elementary school are in general not ready to ecologize. That is, they are operating mostly from an egocentric frame of reference. The causes of this behavior are many and varied, but all focus on personal needs. If we accept the assumption that living in a social situation necessitates concern for others, we must nurture that concern. The outcome will be behaviors which show that the child perceives himself as one part of a large system. In addition, he will demonstrate awareness of the fact that just as actions by others affect him, his actions also affect others. We choose to label the function these behaviors fulfill ecologizing. But what is readiness for ecologizing? Readiness is summed up in the following assumptions:

For a person to function in an ecologizing manner:

1. The person's primary personal needs must be satisfied.
2. The individual must possess sufficient ego-strength (positive self-concept) to choose and act on the basis of personal priorities whether the choice or action is consistent with or in conflict with the choices or actions of the rest of society.
3. The person must be able to move cognitively from immediate stimulus to abstraction in a given situation.

Assumption 1: Needs Level

The essential significance of the taxonomy of needs is this: children who have unmet primary needs cannot be expected to function in a manner designed to meet higher needs. It is not a matter of playing the game poorly but rather of simply refusing to play at all. Hungry children do not understand questions of good citizenship! They are not on that needs level.

The following scenario from a real classroom may be helpful.

A LESSON IN CARING

A second-grade teacher in Bay City, Michigan, was concerned about her children's apparent lack of consideration for each other, for her as a teacher, school, and for the school facilities. She sought to use "Be Kind to Animals" Week as an entree to deal with caring. She prepared and carried out the sequence of activities described below.

One day the teacher arrived in class with a kitten and a bag of lollipops. She stated that she had found the kitten on the way to school, that it apparently had no home and was uncared for. Mrs. Lindow explained that since she had an infant daughter at home she could not care for the kitten. As a result she asked members of the class of 26 children to decide whether they wished to care for the kitten or not. Those who chose not to would receive a lollipop. The children were asked to write their choice and one or two sentences explaining it on a sheet of paper.

The class split, with 14 children electing to care for the kitten and 12 selecting the lollipop. What were the reasons why children selected lollipops? There was a range of reasoning and caring exhibited, but several stand out.

"My dad's allergic to furry animals."
"Because I don't feels good and my mum knows it."
"Because when I was a child a cat scratched me."

The children were allowed to care for the kitten during the next two weeks. During that time several of the lollipop group asked if they might help with the kitten. Mrs. Lindow accepted their request but reminded them that they had made a decision and would have to stand by it. An interesting individual effect was revealed as the "class bully" took a leadership role in planning and supervising the care of the kitten.

On Monday of the third week Mrs. Lindow's class was visited by Mr. Lindow and their baby daughter. Mrs. Lindow reviewed the process of decision-making used in the kitten incident. She pointed to the real choice the children were forced to make. Then she asked them to consider a new situation and to use the same process to make a pretend decision.

Referring to her baby, Mrs. Lindow asked the children to consider whether they would choose to care for the baby or to receive one of a list of material objects. Again the class chose and wrote brief reasons. This time the group split 25 to 1 in favor of caring for the child. It was not possible to analyze precisely why the choices were made. Undoubtedly, some children played a kind of word game where they gained by behaving in an expected manner.

However, one child voted for the "object." His reason — "There are six kids in my family and each one takes care of himself. Nobody takes care of me and I can't take care of somebody else. That's the way it is."

In this lesson the teacher made a decision regarding a personal value disposition. Her belief that caring is important led her to develop a learning experience in which the children in her class faced the question, "What do I care about?" The experience was based upon several assumptions:

1. The affective dimension of a child's education deserves specific planned attention.
2. The children and the teacher must trust each other before a lesson which focuses on feelings or values can be attempted.
3. The level of cognitive as well as affective development of preschool and primary-grade children makes them dependent upon the teacher to structure the learning situation.

This second-grade teacher had previously worked with the children in a straightforward open manner. Thus, she had established a trust relationship which enabled her to approach a question which has a very personal dimension. She had to consider the level at which each child was operating in order to design a successful lesson.

Further analysis of this lesson appears later in this section.

We can only speculate on the choice of the child who voted for the object. However, it seems clear that he was operating much more in the "I" realm than in the "we." Apparently his priorities of the moment were centered in the primary physiological-security realm which precluded movement to the love-esteem area.

Assumption 2: Cognitive Development

The second assumption operant in our notion of readiness for valuing activities involves cognitive development. Values were defined in Chapter 2 as being freely chosen from among alternatives after considering the consequences; further, these choices were acted upon consistently over a period of time and the individual felt good about his choices as well as consequent actions. It was noted that values are the epitome of constructs which shape behavior. Values thus are defined at an advanced level of abstraction. Other determinants of behavior such as attitudes, beliefs, and opinions approach values in degree of abstraction. We have argued consistently that children operating in the preoperational or concrete stages of cognitive development cannot deal with the abstractions that are values. The essential cognitive element requisite to valuing is the ability to extrapolate, that is, to see relationships between situations and to make the transfer from one to the other. Such transfer may be observed in a very basic way at the earliest stages of development. For example: The child becomes *aware* that certain foods "taste good" or that particular others make him feel good.

An important dimension of transfer required for valuing is *time*. (Reexamine the definition of value noting the reference, either stated or implied, to time.) A lesson involving the use of a piñata is illustrative. The lesson follows; thereafter, an account of experience in using it;

then an analysis of the learnings, affective and cognitive, in the preceding lesson in caring and in this piñata lesson in sharing.

A LESSON IN SHARING

Objectives

1. The children are presented with the problem of sharing and will state alternatives to the problem.
2. The children will describe their actions and feelings when being involved in a sharing situation (as either the person doing the sharing or the person receiving).

Materials

Piñata filled with candies, a few less than the number of children; stick.

Procedure

1. **Motivation:** Show the piñata and ask the class what they think it is. Let them guess what it is, but do not tell them it is a piñata until the story has been read. Tell the class it has something to do with birthdays. Then ask the class, How do you celebrate your birthdays? Following this, tell the children a story about children in another country where they use piñatas at their birthday parties.
2. Read the story, "Getting Ready for a Birthday," by Nina Millen, found in **Children and Their Homes around the World.**
3. Ask the following questions:

   a. What do you think would happen if Pablo's mother didn't put enough candy in the piñata?
   b. If everybody got a piece of candy except one little girl would you share your candy with her?
   c. Why would you share your candy?
   d. How would you feel if you shared your candy?
   e. How would the little girl feel if you shared the candy with her?
   f. How would you feel if you didn't share?
   g. How would the little girl feel if you didn't share with her?
   h. What do you think about sharing with people? Is it a nice thing to do?

4. **Evaluation:** Break the piñata and see whether the children will share.

In this piñata lesson as designed, the time component is relatively brief between the discussion and the experience to which the children can apply the discussion. But the interval can be made longer. If it is, will there be any effect on need-satisfaction behavior?

Two student teachers tried the piñata lesson with a group of children in an inner-city school in Philadelphia. On day one, the teachers talked with the children about the importance of sharing. They emphasized the interdependence of people living in a society, pointing to the sharing concept as a prerequisite for survival.

On day two, a piñata was hung in the classroom. The teachers had placed eleven pieces of licorice in the piñata. There were twenty-two children in the class. After reviewing some of the points made in the discussion on sharing, one of the children was blindfolded and the teachers stood back to observe.

The piñata was broken and the candy spilled out. In the scramble that followed the shortage of candy was immediately noticed. Most of the children made the transfer and began dividing their licorice and sharing. However, one little girl sat in the corner stuffing licorice into her mouth obviously unconcerned about the shortage involved. At this point she was challenged by another child in the class, who reprimanded her for failing to recall the importance of sharing. With that the girl took the licorice which remained and offered it to another child. (In a similar situation a boy challenged refused to share. His response was that he had not had anything to eat all day and was hungry.)

An analysis of children's reaction to the piñata lesson shows that they had transferred the understanding of sharing developed in a discussion session to a relatively informal partylike setting. The time factor remains relatively short. In addition, one might hypothesize that the children's behavior is not valuing at all but really an attempt to satisfy esteem needs by pleasing the teacher, or perhaps love or security needs by pleasing a classmate.

Since the number of alternatives open to the children is limited by the teacher the notion of free choice among alternatives fades. In truth we have presented the child a dichotomous situation. He chooses one path or the other.

The kitten and piñata lesson assume a low level of cognitive development and thus limit the number of variables which must be considered. Each lesson did, however, provide an opportunity to inquire into the situation. Thus:

Problems were identified: not enough candy.
Data were analyzed: most children were sharing; one was not.
Behavior was analyzed: Reference was made to sharing as discussed in a previous day's lesson.
Conclusions were reached: "We ought to share. The nonsharing individual is acting inappropriately."
Action was taken: The nonsharing child was challenged. One nonsharing child relented and shared. The other nonsharing child refused to share.

In these contrived situations children were asked to make a choice from two alternatives. The alternatives were either contradictory or complementary to their personal wants, which reflect priority of need fulfillment.

As a postscript to each lesson the children were asked to consider what they had done. The children were also asked to consider the effect of their choice both on their own life and that of others. The kitten lesson was followed by the questions and activities described below.

ANALYSIS

Why did you make the choice you did?

Would you make the same decision again?

How do you think the kitten feels towards those who took the lollipops?

How do you feel when someone has been nice to you?

How do you feel when someone has not been nice to you?

Why do you take care of animals?

Why do we feel we should help animals?

Why do we feed hungry animals?

Would you have made the same choice if it were a puppy? A rabbit? A rat?

What if it were a real baby? A sick person? An old person?

How do we know when we are doing the right thing? The wrong thing?

SYNTHESIS

Think about the many ways you can be nice to animals, the different things you can do for animals; then write about them.

Write about the different ways you can be nice to each other. Let us talk about the different ways we can be nice to each other. Write all you know about kindness. What is kindness?

Tell about or write an experience you have had with helping an animal or some kindness you did for someone. Discuss why you chose the lollipop instead of the kitten or why you chose to feed the kitten instead of eating a lollipop.

EVALUATION

To develop the idea that not everyone likes the same animals, have each child write about his favorite pet. Have them share their stories with each other.

Discuss the reasons why several of the children did not choose to feed the kitten. Approval or disapproval is not the important thing to be developed here, but rather that everyone has difference of opinions.

Why is it important to be kind to animals? How does it benefit us? Why is kindness to one another important? What if everyone in the world were kind to everyone else?

To the question, "What if everyone in the world showed kindness to everyone else?," these answers were given: "People would have more pets." "A lot of animals wouldn't be extinct." "It would be a nicer world." "The world would turn into the shape of a heart." "Everyone would have a lot more friends." "There would be no more wars." "People would live a lot longer." "There wouldn't be any burglars or strangers to worry about." "There would be no more fights." "There wouldn't be any more divorces and there would be a lot more weddings." "The churches would be full of people."

Later, when the children were told that the kitten really had a home and was not starved, these comments were made: "You were just fooling us." "No, she just wanted to see what we would do."

Combining the two elements—a dichotomous situation and an opportunity to choose—creates what might be called a needs lesson. By assigning the label "needs lesson" we clearly indicate that we do not expect the level of intellectual activity implied by the notion of a value lesson. This is a first step in applying concern for personal needs and awareness of cognitive development in the most significant dimension of social study.

THE REFLECTIVE DISPOSITION

Lest we authors be accused of advocating the moralizing we spoke against in Chapter 2, let us consider the question of dichotomous choice. Our first defense lies in the choice presented. Experience has shown that no matter how a lesson plan stacks the cards to produce a desired tendency, some children follow their own path; witness the piñata lesson.

Second, we argue that there are some attitudes, beliefs, opinions and/or values that we must nurture. One group of these has been labeled *procedural;* it includes such notions as taking turns and following directions. We also feel that there is general agreement on another set of values or priorities suggested by the goals of the National Council for the Social Studies and the Wyoming Social Studies Curriculum cited earlier. Among these are concern for the individual and the intelligent use of resources. In addition, we have set out in Chapter 1 a number of *personal, social,* and *cultural* behaviors as desirable terminal behaviors for elementary education. These reflect our personal commitment. Although we maintain that we must provide an open atmosphere in which children can make their own decisions we also claim the right to have a personal set of attitudes, beliefs, opinions and/or values. Where these are clearly consistent with the attitudes, beliefs, opinions and/or values reflected in the ideals of the community we serve, we accept the responsibility to nurture them in our students.

Note the use of the term "nurture." We do not suggest that children should be taught values in a moralizing sense; rather, that the environment can be structured to increase the probability that these so-called consensus values will be chosen. Even then it may be wrong to assume that a "valuing process" is operative. The child may be acting only to please the teacher in order to gain praise or to show love for the teacher. Recall that we are building readiness for valuing. The assumption is that as he develops the child's value constellation will evolve and that choices made to satisfy primary needs today in the early years may later transfer to other situations and emerge as true values. For example, the child exposed to the kitten lesson in grade 1 who chooses to care may later choose a career in health service. Caring could then be identified as a personal priority — a value.

Although we recognize the limitations of these need lessons, we maintain the importance of the choice involved. As teachers we must not only provide the opportunity to choose but must also be prepared to accept the choice the child makes. It is in this accepting that we begin to establish an atmosphere in the classroom conducive to the free exploration of ideas. We cannot replay the hand if the child chooses a path contrary to our own.

The children who resisted peer pressure in the kitten and piñata lessons felt the freedom to be different. Their personal worth had been established by teachers who made conscious efforts to develop ego strength, by adhering to the dictum that "children are people!" Acceptance of this generalization as a guide to action fosters establishment of a trust relationship between class members including the teacher. Praise and criticism are accepted as honest reactions to behavior given by people who respect and care about each other. The activities which we have described will not succeed in a classroom devoid of trust. Trust fosters the reflective disposition. A child's disposition or tendency to reflect upon alternatives, considering consequences and formulating a reasoned plan of action, fails if the child does not have the tools to accomplish the tasks involved. The task has been described as an inquiry by the student into his environment.

WHERE THE ACTION IS

As we return to the reality of the classroom, prepared to analyze various means of supporting student inquiry, let us recall that in Chapter 2 the description of a model of psycho-social development included a discussion of elements called cross-currents. These cross-currents included awareness, consequence, cause-effect, and values. Each plan of instruction or activity described in Chapters 4, 5, and 6 included these elements. Emphasis was correlated with the particular stage of development and function. This relationship is shown in this table:

Stage of Development	Function	Cross-Current
Initial-exploratory	Egoizing	Awareness
Structured-dependent	Governing	Consequence
Structured-independent	Exchanging	Cause-effect
Independent-exploratory	Ecologizing	Valuing

In the remainder of this chapter, instructional activities are considered with reference to the cross-current they tend to focus upon. The intent represented by the selection of these activities is to illustrate the student's movement toward the moment when he can be turned loose to pursue his personal interest, confident that he has the requisite skills and a well-founded frame of reference.

INSTRUCTIONAL ACTIVITIES FOCUSED ON AWARENESS

The first item presented is a plan of instruction dealing with attitudes toward individual differences, rejection, and ostracism; presumably it will heighten awareness in the students who take part in the instruction. It is followed by an individualized learning package (ILP) designed to heighten awareness in a different way. Individualized learning packages (ILP's) have been included in earlier chapters without discussion of their characteristics. Here, therefore, note that an individualized learning package is designed to enable students to work individually or in small groups toward a stated objective. Most ILP's can be typed on a single sheet of paper. They are then stored in the classroom in a place accessible to the students. Usually the student initiates the ILP; however, the teacher may include ILP's as integral parts of a plan of instruction. ILP's vary in time needed to complete them. They may require as little as one class period or as much as a week or more; the key is individual needs.

A PLAN OF INSTRUCTION — OSTRACISM
(A Strategy to develop empathy for and identification with individuals placed in a situation in which they are ostracized)

Behavioral Objectives
Given the opportunity to participate in the role-playing activity below, each student should be able to:

1. List some reasons why one person might avoid being around another person;
2. Explain whether or not the reasons listed justify avoiding association with another person;
3. Describe how one feels when he deliberately ostracizes another person;
4. Describe how one feels when others are deliberately ostracizing him;
5. State what he believes is a warranted generalization about how people feel in similar real situations.

How to Complete the Objective: Role-Playing Activity
Introduce the activity by interjecting the idea of a new student entering a class. The members of the class know nothing about him or her, but they hope that he or she will be worthy of their friendship.

Now propose the question: "What qualities might this student possess that would make him or her a desirable friend? An undesirable one? List both." Most likely, the class will name such things as intelligence, appearance, sportsmanship, behavior. (This list should be kept for later reference.)

After this work is complete, explain to the students that they are going to be this class for one day. Each of them will also have an opportunity to be the newcomer for one-third of the day. However, this new child does not possess the desirable qualities that they listed—only the undesirable ones. Therefore, he or she will not be their friend for this period of time. They are to avoid him or her completely.

To determine who is to be ostracized and the ones who are to do the ostracizing, and to allow everyone an opportunity to do both, a common attribute must be used—in this case, hair color. For the first third of the day, each student that has blonde hair will be the new student. Blonde will represent all the bad qualities listed. The other students will avoid all the blondes in the role-played class during this time.

The second third of the day, the blondes will join the black-haired people in ostracizing the students with brown hair. In the final third of the day, those people with black hair will be the undesirables and thus be avoided.

After each student has had the opportunity to participate in both roles, the class will then have a discussion concerning their feelings as they acted out these roles. Later the discussion will be extended to other children in real situations and how they feel when they are avoided.

Hopefully, each child will have met with some frustration during this activity—especially when he was ostracized through no fault of his own. If they do, then perhaps each of them will be able to look back at the lists they prepared and delete those qualities that children have little control over (intelligence, appearance, for example).

Evaluation

The immediate evaluation will be done by listening to the discussion and observing the students final lists. The teacher will be observing each child in his associations with others to really determine how effective the activity was.

Role-playing starts with a description of the specific roles involved. The outcomes which occur are not specified. Success in role-playing depends on the classroom atmosphere and the ego-strength of the participants. Role-playing may be appropriate in a wide range of situations. The open-ended aspect of this activity provides a relatively safe opportunity to create awareness of attitudes about self, others, institutions, and events.

The following ILP is based on the analysis of pictures. It could, however, provide a basis for role-playing. The activity is designed to develop awareness of the myriad learning experiences provided by non-school activities. The central ideas are that (1) we are all educators and (2) life is a continuous process of learning. Creating this dual awareness increases the probability that students will explore and value their own experiences.

AN INDIVIDUALIZED LEARNING PACKAGE—WAYS OF LEARNING

Objectives

This ILP is centered around three varied learning situations: a boy watching a shoe repairman, a girl reading a storybook with her father, and boys watching television. These are the materials.

By the end of this experience each student will demonstrate understanding that:

1. People learn from each other.
2. People can learn in many different situations.
3. People can learn by observing varied learning situations.
4. People can learn by comparing ways in which people learn and help others learn.

How to Complete the Objectives

1. Cut out of magazines pictures of people involved in learning situations.
2. Explain what you have learned best from the pictures you choose.
3. Answer the following questions about the picture of the shoemaker:

    a. What is the man doing?
    b. What is the boy learning about fixing shoes?
    c. Will the boy learn if the shoemaker does not speak? Why?
    d. Can he learn by just watching? What can he learn?

4. Answer the following questions about the picture of a little girl with the storybook.

    a. What is the girl doing?
    b. Who is teaching?
    c. Do people learn from books?
    d. Can they learn from any book?
    e. Do you like books?
    f. Does anyone read to you? Who?

5. Answer the following questions in relation to the picture of the boys watching television.

    a. What are the boys doing?
    b. What kind of program are they watching?
    c. Can people learn from television?
    d. Can they learn from any television program?

e. Can they learn more from some things than others? What could the boys be learning?

f. Could they learn the same things somewhere else?

6. Now answer the following questions about your own learning experiences.

a. Have you learned anything from watching television? What?

b. Have you ever watched someone work? Have you learned how he works?

c. Have you learned how to do it?

d. What could you learn from a picture?

e. What could you learn at home on a rainy day?

INSTRUCTIONAL ACTIVITIES FOCUSED ON CONSEQUENCE

Drug-Abuse Education

Drug abuse and its consequences represent one of the most pressing concerns of society. The age old use of artificial means to accomplish a desired state of euphoria has produced drug dependency in many forms. In the advanced technological societies of the twentieth century drugs have reached a degree of pervasiveness which commands urgent considered attention. Henry Thomas Van Dyke (1970) encapsulates the ubiquitous nature of drugs (From *Youth and the Drug Problem,* by Henry Thomas Van Dyke, © Copyright, 1970, by Ginn and Company. Used with permission).

John lived in a noisy, traffic-filled section of the city, and frequently suffered from headaches that made sleep a problem. Tomorrow would be Friday, a big day at the office. "I think I'll take a couple of aspirins and one of your sleeping pills," he said to his wife at bedtime. "That ought to make me sleep."

John did sleep quite well, but in the morning he had the sniffles and a slightly sore throat. He took a rather sizable multi-purpose cold capsule and inhaled some nasal vapors to clear his breathing. On the way to the office he stopped at the drugstore for some antibiotic cough lozenges and liquid cold remedies, for which he did not need any prescription.

The Friday work load was difficult, but John had to keep going. He took some more cough lozenges and swallowed twice the recommended dosage of the cold remedy. The latter contained antihistamines which made him quite sleepy in the warm office.

After dinner at home, John tried to relax by reading the evening newspaper, but felt uncomfortable from "heartburn." He took a few acid-reducing tablets. The period of rest was short. "Don't forget that we have to go to that party tonight, dear," John's wife reminded him. Still half asleep, John nodded in agreement. "A few drinks and I always feel better," he said.

John felt so much improved at the party that he accepted an invitation to go deep-sea fishing the next morning. He felt tired, however, when he got up the next morning, so he took a "pep" pill and drank some black coffee in order to be ready for the arduous task of fishing in a choppy sea.

Out at sea, John worried about becoming seasick, causing the skipper to give him several pills to control motion sickness. Life became much more pleasant about noon when the gang brought out the sandwiches and the beer. John drank several beers.

By the time the boat docked late in the afternoon, John admitted that he was quite exhausted. "Office men aren't used to this kind of activity," he admitted.

John got into his car and headed for the superhighway. The steady movement of the cars at 60 miles an hour, the soothing music of the radio, the relaxed feeling of warmth after the bracing fresh air of the sea—all made John feel sleepy. He turned down the window and reminded himself not to fall asleep.

✿   ✿   ✿

The autopsy revealed that John was not drunk when he drove off the highway and down an embankment, but that clinically his body was overdosed to the point that his mind could no longer control the impulses to sleep.

Some may argue that a theory of psycho-social development based largely on human needs must tolerate an individual's right to use of substances such as tobacco, alcohol, or narcotics to satisfy those needs. But, morality aside, it is equally arguable that this right is forfeited when it impinges upon the rights of others. In the example, John drove off the road. In the real world he might have driven head-on into you or me.

A more invidious consequence of drug abuse is revealed in the following story distributed by United Press International (UPI) April 15, 1971.

An LSD-spiked shaker of grated cheese at an Italian restaurant caused hallucinations in a woman and her son after they sprinkled the contents on their spaghetti, police disclosed Wednesday.

A spokesman for the vice detail said a "widespread investigation" was underway into the incident Easter Sunday at the Two Guys From Italy restaurant in Hollywood.

Helen Jones and her 16-year-old son Michael became ill at home after eating the tainted cheese and were taken to a hospital by a neighbor.

Mrs. Jones said at first she thought she was having a heart attack and she told Michael she thought she was going to die. The youth replied to her, "I'm going to kill myself," and went to get a knife.

That was when she grabbed the boy and rushed next door to the neighbor's house.

"I got it worse than Michael did because I love cheese and put a lot of it on my spaghetti," she said.

Mrs. Jones said she saw "strange animals coming from my skin and body." Michael saw varied geometric patterns of different colors.

A thorough presentation of information regarding appropriate materials and approaches by which teachers can develop awareness of the consequences associated with use and abuse of drugs is beyond the scope of this text. We do feel obligated to note the problem and to direct the reader to sources of information and assistance. Descriptive materials have been selected from a drug-education curriculum as illustrations. Selections are taken from the *Drug Abuse Education Unit — Grades K-12* of the South Bay Union School District, Imperial Beach, California (South Bay, n.d.). These materials were chosen because of the succinct introduction and the overview presented in the "Strands — Time Schedules." The objectives also contribute to this overview.

A PLAN OF INSTRUCTION — DRUG ABUSE
Introduction

We live in a drug oriented society, where children are saturated with the wonders of drugs from the time they are first able to see television commercials on aspirin and Geritol. Children accept drugs as a necessary part of society. The problem arises when they have to differentiate between the legal and the illegal. How are we to explain the difference between the drugs the doctors prescribe for them and the drugs that are used for illegal purposes? How do we explain the drugs accepted by their parents and the drugs they learn about in school? The teacher's role is one of prevention, familiarizing pupils, making them aware and to build a base in human values. **We cannot and must not use fear tactics.** Research indicates that police tactics and negative attitudes are not effective. Children's attitudes are not changed by these methods. Neither must we dwell on hard narcotics, but especially at the elementary school level, we must approach drug abuse problems from a positive viewpoint. The secret is the **how,** the **why,** and **with what attitudes** you present Drug Abuse Education.

The key is one of building proper attitudes, teaching decision making, working from the concept and appreciation of the human body. Basic to developing attitudes and appreciation is how do you solve your problems, what do I have with which to meet life?

Citizenship needs to be stressed. Another of the teacher's responsibilities is to point out the relationship of drugs and being a good citizen. The basic concept of the laws being challenged is another aspect on which we must work. As citizens we need to learn respect for the law.

The problem with our age level children is not so much one of marijuana, heroin, and hard narcotics, but one of teaching values, and one of producing mentally healthy and socially adjusted children.

We are already teaching the effects of alcohol and tobacco, as required by State Law. In teaching about drug abuse, as in all curriculum areas, we must avoid lecturing and moralizing. The underlying concept of the program is one of responsibility, responsibility to ourselves and to others. We must stress reason and awareness as opposed to punishment, fear and morality. Positive and negative aspects must be stressed, but not dwelled upon. These concepts are not only about drugs, but about people. We want to produce behavioralistic change. Guidance of the child's emotional and social development is most important. The strongest deterrent to drug abuse in the child's future lies in his strength of character in his ability and determination to face life and enjoy it through the wholesome understanding and constructive use of his own resources.

Objectives

Drug abuse education as part of the total curriculum in the South Bay Union School District has the following goals:

1. To build the self concept; good attitudes towards self.
2. To give instruction in decision making to children to enable them to make decisions.
3. To develop appreciation for the human body.
4. To develop responsibility to self and to others.
5. To build good citizenship — respect for the law.
6. To promote parent involvement: (a) by creating an environment in the home where there is a positive value orientation. (b) by bringing enlightenment and correct information into the home . . . in order to help eliminate misinformation.

Strands — Time Schedules

There are four strands included in the program:

1. Volatile Chemicals
2. Health and Appreciation of the Human Body
3. Advertising Propaganda
4. The Law

Time schedules are as follows:

Kindergarten . . . . .Two weeks — 15-30 minutes daily
Grade One . . . . . .Two weeks — 15-30 minutes daily
Grade Two . . . . . .Two weeks — 15-30 minutes daily
Grade Three . . . . .Six weeks — 30-45 minutes per day — Three times per week
Grade Four . . . . . .Six weeks — 30-45 minutes per day — Three times per week

Grade Five ......Six weeks—60 minutes or more per day—Three times per
week

Grade Six ....Six weeks—60 minutes or more per day—Three times per
week

Length of time, daily, is dependent upon pupil interest.

The second selection taken from the Imperial Beach unit describes a number of actual lessons designed to meet stated objectives. The lessons are representative of the total unit. Note the three distinct yet related thrusts of these lessons; awareness, decision making, and parent involvement. Lessons are placed at grade levels and correlated with other curricular components. (Physical arrangement has been changed to facilitate printing in a book; aside from this, there are no editorial changes.)

LESSONS FOR DRUG-ABUSE EDUCATION
Grades: 4, 5, 6

Correlated Areas: Health, Language Arts, Art

Broad Objective
Children recognize that nonfood substances are potentially damaging to the body and should be used only under special circumstances and with extreme care.

Learnings
Children describe substances that are potentially damaging to the body which are found in and around their homes.

Pupil Experiences
Let children make a list and discuss household substances which are potentially harmful to the human body.

Have the pupils ask their parents to make a list with them of substances in their own homes which are potentially harmful to the human body, such as detergents, insect poisons, volatile chemicals, lye, and snarol [snail poison].

Let the children make a display exhibit of dangerous household substances and describe their use in class.

Invite a chemistry or biology teacher to talk to the class about the nature of dangerous household chemicals and the precautions that should be observed in their use.

Have the pupils read the labels and determine what each substance contains which might make it dangerous.

Let the children design labels which might be placed on containers as warnings.

Let the children choose committees to do reference work on poisonous plants. Here are some suggestions: Consult the color plate, "Poisonous Plants," opposite page 1768 in the Third Edition of Webster's unabridged New International Dictionary. Make drawings of plants that are found growing in California, such as the castor-oil plant, loco weed, and Jimson weed or datura. Try to locate pictures in books, magazines, or other sources, too.

References
MP 1900 **Make Your Home Safe**
T 1358 **Safety House**
FS 1106 **Hidden Enemies in the Home?**
T **Glue Sniffing**—California State Department of Education; MacDonald—
A. Kitzinger

Broad Objective
Children gain experience in the whole realm of decision making through group discussion, student involvement, games, TV commercials.

Grades: 4, 5, 6

Correlated Areas: Health, Language Arts

Learnings
Children learn that they are always making decisions and learn some principles for decision making.

Pupil Experiences
The pupils may wish to organize committees responsible for informing the class about some of the drug-promotional efforts that are carried on in the modern world. The committees might do the following:

1. make a bulletin-board display of drug advertisements.
2. make a tape recording of drug advertisements on TV and radio and play the recording in the classroom.
3. discuss the meaning of various slogans that are used in advertising drugs and tell how some of this slogan information gives wrong ideas.
4. list suggestive types of advertising.

The pupils may wish to write limericks on the comical side of drug advertisements.

Some pupils may wish to rewrite some TV or radio commercials and offer factual information.

Other pupils may wish to clip advertisements from magazine and newspapers on drugs and then develop their own format using factual information.

Through class discussion help the pupils to realize that the important decisions of life are the ones they are making right now.

They may write an essay on "My Decisions Are Important Today." In the essay have them include some of the afore-mentioned decisions and what bearing their decisions today have on tomorrow. Some of these may be read to the class and then discussed. A contest for the BEST essays could be planned.

Make a vocabulary list of words used in advertising.

Broad Objective

Parent involvement—creating positive attitudes at home and bringing correct information into the home, creating an awareness of the drug problem.

Grades: 4, 5, 6

Learnings

Children learn to involve their parents in Drug Abuse problems so that together they can face the issues and resolve them.

Pupil Experiences

Pupils might take a letter home at the beginning of the Drug Abuse Course which explains the purposes of the course, some of the content, and some brief suggestions about how the parents can help their child.

As the children make their Scrap Books of magazine and newspaper articles on Drugs You Use and Abuse they should be encouraged to discuss these articles with their parents and make notes of what reactions both parents and child had—any disagreements felt and how they resolved their differences, how their parents helped them understand the articles and any other outcomes. These should be discussed in class.

Parents could be invited to school to view some of the films used in the Drug Education Program.

Teacher should be aware of TV Programs planned on Drug Abuse and make recommendations to the class, always suggesting that the parents watch too. The same procedure can be used here as was used by parents and children with the articles for the Scrap Book.

Parents and children could go to the San Diego Police Department and view together their display of drugs—reactions should be brought back to class and discussed.

Throughout the course children should be encouraged to discuss issues with parents and **ask** their opinions and draw from their knowledge.

References

Drugs, Your Child & You, Peter R. Frank, Curriculum Coordinator, San Diego County Department of Education.

San Diego Police Department, San Diego, California.

Sample letter home.

The National Council for the Social Studies has published *Drugs and Youth* (Wolk, 1971) as the first in a series of publications dealing with Teaching Social Studies in an Age of Crisis. This publication is recommended to all teachers as an initial step in self-education regarding drug abuse. Background materials and references are presented as well as ground rules for classroom activities. An annotated bibliography of curricula currently available is included.

INSTRUCTIONAL ACTIVITIES FOCUSED ON CAUSE-EFFECT

It would be a serious error to overlook the child's need to be aware of drug use and its consequences. In the early years of elementary education, attention to consequence would constitute the major focus of activities dealing with drugs. As the child grows, developing both psychologically and socially, the focus expands and attention to causal factors takes priority. Readers may have discerned evidence of such movement in the progression of lessons presented above. Rather than play out the idea of cause-effect relations using drugs, it would seem more profitable to introduce another current content area as vehicle.

Pollution

O Beautiful for smog-filled skies,
Synthetic waves of grain.
For dump-heap mountain majesties
Above thine asphalt plains.
America, America,
Man does his worst to thee,
And crowns thy mess with filthiness
From sea to slimy sea.

This poem, written by a group of sixth-grade children in Atlanta, clearly points to causal relationships to the problem of environmental pollution. The children have applied Pogo's conclusion: "We have met the enemy and he is us!" Their poem was written as one activity in a unit on water pollution developed by their teachers, Ercell McIver and Rose Drake. The entire unit plan is presented below. The ideas may be successfully developed with children in the upper elementary grades.

A PLAN OF INSTRUCTION—WATER POLLUTION

Main Idea: The biosphere is not running out of water. Because of the hydrologic cycle—evaporation, condensation, and precipitation—the actual amount of water remains constant. However, it is running out of usable water, and when water loses its usefulness, we say it is polluted.

Organizing Idea: It is nature's plan that water recycle and purify itself. In its recycling process, however, water picks up more materials than anything else known on earth. When water falls as rain or snow, it picks up particles and gases in the atmosphere. When it percolates through soil, it collects land contaminants, and when it splashes over rocks, buildings, bridges and roads, it carries still other materials along with it. All these materials, and hundreds more, eventually find their way into larger and larger bodies of water.

Child-Level Concept: In American homes, each person uses about 50 gallons of water a day for drinking, bathing, cooking, cleaning, toilet-flushing, and lawn-watering. Within this decade, some aspects of the "good life" — enjoyed by most of us — will disappear unless drastic corrective measures are taken on a large scale to combat water pollution.

Cognitive Objectives
1. Dust, terpenes, pollen, industrial gases, hydrocarbons and radioactive particles enter our water supply when rain washes them out of the atmosphere.
2. Insecticides, fertilizer salts, and decaying vegetation, are washed from the soil by rain, floods, and underground "rivers."
3. Domestic septic tanks, storm sewers and industrial plants wash pollutants into our water supply.
4. Oil from boats, ships, and drilling operations adds to pollution.
5. Human litter of broken glass, old mattresses, junked cars, rusting metals, all add their special taint to our waters.

Behavioral Objectives
At the end of the unit, the students should show the following behaviors:

1. The student should be able to identify pollutants in local creeks, streams, ponds, lakes, and rivers.
2. The student should demonstrate willingness to help combat pollution through controlling personal behaviors such as proper disposal of trash.
3. The student actively discourages improper usages of detergents, fertilizers, insecticides, and other pollutants.
4. The student actively seeks, through contact with governmental agencies, for proper disposal of industrial and municipal wastes.
5. The student can demonstrate through creative writing or drawing that he has knowledge of the hydrologic cycle.
6. The student actively solicits behaviors in his family, friends, community business operations, factory operations, and governmental officials to conserve our usable supply of water.

Activities
1. Hike through the neighborhood inspecting polluted streams, creeks, rivers, ponds, lakes, etc.

2. Collect samples of water for viewing under the microscope.

3. Identify and list pollutants observed—have children draw, or cut out of magazines, pictures of pollutants to be put on bulletin board.

4. Make folders of newspaper and magazine articles concerning pollution.

5. On the chalkboard, write, "The water you bathe in tonight may contain some of the same water that Moses was hidden in as an infant . . . or that Daniel Boone crossed on his trip west." Instruct children to read the comment carefully and then write one or two paragraphs explaining its meaning and why they think it is true or false.

6. Write poems, slogans, stories, TV commercials about pollution.

7. Plan a mural as a group activity showing the different phases of the hydrologic cycle.

8. Ask children to speculate on the meaning of the following caption: "The Death of a River." Ask: What is a river? Where do rivers start? Where do they end? How can a river die? Who uses a river? What structures might be built near rivers? Why? What might be on the river? Over the river? Under the river? In the river?

9. Sketch the flow of a river from source to mouth on a large sheet of newsprint. Divide the class into groups to add to the sketch various things they might find along the river route if they sailed up the river in a boat, such as: mountains, factories, houses, parks, people, grass, trees, clouds, raindrops, animals, etc.

10. Each child constructs a booklet consisting of about 20 lined pages with an oaktag covering. Ask each student to imagine that he is a body of water (a pond, stream, lake, brook, river, etc.) and to keep a daily account—a diary—of things that happen to him. Each entry must be dated and may be a simple sentence or a whole paragraph.

11. Allow one group of children who exhibit interest in civic affairs to set up a file of addresses of local and state committees or groups who are working on the water pollution problem. Keep an up-to-date list of names and addresses for future class references.

12. Visit local industries and inquire about how they dispose of waste.

13. Play the game of "Ad-Verse" as an enrichment activity. (The first player starts to tell a story of water pollution in a rhymed jingle. For example, "I saw a stream as sweet as cream." The second player continues, "It was clear and blue and sparkling too." The third player might add, "The stream soured and algae flowered." Continue the jingles until the story ends. The jingles can be typed and placed on the bulletin board.

14. Take pictures of polluted streams throughout the community.

15. Visit the nearest water supply plant. After the tour, have the children interview the person in charge, asking questions from a prepared sheet. Have a student record the responses to such questions as: How many gallons of water a day are used? Where does the water come from? How is it collected? What is added to the water? How does the water get to my home? Are there any controls about water usage?

16. Visit the nearest sewage treatment plant. Interview a person in charge there asking similar questions as those asked at the water supply plant.
17. Construct a map of the local area, locating and labeling water areas, the water supply, sewage plants, watersheds, and dumping areas.
18. Write a class letter to persons and groups engaged in clean-water projects and ask how class members may help.

Culminating Activities
1. Write a play or short drama about pollution. Let class members act it out.
2. Write a TV commercial about combating pollution, and ask for permission to actually dramatize the commercial on a local station.
3. Hold a panel discussion about the effect of water pollution. Invite civic leaders and industrial managers to serve.
4. Make a class bibliography of research sources used during the unit.

Descriptive Level Questions
The following are additional questions which may be considered by the class. Other descriptive-level questions have been included within the activities section.

1. What uses does your family make of water in your home?
2. How much of the earth contains water areas?
3. How much of this water is suitable for drinking?
4. How long can humans live without water?
5. How do rivers and streams become polluted?
6. What are pollutants?
7. What can I personally do to combat pollution?
8. How can I enlist the aid of others in helping to combat pollution?

As a topic of concern for all mankind, pollution occupies a central place. The emotional impact of the problem provides motivational impact. From an instructional standpoint, its importance as an issue is secondary—the primary utility of a unit such as the one illustrated lies in the opportunity for children to explore causal relationships between man's acts and their effects.

Inquiry into the causes of pollution requires children to:

1. Define the meaning of pollution.
2. Hypothesize about the possible causes.
3. Collect data related to the problem.
4. Analyze the data, screening out unimportant data and retaining relevant data.
5. Synthesize the data into a clear definition of the causes.
6. Propose a course of action.

These activities have been field tested by the teachers who designed them and proved very successful. In addition the authors have visited classrooms where other teachers have implemented their instructional procedures. We found the activities equally successful. In each case the motivational quality of the activities provided the major impetus to learning.

Survival

Three ILP's dealing with the concept *survival* may be used to stimulate an inquiry into cause-and-effect relations. In each case a living organism is faced with the problem of surviving in an apparently hostile environment. Two of these ILP's are designed to show the effect of man's attempts to satisfy his most basic needs. Another uses the case of the bald eagle to show parallels between the human species' attempts to meet needs and the corresponding attempts of other animal species. In addition, a simulation exercise, developed by the National Aeronautics and Space Administration, provides an opportunity for the student to explore the unknown, hypothesizing about the value of each of 15 items for survival.

AN INDIVIDUALIZED LEARNING PACKAGE— SURVIVAL IN A FRONTIER ENVIRONMENT[1]

Objectives

This is an ILP about the adjustment of the frontiersmen to his environment. Because there was no fast method of transportation and no factories in the new land, the people had to use what was available and "make do." The frontiersmen made blockhouses and log cabins for homes; log rafts for transportation; and palisades for protection. When you have completed this objective you should be able to do the following:

1. Tell why the frontiersmen made blockhouses, log cabins, palisades and log rafts; how they were made; and why they were important for survival in the West.
2. Draw a picture of each of the above structures, or make models of them.
3. Pretend that you are lost in a heavily wooded mountain area. Tell what you would do and what you would use to make a shelter to protect yourself from the cold and rain. Tell also how you might be able to get food from the surrounding area.

How to Complete the Project

1. Look in the library card catalog for materials about:

---

[1] Written by Frederic Watson, ILP Development Project, Ruby S. Thomas Elementary School, Las Vegas, Nevada. Program Directors: Frederic Watson, Dallas Owens, Mary Bogard. This is used with the kind permission of Mr. Watson, as are numerous other ILP's prepared in the same Project.

Westward Movement	Log Cabins
Houses	Palisades
Forts	Boone, Daniel
River Transportation	

2. Use any reference books available, such as encyclopedias, history books, unabridged dictionary, etc.
3. Talk to the United States Forestry Office.
4. Consult the Boy Scout Handbook, and Boy Scout leaders.

AN INDIVIDUALIZED LEARNING PACKAGE—
SURVIVAL OF AN ENDANGERED SPECIES[2]

Objectives

This is an ILP about survival, how well a living thing is prepared to live on our earth. The bald eagle is the national bird of the United States. We have always thought of it as a strong bird that is safe because it is such a good hunter. Conservationists are beginning to think the bald eagle might die out in this country. When you complete this lesson, you should be able to:

1. Tell where in the United States the bald eagles live.
2. Tell what they eat.
3. Tell how they protect themselves and their young.
4. List the reasons American bald eagles are dying faster than they are being born.
5. Write a discussion of this statement: "Progress is killing the bald eagle. We need more land for farms, factories, and homes. If the bald eagle dies, that is just the price of progress."
6. Write about a plan that would save the eagle from dying out in America.

How to Complete the Objectives

1. In the library card catalog, find cards that on the top line say:

Eagles
Birds of Prey

Some cards may tell you about **books,** others about **nonbook media.** You will see cards for **all the media** right together in the card catalog. You will not have to look in any other lists to find media such as filmstrips, transparencies, tapes, charts, 8mm loops, study prints, slides, etc.

AN INDIVIDUALIZED LEARNING PACKAGE—
SURVIVAL WITHOUT SOCIETY[3]

Objective

This is a lesson about survival—how men, animals and other things seek to go on living. When you are finished with this lesson, you should be able to

---

[2] Written by Frederic Watson, ILP Development Project, Ruby S. Thomas Elementary School, Las Vegas, Nevada. Program Directors: Frederic Watson, Dallas Owens, Mary Bogard.

[3] Written by Frederic Watson, ILP Development Project, Ruby S. Thomas Elementary School, Las Vegas, Nevada. Program Directors: Frederic Watson, Dallas Owens, Mary Bogard.

tell how Robinson Crusoe changed his island surroundings so that he could survive. Remember Crusoe had to think about keeping his mind healthy, as well as his body.

How to Complete the Objective

1. Get the book **Robinson Crusoe.** Read it carefully, keeping in mind the points in the objective.
2. You may perform this objective in two ways. In either case, be sure your work is neat and attractive.

   a. Write a book report, being sure to include the points in the objective.
   b. Build a model of Crusoe's island and living quarters. Be sure they look exactly as the book describes them. Then be able to show how the different parts of your model helped Crusoe survive.

A teacher might wish to supplement this ILP by explicitly exploring the effects of a person's being alone.

The moon game was designed by the National Aeronautics and Space Administration. Although ostensibly a survival game requiring good judgment in applying one's knowledge of the moon's environment in making the requisite decisions, this simulation provides additional learning activities.

A SIMULATION ACTIVITY—THE MOON GAME

Procedure

Initially each game participant is asked to compile, without consultation, his own survival list as outlined by the game rules. [See instructions, below.] Upon completion of their lists, the participants are divided into teams of approximately five to eight members. Each team is then given 15 to 20 minutes to discuss the merits of the alternative decisions available and to then submit one team survival list. A nonparticipant is assigned to each team to observe and record the actions of the participants. After submission of all group lists, the answer lists are compared.

Evaluation

1. Did each participant do better on the list where he made his own decisions or on the list where he worked as a team member? How does each participant explain this result?
2. Feedback from observers.

   a. How were decisions made on each team? (i) by consensus of group members? (ii) by one or two influential team members? (iii) by any other means?
   b. Was there any correlation between how decisions were made and the team which had the best score?
   c. How did each team member interact with the other? (i) Did any one

person emerge as a team leader? (ii) Who was most helpful to the group? (iii) Who was least helpful? (iv) What actions hindered the group? (a) Joking? (b) Arguing? (c) Tangential discussions? (v) At what stages did individual participants seem most involved? Least involved?

Instructions

You have just crashed-landed on the light side of the moon. No one has been hurt, but only this list of 15 items has survived the crash. You must travel 200 miles to a space station. No one can come from the station to help you. Each person, **without consulting** with anyone else, should now look at this list and decide which things are most important to take on your trip to the space station. This list is scrambled. Rearrange it so that the most important item is first, the next important item is second, and so forth, so that number 15 is the least important item. Do this individually. You may write your list on the sheet marked "First Listing."

1. First-aid kit
2. Food
3. Rope
4. Flares
5. .45 Caliber pistols
6. Heat units
7. Compass
8. Matches
9. Oxygen
10. Map
11. Radio
12. Life raft
13. Milk
14. Parachute silk
15. Water

It might be useful to keep some discussion going after the lists are compared. For instance, if the pistol was deemed worthless or put very low on the list, why? Is there anything to shoot on the moon? Could the pistol sound serve as a signal? Would the pistol's recoil be valuable as a means of propulsion? Would the pistol shoot where there is no atmosphere?

INSTRUCTIONAL ACTIVITIES FOCUSED ON VALUING

Valuing and Inquiry

The ultimate goal of social study is the self-motivated inquiring individual. Such an individual possesses the skills necessary to process information through rational inquiry in order to define a base of personal action. He is aware of himself and his environment and can identify consequences through causal relationships. The capstone of the inquiry is valuing. Through valuing, as defined earlier in Chapter 2, an individual clarifies his personal feelings, attitudes, beliefs and values. He is now ready to act secure in the knowledge that his priorities are well founded, that they are valid for him.

Children who have reached this stage of psycho-social development need freedom to explore. Their exploration should be self-initiated. However, they may require some initial suggested activities or stimuli from which to branch outward. The use of ILP's provides an approach which suggests broad categories of learning activities while at the same time avoiding individual restriction.

A Current Event as an Invitation to Inquiry

A current concern of your specific community may offer a profitable stimulus.

AN INDIVIDUALIZED LESSON PACKAGE—VALUES AND VALUING

Objectives

This is an ILP about personal and community priorities. Economic concerns often influence the actions people take as individuals and as groups. When you have completed this ILP, you should be able to do the following things:

1. Analyze actions taken by community representatives to determine priorities.
2. Identify similarities as well as differences between your personal priorities and those of your community.
3. Determine an appropriate course of action you might take to influence a current concern in your community.

How to Complete the Objective

Read the situation below and try to identify what you would do if you were faced with such a situation. Try to be as realistic as possible in your choice of actions.

Situation

A profitable industry wants to locate in a small town because a river running on the outskirts of the town would be an excellent and inexpensive way to dispose of industrial wastes. The town has many poor people who would be willing to work for just about any wage. The industry would be a boon to the town and increase its economic standing in the state.

You have been invited to the meeting of the town council to voice your opinion about the possible location of the industry in your community. You are aware of the possible pollution of the river which presently provides you with clean drinking water and recreational activities. However, you also are aware of the opportunities for low-income families to get better incomes, thereby increasing the economic standards of the community as well as enabling the poorer families to enjoy some of the finer things of life. You are personally acquainted with poorer families who desperately want the industry and the opportunities it will bring.

Questions to Consider

1. At the council meeting will you take a stand for or against the new industry coming into the community?
2. List arguments you will use to help persuade fellow citizens to see your side of the issue.
3. Will your relationships with any of your friends be affected by your decision?
4. How will you feel toward those who oppose you?

Any daily newspaper or local television news broadcast provides ample material to stimulate inquiry into local political, economic, social, cultural, and historical phenomena. Each of these affects students, teachers, and their communities in a variety of ways. The kinds of broad activities suggested in this ILP might be useful in an examination of any community issue.

Topics or Concepts as Invitations to Inquiry

Often specific topics or concepts can be developed to focus on value conflicts. A topic such as *protest music* provides an opportunity to inquire into relationships of individuals or groups to the institutions of their culture. The following ILP provides a basis for such an inquiry. The individual student may wish to expand the suggested activities to include many other songs or demonstrations of protest.

AN INDIVIDUALIZED LEARNING PACKAGE—PROTEST MUSIC[4]
Objectives

People have many ways of expressing themselves when they are unhappy. Since man learned to sing, songs have been used to express unhappiness. Probably the most interesting of these songs are those protesting something. Sometimes they are critical of the way a country is being governed. Sometimes they tell of unfair treatment of certain groups in a country. When you have completed this lesson, you should be able to:

1. Choose two types of protest songs from the list below:

[4] Written by Frederic Watson, ILP Development Project, Ruby S. Thomas Elementary School, Las Vegas, Nevada. Program Directors: Frederic Watson, Dallas Owens, Mary Bogard.

a. folk songs sung by American slaves.

b. songs protesting war.

c. folk songs about the depression of 1929.

d. songs protesting school segregation.

e. songs protesting atomic weapons.

f. songs protesting hatred and violence.

2. Listen to the songs and

a. Tell the main idea the song is trying to get across.

b. Discuss how you feel about the ideas in the song.

How to Complete the Objectives

1. There are many songs popular today that are protest songs. Listen for them on the radio.

2. The library has three albums that might help you. Ask for the albums: "American History in Ballad and Song" (vol. 1 and vol. 2); "The Burl Ives Sing Along Book."

Intolerance is a concept which is particularly well suited to wide-ranging inquiry. The example that follows focuses on ethnic groups. However, the model may be adjusted to explore intolerance based on sex, religion, race, dress, or any other attribute the student selects.

AN INDIVIDUAL LEARNING PACKAGE—INTOLERANCE[5]

Objectives

This is an ILP about hatred and bad treatment among men. Throughout history groups of people have shown prejudice against other groups of people for no good reason. When you have completed this ILP you should be able to do the following things:

1. Tell the meaning of the word **prejudice.**

2. Choose **one** of the eight groups listed here:

American Indian   Cubans

Mexican-American   Japanese-Americans

Puerto Ricans   Chinese-Americans

Black Americans   Jews

Write in your own words a short history of the group you chose. Be sure you bring out the following:

a. When and why the group you are reporting on came to this country.

b. How they were treated by other Americans.

c. What reasons did people give for hating the group you are reporting on.

[5] Written by Frederic Watson, ILP Development Project, Ruby S. Thomas Elementary School, Las Vegas, Nevada. Program Directors: Frederic Watson, Dallas Owens, Mary Bogard.

    d.   What is wrong with the thinking behind the reasons you listed.

3.   Pretend that you are married. Six months ago you became the proud parent of triplets (2 boys, 1 girl). You want your children to be tolerant and to respect the worth of all men. Set up a plan explaining how you will raise your children to be tolerant as you want them to be.

4.   Discuss all of the points in the objective.

How to Complete the Objective

1.   In the library card catalog, find cards that on the top line say:

Indians — American	Cuba	Prejudice
Mexican-Americans	Japanese-Americans	Intolerance
Puerto Rico	Chinese-Americans	Bigotry
Negroes — American	History — U.S.	Racism
		Ku Klux Klan

Some cards may tell you about **books,** others about **nonbook media.** You will see cards for **all the media** right together in the card catalog. You will not have to look in any other lists to find media such as filmstrips, transparencies, tapes, charts, 8mm loops, study prints, slides, etc.

Very personal perceptions based on values influence the aesthetic sensitivity of our students. Music, art, drama, dance, language and literature — the whole range of human studies offers a rich arena for inquiry. Exploration of the humanities nurtures the child's values of self and of the contributions of others.

The topic in the two examples may be viewed as encompassing a wide-ranging variety of concepts, or as discrete concepts in and of themselves. The reader may wish to refer to Chapter 3 in order to categorize *intolerance* and *protest music.*

People as Invitations to Inquiry

Traditional elementary social study has included exposure to numerous biographical experiences. Most often these were used as models for "good citizenship" or to nurture "democratic values." In recent years the significant contributions of little-known individuals have been included in the curriculum. Particular emphasis has been placed on representative members of various minority groups who have contributed to the advancement of their fellow man. These individuals tend to be viewed discretely, that is, in terms of their own life and times. Children operating at the highest level of psycho-social development should be able to analyze not only the specific incidents of an individual's life but also the motives which stimulated his action. They should further be able to synthesize these discoveries in order to evaluate numerous individuals living in different time-space frames. Three ILP's are presented as examples. It may be profitable for teachers to explore for themselves the common attributes of Crazy Horse, Jane Addams, and Martin Luther King, Jr.

AN INDIVIDUALIZED LEARNING PACKAGE — CRAZY HORSE[6]

Objectives

This is an ILP about one of America's greatest soldiers. He was a war chief of the Ogalala Sioux. Superstition was a driving force in his life. When you have completed this ILP, you should be able to show an understanding of the part superstition played in the life of Crazy Horse by answering the following questions in a discussion:

1. How did Crazy Horse get such a strange name?
2. Most boys have many different plans for when they grow up. Crazy Horse had only one. How did he know what he would be when he grew up?
3. Shannon Garst says that Crazy Horse wore a strange costume when he went into battle. What did Crazy Horse wear? How did his battle gear show he was superstitious?
4. What is a prophecy? Was there a prophecy about the death of Crazy Horse?

How to Complete the Objectives

1. In the library card catalog, find cards that on the top line say:

   Crazy Horse, Ogalala Indian
   Garst, Shannon
   Indians of North America — Wars
   Indians — Plains
   Indians of North America — Biography

   Some cards may tell you about **books,** others about **nonbook media.** You will see cards for **all the media** right together in the card catalog. You will not have to look in any other lists to find media such as filmstrips, transparencies, tapes, charts, 8mm loops, study prints, slides, etc.

AN INDIVIDUALIZED LEARNING PACKAGE — JANE ADDAMS[7]

Objectives

This is an ILP about a famous woman who spent her entire life helping people not as lucky as she was. To complete this ILP, pretend that you can talk

---

[6] Written by Frederic Watson, ILP Development Project, Ruby S. Thomas Elementary School, Las Vegas, Nevada. Program Directors: Frederic Watson, Dallas Owens, Mary Bogard.

[7] Written by Frederic Watson, ILP Development Project, Ruby S. Thomas Elementary School, Las Vegas, Nevada. Program Directors: Frederic Watson, Dallas Owens, Mary Bogard.

to Jane Addams and write an interview of your visit with her. Be sure the interview contains information about the following:

1. How Jane Addams first became interested in helping the poor.
2. The things she did that helped poor people.
3. What people in her life helped her become the kind of person she was.
4. What Jane Addams thinks are America's two worst problems.
5. How she thinks those problems should be solved.
6. Why did she bother with poor people when many people think poor people are lazy or they would not be poor?

How to Complete the Objective

1. In the library card catalog, find cards that on the top line say: Addams, Jane; Hull House. Some cards may tell you about **books,** others about **nonbook media.** You will see cards for **all the media** right together in the card catalog. You will not have to look in any other lists to find media such as filmstrips, transparencies, tapes, charts, 8mm loops, study prints, slides, etc.

AN INDIVIDUALIZED LEARNING PACKAGE—MARTIN LUTHER KING, JR.[8]

Objectives

This is an ILP about a famous civil-rights leader. He taught Americans how men can work for justice when the law and government have failed to move. When you have completed this lesson, you should be able to rewrite in your own words the life of Martin Luther King, Jr. Be sure to include information about:

1. How Martin Luther King, Jr. was touched by unfairness in America while he was growing up.
2. King's education and the work he chose.
3. How the bus boycott started and how it changed the unfair rules the bus company used against black people.
4. What Dr. King meant when he urged black people to use "nonviolent protest."
5. Why Dr. King received the Nobel Peace Prize.
6. What Dr. King might have done with the rest of his life if he had lived to be 86 instead of 39.

How to Complete the Objectives

1. In the library card catalog, find the cards that on the top line say:

King, Martin Luther, Jr.
National Association for the Advancement of Colored People

---

[8] Written by Frederic Watson, ILP Development Project, Ruby S. Thomas Elementary School, Las Vegas, Nevada. Program Directors: Frederic Watson, Dallas Owens, Mary Bogard.

Segregation
Rights — Civil

Some cards may tell you about **books,** others about **nonbook media.**
You will see cards for **all the media** right together in the card catalog.
You will not have to look in any other lists to find media such as filmstrips,
transparencies, tapes, charts, 8mm loops, study prints, slides, etc.
2. In the social studies room see the book **American Biographies.**

The ILP's may be presented individually for specific inquiry or as
a group for more thorough exploration. The objectives suggested are
designed to move the student from initial awareness of the individual
to a situation in which he, the student, makes an evaluation. Students
are also provided an opportunity to propose alternative courses of action
and to evaluate their relative merits.

CONCLUDING REVIEW

We authors believe that the only appropriate conclusion to this
chapter lies in activity. We suggest that each reader complete at least
one of the group of ILP's labeled *Options* and that every reader complete the ILP labeled *Required.* Upon completion of these activities he
should analyze his response in terms of the following question: Where
do you stand on the continuum of psycho-social development from
egoizing to ecologizing?

Options

AN INDIVIDUALIZED LEARNING PACKAGE — VALUES
Objectives
Imagine you have been isolated on an island since birth. You have just
been rescued. Upon returning to civilization, you are totally unaware of the
present existing life (the laws, customs, cultures, habits) and how each of these
evolved. You have governed yourself all these years and formulated your own
concepts and ideals of what you hold as most important in fulfilling your goals
in life.

Upon completion of this ILP you should be able to draw the following
conclusions and be able to support them.

1. You would have a complete "cultural shock."
2. Man continuously has laws to govern him.
3. Change is ever-present . . . always for the betterment of man? Is it?
4. Concepts of good and evil basically never change.
5. You need some values and ideals to guide you in fulfilling your goals.

How to Complete the Objectives

1. Use the library catalog under such titles as

Culture	Values
Laws	Concepts
Primitive Man	Evolution
Contemporary Man	Civilization
Citizenship	Mores

Make a list of similarities between you and the people of the community to which you have come, and the differences. The lists should be concerned with attitudes toward law; concepts of themselves; goals; values; cultures; and customs.

AN INDIVIDUALIZED LEARNING PACKAGE— ETHNIC ORIGINS AND VALUES[9]

Objectives

The chances are that your great-grandparents or their parents before them came to America from a foreign country. Families hand their history down from parent to child. A person can learn a lot about the ethnic group he is from and about his country's history simply by listening to the stories his parents and elders tell. When you have completed this ILP, you should be able to:

1. Write the history of your family, going back as far into the past as you can.
2. Tell what ethnic group your ancestors were a part of when they came to America (German, Irish, Italian, African, Chinese, or other).
3. Draw two maps, one showing where your ancestors came from and one showing where they settled in this country.
4. Tell whether your ancestors suffered from prejudice when they got to this country and whether they still are treated with prejudice.

How to Complete the Objectives

This is a lesson you can do with your parents and relatives. Old snapshots and other souvenirs will be helpful.

AN INDIVIDUALIZED LEARNING PACKAGE—TRANSPORTATION IN 2001

Objectives

Pretend that it is the year 2001. Your city has a population of three million people. It is the terminal for large hypersonic passenger planes carrying hundreds of people from all over the world. A special problem has arisen. These people who arrive at your city want to continue on to other parts of town and to nearby towns and cities quickly, but no rapid-transportation system has

---

[9] Written by Frederic Watson, ILP Development Project, Ruby S. Thomas Elementary School, Las Vegas, Nevada. Program Directors: Frederic Watson, Dallas Owens, Mary Bogard.

been installed. You have been hired to plan a rapid-transportation system to connect all parts of the city and to connect the city to another nearby metropolitan area. The air lanes are already overcrowded so your plan must be some kind of fast ground transportation. Try to think of systems nobody has yet thought about. In finishing the plan to be presented, be sure to include the following items:

1. Drawings of the proposed high-speed systems.
2. Maps showing the location of the system within the city and connecting it with other cities.
3. The cost of your systems and how you intend to pay for them.

How to Complete the Objective
1. In the library card catalog, find cards that on the top line say: Monorail; Transportation; Airplanes.
2. Write or call the city planning commission and find out the future plans for your city.
3. Read the September 1969 edition of the **National Geographic Magazine.**

Required

SETTING INTELLECTUAL PRIORITIES FOR THE SCHOOLS
Instructions

Below is a list of behaviors (drawn from many possible) which could be set as priorities for our public schools of the future. Please read the entire list and then indicate which of the behaviors you believe should take precedence over others. Assign a 1 to the behavior of highest priority, 2 to the next highest priority, and so on. You need not assign numbers to all behaviors, but you should indicate at least the three top priorities you would leave as well as the three behaviors which you feel are least important. Assume that all of these behaviors are measurable and that all students would be capable of attaining these behaviors before graduating from out public schools.

___ Can identify propaganda techniques used by an author or speaker.
___ Can read and interpret various map and globe projections.
___ Has a minimum of 15,000 words in his word recognition-vocabulary.
___ Can identify, within selected materials, the conclusion and supporting statements of the writer.
___ Can translate a high percentage of mathematical formulas into their verbal equivalents.
___ Can distinguish between factual claims and opinions using logical argumentation in establishing the former.
___ Demonstrates empathy for people within or outside his own ethnic, racial, or socioeconomic group.

___ Can use a language other than English at an eighth-grade comprehension level.

___ Demonstrates skills of leadership (organizing, implementing and evaluating).

___ Has read and can discuss many of **The Great Books.**

___ Can arrange personal ideas he has written in a logical order.

___ Can set up criteria for identifying examples of "good" art in judging his own work as well as the work of professional artists.

___ Can list those rights and responsibilities stated in the United States Bill of Rights.

___ Can identify and defend his personal system of beliefs in areas where social and political conflict exist.

___ Uses standard rules of language in his writing and speaking.

___ Can identify crucial incidents related to the problem of growing alienation in our society.

___ Can draw reasoned conclusions from physical science experiments he has observed.

___ Can recall 90 percent of the information in works he selects to read.

If you compare the rankings of several people, you will undoubtedly discover disagreements and differences. Reflect on the differences and make use of them, if possible, but do not waste time on efforts at statistical analysis such as averaging. It is our opinion that when a teacher engages in honest reflection on educational priorities he holds, much can be revealed concerning his ecological "leanings." Comparing your impressions above with the *What Do You Value* section in Chapter Two can add deeper analysis to the above.

PART THREE

Evaluating Instruction; Materials for Instruction

CHAPTER 8

Assessing for Psycho-Social Outcomes

The theory of psycho-social needs upon which this textbook was constructed raises some knotty problems in the area of evaluation and particularly in the area of measurement. Before looking for ways of assessing student progress, we must first question the *why* of evaluation and measurement, for what purpose(s)?

Traditional measurement and evaluation in social studies were relatively simple. The intent was to objectively (actually intersubjectively) measure students over certain facts and generalizations which were seen as inherently "good." This practice still is perpetuated in some standardized tests and unfortunately in many teacher-made tests. Names, dates, places, and events must be recalled, matched, underlined, correctly selected, and so on and on.

This traditional method of evaluation must be rejected as the mode of measurement with reference to the theory of psycho-social development on at least two counts. First, the measurement of "things" rather than ways of processing and utilizing knowledge is inconsistent with the future personal and societal needs that we authors envision. Chapter 3 hopefully provides an elaborated rationale for this rejection. Facts and loosely controlled generalizations (those selected arbitrarily rather than structurally) are seen as the measure of miseducation and ineffectual instruction, not of effective teaching and learning.

We need to raise a second reservation regarding this type of assessment. While the *what* and *how* in regard to this type of measurement were found highly objectionable, the *why* of such measurement is also unacceptable with reference to our model of instruction. Such measurement often had as its primary aim the separation of students on the basis of one cognitive dimension. Those few who could memorize felt good about themselves. The rest saw themselves very often as inadequate, as failures in social studies. Such massive failures are essentially counterproductive in the needs theory – people do not need continual wide-scale failure!

PURPOSES: WHY EVALUATE?

We, as social studies educators, must reject a method of evaluation which often reduced the uniqueness of human beings to the scale-point where they fall in a distribution of raw scores on a factual-recall test. What then, should be the nature and purposes of evaluation in our model of instruction? We posit the following list of suggestive, not prescriptive, criteria.

1. *Evaluation is needed to get clues for future instruction.* Hence it is necessary to assess the initial and the changed physiological-psychological-social needs of youngsters, and means for making such assessments should be established.
2. *Evaluation is needed to determine the effectiveness of the teacher's instruction.* Hence the means for making the assessment should be established.
3. *Evaluation is needed to appraise the students' attainment of skill in intellectual processes.* Here, bear in mind that memory is only one of the intellectual skills; the need for evaluation applies to mastery of high-level social-science concepts and generalizations to the higher-order skills of interpretation, application, analysis, synthesis, and evaluation. If developing such skills is an objective of social studies teaching/learning, then means for assessing the degree of development should be established.
4. *Evaluation of the psycho-social development of children is needed, to know what is happening to the child.* Since the teaching/learning process affects student feelings, opinions, attitudes, and values, we teachers need to assess the effect,

hence must be concerned with the diverse attempts to make both quantitative and descriptive assessments of psycho-social development.

The remainder of this chapter will review both formal (standardized) tests and informal measures in an effort to provide some insight in selecting and/or building a psycho-social testing program. Three major limitations must be kept in mind.

First, the state of the art. Measurement according to the criteria above stated is relatively new. No standardized test in social studies has addressed itself to these four criteria. A number of writers point to evaluation and measurement as the weakest link in social studies curricula. The rapid transition in social studies-social science has resulted in confusion of aims and purposes which is necessarily reflected in evaluation and measurement. While some disagreement and confusion of direction will no doubt continue, owing to the fact that social studies education is so broadly defined, more clearly defined models of instruction with resultant more precise measures for evaluation can be expected to emerge in the near future.

A second limitation regarding setting forth a picture of measurement and evaluation resides in the fact that each child's educational situation will be unique. Limitations of language and reading development in one situation may, for example, be a major constraint in regard to the "what" and "why" of measurement and evaluation, while of relatively limited importance in another situation.

A third limitation resides in the authors' own collective knowledge concerning "what" exists. The wide range of disciplines to explore in identification of measures of evaluation is staggering.

COGNITIVE ASSESSMENT: REVIEW OF STANDARDIZED MEASURES

Social studies education is in the midst of a revolution. As the pluralistic aims which are beginning to emerge dictate different emphasis of instruction, some direction toward what should constitute the make-up of standardized achievement tests in social studies is clearly needed.

Richard Gross raises these challenges to persons charged with the construction of standardized tests in social studies when he lists the following key questions.

How well do our students read and comprehend in the social studies area? How well can they differentiate cause and effect? How well can they demonstrate the understanding of basic concepts and generalizations? Can they recognize propaganda? Can they decide if conclusions are warranted by the evidence? Can they state the relationships between former events and current events? Do they hold the essential capabilities of analysis and attitudes of openmindedness fundamental for the resolution of social problems? These are the queries I would want to put when examining pupils for true achievement of my social studies goals and these are elements upon which these tests throw very little light. (Gross and Allen, 1965, 607)

In the same work, Gross and Allen express skepticism that tests can be constructed to measure some of the fundamental skills stated above.

Yet even as we build the necessary measures of skill, we remain dogged by a doubt that has not been alleviated to date. Are such tests of competency actually measures of the qualities implied or are they largely indexes of ability to apply knowledge previously learned?

How well do existing measures of social studies achievement in elementary education meet the requirements Gross articulates as desirable? We have selected four standardized measures for analysis in the light of this question, using two specific criteria:

1. The tests had to address themselves *within the test manual* to at least one of the following areas:
   a. Comprehension of social studies material (such as reading, development of map and globe skill).
   b. Emphasis on structural learnings (such as concepts and generalizations drawn from the social science disciplines).
   c. Emphasis on intellectual processes (cognitive skills as opposed to recall of specifics).
2. The *tests themselves,* as ascertained by our personal inspection or from comments of reviewers in *The Sixth Mental Measurements Yearbook* (Buros, 1965),[1] had to reflect some effort to deal with the areas identified in the preceding criterion.

A list of the tests which appear to meet parts of the selection criteria follows, with comments.

Metropolitan Achievement Test: Social Studies, 1964 revision. Harcourt Brace Jovanovich. Emphasis, while confined to the traditional social science disciplines of geography, history, and civics, does touch upon major concepts and generalizations. Barbara Peace (in Berg, 1965, 234) states, "Items are essentially factual, though a good number of broader issues are touched upon."

---

[1] *The Seventh Mental Measurements Yearbook* (Buros, 1972) was not available while this evaluation was in progress.

Gross criticizes the history items, indicating that they "are sadly short of what should be included for a comprehensive assessment of knowledge in this discipline. Twenty items are included in each form to survey knowledge of the world, as well as United States history from the Stone Age to the United Nations." (Buros, 1965, 221)

The strongest area of the Metropolitan Achievement Test in Social Studies appears to be the section dealing with study skills. Map, table, chart, and graph reading are tested.

Sequential Tests of Educational Progress, 1963 ed. Educational Testing Service. Donald Oliver, in reviewing this test in Buros' *The Sixth Mental Measurements Yearbook* (1965, 1224) states that it was

> . . . developed upon the assumption that the focus of education is upon the development of critical skills and understandings rather than upon teaching only the facts of lesson material and that success in education is to be measured in terms of the student's ability to apply school learned skills to the solution of "new problems."

There seems to be little question that this test comes closest to the criteria mentioned by Gross and quoted at the beginning of this section. Jonathon McLendon, another prominent social science educator who has reviewed the test, calls it "the best standardized series of skill tests in social studies." (Buros, 1965, 1225)

Items from economics and sociology are included along with the traditional disciplines. The student's ability to identify generalizations and values, distinguish fact and opinion, and assess and compare data in drawing conclusions is tested. Excellent maps, graphs, cartoons, photographs, drawings, and text materials are utilized.

Primary Social Studies Test, 1967 ed. Houghton Mifflin Company. This test addresses itself specifically to testing how well primary-grade students can understand major concepts and generalizations drawn from the social sciences. It does not include any items drawn from sociology, a glaring weakness.

One advantage of the test is that it does not require any reading on the part of the children. Pupils are shown a series of three pictures and asked to circle the one which correctly answers a question posed by the teacher. For example, three pictures of weapons used in three different time periods are presented to the children. They are then asked to "Fill in the oval under the picture of the weapon that men used first." (Preston and Duffy, 1969, 10) In reviewing the social science generalizations at the back of the teacher's manual under History, one finds the statement which this item is supposedly testing. "Events occur in a sequence, and they influence the present." (Preston and Duffy, 1967, 19)

The teacher's manual for this test includes respectable validation and some reliability data. Its weakness appears to be centered around the fact that only 142 items were used in a national tryout, of which ". . . the best seventy were used in constructing the present test." (Preston and Duffy, 1967, 20) No alternate forms are available.

Stanford Achievement Test, Intermediate I Battery, 1965 revision. Harcourt Brace Jovaᵤovich. Emphasis is much like that in this publisher's other major test, the *Metropolitan Achievement Test: Social Studies*. Its major strength lies in its study-skills section. Very few items (24 in the Intermediate I edition) are used to test a fantastically wide range of social studies concepts. Emphasis again is upon the traditional social science disciplines.

This concludes the review of existing tests which, in part, meet the criteria cited at the outset. Gross's conclusions relative to the limitations of current standardized tests in social studies are largely confirmed. While no one test was found which was entirely appropriate and, indeed, several others not reported here were found to be entirely inappropriate, the following recommendations for utilization of present tests are posited.

Primary-grade teachers must be content with using the *Primary Social Studies Test* developed by Preston and Duffy in assessing knowledge of major concepts and generalizations.

Intermediate teachers could best profit from using the *Sequential Tests of Educational Progress* which assess both study and critical-thinking skills as well as knowledge of major social science ideas.

We authors served on a writing team which generated test items for the 1973 Stanford Achievement Test. While these items are more clearly in line with some of the present aims in social studies education, as no doubt are other major revisions, teachers of social studies are faced with some immediate assessment. The obvious drawback of revisions every eight years is clearly evident. There is a definite need for such tests today, not in four or five years. Standardized achievement tests in social studies are not needed to mirror the present, that is, to test the isolated facts often taught in our schools, but are needed to set the goals of instruction. As Gross has so cogently stated,

> As long as standardized tests are so lacking in scope of measurement they promise not to provide the needed leadership towards improvement in curriculum and instruction, but rather to further inculcate the distressing fact-depository school of social studies "education." (Buros, 1965, 1221)

COGNITIVE ASSESSMENT: TEACHER-MADE TESTS

We authors maintain the considered opinion that evaluation ought to be in the form most necessary for high-level cognition and valuing, and that much more emphasis should be placed on verbal expression. These linguistic skills are extremely important. The ability to see relationships, to make application to other situations, to analyze some message, to choose freely and to defend logically, these and other high-level skills are not gained primarily by answering true-false or fill-in-the-blank memory tests. In fact, when youngsters answering fact-recall questions do some thinking above the recall level, their answers are frequently marked wrong! An example of this was a fifth-grader's answer to the question: "Abraham Lincoln was born in _____." "Log cabin?" But one young fellow put down "original sin," making application from his religious training—a higher-level transfer!

The levels of thinking presented in Chapter 3, if utilized in setting objectives and devising means of evaluation, can produce results more consistent with the psycho-social model this textbook advocates.

Levels of questioning were mentioned in Chapter 3, with reference to some of Norris Sanders' work. (See Sanders, 1969 and Sanders, 1966.) Sanders uses Bloom's taxonomy (Bloom, 1956) in establishing a hierarchy of thinking levels. Teachers who wish to assess the cognitive growth of their youngsters need to construct questions at the higher levels of thinking. An excellent book which will provide the necessary background in test construction is the 1965 yearbook of the NCSS, edited by Harry D. Berg (Berg, 1965). Chapter 3, written by Dr. Berg, is particularly strong in providing a test-construction background for teachers of upper-level students. In the same yearbook, Maxine Dunfee sets forth some activities for use as guides to measurement of some higher-level educational skills. These include:

> To match statements of cause and effect.
>
> To distinguish between facts and generalizations in a given list of statements.
>
> To supply the generalization to be drawn from a given set of facts.
>
> To select the conclusion to be drawn from a chart, diagram, or graph.
>
> To support a given generalization with facts.
>
> To state the generalizations that can be drawn from a field trip or other project.
>
> To match a generalization with its supporting data.
>
> To select the generalization that may explain why a given situation exists.
>
> To draw conclusions from an imaginary dialogue in which an issue is discussed, [such as] what person has inaccurate information, what person's comments reveal prejudice, etc.
>
> To state the most important ideas learned from a unit of work.
>
> To state an opinion about why a particular unit of work was chosen for study.
>
> To select responses to multiple-choice items which emphasize why something happened or why a condition exists.
>
> To match pictures with the generalization they represent. (Dunfee, 1965, 165)

While current elementary social studies textbooks are increasingly placing more stress of teaching for high level thinking, their authors usually do not supply high-level text questions for the purpose of measuring pupil growth. One notable exception can be found with the Fideler Company (Grand Rapids, Michigan) textbook series. The following questions were drawn from several they raise within their *Asia and Africa Social Studies* (Teacher's Guide edition, 1969). Source-page references are to this book.

Translation Question: Explain the term "delta" in your own words. If you wish, you may draw a picture to help explain the meaning of this term. (p. 63)

Application: Determine what you believe to be some of the problems faced by the newly independent countries of Africa. If you were a citizen of one of Africa's new nations, how would you try to solve these problems? (p. 65)

Analysis (Sample Question): Read the following two paragraphs, distinguishing statements of fact from opinions. When you have completed your reading, answer the following questions: (a) Are the statements of fact in these two paragraphs contradictory, or could the facts given in both paragraphs be true? (b) What can you tell about the beliefs or attitudes of the writer of each of these paragraphs?

"During recent years, great changes have been taking place in the way goods are produced. Machines have been invented that require few, if any, human operators. The use of such machinery is called automation. With automation, our factories are now able to produce greater amounts of goods with fewer workers than ever before. Although automation has reduced the number of jobs available for unskilled workers, it has opened up many new and different jobs for highly trained workers. For example, large numbers of engineers and other technical workers are needed to design and build the new machines and to keep them running."

"During recent years, a serious problem has arisen. In many places thousands of workers have been thrown out of work by machines. The use of machines that require few, if any, human operators is called automation. With automation, factories are able to make profits for their owners with fewer workers than ever before. Although some engineers and other highly trained technical workers are kept busy designing, building, and running the new machinery, there aren't many jobs left for the unskilled workers whose work has been taken over by these mechanical monsters." (p. 66)

Synthesis: Read the information about propaganda on page 168 of **Africa.** Now, imagine that you are working for an advertising agency. Choose a product such as toothpaste or an automobile and write a radio commercial or a magazine advertisement that will help to sell the product. Display your advertisement in class or read your commercial to your classmates. Ask them to answer these questions: (a) Did this advertisement or commercial make use of any propaganda tricks? If so, which ones? (b) Would this advertisement or commercial influence them to buy the product advertised? Why, or why not? (p. 67)

Evaluation (Sample Question): Read about the Boxer Rebellion (**China, page 57**). Now, imagine that you are going to write a report about this uprising. You decide that your report should include the following information: (a) the causes of the Boxer Rebellion (b) a description of events during the rebellion (c) a summary of the results of the rebellion. You go to your community library to find the information you need to write your report. At the library you find the following:

a. the translation of a diary written by one of the leaders of the Boxer Rebellion.

b. a novel for young people, telling the story of an American family attacked by a group of "Boxers."

c. a book entitled **China: 1840-1945,** written by a professor of Chinese history.

d. an encyclopedia article about the Boxer Rebellion.

e. issues of a New York City newspaper (June to September, 1900) containing articles and photographs describing the rebellion.

f. the autobiography of a British government official who lived in China during the rebellion.

g. a United States government publication containing a copy of the agreement signed by China and other nations after the rebellion.

Which of these sources of information do you think would provide the best information for your report? Which would be least useful? Give reasons for your answers. (Keep in mind the suggestions for evaluating information found on pages 167 and 168 of **Africa.**) (p. 68)

Measuring Ability to Interpret Nonverbal Materials

Helping youngsters to interpret pictures, charts, cartoons, graphs, and tables, as well as maps and globes, often becomes important for teaching/learning when the materials to be studied rely heavily upon such devices. The section on map and globe skills in Chapter 6 hopefully provides some insight in the promotion of these skills. In utilizing graphs, charts, and the like, one excellent teaching practice is to ask children to present the information in another way. Building children's ability to translate a chart into "their own words" or asking a child to write a short essay explaining the meaning of some political cartoon or similar item can be a useful objective. Teachers are again admonished to stress and to assure success of children in such endeavors. The use of activities or tests "to show children how little they know" can have severe consequences for the psycho-social development of a child. Emphasis on one-to-one teaching situations and/or doing a few examples with the total class will greatly increase success.

ASSESSING AFFECTIVE DIMENSIONS:
COMMERCIALLY AVAILABLE INSTRUMENTS

An excellent reference for use in selecting tests of affective qualities and growth is *Improving Educational Assessment: An Inventory of Measures of Affective Behavior* (ASCD, 1969).

Here we present a list of ten tests that are close to meeting the criterion for diagnosis and evaluation of the students' feelings, attitudes, opinions, and values. The names of the tests are given, with information about their authorship and related facts, and some suggestions about ways in which they might be used.

Torrance Tests of Creative Thinking. E. Paul Torrance, Department of Educational Psychology, College of Education, University of Georgia, Athens, Georgia 30601. Specimen set available from Personnel Press, Inc., 20 Nassau Street, Princeton, N.J. 08540. Forms for norms from age 4 up. Useful in establishing those children with high creative potential. Clues to individually strong areas of perception can be helpful in selecting appropriate types of learning strategies.

Interaction Analysis. Ned A. Flanders, College of Education, University of Michigan, Ann Arbor, Michigan 48104. This is a system of recording types of teacher and student responses. It provides feedback to a particular teacher concerning such matters as, what percent of time does he talk compared to his students, how non-directive is he in his behavior toward students, etc. Teacher can learn the coding system, tape record his own lesson, thus review the tape and make his analysis. For a more detailed explanation of the system refer to Amidon and Hough, *Interaction Analysis: Theory, Research and Application* (Reading, Massachusetts: Addison-Wesley Publishing Company, 1967).

Draw-A-Classroom Test. E. N. Wright, Toronto Board of Education, 155 College Street, Toronto 2B, Ontario. A great test to get inferences about a student's development of concepts in regard to his mental, emotional, and social areas of growth. A manual regarding the theory and purpose of the test and a manual regarding administration and interpretation are available; price $2.00.

Hayes Pupil-Teacher Reaction Scale. Available from Robert B. Hayes, Director, Bureau of Research, Administration, and Coordination, Pennsylvania Department of Public Instruction, Box 911, Harrisburg, Pennsylvania 17126. The scale consists of 20 items designed to measure a teacher's ability to establish an intellectually stimulating climate, set up on 4-point agree-disagree scale on which the child evaluates his teacher. Items deal with such things as the ability of the teacher to get the child to think, how much the teacher challenges the student, etc.

What I Like to Do (An Impulsivity Scale). Sutton Smith and B. G. Rosenberg, Bowling Green University, Bowling Green, Ohio. Twenty-five items in which a child responds "true" or "false" to statements about the nature of his home, behavior in school and outside, etc.

Early School Personality Questionnaire (6-8 years) and *Children's Personality Questionnaire* (8-12 years). University of Arizona, Tucson, and Raymond B. Cattell, University of Illinois, Urbana. Write for further information to I.P.A.T., 1602-04 Coronado Drive, Champaign, Illinois 61820. Provides 13 personality dimensions with a minimum of testing time. Constructed for ages 6 to 8. Eighty items are read to children and they record their answers on nonverbal answer sheet (C.P.Q.). The test for children of 8 to 12 years yields 14 personality dimensions.

Levine-Elzey Preschool Competency Scale. San Francisco State University, San Francisco, California 94132. A rating scale of social competence for children 2½ to 5½ years old. Makes observation of the child's behavior on such things as ability to identify certain things (his name, for example) to his ability to deal in social peer relationships.

What I Am Like. Cincinnati Public Schools, Division of Psychological Services and Division of Program Development, Cincinnati, Ohio. Based upon Osgood's concept of semantic differential. Attributes about perceptions of physical appearances, psychological acceptance, and social attributes are included.

How I See Myself. Ira J. Gordon, College of Education, University of Florida, Gainesville, Florida 33601. Two forms (elementary and secondary) are available. Easy to administer and interesting to interpret in reference to the teacher's own perception of the child. (The use of this is discussed in our Chapter 6 as part of an illustration of personal-social exchange.)

About Me. James Parker, Department of Education, Georgia Southern College, Statesboro, Georgia 30458. Similar to *How I See Myself,* preceding. This has 30 items which can be used at various levels in elementary school. Many clues about physical, psychological, and social needs emerge.

An excellent index of physiological, and social needs was developed by Elizabeth Léonie Simpson in her book *Democracy's Stepchildren* (1971). The scale was used to determine prevailing needs based on Maslow's hierarchy. The scale, and results from three socioeconomic samples, are reported in the book.

An excellent attitude test for obtaining values preferences of children of upper-elementary age and above is *Survey of Ethical Attitudes.* In this, decisions are made by respondents which show how the youngster is oriented with reference to natural and man-made laws. The test is used in Simpson (1971). It originates in Hogan (1967).

AFFECTIVE MEASURES: TEACHER-MADE

When a teacher clearly identifies the specific information she needs about some youngster, a number of informal measures usually exist that can be used when formal measures are not readily available. Interviews with the child under study or with others who know him intimately are often successful. Use of interest inventories also are seen as imminently useful in the model upon which this book has been based. Having children keep a personal record of emotional, physical, and social growth is also desirable. The remainder of the chapter provides some examples of informal measurement which the authors found to be consistent with the psycho-social development theme.

Attitude and Value Tests

A teacher identified fourteen seventh-grade students who were not able to function effectively in her American History course. In attacking this problem she constructed an instrument to obtain more data about the children. Her results gave clues to better meeting the needs of these potential "failures."

A SELF-REPORT OF ATTITUDES AND VALUES[2]

Please follow instructions in regard to method of answering.

1. (Choose one) My parents think education:

    _____a. Is a good thing.
    _____b. Something you have to do.
    _____c. A waste of time.

2. (Check one) I would rather:

    _____a. Read a book.
    _____b. Watch television.
    _____c. Play games.

3. (Rank in order of preference, 1 for top choice) I would rather learn from:

    _____a. Book with no pictures.
    _____b. Movie film.
    _____c. Records.
    _____d. Books with pictures.
    _____e. Lectures.

    Answer **sometimes, always,** or **never** to the following:

[2] Constructed Winter 1971 by Mary R. Perkins, graduate student at Georgia State University, whom the authors thank.

4. I understand completely our American History assignments. _____

5. I know as much as any other student in the class about American History.
   _____

6. Any student would cheat to get good grades. _____

7. I would like more help in our assignments. _____

   Rank in order of preference (top choice is 1):

8. _____My teacher could help me more.
   _____My parents could help me more.
   _____My friends could help me more.
   _____None of the above.

9. _____I could help the slower students.
   _____The smarter students could help me.
   _____Neither of the above.

10. _____I am a below-average student.
    _____I am an above-average student.
    _____I am an average student.

11. _____I could do better if I really wanted to.
    _____I am doing about as well as I want to.
    _____I could do better if I had extra help.
    _____I cannot do any better than I am doing.

12. _____I have just a few special friends in class.
    _____I like all the students in the class about the same.
    _____My friends are not in my class.
    _____My friends live in my neighborhood.
    _____None of the above is true for me.

Teachers can combine tests of their own design with tests already established to explore attitudes children have. Here a teacher resurrects a 1929 test by Clark and Clark (1947) to appraise the attitudes of her youngsters regarding racial inferiority. The total study, including her method of attacking the problem, is presented here. Note the use of a pretest to establish where her youngsters "are," followed by treatments, and finally a post-test to measure growth.

AN ATTITUDE SURVEY AND PLAN OF INSTRUCTION TO ALLEVIATE RACIAL INFERIORITY[3]

Problem: How can I provide educational experiences to show that membership of a minority group does not have to be a severe hindrance in rising socially or intellectually?

[3] Developed Fall 1970 by Miss Patricia Daniels, graduate student at Georgia State University, whom the authors thank.

Backgrounds

The studies of Clark and Clark [1947] several years ago revealed some significant findings. They used white and black children of low economic standards, overcrowded dwellings, and large families. Each child was presented four dolls, alike in every respect except for skin and hair color. Two dolls had brown skin and black hair and two had white skin with blond hair. The children were given eight directions, as follows:

Give me the doll that:

1. you would like to play with.
2. is a nice doll.
3. looks bad.
4. is a nice color.
5. looks like a white child.
6. looks like a colored child.
7. looks like a Negro child.
8. looks like you.

The results of this study showed that the black children had the tendency to choose the white doll just as white children did. To question 3, both the black and white children of the background description they [the Clarks] used were rather unwilling or psychologically unable to identify with the brown doll. The report also stated that aspirations were low and self-esteem significantly low.

In the article "Black History, Negro History, and White Folk," Larry Cuban [1968] explains how books glorify such individuals as Crispus Attucks, but he is a shadowy historical figure. He is not created in the image as Nathan Hale and other whites. He goes on to explain that Blacks need a pantheon of black heroes that children can point to with pride.

The idea of Negro History brings up the question of whether studying "Black" History will improve self-concept and instill pride. It is known that attitudes do change.

Background of My Students: My class consists of 30 black four- and five-year-old students. All of these students live in government projects. The incomes of most of these families are significantly below normal subsistance level. There are more than two children in the homes and the male is absent in over 65% of the cases. Most of the mothers work from eight to twelve hours daily and the institution for which I work provides educational services for these children as well as day care.

The institution functions from government funds as well as donations from other charitable organizations. Over one half of my children are interested in learning. For the remaining half, limited interest prevails. School for some of them already appears to serve no real purpose.

My concern grew when I heard a little five-year-old boy telling another boy that "When I get big, I'm gonna get my big brother's gun that is in the service and kill people." I asked him if he had ever considered being a doctor, teacher, brick mason, etc. His reply was "I can't do none of that stuff." I went on to explain that there are schools that teach you how to do whatever you want to do. After explaining in vain, I realized that explaining or verbalization was not effective. This prompted me to take other measures towards solving my problem.

I plan through the solving of my problem to reach this child and shed light upon others who may have other skeptical ideas about life. This is to be done indirectly and not obviously.

Procedures
I plan to solve some of my problems by:

1. Giving a doll pretest.
2. Having children discuss the test.
3. Using bibliotherapy.
4. Using films (black oriented).
5. Role-playing.
6. Letting children discuss everyday successful blacks.
7. Taking educational field trips.
8. Giving individual conferences.
9. Evaluating procedures and success.
10. Giving a doll post-test.

Test and Results (Daniels Test)
Show me the picture of the doll that

1. Is the prettiest.
2. Looks like you.
3. Is the ugliest.
4. Is a bad doll.
5. Has the prettiest face.
6. Is a nice color.
7. You would like to be.
8. Looks like a black child.
9. You would like to play with.
10. Looks like a white child.

The students were shown four drawings of four dolls exactly alike except the color of the skin and hair. Two of the dolls had brown skin and black hair and the remaining two had blond hair and white skin. Each child had to point to the doll that he thought fit the category mentioned. The girls had a girl doll to point to and the boys had a little boy doll to point to (in all, eight pictures were used, four of girls and four of boys.)

The results of the pretest are as follows:

1. 85% of the children thought that the pictures of white girls and boys were the prettiest.
2. 75% identified with the white doll.
3. 95% chose the black doll as the ugliest.
4. 98% picked the black doll as the bad doll.
5. 100% picked the white doll as the prettiest face.
6. 50% said the white doll.
7. 85% would like to be white.
8. 100% knew which doll was black.
9. 86% said the white doll.
10. 100% knew which picture was a picture of a white child.

Working on My Problem

The results of the pretest made me realize that immediate attention should be directed towards the problem. The first step toward the resolution of my problem was to read stories involving black children and their culture. One particular book that the children enjoyed was **Harold (and His First Day in Kindergarten).** The children enjoyed dramatizing this story for this was something all of them had experienced. Other books were used. Some were obtained from the West Hunter Branch Library on Hunter Street and some from the downtown branch.

Another thing done was to make cutouts of felt material for use with the flannel board. The children made up stories and told them to the class. Bibliotherapy was very effective and the children enjoyed the series of black stories.

Some black children models were invited to come out and present a fashion show. The children really enjoyed it and wanted to present one themselves. The children presented and narrated their fashion show with humorous success.

Great individuals such as Martin Luther King, Jr., Langston Hughes, Mary M. Bethune, and Frederick A. Douglass were told about and the children acted out some of the things in the short stories. One of particular success was the acting out of "The Black Moses of Her Race"—Harriet Tubman. The children really enjoyed pretending that they were escaping slaves. At gun point, Harriet had to force some of the slaves to move on and she would comfort them by saying "You'll be free or die." We had children pretending to be slave owners who looked for Harriet but didn't find her. The children did a fantastic job!!! Another dramatization done by the children I must mention was that of Madame C. J. Walker, who spurred the interest in beauty among blacks. The girls acted out how it must have been when Madame Walker invented the first straightening comb and a hair softener. The girls presented it without any consultation. The boys really enjoyed it. Even though it is looked down upon to have straight hair now, the children acted out how it must have been then to find out your hair could be straightened or "dekinked."

Martin Luther King, Jr. has always been a favorite of the children for he was born right here in Atlanta. We learned his favorite spirituals and sang them with accompaniment. We all discussed what was meant by "Free at Last" and the conditions that probably prevailed before the blacks could have sung this popular spiritual.

Field trips were also a part of the project. Some of the places we visited were: Dr. King's grave; the Citizen Trust Bank [a bank operated and owned primarily by blacks] on Hunter Street, The West Hunter Street Library to see the Black Children's Hour presented weekly. We had a brunch at Pascals Brothers, a Black-owned and -operated restaurant (compliments of a white volunteer working in the center) and also saw two plays presented at Spellman College, entitled: "Anse and the Glueman" (an African play) and "Junction Village." The children were fascinated by the make-up, dancing, and music. We made home-made drums and the children used paint and water colors for make-up and the children did little African dances (that they themselves made up.)

The children also discussed famous blacks in the world of sports. The one that really deserves mentioning is Cassius Clay. The children presented a fight as they thought it happened or had heard that it happened. Two of the boys acted as boxers, some acted as spectators who were to cheer the fight on and some acted as the finely dressed people to see the fight on the outside.

To culminate the activities, I gave the children individual conferences to discuss what we had done, but the motive was not made clear to them, which I felt would make the post-test results more interesting. If they didn't understand the motive, they would answer the post-test innocently.

The post-test revealed the following results.

1.   55% thought that the white doll was the prettiest.
2.   69% identified with the black doll.
3.   45% chose the black doll as the ugliest doll.
4.   98% still picked the black doll as the bad doll.
5.   The same as on the pre-test.
6.   The same as on the pre-test.
7.   20% wanted to be white.
8.   The same as on the pre-test.
9.   50% said the white doll.
10.   The same as on the pre-test.

Results

I found that attitudes do change when attention is focused on the positive aspects of minority groups to minority groups. (I can say it did for the black children I used.)

All of the attitudes did not change in all areas, but they did in some of them. Children do enjoy reading about their people and contributions. I had not seen such enthusiasm until I pursued this project. The children enjoyed acting or role-playing. They enjoyed learning that we have beauty in our race.

I cannot say how long the lesson taught will continue to influence these children, but I hope constant follow-up work will prove beneficial. I plan to give the same test at the end of the school year and see if the percentages reflect improvement.

I can say that this has been one of my most enjoyable educational experiences I have done for a class. I am only sorry that it took a compulsory requirement to make me see there is a need of attention to be directed toward this problem and there may be some resolutions feasible or steps toward resolutions. No absolutes came out of this research but there are implications that attitudes can be changed at least temporarily.

Using a Rating Scale

R. Murry Thomas, in an article entitled "Education, The Case for Rating Scales" defines a rating scale as "a sheet on which a teacher or pupil records his observations of how adequately someone has performed." (Thomas and Brubaker, 1971, 364)

In the following example, a teacher was concerned with some of her students who exhibited general irresponsibility concerning class assignments, home work, and carrying out classroom responsibilities. She developed the following behavior checklist. Students were asked to evaluate their own behavior. One student's weekly report is included here.

HOME OWNER _____ *Gail* _____

	Mon.	Tues.	Wed.	Thurs.	Fri.
1. Books organized neatly in desk	✓	✓	✓	*No*	✓
2. Books on the floor under desk	✓	✓	✓	✓	✓
3. Paper on floor around desk	✓	✓	✓	✓	✓
4. Have needed materials for school work day. (paper, pencil)	✓	✓	✓	*no pencil*	*no notebook*
5. Have homework for today	✓	✓	✓	✓	✓
6. Completed all work for the day.	✓	✓	✓	✓	✓
7. General conduct for today S = satisfactory, P = poor	S	S	S	S	S

Thomas suggests some other uses of this technique. These include rating a student's performance in role-playing, in a simulation game, or in other activities that permit.

An example of this use can be seen in a rating scale used by a teacher who developed a mock-trial simulation game. Such use must be approached cautiously; students should be quite willing and comfortable about being so evaluated by their teacher and/or their peers. The score card is illustrated on p. 280.

Performance on certain other learned skills can also be evaluated through use of a rating scale. An example will be explained shortly.

Thomas indicates that six concerns are usually involved in construction of a rating scale. Summarization of these appears to be:

1. Start by selecting the specific purpose for which you wish to employ the scale.
2. Determine the focus of behaviors you wish to record. For examples: Will you record all positive instances of the behavior, all negative, both? Strength and/or weaknesses of students?
3. Determine the range of observable behaviors under each general area. If a teacher is concerned with recording observations about her childrens' self-concepts, for example, a more specific area of self-concept she may wish to check could be "physical presentation of self." Under this category, numerous behavior specimens might be possible. One of the specific behaviors she may wish to scale might be: "Makes derogatory

MOCK TRIAL SCORE CARD

How Well Did the Student Play the Role?		OUTSTANDING	ABOVE AVERAGE	AVERAGE	SOMEWHAT WEAK	VERY WEAK	
Role	Student's Name	1	2	3	4	5	Notes
Judge							
Recorder/Clerk							
Plaintiff's Attorney							
Plaintiff							
Ecologist							
Health Official							
Defense Attorney							
Defendant							
Union Official							
Mayor							
Engineer							
Juror 1 (Foreman)							
Juror 2 (store clerk)							
Juror 3 (housewife)							
Juror 4 (housewife)							
Juror 5 (retire man)							
Juror 6 (plant worker)							
Juror 7 (teacher)							
Juror 8 (housewife)							
Juror 9 (secretary)							
Juror 10 (doctor)							
Juror 11 (gardner)							
Juror 12 (banker)							

comments about appearance. (Circle one) Never observed, occasionally observed, frequently observed."

4. The fourth concern deals with format—placement of items, sequencing of items, methods of checking items, placement for additional information, inclusion of personal data, etc.

5. The final format should be selected after the above four matters are decided. Thomas supplies an example of three possible single-item formats around a logical-thinking-skill item. [illustrated]

"How often does the pupil support his opinions with evidence from reliable sources?"

Option 1: _____

| Never | Rarely | Sometimes | Usually | Always |

Option 2: _____

| 0% | 25% | 50% | 75% | 100% |

Percent of the time evidence is given

Option 3: _____

| ☐ | ☐ | ☐ | ☐ | ☐ |
| Never | ¼ of time | ½ of time | ¾ of time | Always |

6. The rating scale should then be used with a small group of students to determine its appropriateness. (Thomas and Brubaker, 1972, 364-378)

Teachers should be aware of the vast possibilities of such scaling with regard to the model projected in this book. Nearly all areas of student growth and development could be recorded to help the child see his own patterns of development. Such measurement should instill confidence and trust in each child. Comparisons of where each child was before and after some planned experience is the important dimension.

Two examples of how our students have applied the rating-scale principle may be useful.

1. A first-grade teacher was interested in having her children discover some of the psycho-motor changes taking place during the year. She and her aide helped children to record individual records in regard to some things as distance in throwing a softball, success in kicking a football, and success in catching a volleyball; ten events were included. Periodic checks were made as the children participated in a planned physical-education program. All children reflected some growth at some point in the year.

2. A sixth-grade teacher interested in applying valuing lessons to her teaching allowed her children to record personal opinions they had related to

each issue the class was to discuss. During the trial of Lieutenant William Calley (My Lai Incident) she clipped parts of newspaper quotations dealing with the issue of whether Calley was "a hero," "a victim," "a coward," etc. After each quotation, the student responded by circling one of the following: strongly agree; agree; no opinion; disagree; strongly disagree. Students were then asked to place their responses in their desks to be analyzed later. She then had students observe a television program attempting "objectivity" concerning the Calley trial, and eventually had the youngsters participate in a mock trial. Four weeks later the youngsters again responded to the opinion checklist. Each child was then asked to compare his answers with the ones he originally circled. Students were encouraged to write a brief paper describing changes and/or stability of answers. Opinion sheets aimed at determining the sources of beliefs were also circulated. An example of this type of device is included in the Appendix as part of a unit on civil rights.

Using Interest Inventories

One very important technique that teachers can use when concerned with awareness of students' psycho-social needs is an interest inventory. Many teachers have tapped a particular interest of some child and discovered many clues to further the intellectual and emotional growth of a child. An example of an interest inventory follows. (If it is used, provide at least a line of space for each answer, and space the lines for children's handwriting.)

AN INTEREST INVENTORY—WHAT I WANT AND HOW I FEEL

Directions: Complete the following sentences to express how you really feel. There are no right or wrong answers. Put down what first comes into your mind and work as quickly as you can. Try to complete all the sentences and to do them in order.

1. Today I feel _____
2. When I have to read, I _____
3. I get angry when _____
4. To be grown up _____
5. My idea of a good time _____
6. I wish my parents knew _____
7. School is _____
8. I can't understand why _____
9. I feel bad when _____
10. I wish teachers _____
11. I wish my mother _____
12. Going to college _____
13. To me, books _____

14. People think I _____
15. I like to read about _____
16. On week ends, I _____
17. I don't know how _____
18. To me homework _____
19. I hope I'll never _____
20. I wish people wouldn't _____
21. When I finish high school _____
22. I'm afraid _____
23. Comic books _____
24. When I take my report card home _____
25. I am at my best when _____

CONCLUSION

This chapter attempted to present some insight into the nature and purpose of evaluation and measurement that might fit the theory of instruction posited in this book. Assessment of social, language, and intellectual skills, needs, and values are deemed desirable both when their measurement is used for diagnosis of students needs and for measurement of success of instruction — for both teacher and learner. Dichotomy between the roles of Teacher with a capital "T" and learner should not exist in a psycho-socially based curriculum.

The second portion of the chapter attempted to provide some examples of what exists in affective and cognitive measurement. The implementation of a truly meaningful testing program will require the efforts of a number of staff members in a school district because of the enormity of the tasks of selection, construction, administration, record keeping these at the least. Our attempt was to provide a place to begin developing some program of measurement and evaluation. Examples of teacher-constructed means of evaluation were provided to aid the classroom teacher who may be undertaking development of a psycho-socially based program of instruction in her classroom.

CHAPTER 9

Materials to Support Instruction in the Psycho-Social Approach

There are no materials currently available which are *based on* a psycho-social approach to social studies. (Note: This is not synonymous with the statement, "There are no good textbooks.") Most materials currently available are *adaptable for* instruction based on the psycho-social approach. Materials suited for use in instruction based on the psycho-social approach are available and can be identified. These materials vary in accessibility and expense but the range allows for inclusion in most budgets.

MATERIALS FOR THE INITIAL-EXPLORATORY STAGE

The Child as a Materials Source

The single most useful source of materials is the child himself. As he comes to the elementary school he has lived five or more years. Think for a moment just what that means—lived five or more years! That translates into 1,816 days (don't forget at least one leap year), 43,584 hours. Consider the billions of stimuli which have impinged on each individual, shaping and molding his frame of reference, his perception of reality, his very self.

Though much of the stuff of life has gone unassimilated or misunderstood by reason of the child's lack of cognitive or affective development, the impressions left on him remain a rich source for growth. Recall the unit on Feelings presented in Chapter 2. The basic materials component of the unit was the individual child. He can help direct and focus instruction with answers to the kind of questions suggested in the Feelings unit. Additional information may be gleaned from his responses to instruments and activities such as those described in Robert Mager's useful book *Developing Attitude toward Learning* (1968). Mager describes ways of increasing approach behaviors — interest or motivation — and decreasing avoidance behaviors in the classroom. The key to these behaviors is the individual child. Thus the search for materials starts with the learner.

The Community as a Materials Source

The second element in the inventory of materials is the community the teachers serve. What kind of a community is it? How is land used? Why does this community exist in this place at this time? These and other questions asked in the unit on the Community offered in Chapter 4 are only a part of the potential.

Residents of the community have experienced many of the same things the pupils have, and more. As teachers help children grow in skills of communication and group process as well as in their knowledge of the economics, politics, social interactions, historical perspective, and other aspects of their culture, they may call on the adults of our community who have learned these things and utilized them.

Beyond the normal experiences associated with personal survival and relative prosperity, residents in a school's community may be able to furnish a great deal more. Some may possess special skills or competencies of interest to our children. Representatives of particular kinds of occupations or businesses provide rich input for classes. Institutions in the community should not be overlooked. Other schools, churches, corporations, clubs, and service agencies have vast potential. Potential resources may be catalogued to provide a community resource file.

The process used to compile a community resource file can provide a rich learning experience. An interview schedule or questionnaire designed and administered by the students — even very young students — can be used. Questions will reflect the particular interests and needs of the pupils. Answers will give insight to the unique character and needs of the community. These activities develop skills in language and interpersonal relations and the students inevitably gain a new perspective of their community. Upon completion, the resource file should include invaluable sources of information on travel, occupation and experience.

MATERIALS FOR THE STRUCTURED-DEPENDENT STAGE

Materials judged appropriate for the structured-dependent stage are categorized as Project Materials and Commercial Materials. There is no inherent superiority in either category. The role of focus or emphasis must be kept in mind during discussions of methods and materials; each item is useful in a wide range of situations, although it is necessarily discussed in a specific place.

PROJECT MATERIALS FOR THE STRUCTURED-DEPENDENT STAGE

Throughout the country local school districts, colleges and universities, and government agencies acting alone or in concert have sought to provide instructional materials suited to the needs of students and teachers. We choose to refer to these efforts as projects. The efforts of the various social studies curriculum projects operating during the period 1964-1971 have been based on widely diverse assumptions about what children "ought" to learn.

Careful examination of the products of curriculum-development projects reveals that they tend to promote inquiry-oriented and conceptually-based study. There is heavy emphasis on the procedures or processes of social sciences in attempts to define problems, formulate hypotheses, gather and analyze data, and draw reasoned conclusions.

Only a very few projects chose foci related primarily to the psychosocial development of children. None have completely succeeded in developing materials sufficient to sustain instruction in this vital dimension of growth. As this is being written some of the most promising materials are at the pilot testing stage. There appears to be particular cause for optimism regarding the products of the "Humanistic Education" movement. Readers are urged to examine Fantini and Weinstein's book *Toward Humanistic Education: A Curriculum of Affect* (1970) or George Brown's *Human Teaching Is Human Learning* (1970). The products of the Centers for Humanistic Education at the University of Massachusetts and in Santa Barbara, California will be of particular interest.

Materials developed in actual classrooms using assumptions of psycho-social development have been used to illustrate earlier chapters;

these are very compatible with many elements of the curricula discussed as useful in the initial-exploratory stage.

The Human Development Program

Bessell and Palomares adopted the development of a child as a complete human as the focus for their *Human Development Program* (1967) for kindergarten and grade one, summarized here. Note the relationship between this program and the unit on Feelings in Chapter 2. The team of teachers who developed the Feelings unit seem to have intuitively understood and sought the general purposes set out by Bessell and Palomares.

1. The principal reasons for devising a human development program is to place in the hands of those classroom teachers who have either special competence or special training an easily administered methods manual, which can be used to promote personal effectiveness in children.

2. The over-all program consists of a series of teacher's guides beginning at age 4 or 5 and going on up through all of the grades to junior high school, with each age level offering successively advanced material. At any grade level after the first there is sufficient flexibility in age-range challenge so that the guides may be used in direct sequence, once the program is begun.

3. Can there be any disagreement with our nation's conviction that human beings are our most valuable resource? Our children, as an undeveloped resource, therefore merit every possible attention if their potential talents and personal satisfactions are to be realized to the fullest.

4. Self-realization does not occur by chance. Academic realization which culminates in meaningful work performance results from carefully planned and administered curricular sequences. But research has shown that far more often people lose their jobs because of personal ineffectiveness than because of technical incompetence. It would seem wise, therefore, to provide a program to assure personal effectiveness to go along with the usual academic (or technical) education. And this should be supplied as a carefully planned program of learning experiences.

5. Personal effectiveness at each grade level is defined as a set of principles. At the first level, lesson sessions are prepared which provide developmental opportunity in three areas which have been demonstrated to be of critical significance in the acquisition of patterns of personal effectiveness. These are Communication (the aware perception, reception, and transmission of one's own and other people's feelings, thoughts, and behavior), Mastery (capability coupled with self-confidence), and Social Interaction (a practical comprehension of what leads to social approval or disapproval).

6. The program is so designed that it is assured that each child will markedly and measurably increase his awareness of himself and of others. Tasks of graduated difficulty are presented which offer an interesting challenge but also assure mastery of skills. While the mastery ingrains a feeling of capability, the socially reinforcing remarks of the teacher assure a growing sense of self-confidence. Presentation of structured social interactions promotes the acquisition in each child of a first-hand appreciation of the causes and effects in interpersonal behavior. These children will inevitably be more effective in all spheres of their lives because each one has had development of those characteristics which demark the effective person from the ineffective one. These children should have a deep personal comprehension of themselves and of the meaning and purpose of their activities. They will naturally and properly come to see themselves as effective. And with this self-concept they will be highly motivated and optimistic in facing new challenges as well as being more effective in actually coping with those challenges.

7. Personal happiness, social usefulness, and technical effectiveness tend to go together. This program offers a special set of methods to further those personal objectives which would be the appropriate companions of technical accomplishment.

8. The Level III Teachers Guide for the third grade offers content and methods in further human development in three basic areas (Self-Understanding, Responsible Competence, and Social Interaction). These are Self-Worth (the effective child values himself), Things I Can Do (the effective child is capable and experiences himself as being capable), and Liking and Being Liked (the effective child knows why people like each other).

9. Further guides offer content and method in other and more advanced areas within the basic themes.

10. The timeliness of this program is attested to by the awareness of the general population of the relationship between the lack of true developmental personality training for effective living and the unsatisfactory results they see in the lives of ineffective individuals.

11. It might be hoped that some of the social consequences of this curriculum sequence will be a reduction of prejudice and other group tensions and their replacement by a spirit of mutually enhancing creativity.

The general purposes are translated into suggested teaching-learning activities which become the instructional materials. Consider the three examples set out in the remainder of this section. (See also, for an idea of their place in the curriculum, the overview in Chapter 2.) The first example is the Thursday material from the second week's work in Unit 1, Communication: The Language of Pleasant Awareness and Expression. (Bessell and Palomares, 1967)

A VERY BAD THOUGHT THAT I HAVE

Review for the children the lessons about nice thoughts and bad thoughts.

Then tell them that everyone can think of bad things. Tell them that some people have very funny feelings about their not-so-nice thoughts. Some people feel that they are bad people because they have bad thoughts and they try to hide these thoughts or deny them so that nobody will know.

Tell them that it is natural to have bad thoughts, just as it is natural to have bad feelings.

Then tell them that where people make their big mistake about bad thoughts is that they do not understand the difference between having a thought about doing something that is bad and actually doing that thing. It might be bad to do it, but it is very hard for a thought to harm someone.

Tell them that if they can understand the difference between thinking something and doing it, then they do not have to be afraid of even their worst thoughts.

Ask them if they can tell the difference between thinking and doing, and after each child has shown that he can explain the difference, then give each child a turn to guess something terrible about what could be in the box. Tell them it can be a bad thought, not just a bad thing.

End by re-emphasizing that it is natural to have bad thoughts, but just because we can think a bad thing that does not mean we have to do it. This point does not need to be made if it is not applicable; e.g., if a child tells of something that is frightening to him.

The activity described below calls for each child to think of "something I want to do for myself, but don't know how" and to share this with others in the class. It is the Thursday material from the tenth week's work in Unit 2, The Development of Mastery: . . . I Can Do Things for Myself.

SOMETHING I WANT TO DO FOR MYSELF, BUT DON'T KNOW HOW

One purpose for today's lesson is to promote overt recognition of limitation, but to allow for the presentation of helpful suggestions by the other children. Every child must cope often with his limitation. It is important to protect him, therefore, against developing a negative self-orientation by:

1. Allowing him the benefit of universalization by hearing a great many other children express their inadequacies, and
2. Allowing him to receive many helpful suggestions from the other children, one of which might work.

This should not be conceived as an opportunity to share futility, but as a chance to foster the spirit of cooperation among the children. It also sets the stage for, by giving license to, the seeking of help from other children rather than only from the teacher.

Some kind of summarative remarks should be made by the teacher pertaining to the rationale mentioned above.

We authors have found these activities increase in effectiveness when the teacher plays the game with the children.

The following is the Friday material from the same unit as the preceding.

SOMETHING I'M VERY PROUD THAT I CAN DO BY MYSELF

Every child has some peak experience in which he really surprised himself in finding out that he could do it all by himself.

Since the children have been at this game now for the past four days, they should now be able to give full expression to some important accomplishment, and they should be encouraged to tell about their success at self-sufficiency in a full measure of detail.

Be sure that every child has a turn; even if some of the children cannot recall something special, then they should be encouraged to tell of some item of self-sufficiency of which they are proud.

Compliment the children as usual, mentioning each by name, and make some summarative remarks about how self-sufficient the children are becoming and how they can certainly look forward to developing even more capability.

The Bessell and Palomares materials are particularly useful when the objective is an open trusting classroom atmosphere. Teachers willing to share some of their hopes and frustrations with children tend to find their children increasingly more motivated when more traditional elements of the curriculum are examined. Imagination is an important aspect of materials evaluation. It has been stated that instructional materials are limited only by the creativity of the person using them.

As you examine materials consider their stated purposes and/or objectives, then try to identify additional or alternate objectives. Your perspective is different from that of the materials developer. It may be more appropriate.

A Causal Approach

Ralph H. Ojeman attacked the problem of social studies curriculum development for young children (K-6) from the perspective of causal orientation toward human behavior and the social environment; there was a brief comment in Chapter 2 on the Ojeman materials. This approach seeks to identify cause-and-effect relationships in the child's own experience. Its meaning and purpose are developed in the introduction (here quoted in part) and in the first lesson taken from the handbook for grade one. (Ojeman, 1959)

The present generation of adults takes it for granted that the child from the earliest years will be helped to learn about the forces that operate in his physical environment. The sciences of the physical world in which the child finds himself appear in the suggested curriculum of every grade throughout the elementary and secondary years. The teaching content in the early years is of a very elementary nature, to be sure, but is designed to help the young learner take significant steps in acquiring an appreciation of how his physical world operates. We tend to take it for granted (and there is evidence to support our assumption) that using a "causal approach" toward our physical environment helps the child in living in and adjusting to that environment.

The teaching of a causal approach to the social environment is not so well developed. Much of our past teaching, as it related to the social world, has been concerned with what people do. Only in recent years has there been a growing interest in helping the child understand more about why people do what they do and what some of the effects tend to be of alternative ways of working out social situations.

AN EXAMPLE OF CAUSAL APPROACH—THE NEW MITTENS

To the Teacher

You probably have noticed that when one child does something to another, the latter may make a "snap judgment" or jump to a conclusion as to the meaning of the behavior. For example, one child may hit another. The second child may immediately assume it was deliberate even though circumstances indicate that perhaps it may have been accidental. One child may make some remark and another may misinterpret it completely and not think of the several meanings or interpretations.

The question is, can we help children to look at such behavior more objectively and get the facts as to how it came about before jumping to conclusions?

Misplacing or losing mittens, scarves, boots, crayons, and so on is a frequent occurrence in the primary grades. This story seems to be a good one to use early in the year to help the children stop and think before quickly blaming someone else for taking a lost or misplaced article.

Suggestions for Using the Story

As has been suggested before, early in the year while the children are still adapting to school and group work, it seems best to intersperse short discussion questions in the body of the story rather than having a long discussion at the end. However, it is important to keep these discussions brief so the children will not lose the thought of the story. Questions that might be used have been included in this story.

This finger play poem can be used to introduce the story.

THE MITTENS

I like the way my fingers feel
Inside my mittens.
Only .   .   .   .
I sometimes wonder
If my thumbs all by themselves —
Are lonely.

Introduction

Today, we have a story about two girls who were angry with each other. Let's see how this happened.

[A story follows the introduction. The story, presented in dialogue form and supplemented by pictures tells about two girls and a new pair of mittens. Patty believes Charlotte has taken her new mittens and tells the teacher. In the ensuing dialogue the problem is solved and the girls reconciled. Discussion questions are presented.]

Miss Barry saw the girls coming back to school together. They were laughing and talking to each other.

Later that day when Miss Barry saw Patty and Charlotte, she said, "So the mittens have been found. I am glad about that. It often helps when we can talk over with each other something that is bothering us. It often makes it easier if we can do it at the beginning."

Suggested Discussion Questions

1. What did you think about the story?
2. Is there anything you would like to tell about the story? (Let them relate personal experiences if they care to.)
3. How did it happen that Patty thought Charlotte had taken her mittens?
4. What did she do about it?
5. What did the teacher think when Patty told her about it?
6. How did Charlotte feel when Patty wouldn't talk to her?
7. How did Miss Barry help to find the mittens?
8. What might Patty have done in the beginning when she couldn't find her mittens?

[Further suggestions about using the story attempt to increase its effectiveness and build on children's responses.]

Following Through on Each Question

Often children may have a tendency to answer the question with only one word, such as "sad" or "happy." It is usually a good plan to carry the questioning further, helping the children to understand how the behavior came about. Children also may have a tendency to jump to conclusions or decide what is to be done before they think of what caused the problem. Through further discussion, help them to see how the behavior developed.

The children may need help in bringing out what some of the possible causes may be for the behavior. If the teacher doesn't guide the discussion, pointing out the causal factors, the children may tend to think only of the surface approach to the behavior. They may tend to think of ways to help children — such as ways of overcoming shyness — without thinking of the underlying factors producing the behavior.

Following Through	**Not Following Through**
T. What do you think of the way Patty was trying to solve her problem?	T. What do you think of the way Patty was trying to solve her problem?
P. It was good.	P. Good.
T. Why do you think it was good?	T. Yes, it was good.
P. Because she let the teacher know right away what was bothering her.	T. If you were Patty, would you have done the same thing, that is, let your teacher know what is bothering you?
T. If you were Patty, would you have done the same thing and let your teacher know what is bothering you?	P. Yes.
P. Yes.	
T. How would you have done this?	

The teacher does not even attempt to "get behind" the responses given by the pupils. She does not find out what led the pupils to respond the way they did.

These materials possess unquestioned potential for social learning. However, the questions raised in Chapter 2 regarding their use with very young children including kindergarten and first grade remain. Children must possess the intellectual equipment to understand causal relationships. Beware of verbalizing.

The "Becoming" Curriculum

A program developed by Wells for the ASSIST Center of the Wayne County Intermediate School District, Wayne, Michigan, presents an encouraging attempt at a psycho-social program for K-6 termed the *Becoming Curriculum*. (Wells, 1969)

The **Becoming** Curriculum is a comprehensive psycho-social-educational program to help children move toward self-actualization. . . . The theoretical model for self-actualization comes from such existential-humanists as Fromm,

Rogers, Buber, May, Jourard, Shostrom, and particularly Abraham Maslow. . . .
The program is based on the following premises:

1. Life's most important and exciting journey is **Becoming** — the quest for actualization.
2. **Becoming** has the potential for being the goal or ideal that can capture the imagination of our youth and free them from the present destructive trends toward alienation for productive lives of commitment and growth.
3. The primary goal of education of all levels is the continuing development of authentic, fully functioning people.

The general design of this curriculum is such as to emphasize many elements from the entire behavioral science field. Students are expected to collect, analyze, and generalize about data. They are asked to examine many alternative ways of solving problems and hypothesize on the consequences of acting on the alternatives. The value issues involved in the many problem areas are studied and students are expected to make a commitment on an issue and **do something about it!** This requirement to take a stand, select a goal and act is directly related to our conviction that the present absence of these expectations for the children in our schools has contributed to the anomie and alienation so prevalent among our young men and women.

The ASSIST materials begin with self-awareness, capitalize on what the child knows, and move on to reinforce strengths and eliminate weaknesses. Each lesson includes a title and a time estimate. Instructional goals are stated in performance terms. The evaluation component of each lesson is impressive. Evaluation is focused on the effectiveness of the lesson rather than on the assumed adequacies or inadequacies of the child.

COMMERCIAL MATERIALS FOR THE STRUCTURED-DEPENDENT STAGE

In 1970 a number of federally funded curriculum development projects were terminated. Their products were purchased by commercial publishing companies for packaging and distribution. Thus, in 1971 there are at least seven new elementary social studies curricula available for purchase. In addition, a number of projects have published their own materials.

Too many commercial materials are available for exhaustive listing here. Those materials selected as illustrations or examples represent the authors' frame of reference and leave room for teachers' personal creativity. The fact that materials cited here are absent from a classroom does not prohibit the teacher's conducting the kind of instruction suggested by a psycho-social approach.

Materials discussed in this section were selected to reflect the earliest stage at which they were judged appropriate.

The Taba Social Studies Curriculum

The late Hilda Taba directed one of the best known curriculum-development projects in cooperation with the Contra Costa County Schools in California. This curriculum, published as the *Taba Social Studies Curriculum* (Durkin and colleagues, 1969 A) reflects the concept of the spiral curriculum illustrated in Chapter 3. Taba selected eleven constructs, referred to in the materials as key concepts, which serve as threads for this K-8 curriculum. The constructs include: causality, conflict, cooperation, cultural change, differences, interdependence, modification, power, societal control, tradition, and values.

Each concept is supported for purposes of instruction by a generalization referred to as an organizing idea appropriate to the given grade level. Each concept reappears in each grade at an increasing level of sophistication. The Taba materials here discussed are contained in handbooks for the teacher, not in student texts. However, the materials represent the expanding-horizons approach to social studies curriculum and are therefore correlated to most traditional and many new materials. An illustrative example of this program was presented in Chapter 3.

This approach permits the teacher to move one step from a textbook curriculum. Since only one book is required per classroom the program is relatively inexpensive.

A classroom teacher offers this appraisal of the Taba curriculum:

> Hilda Taba bases her program on eleven key concepts which represent highly abstract generalizations. The concepts are single-word labels standing for abstracted characteristics that a number of instances have in common, such as causality, conflict, cooperation, etc. Each unit of the program is headlined by a main idea that is, in essence, a generalization. This generalization is usually less abstract than the key concepts.
>
> The Taba Project is highly inductive. Many of the learning activities in her program begin with the teacher asking an open-ended question. This means that a teacher is not searching for specific facts but rather answers from many class members that are resulting from thinking and experiences of the members. Dr. Taba stresses that the teacher must establish a focus by her opening question or unproductive discussion will result. She also emphasized that when a teacher is attempting to keep children on the track, she is attempting to control the process, not the content, of the discussion. The beginning question must also elicit the kind of data that is needed for the task at hand and should also help children make comparisons of events.
>
> The Taba Curriculum makes use of films, filmstrips, and books, as do

most other series. However, her program literally forces participation from children through discussion and learning activities, while children tend to be passive recipients of social studies content with the use of other series. But the Taba Curriculum forces the teacher to think and be more explorative in her teaching also.

It was rather hard for me to see the starting and stopping of each lesson because content is based on sequential, numbered learning activities. The first unit had 45 learning activities plus evaluation exercises. I concentrated on the opening and first four learning activities which assesses the background of the child on homes leading up to the Eskimo home and seeks to have the children suggest some hypotheses. The opening question causes the children to group and label, the basis of concept development. The first activity leads to the organization of material in chart form. Further activities include artistic expression and hypotheses formulation.

The Social Science Laboratory Units

The Social Science Laboratory Units (Lippitt and colleagues, 1969) were developed at the Bureau of Social Research of the University of Michigan. The basis of the program is in field psychology. Each child's life, for that matter each person's, is viewed as being in balance beam while acted upon by numerous forces and counterforces. Thus the field — life — becomes a force field.

Change in the relative impact of these interacting forces results in an imbalance, disequilibrium. There is a basic human tendency to seek equilibrium. If an individual perceives imbalance he attempts to remedy it by removing or countering the source.

These units utilize extensive role-playing, dramatic play, and visual stimuli to create social situations in which an imbalance is present. Students are asked to examine the situation very carefully in order to define the precise nature of the problem. Through discussion, hypotheses are generated which attempt to predict the eventual outcome of the situation. Data which might shed light on the situation are collected and analyzed. Particular emphasis is placed on analysis with regard to specific social science constructs, concepts, and generalizations. The end product of these investigations is the child's ability to act to resolve common social problems.

The Field Enterprises Social Studies Program

Field Enterprises has published a K-12 social studies program (Gross and Michaelis, 1970) which reflects much of the current move in curriculum development. The program, under the direction of Richard Gross and John Michaelis, is conceptually based and is susceptible to an inquiry approach. This series has several particularly exciting characteristics. Initial units of the first text require little or no reading. They are essentially picture-book units. Each picture is selected for the concepts it may unlock.

Cross-cultural study, a Michaelis trademark, plays an important part in the development of this series which might be referred to as multidisciplinary in approach, employing data or techniques from various social or behavioral science disciplines as the particular topics of study. For example, "City Problems in America" (Chapter 7 of Book Three, *Towns and Cities*) contrasts life in the United States and in Latin America. Contrasts are not limited to the families of the areas who are members of relatively similar middle or upper socio-economic classes. Examples of slum housing and life are included along with contrasting upper-class situations. Each example is supported by many up-to-date pictures and other illustrations. A real attempt is made to deal with the important social, economic and political problems of urban life.

For example, a picture of slum housing in Puerto Rico is captioned, "Why might people who live in these homes in Puerto Rico want to move to New York City?" Another photograph of a poor white rural family asks the question, "Why would this family leave the farm and move to town?" The questions of adjustment to a new environment and retention of personal ethnic identity are also covered.

Each question includes dimensions of anthropology, economics, history, law, political science, psychology, sociology and so on. The emphasis selected will vary with each group using the materials.

The Social Sciences: Concepts and Values

The Social Sciences: Concepts and Values (1970) is designed to create a classroom environment in which children may learn to understand human behavior and become responsible participants in the social order. The content of the program is drawn from the social sciences — anthropology, sociology, geography, economics, history, and political science — and is structured on five conceptual (cognitive) schemes:

1. Man is the product of heredity and environment. (Anthropology)
2. Human behavior is shaped by the social environment. (Sociology)
3. The geographic features of the earth affect man's behavior. (Geography)
4. Economic behavior depends on the utilization of the resources. (Economics)
5. Governments resolve conflicts and make interaction easier among people within their environments. (History, Political Science)

These schemes, with the desired behavior of the users of the program at a given grade level, are clearly outlined.

In Unit One the major concept to be taught is *adaptation*. A clear definition of the teaching objectives for each section is outlined in terms of concept-seeking, value-seeking, and methods of intelligence. For example, these teaching objectives for Section 1 are as follows:

> Concept-Seeking: Children begin to grasp the concept of adaptation by recognizing that communities adapt to their physical environment.
>
> Value-Seeking: Children begin to be aware that the values held by communities are related to their environment.
>
> Methods of Intelligence: **Observing** ways in which the Eskimos adapted to their physical environment. **Categorizing** different materials man uses for food, shelter, and clothing in different environments. **Inferring** that men adapt to their environment.

This structure enables the teacher to deal positively with the "explosion" of human knowledge, for concepts have a stability which transcends a topic-centered, fact-oriented curriculum. Concepts and values — the concepts of man as a social being, and the values that make him human — are the substance of this program.

This program permits the child to seek orderly explanations of human behavior as does the social scientist. The lessons in the series include the following aspects: the teacher creates a situation (a problem situation or a setting); the children are encouraged to explore human behavior and the human environment; they seek orderly explanations of the behavior under inquiry; they test their explanations.

A classroom teacher discussed a portion of *Social Sciences: Concepts and Values* as follows:

> Unit Three in the Level One text is entitled "The People We Learn From" for it deals with the concept of interaction. In the first lesson of this unit, the children were exposed to a setting of two groups of children involved in the learning process. Through exploration of this problem-situation they were to grasp one attribute of the concept of interaction, namely, that man learns skills and ideas from others around him. Lesson Two, on which this evaluation will focus, attaches the quality of time to this learning development which was introduced in the previous lesson. Learning development is to be perceived as a gradual process requiring an interaction with others. It is a process that builds on former experiences.
>
> This lesson is primarily inductive in nature. The teacher does not begin with a statement or generalization to be examined by the students but rather provides a situation in which an idea can be formed. She assists this self-discovery through an array of questions (memory, interpretation, evaluative, etc.) which allows the child to use different learning skills in the process. The discussion patterns begin with the general and lead to the specific — focusing on

the child personally. This facilitates the incorporation of the idea under study into the child's personal mental framework.

An inductive lead-in is suggested to create a learning situation for this lesson. Children have brought or the teacher has brought in baby pictures. (visual stimulation) The children are asked to discuss among themselves the activities an infant can perform. Through the use of memory questions such as "What can babies do?" the teacher initiates a general discussion on infants and gradually shifts the discussion toward the child's personal growth. "What have you learned?"

The lesson is developed through the pictures in the text of problem-situations showing some of the activities a six-year-old girl has learned. The children are encouraged to describe the obvious physical changes between the six-month-old infant and the six-year-old child. The teacher may assist this observation through interpretation questions such as "How has she changed?" Focus is shifted to changes in skills and intellectual development through questions such as "Can Joan understand what her mother says?"

The children are then led to infer other skills that Joan has probably learned. Following this discussion, concentration is once again placed on the children's own learning. They are influenced to associate persons with their learning through questions such as "Who taught you to use a knife and fork?" This discussion leads to a summary of all that has been discussed. A question such as "How did you learn?" gives the children the opportunity to synthesize this information individually. Their responses will reflect various ways of learning—learning as a gradual process through the interaction with others.

The lesson contains a list of alternate experiences which can be used in further developing this idea in a variety of ways. Children are unique individuals with a wide scope of interests. Perhaps one of these experiences would prove more suitable for arousing the interest of your particular class.

This lesson is indicative of the conceptually oriented format used throughout the text. It deals with the time aspect of development which results from interaction. (The concept developed in this unit.) Yet this concept could not be fully grasped until the child had some understanding of man and his environment. These ideas were developed in the first two units based on the concepts of human variability and adaptation to environment. Thus these concepts are introduced in an orderly fashion and interrelated as one moves through the text. Concepts encountered earlier are used to introduce the new ones and aspects related to them. The lessons remain within the framework laid out—working with the familiar to learn the new. This method makes the assimilation and accommodation processes much easier.

MATERIALS FOR THE STRUCTURED-INDEPENDENT STAGE

As children move into the structured-independent stage of psycho-social development their skills and knowledge competencies have advanced markedly. Most are reading at or near grade level. The activities and materials utilized during the first two stages contained significant language-development components. At the same time children have been brought to an awareness of themselves as individuals and as participating members of various communities.

The materials available to support instruction have also changed. Generally speaking, those programs discussed in the earlier sections include materials appropriate for the more advanced developmental stages. For example, both the Field Enterprises and Harcourt Brace Jovanovich programs are K-12. Materials to be noted in this section represent the input of material—data, concepts, technique—associated with a specific social science discipline. None of the materials to be discussed here are designed specifically to promote psycho-social development.

As in the preceding section, materials are distinguished as project materials and commercial materials.

PROJECT MATERIALS FOR THE STRUCTURED-INDEPENDENT STAGE

University of Georgia Anthropology Curriculum Project

The University of Georgia Anthropology Curriculum Project (*A Sequential . . .*, 1969) seeks to introduce young children to the science of anthropology. Teams of anthropologists and educators have developed materials designed to reveal the structure of the discipline as well as the method of the scientist. The first materials produced represented an extremely high level of scholarship; second-generation materials were modified to increase "teachability."

Materials include thoroughly developed teacher's manuals and resource books. The resource books are particularly helpful to the teacher whose background in the discipline may be inadequate.

Packets of materials for students include vocabulary lists as well as narrative. Much of this material is deductive in nature. The following lesson on New World Prehistory is representative of the deductive element.

A. **Introduction:**

Indians had been in the New World many thousands of years before the white man came. Some of them had built large and beautiful cities. Some of them were still hunters and lived in small villages. Many of them were farmers and grew corn. The material in this section will tell you about the Indians of the New World. It will tell you where they came from. It will tell you how their life changed over the years. Study the vocabulary carefully. The words will help you learn about the Indians of the New World.

B. **Anthropology words I must use:**

agriculture

Archaic Stage

astronomer

Classic Stage

climate

domestication

environment

extinct

Folsom point

Formative Stage

glaciers

inhabited

maize

Paleo-Indians

plateau

plaza

Pleistocene

Post Classic

priests

pueblo

pyramid

reservation

surplus

C. **Key ideas I am to look for and learn about are:**

1. Where did American Indians come from?
2. How did the life of the Indians change during the many years before other people came to the New World?
3. Were Indians all over the New World alike?
4. Who were the last people to come to the New World before the people from Europe?

D. **Things I can do:**

1. Collect pictures of Prehistoric Indians. Make a scrap book with the pictures.
2. Write a play about a day in the life of a prehistoric child. Write about a certain group of Indians. (Ask your teacher to help you. Give the play for your class.)
3. If there is an Indian reservation near you, visit it. Give a report to your class about your trip. Tell them what you saw.
4. Draw pictures of the tools used by Indians. Put the pictures on the bulletin board.

E. **Questions to help me think:**

1. Do you think that the first Indians in the New World knew they were in a New World?
2. Why did the life of the Indians change over a period of years?
3. Indians that lived in the desert lived one way. Indians that lived in the woodlands lived another way. Why were the ways they lived different? Was the land around them the only reason their lives were different?
4. Some Indians hunted large animals. Some Indians raised corn and other things. Some Indians gathered roots and berries. What was the best way to get food? Why?

F. **Review Questions:**

1. Where did the American Indian come from?
2. Indians have been in the New World for about 20,000 years. Did the way they live change during this time?
3. Did all Indians live the same way at the same time?
4. When did the Plains Indians get their horses?

In this lesson the major idea is presented and then examples are examined. The inductive portion of the program takes two forms. The first involves study of two primitive peoples, the Kozak and Arunta. Children are encouraged to generalize from this study to their own community.

The second inductive element involves study of archeological techniques. Application of the procedures of the archeologist in real or artificially constructed "digs" provides opportunities for a wide variety of discoveries. The materials for students are occasionally overloaded with technical language. Recent editions of these materials have been revised with the help of classroom teachers. In the process many difficulties have been overcome. The Georgia materials remain the single most complete program for elementary students dealing with a single social science discipline.

Economic Education: A Guide for New York Schools

The Joint Council on Economic Education has sponsored a number of projects designed to increase the effectiveness of instruction in economics at all grade levels. One element of the over-all attempt to enhance instruction was the establishment of Centers for Economic Education at colleges and universities around the country. The Center for Economic Education, State University College at Oneonta, New York developed *Economic Education: A Guide for New York Schools* (Bandy, 1970) under an ESEA Title III project grant. The philosophy of the program is embedded in the directions regarding *How To Use This Guide.*

> Planning for learning is the essence of teaching. What and how you plan are excellent indicators of what you believe school is for. The process by which plans are implemented provides further knowledge of what you believe is the role and purpose of a teacher in the classroom environment.
>
> This guide is a series of plans for learning. It includes the plans for conducting the learning process in and outside of the classroom. It has been constructed from the beliefs which the authors hold about learning and the role of the teacher in that learning process. This guide should not be viewed as a total program for social studies in any grade. It is intended only as a

beginning, but with this difference. The kind of learning environment created by these materials is applicable to all other learning in the social studies.

Planning for learning begins at the end and works backward to where learning by the students starts. The process of planning for learning begins by stating the goals to be accomplished at the end of a given time period. When goals have been defined, the specific objectives involved in reaching those goals must be identified. These are followed by the planning of strategies to reach those objectives. The strategies define the materials that will be necessary, and it is in these materials that the content which the class will be exploring is to be found. In general terms, this was the process followed in constructing this guide.

It would appear, from the previous description, that content was the last consideration in the preparation of these materials. That is very close to the truth. As stated in the philosophy earlier in this guide, public school education should be dealing more with the business of how to learn and less with what to learn. We are not in the business of training economists. That is the responsibility of institutions more specialized than our public schools. Our responsibility is to children and their communities, and it involves the systematic development of learning and thinking skills. That the discipline of economics offers an excellent vehicle by which these skills can be developed is fortunate; otherwise, there would be no reason to include the discipline in the curricula of our public schools.

The program is one of the most usable that the authors have examined. Objectives are clearly defined, appropriate instructional strategies are described, and evaluative techniques are discussed. The program is based on a model of inquiry. Therefore content is generally developed by the student as part of the process of doing inquiry. However, where it seems appropriate content samples or references are included. Topic I of the sixth grade deals with an exploration of the methods man uses to organize the economic life of his community. Economic systems of various world regions are introduced. After the systems and their characteristics have been explored, the students are asked to construct a series of pertinent questions that can be used to investigate the economic systems of other regions.

Seven objectives and instructional strategies for Topic I are listed below. They are followed by the instructional strategies designed for those objectives.

Objectives

1. Given several pictures that depict life in a region,
   —the student will demonstrate his ability
   —**to abstract information** from pictures
   —**by listing** at least five phrases that describe what life is like in the pictures under consideration.
2. Given several pictures that depict life in a region,

—the student will demonstrate his ability

—**to recognize similarities and differences**

—by categorizing under proper labels, at least three ways that life is different, in the pictures, than in his own life.

3. Having categorized the similarities between his life and life depicted in the pictures,

   —the student will demonstrate his ability

   —**to generalize** based on sample evidence

   —**by summarizing,** in his own words, the similarity of man's needs throughout the world and include at least three examples of similar needs.

4. Having categorized the differences between his life and life depicted in the pictures,

   —the student will demonstrate his ability

   —**to recognize cause and effect** relationships

   —**by listing** at least two items that act to cause men to live differently in different parts of the world, and be able to cite evidence to support his position.

5. Given case studies that describe how societies assign jobs to their members,

   —the student will demonstrate his ability

   —**to abstract information** from case studies

   —**by citing evidence** from each case study that identifies the methods used for assigning jobs to people in the societies described.

6. Having discussed three methods which societies use for assigning jobs to their members,

   —the student will demonstrate his ability

   —**to recognize cause and effect relationships**

   —**by explaining** in his own words, what effect each of the three methods (used by societies to assign jobs to their members) has on what jobs will be done, and be able to cite one example of each method.

7. Given a situation that describes a method for assigning jobs,

   —the student will demonstrate his ability

   —**to apply ideas** learned in one situation to other situations

   —by selecting from the three methods for assigning jobs the one most like the situation described.

Instructional Strategies

A. (Strategy for Objectives 1-7)

Post a variety of pictures that depict life in various areas of the world. After students have had an opportunity to view these in some detail, ask:

1. On a piece of paper, write several phrases that describe, in your words, what you feel life is like in the area where these pictures were taken.

2. On the back of the page, make two columns — one entitled Similarities, the other entitled Differences. List under each heading, the ways in which

life in the area shown in the pictures is similar and different from life in your own region.

After these lists have been compiled, discuss the following questions:

1. In what ways is life in these pictures similar to your life? (Should include need for food, clothing, and shelter, families, etc.)
2. Why is it that these similarities exist?
3. If we were to look at pictures of people in South America, Europe, or other parts of the world, would these similarities which we have identified be there also? Why? (Man's needs are similar.)
4. On your paper, write a statement that summarizes the similarities of man's needs throughout the world. (You could evaluate the student's ability to apply this generalization by asking if it applies to several specific places in the world: e.g., Japan, China, Germany, Canada, man on the moon, etc.)
5. Looking now at the differences you have listed, name some of them.
6. What causes these differences to occur in people's way of living? (topography, climate, resources, traditions, or culture)
7. If "traditions" or "culture" is not stated by students, ask: How do the things that people learn from their parents and elders affect what they do?
8. How are the things that you do affected by the things that your parents or teacher tell you? (e.g., school, church, clubs, TV)
9. How many of you really know very much about life, and how people decide to do things in other parts of the world? For example, in our system, as one grows up, one can practically choose any job he wants, provided he can quality for it; e.g., engineer, teacher, salesman, mechanic. We say that we have freedom of choice in this country, and we think it is the only way. But is it really the only way?
10. Do you know of any other ways that societies decide who will do what jobs? (If students can't identify examples that show Command and Tradition, give them Case Study 1 from Appendix at the end of this grade level. If they can identify examples of Tradition and Command, use case studies to see if they can identify which is which.)
11. After having discussed the case study, ask: We have now discussed three different methods that societies use to decide who does what jobs; e.g., freedom of choice, Command, and Tradition. Will the method that a society uses help to determine who does what job in that society? Give some example that you know about.
12. In Virginia, when our colonies were first being settled, many men were so interested in looking for gold that all men nearly starved. Their leader told them that anybody who didn't help get food and build shelter wouldn't be permitted to share these things when they needed them. (a) Why do you suppose he said that? (needs to be fulfilled) (b) Which of the methods we discussed earlier was most like that system in Virginia? (Many other examples can be used: e.g., slavery, military service, "I'm going to be a doctor like my dad.")

13. Which of these methods is best? (It depends on what is being done vs. what needs to be done. Command was best for Virginia, at that time.)

Our Working World

Economics serves as the organizing or focusing discipline for *Our Working World* (Senesh, 1967), the three-level social studies program published by Science Research Associates. This program is of interest for several reasons. First, it is the product of one of the earliest and best conceived social studies curriculum-development projects. Begun under the leadership of a professional economist, Lawrence Senesh at Purdue University, the project was developed and tested in cooperation with the public schools of Elkhart, Indiana. Thus, it was the first major project to receive thorough field testing in actual classrooms.

Second, it offers a social science discipline, economics, as a thread from which hangs or around which develops a much wider inquiry into personal and societal institutions and relationships. The structure of economics is presented in an intellectually honest manner clothed in material that children in grades 4 through 6 can comprehend. For example, examination of the various roles played by family members focuses on producer and/or consumer functions. The student, using a text made up almost entirely of drawings, moves quickly to differentiating between producing and consuming goods and/or services. Additional economic concepts are also examined. However, in the process many ideas representing the broad range of social and behavioral sciences are encountered. Concepts of role-identification and interpersonal relationships associated with sociology or social psychology are readily apparent.

Third, the materials are designed to include a wide variety of activities. Children maintain a high level of involvement resulting in sustained interest. The student texts are brightly colorful, which helps to maintain the motivational level. The series includes three levels—*Families at Work, Neighbors at Work* and *Cities at Work*. The series is an excellent example of a concept-based discipline-oriented curriculum. The following is an evaluation of Lesson 6: "What Keeps People Together? What Keeps People Apart?" found in the *Cities at Work* text.

CONCEPT BEING DEVELOPED

The concept being developed is that in the nature of the development of a city there are some forces which draw people together and others which force them apart. Some of the generalizations presented in this lesson are the following:

1. That there are forces within the city which cause people to form groups based upon economic, political, racial, and cultural interests;

2. that these groups of people may have conflicts with each other;
3. that for a peaceful environment within a city lines of communication must be kept open; and
4. that when these lines of communication are kept open there is a greater chance for lessening conflicts and easing problematic situations.

DEVELOPMENT

The children are presented with the idea that there are some forces within the city which draw people together and others which draw them apart. In the first part of the lesson through analogies, reasons, and examples children are presented with the ideas that the division of labor keeps people together in a city, that common interests draw people into groups, that groups may not agree with each other, that common interests of a neighborhood may keep people together, that different neighborhoods may have conflicts with each other, and that cities today are trying to find ways to help neighborhoods live in peace with each other.

In the second part of the lesson, the book introduces one city, Atlanta, and discusses several methods it has used in trying to cope with the problems of the city. It shows actual pictures of the city and some of its people who have tried to help alleviate the problems in Atlanta.

In the third part of the lesson the book presents a hypothetical situation in story form which incorporates some of the problems suggested in the first part of the lesson and shows the solutions of one family in trying to cope with city life.

Stories of men such as Martin Luther King, Jr., Ivan Allen, Ralph McGill and other Atlantans are presented in the resource unit in connection with their contributions to the problems of the city. In the activity book which accompanies the text, children are given a variety of examples similar to those discussed in the text and yet quite different. The children are asked to interpret the information and to form their own solutions.

VALUE JUDGMENT

The concept presented is one that is of interest and relevance to children today. The concept—there are forces within the city that keep people together and others that force them apart—is presented in a variety of ways. The generalizations present a fair picture of a societal problem; the solutions do not limit themselves nor suggest absolute resolutions. The information given lends itself to inductive learning situations. The textbook provides important generalizations and background by building on statements made through examples and situations. The activity book provides the opportunity for children to "do" something with the material through critical thinking and their own interpretations.

The "activity book" referred to above is a teacher's guide and resource which accompanies each level of the program.

COMMERCIAL MATERIALS FOR THE
STRUCTURED-INDEPENDENT STAGE

Follett Social Studies Program

The Follett Educational Corporation has developed an elementary series focusing on the idea of exploring. (*Follett,* 1969) Exploration becomes the process by which the child moves through an expanding world from his own needs to world regions and finally into United States history and government. Throughout the various texts in the series, elements from the various social and behavioral sciences are introduced as they shed light on the subject at hand. The net result is a multidisciplinary approach.

For example, a unit dealing with Mexico is introduced through the historical perspective of the nineteenth and early twentieth centuries. Interwoven in the historical account are major concepts and data regarding the economic and social-class systems. The role of class in the struggles of 1910-1920 is developed in terms of historical perspective and consequence. At the same time the student encounters many anthropological concepts and is required to demonstrate geographic understandings. Periodically, special sections dealing with specific social scientists are included.

The annotated teacher's editions of the Follett series provide clear statements of objectives and helpful suggestions for learning activities. Evaluation techniques are thorough but not significantly different than other textbook series.

Concepts in Social Science

Concepts in Social Science (King and colleagues, 1968) is the series title for the Laidlaw Brothers elementary social studies program. The program is built on concepts from each of the social science disciplines. The authors prefer to call their program interdisciplinary in nature, emphasizing the overlap and interplay among the ideas introduced.

The texts contain a high inquiry component. Throughout the narrative, questions are introduced to challenge the reader's thinking. Individual texts deal with an expanding world theme, moving from the home through family needs to regional concerns and finally to social studies. This material is somewhat different from most social studies texts.

Each of the six major social science disciplines is introduced in a separate unit. Major ideas which give the discipline its unique structure are introduced as well as the particular method of the scientist. Representative people and instances from real life are used to illustrate the work of the scientist. Materials are bright and cheerful, using both contemporary photographs and drawings.

Annotated teacher's editions provide useful aids in organizing the units. Annotations are particularly strong on teaching activities and evaluation techniques.

Investigating Man's World

Investigating Man's World (1970) is a four-volume series produced by Scott-Foresman as a supplement or alternate to their regular series. The approach is multidisciplinary, drawing ideas from the various social science disciplines.

The program is very strong in the area of concept development. The format is designed to set out on each page the major concept to be learned. Concepts are followed by questions which may serve to open the discussion to further inquiry. In the main, inquiry is treated as a process helpful in creating orderly procedures or patterns for examining data. Questions are used throughout the text to establish a dialogue with the children and to guide them in rational decision making.

MATERIALS FOR THE INDEPENDENT-EXPLORATORY STAGE

As children enter the final independent-exploratory phase of psycho-social development there is a need for both more and less material. Less material of a structured convergent limiting type. More material to stimulate students and encourage them to explore their own concerns. Here we seek invitations to inquiry.

Man: A Course of Study

Man: A Course of Study (Dow, 1971) was developed for upper-elementary and middle-school children under a grant from the National Science Foundation. The curriculum is based on the notion that anything can be taught to anyone in some intellectually honest manner. Thus, many concepts and procedures formerly consigned to college courses in anthropology, sociology, natural science, and other fields, are communicated to elementary-school youngsters.

Man is the subject to be considered. Guiding questions are: What is human about human beings? How did they get that way? How can they be made more so? Children study the biological and social growth and development of animals and other men in order to gain insights into the three defining questions. Four units make up the course.

The intellectual frame of reference for the course is presented in the first unit, dealing with the salmon. Questions related to qualities inherent in a species and their presence or absence in man are considered, with emphasis on how organisms develop. Unit two focuses on the herring gull. Children examine adaptive behavior and what may be referred to as the institutions of the gull.

Group structure and behavior of baboon tribes of Kenya provide the data for unit three. Parallel or analogous social behavior provides the students with data to compare and contrast with human behavior and institutions. The final unit focuses on the Netselik Eskimo, presenting an extremely thorough picture of another culture. Children may be able to see more clearly the reasons for culture-based institutions when the number is reduced, as in a culture where the need for survival dominates man's life.

Materials for *Man: A Course of Study* are mostly visual and do not lend themselves to written description. Interested teachers should view the films and other materials. A teacher would profit also by considering the relationship of this program to the science curriculum in his school.

Environmental Studies

The *Environmental Studies* (1970) come out of a project sponsored by the American Geological Institute and supported by the National Science Foundation. Although the program would seem at first glance a science curriculum supplement, it is more.

Materials prepared to date consist of what might be considered invitations to inquiry. The project developers do not label the group, preferring to identify each activity separately. The essence of the activities is increased awareness of environment and self, with consequent repatterning of behavior.

A packet of materials includes twenty-five activity cards (invitations). The action, as it is called, is limited only by the imagination of the actors. The invitation may ask children to identify things they cannot map — then go out and map them. Some examples might be love, power, status, and so on.

The technique resembles the individual learning package but is considerably more open. Each card in the packet contains suggestions to open the way for more exploration. In many of the suggested activities, the children take photographs.

The two most important sources of instructional materials in the Independent-Exploratory stage of psycho-social development are the community and the student himself. As a student identifies the elements of reality which impinge upon his personal opportunities and expectations he defines unique concerns. These concerns provide a stimulus for exploration.

SIMULATION GAMES[1]—MATERIALS FOR ALL STAGES

Children at all stages of psycho-social development may profit from participation in simulations. Since these activities cross the various phases they are set out here as a discrete set of materials.

The use of games and game-like simulations is becoming increasingly popular in elementary social studies instruction. A simulation game recasts some element of reality in a game format. The format provides for total involvement through participation in what children perceive as a "fun" activity. Readers will recall the Gold Mining game described in Chapter 6 and the N.A.S.A. Survival Game in Chapter 7.

In the last decade educational games have caught the fancy of teachers in both elementary and secondary schools, especially social studies teachers. As is true of every educational innovation, gaming is not a remedy for the evils which plague us in education. Evidence exists, however, to indicate that it can be a very effective teaching tool for teachers and learning vehicle for students. With these potential contributions in mind, it behooves us to learn how to utilize games to obtain their greatest contribution.

One acceptable definition of a game is: Any contest (play) among adversaries (players) operating under restraints (rules) for an objective (winning, victory, or payoff). There are at least four types of games; see the table on p. 313.

It is important for a teacher to recognize the nature of each type and its advantages and disadvantages. In some circumstances, a game of skill would be desirable; in other situations, a game of reality would be a better teaching device. The objectives a teacher has established will determine his choice of the type of game to be played. Simulation games are in the reality category. So also, it may be usefully mentioned, are simulation activities that are not games by reason of lacking the contest aspect.

Because gaming, especially reality gaming, is a teaching device with which many teachers are experimenting, it seems appropos to suggest procedures which may increase the effectiveness of the game. The four categories of procedures are: (1) deciding which game to use; (2) what to do before beginning the game; (3) the teacher's role during the playing of the game; (4) what to do after completion of playing the game.

In deciding which game to use, the following points should be considered:

---

[1] The authors wish to express their thanks and give acknowledgment to Mrs. Nora Crawley for her contribution to the comments dealing with simulation, including the select bibliography.

1. Acquaint yourself with the commercially available games and if funds are available, purchase appropriate ones for your school. (Talk with people who have used them.)
2. After looking at commercially available games, you may decide to make your own. This is easier than you may think. (See following section on designing simulation games.
3. Fit the game into an appropriate unit of study and decide what assignments will precede, accompany and follow the game.
4. Allow adequate time for the game but don't drag it out.
5. Take into consideration the number of students who can participate in a game and if anyone isn't to be involved, plan some other activity during the playing of the game.
6. Most important—pick a game for its *educational* value for a student or a group of students.

The following must be done before beginning the game:

1. Consider the nature of your students before assigning roles. Some oversensitive students may, for example, be given responsibility as scorekeepers. Also, don't place all your able students in the same group.
2. Specify each participant's aims and objectives and where

TABLE OF GAMING TECHNIQUES

Type	Definition	Example	Advantages and Disadvantages
Skill	A game in which the outcome depends on the capabilities of the players	Chess	Adv.: Rewards achievement Disadv.: Discourages slow learners
Chance	A game in which the outcome is independent of a player's capabilities	Dice	Adv.: Dramatizes the limitations of effort and skill Disadv.: Minimizes personal responsibility
Fantasy	A game in which both skill and chance affect the outcome	Poker, Bridge	Adv.: Provides release from conventional perceptions and inhibitions Disadv.: Low cognitive content
Reality	A game which models a real-world operation	Monopoly	Adv.: Highly motivational, with potential carryover to the real world Disadv.: Danger of learning spurious analogies

necessary his resources. Each role must be clearly defined.

3. Check the game kit to be certain all the required pieces are together. In some cases, a trial run with a small group of students is desirable.
4. If the game is a controversial one, talk with any necessary administrative personnel.
5. Warn teachers in the rooms near you that there may be some noise resulting from the gaming activities.
6. Talk with the custodian about desk arrangement if there will be change from the ordinary setup.
7. Consider the designing and administering of a pre-test and post-test to measure any changes as a result of the game. The nature and purpose of the game will determine the desirability of a test and the type of questions asked.

The actual game itself will occupy your attention during the playing, but there are a few very important procedures which may make the play more meaningful:

1. Take periodic "breaks" from the game and evaluate the situation from the students' viewpoints. Make any necessary adjustments.
2. The students should be in the limelight and the teacher in the background. This is a time in which we teachers can learn about our students and how they might react in social situations.

The fourth and final procedure for consideration in gaming is what to do after the completion of the gaming exercise. Among the after-the-game procedures:

1. Ask the students to evaluate the game by suggesting what should be added and/or omitted.
2. A student should never receive a grade on the basis of his game score. Make this clear to the students at the beginning of the play.
3. Return all game items to a special container by checking the list of all the necessary components.
4. Utilize skills and data acquired by the playing of the game to further the development of your students.

If this list appears brief, remember that much of what is learned in gaming is in the affective area of learning and this is an area which we as teachers are just beginning to understand.

Criticism of gaming is usually based on the premise that students do not learn substantive material as a result of participation. Recent research has indicated that this opinion is not correct. (The best reference on this is the article by Heinkel which is mentioned in the bibliography.) In addition to the research which indicates that cognitive learning is not "injured" by gaming, there is also considerable evidence to indicate that gaming is especially effective for affective learning. (See the Heinkel article and the one by DeKock.) The thrust of this discourse is that every teacher should at least consider the use of gaming for classroom instruction; the potential results are student involvement, enjoyment of learning, and better-satisfied teachers.

Designing Simulation Games

There are numerous commercial and project materials for simulations and simulation games; some are listed in the next section. However, it is advantageous or even necessary to design and use games to fit special situations. Five major considerations[2] are usefully observed in doing so.

1. *Procedure.* Decide how the game is to be put into play and the general order in which play proceeds.
2. *Behavior constraint.* Specify what each player must do and what he cannot do.
3. *Goal.* Define the goal and the means and measure for each player's achieving the goal.
4. *Environmental response.* If the environment is part of the game, specify how the environment will behave.
5. *Police rules.* Specify the consequences of violating the designed procedures or behavior constraints.

Commercial and Project Simulation Games

Here is a relatively brief list[3] of simulation games available about the time this book was prepared for publication. The sequence is alphabetical, by title.

Bushman Exploring and Gathering. A two-phase board game to teach the concept of cultural adaptation to a harsh environment. Illustrates the subsistence economy of the Bushmen in the Kalahari Desert. Education Development Center, 15 Mifflin Place, Cambridge, Massachusetts 02138.

Campaign. Deals with nomination and election of state legislators.

---

[2] These are essentially as presented in Sarane Boocock and E. O. Schild, *Simulation Games in Learning* (Beverly Hills, California: Sage Publications, 1968).
[3] Compiled by Sherry Blakely.

Instructional Simulations, 2147 University Avenue, St. Paul, Minnesota 55114.

The Cities Game. Students represent four groups—business, slum dwellers, agitators, and government—and attempt to form coalitions to solve problems. The Cities Game, 1330 Camino Del Mar, Del Mar, California 92014.

The Columbia River Game. Builds an understanding of the industries, agencies, and farming interests along the Columbia River in their relationships to each other and to the river. Teaching Research, Monmouth, Oregon 97361.

Community Response (Disaster). Simulates problems which face individuals when a community is hit by a storm, earthquake, or hurricane. Western Publishing Co., 850 Third Avenue, New York 10022.

Consumer. Installment buyers and credit agents compete in a model of a consumer buying process. Western Publishing Co., 850 Third Avenue, New York 10022.

Dangerous Parallel. The principal objective is to teach students foreign-policy decision making as students play ministerial roles for six fictionalized countries facing a situation similar to the Korean War. Scott-Foresman & Co., 1900 E. Lake Avenue, Glenview, Illinois 60025.

Democracy. Eight games that simulate various aspects of the legislative process of Congress. Western Publishing Co., 850 Third Avenue, New York 10022.

Disunia. Students attempt to cope with problems of the kind Americans faced in the period 1781-1789. The setting is a new planet in the year 2087. Interact, P.O. Box 202, Lakeside, California 92040.

Economy. Designed to develop an understanding of the circular flow of goods and services in the economic system.

Election. A board game for four persons, simulating the steps usually followed in a political career and the procedures involved in the election of a United States President. Educational Games Co., P.O. Box 363, Peekskill, New York 10566.

Free Enterprise. Students learn about the free-enterprise system by assuming roles in various corporations. Instructional Innovations, Redlands, California 92373.

Generation Gap. Simulates the interaction between a parent and an adolescent son or daughter with respect to certain issues on which they may have opposing views. Western Publishing Co., 850 Third Avenue, New York 10022.

Ghetto. Simulates ghetto conditions as students play the roles of fictional persons who seek to improve themselves and their neighborhood. Western Publishing Co., 850 Third Avenue, New York 10022.

Impact—A Community Simulation. Participants play the roles or community members who deal with problems and change. Experience in decision making and problem solving. Instructional Simulations, 2147 University Avenue, St. Paul, Minnesota 55114.

Kolkhoz. Teaches the economic philosophy upon which the collective farm operates. Abt Associates, 55 Wheeler Street, Cambridge, Massachusetts 02136.

Life Career. A simulation of certain features of the labor market, the education market, and the marriage market. Western Publishing Co., 850 Third Avenue, New York 10022.

Manchester. A historical simulation on the Industrial Revolution. Abt Associates, 55 Wheeler Street, Cambridge, Massachusetts 02136.

Market. Focuses on the concept of supply and demand. Students bargain over prices of goods. Abt Associates, 55 Wheeler Street, Cambridge, Massachusetts 02136.

Napoli. A simulation of the legislative process and its interrelationship with political parties. Western Publishing Co., 850 Third Avenue, New York 10022.

Neighborhood. Development of an urban area. Abt Associates, 55 Wheeler Street, Cambridge, Massachusetts 02136.

Panic. Students play the roles of members of economic pressure groups in the United States in the period 1920-1940. Interact, P.O. Box 202, Lakeside, California 92040.

Pollution. Teaches the social, political, and economic problems involved in attempts to control pollution. Abt Associates, 55 Wheeler Street, Cambridge, Massachusetts 02136.

Seal Hunting. Demonstrates the chance interaction of the worlds of seals and the Eskimo. Abt Associates, 55 Wheeler Street, Cambridge, Massachusetts 02136.

Sierra Leone. An experimental, computer-based game in which the student assumes the role of an American economic advisor attempting to improve various aspects of the economy. Abt Associates, 55 Wheeler Street, Cambridge, Massachusetts 02136.

The Slave Trade Game. Deals with the slave trade in the eighteenth century. Abt Associates, 55 Wheeler Street, Cambridge, Massachusetts 02136. (This is a one-day portion of a larger game called the Empire Game.)

Star Power. Simulates the uses and abuses of power in a three-tiered society where the wealthiest group makes the rules. Western Behavioral Sciences Institute, 1121 Torrey Pines Blvd., La Jolla, California 92037.

Sunshine. Students become members of different races in a mythical city and face various urban problems. Interact, P.O. Box 202, Lakeside, California 92040.

War or Peace. Designed to introduce students to the dynamics of international relations. *Scenario in Social Education,* November, 1966, 521-522.

A Select Bibliography on Simulation Games

Barton, Richard F. *A Primer on Simulation and Gaming.* Englewood Cliffs: Prentice-Hall, 1970.

Boocock, Sarane S., and E. O. Schild. *Simulation Games in Learning.* Beverly Hills, California: Sage Publications, 1968.

Chapin, June R. "Simulation Games." *Social Education,* XXXII (December, 1968), 798-799, 803.

Christine, Charles, and Dorothy Christine. "The New Social Studies: Four Simulation Games that Teach." *Grade Teacher,* LXXXV (October, 1967), 109-120.

Christine, Charles, and Dorothy Christine. "Simulation: A Teaching Tool." *The Elementary School Journal,* LXVII (May, 1967), 396-398.

Coleman, James S. "Academic Games and Learning." *Bulletin of the National Association of Secondary School Principles,* LII (February, 1968), 62-72.

Coleman, James S. "Learning through Games," *NEA Journal,* LVI (January, 1967), 69-70.

DeKock, Paul. "Simulations and Changes in Racial Attitudes." *Social Education,* XXXIII (February, 1969), 181-183.

"Foreign Policy Association Bibliography on Simulation." *Social Education,* XXXIII (February 1969), 195-199.

Guetzkow, Harold S. *Simulation in Social Science: Readings.* Englewood Cliffs: Prentice-Hall, 1962.

Heinkel, Otto A. "Evaluation of Simulation as a Teaching Device." *Journal of Experimental Education,* XXXVIII (Spring, 1970), 32-36.

Hogan, Arthur J. "Simulation: An Annotated Bibliography." *Social Education,* XXXII (March, 1968), 242-244.

Ingraham, Leonard W. "Teachers, Computers and Games: Innovations in the Social Studies," *Social Education,* XXXI (January, 1967), 51-53.

Ochoa, Anna. "Simulation and Gaming: Simile or Synonym." *Peabody Journal of Education,* XLVII (September, 1969), 104-107.

Raser, John R. *Simulation and Society: An Exploration of Scientific Gaming.* Boston: Allyn and Bacon, 1969.

Ryan, T. Antoinette. "Use of Simulation to Increase Transfer," *School Review,* LXXVI (June, 1968), 242-252.

Sachs, Stephen M. "The Use and Limits of Simulation Models in Teaching Social Science and History." *Social Studies,* LXI (April, 1970), 163-167.

Shirts, R. Garry. "Simulations, Games and Related Activities for Elementary Classrooms." *Social Education,* XXXV (March, 1971), 300-304.

Shubik, Martin. *Game Theory and Related Approaches to Social Behavior.* New York: John Wiley and Sons, 1964.

Tanaey, P. J., and Derick Unwin. *Simulation and Gaming in Education.* London: Methuen Educational Ltd., 1969.

SUMMARY

Implementing the psycho-social model of instruction articulated in this book requires application of many diverse types of materials. This chapter attempted to describe those materials which most closely comport with the four psycho-social stages of development. The selection was necessarily based upon the authors' frame of reference and does not represent an exhaustive review of current materials. Teachers should consider the needs of their specific groups of students in the selection and development of materials.

CHAPTER 10

A Call to Action

In this final chapter, we authors wish to be consistent with the models of teaching posited and illustrated in earlier chapters. An analysis and evaluation of the psycho-social model of instruction will follow. First is an analysis of the authors' assumptions regarding "what is" and "what ought to be" with regard to individual and societal needs. Next follows a description of some of the problems a teacher might anticipate when attempting to implement some of the lessons presented. Finally, a few comments are made regarding possible ways of launching a psycho-social curriculum for children.

WHY BASE INSTRUCTION ON PSYCHO-SOCIAL NEEDS?

It is our opinion that the needs of present societies ("societies" like the United States, which is presently entering a postindustrial age) point to a curriculum based on children's psycho-social needs. Any day's newspaper will report on numerous political and social institutions seeking desperately to manipulate the environment to better meet the physical, psychological, and social needs of people and community.

The *Atlanta Journal* recently carried a feature story entitled "Every Loser a Winner" in which the writer described the Georgia Special Olympics. The event, sponsored by the Joseph P. Kennedy, Jr. Foundation, brought elementary children classified as "retarded" to Atlanta. All youngsters, regardless of where they finished in a variety of events, received a ribbon and a medal. Such an event is one step, perhaps small, to better meet the love and esteem needs of these children. The newspaper account concludes by relating the following incident.

> The little blonde girl apparently was Mongoloid.
>
> She wore a blue baseball cap with a red visor, and around her neck was a bronze medallion hanging on a red, white and blue ribbon, which she won at the Special Olympics held at a junior college Saturday for 17,000 retarded children in Georgia.
>
> The sign she held said "Clayton," though she and her teacher were from South Georgia. She held it over the teacher's head to shade her from the sun.
>
> Finally, she brought it down on the head of her teacher several times and whispered the teacher's name.
>
> The teacher turned, prepared to chastise the child for beating her on the head, but for some reason first said "Huh?"
>
> "I love you," said the little girl. (Beeman, 1971, 3A)

People in all cultures educate their children in order to meet the prevailing needs in that society. Emile Durkheim has stated that "education is the means by which society perpetually recreates the conditions of its very existence. (Durkheim, 1956, 123) In stable small societies, this socialization takes place through training by adults with whom the child is in daily contact and much learning takes place through simple imitation. Education in this type of culture is carried out the same "natural process" through which a parent teaches his child to walk and talk. Farley Mowat, an anthropologist, describes the socialization and educational process in a simple culture as it applies to an Eskimo boy of the Ihalmiut tribe.

> If an Ihalmiut boy wishes to become a hunter, a great hunter, all at once, his parents do not make him feel foolish nor do they condescend to his foolish fancy. Instead the father sets to work to make a small bow that is not a toy but an efficient weapon on a reduced scale. The father then presents the boy with the bow and the boy . . . sets out for his hunting grounds—a ridge, perhaps, a hundred yards away, with the time-honored words of good luck ringing in his ears. These are the same words which are spoken by the people to their mightiest hunter when he starts on a two-month trip for musk ox. . . . There is no distinction, and this lack of distinction is not pretense; it is perfectly

real. The boy wants to be a hunter? Very well, he shall be a hunter — not a boy
with a toy bow! . . . When he returns at last with hunger gnawing at his stomach,
he is greeted as gravely as if he were his father. The whole camp wishes to
hear about his hunt. He can expect the same ridicule at his failure, or the same
praise if he managed to kill a little bird, which would come to a full-grown
man. (quoted in Vander Zanden, 1970, 525)

In this manner the Ihalmiut socialize the boy. Their practice reflects the needs of their society: for good hunters to find food; for men
of strength, bravery, and honesty; for ego-building experience — success,
social acceptance, and humility or realism in failure. Their culture does
educate their young according to their needs. They do not give a boy a
modern math problem; instead they give him a bow and arrow. Thus
education is provided by the family and the community in a rather intuitive manner through daily living. The Ihalmiut, according to their
needs, have no use for such an institution as the school.

But as societies grew it became quite impossible for parents and
immediate associates to accomplish the full task of socialization. Specialization and cultural diversity have developed. Schools, therefore, have
become necessary agencies to assist in the socialization process.

Schools came into existence several thousand years ago in order to
prepare a select few for leadership and certain professions. In contrast,
during the last century, schools were given the duty to educate the
masses. The basic skills were reading, writing, and arithmetic. The over-
all goal was to achieve literacy, literacy to help man fit and exist in his
fast-moving industrial world. Goals such as job training, advanced scientific knowledge, guidance, and self-awareness were nonexistent. The
individual was not of primary concern in a rapidly changing industrial-
oriented culture.

Today has brought another educational phase based on different
societal needs. Education has become the means of national survival.
People are turning to the school for reasons other than the three R's.
Postindustrial societies are looking for the school to handle value-
oriented problems. Education in such matters as race relations, sex,
drugs, and religions is a possibility at least being entertained by large
segments of our society. Vander Zanden (1970, 524) concludes: "Hence,
schools have come to share with the family the responsibility for trans-
mitting those aspects of culture essential for competent social participation — the norms, values, beliefs, and symbols found within the society."

Cuber, Harper, and Kenkel express the function of education for
today's Americans as being not merely to perpetuate the existing culture but

. . . to evaluate it, analyze it, raise questions, and examine many proposals for
the perpetuation or modification of the society . . . and that another function of

education includes directing social change along the lines that seem desirable
in the public interest. (Cuber, Harper, and Kenkel, 1956, 306-307)

While certainly some public-school systems have made significant
strides away from the traditional view of education as a means of selecting and rewarding a few students (stars) in the social-mobility game, far
too many continue to play "I've Got a Secret" or "One Upmanship" with
children. The needs of society no longer call for such games! Even the
most "successful" at playing such games often look at the schools with
disdain and demand a different education for their children.

Picture, if you will, an unemployed Ph.D. in nuclear physics or a
displaced aircraft engineer. Certainly both are painfully aware of the
inadequacies of an educational system which did not accurately anticipate
the needs of its students and those of society. The future needs of society
certainly must include greater emphasis upon the similar needs all men
possess. On those who find their psycho-social needs easily gratified
must fall the responsibility of bringing satisfaction to those not so
genetically or culturally lucky. Making "every loser a winner" ought to
be a felt priority upon which all people act, not just cute rhetoric.

Are school people revealing a deficiency of profession and society
by neglecting children of low socioeconomic circumstances? Such children do not have the same needs as those of the typical middle-class
suburban society. Yet middle-class America sets up their educational
programs. The result has been low achievement, truancy, inadequate
skills, poor conduct, lack of interest in school, poor self-image, and
numerous other misfortunes.

Certainly part of the problem resides in a conflict of "needs" between members of differing cultures. Consider as one illustration the
attitudes about the simple act of physical aggression. Aggressive behavior can be interpreted in two opposite ways. The middle-class idea
would be to channel this aggression in a positive and productive way,
perhaps into competitive sports. Thus a middle-class parent might refer
to the aggression as a bad behavior pattern and as a challenge to achieve
self-control. But a member of a different socioeconomic class might look
on physical aggression as an expression of self and worth, not to be hidden but to be exhibited as a part of normal expected behavior — a tool of
defense and an attribute of manly strength. A middle-class teacher, seeing physical aggression, typically uses her values and training to judge
the action, not thinking of the child's needs, possibly not even knowing
his needs. The result is poor communication, frustration, and conflict.
End results of many such frictional encounters may then be poor education for the child and unhappiness for his teacher. Cultures can and do
educate their children according to the needs of their society if someone
allows them this function.

The sum of these many insights places on educators a responsibility that is well reflected in the following quotation:

> . . . without first gratifying lower needs, how are we to know the higher needs which may exist in the healthy child? Since the environment is controllable, at least within certain limits, it is the ability to manipulate need level which makes Maslow's theory relevant to educational practice. If the needs for self-actualization, knowledge, meaning, and beauty do not occur, is it possible that they may be induced if the tutoring generation cares enough to keep alive this cultural inheritance of values. (Simpson, 1971, 168)

Certainly teachers stand in the "tutoring generation" as key figures.

PROBLEMS TO BE ANTICIPATED

Now imagine what may confront a teacher who does care enough to keep that cultural inheritance alive, especially a teacher who has read this book and has come to feel the imperative importance of molding curriculum to meet psycho-social needs. She may wish to begin this kind of teaching immediately—may indeed stand ready to challenge the authorities and the community on this point. For the community may not agree with her intention (naturally, most of the community will not have read this book). Thus the teacher's needs for self-actualization— she might even say for integrity—may conflict with her needs for psychological and professional survival (even for physical survival—she has to eat). What is to be done in such a situation?

Take thought before answering that question. It may be useful to review a similar problem. You are a sixth-grade teacher. A Jewish child in your class has been persecuted by members of the class. You recognize this as symptomatic of general community feelings. Your immediate reaction might be to have children study about various aspects of Jewish life, on the rationale that more knowledge will bring greater acceptance —a basic need being largely unmet for this child. Such a solution does not make the necessary provisions for dealing with the antisemitism observed in the larger community. (If you happen to be Jewish, the plot gets even more involved.) Better reasoning might include: study of various religious customs, a description of planned lessons to be presented which might be sent to parents and administrators in advance of the teaching, as well as some less direct means of attacking the problem of acceptance (the bibliotherapy techniques described in Chapter 7, for example.) However you set about dealing with the situation, you may be frustrated. You may find, for one very real possibility, that the school district rigidly holds to a prescribed social studies program that provides no time and no room for teaching about religion or cultural acceptance. You may find other kinds of resistance. What do you do? What do you do, correspondingly, if the school district holds tenaciously to a program that frustrates or ignores the children's psycho-social needs?

You must decide what to do, or whether to do anything.

We are not preparing to advocate compliance with such a system. We are recommending that you make yourself fully aware of the predictable consequences of whatever decision you make — that you explore the parameters of the world in which you operate. Here is a framework for the exploration — an analysis for coping with a problem or perhaps even solving it.

THE PROBLEM

It is time for a change, but the change is resisted.

THE KEY QUESTIONS

Who decides the conditions under which I teach social studies?

What can I do to influence decisions which affect my teaching?

HYPOTHESES

I am the master of my own ship.

Decisions are made by an unknown "they" (spoken about often in the teacher's lounge) who are not responsive to my influence.

(Quite possibly neither of these hypotheses is wholly correct; you may make some decisions, "they" make others.)

NEEDED DATA

1. What does the State Department of Education say about the social studies curriculum?
2. Who determines the textbooks and supplementary materials available for use in instruction?
3. Does the school district have a curriculum council? What does it do?
4. Does the district employ curriculum supervisors? Do they recommend or do they direct? Do they evaluate teachers?
5. Is the school principal primarily an instructional leader or an administrator?
6. Are teachers in the district aware of educational developments on the national level, particularly social studies developments?
7. What federal funds does the school district receive?
8. What other groups provide incentive for program development?

SOURCES OF DATA

1. Fellow teachers in your building and district.
2. Your principal — an interview.
3. Your school district's staff directory.
4. State and/or local curriculum guides.

5. Bulletins from the State Department of Education.
6. Local news media.
7. Local parent's organizations.

ANALYSIS OF DATA

You may look at the data in a variety of ways. One method which is both useful and rapid involves the development of a decision table. Set down the people most directly affected by the decision makers you are attempting to identify (you the teacher, and your pupils). Identify the characteristics of the classroom; the building; the instructional materials; the auxiliary services — all the pertinent facilities and services. Break these into components and determine who decides the quantity and quality of each available to you. Check those decision makers whom you can reach, and establish a list of priority items for their attention.

You have probably reached some tentative conclusions regarding the degree of influence exerted on your school district by various government agencies. The degree for each agency or level of government may be placed on a continuum ranging from little or no effect to rigid authoritarian control. Similarly, your own potential influence will vary greatly. There is no pat formula guaranteed to result in the changes you desire.

One inescapable conclusion is that the school curriculum is responsive to its environment. Every elementary school in the United States exists at the pleasure of some kind of governing board. The majority of these boards represent the community which supports the school and their decisions reflect the interests and preferences of their communities. Education has traditionally served as the vehicle by which a society transmits its culture from one generation to another. (Remember the Ihalmiut.) As teachers we have the dual responsibility of employee of the school system and professional educator. On the one hand we must consider the goals of the community we serve and on the other the educational objectives which we, as professionals, establish. In a democratic society there should be little conflict between the interests of society and the objectives of education. The essence of the relationship resides in the community's responsibility for the goals of education and the teacher's responsibility for the implementation of programs to achieve those goals. Put another way, the community largely determines the ends and the professional educators determine the means.

LAUNCHING A PSYCHO-SOCIAL PROGRAM

It should be clear from preceding discussion that the teacher must begin by assessing the nature of community needs as well as the needs of each individual child in the class. Obviously not all lessons illustrated here are appropriate to all communities or all children. A fourth-grade class in an economically disadvantaged area doesn't need lessons concerned with bringing about some understanding of what it's like to be poor. Suburban children, in contrast, ought to be taught something about the effects of poverty. The unit on gangs presented in Chapter 5 is certainly structured in a way that it would be more responsive to the needs of inner-city Philadelphia kids than it would be for rural children in southern Georgia.

If you are undertaking to launch a program based on children's psycho-social needs, you will have to tell the community what those psycho-social needs are. You will need the interest inventories and other assessment techniques already examined and discussed (particularly in Chapters 2, 3, and 8). You may have to go further, as by inventorying the needs of individual children for discussion with all those who claim a voice in decision making (see the example of a form for making such an inventory).

Inventory of a Child's Unfilled Needs. *The needs are discovered through observation and through interviews with the child and with other children. The listed behaviors are examples.*

BEHAVIORS	CLASSES OF UNFILLED NEEDS				
	PHYSIOLOGICAL	SAFETY	BELONGING	SELF-ESTEEM	SELF-REALIZATION
Sleeps in class	✓				
Never talks, in or out of class			✓		
Has no hobbies					✓

In considering the nature of the community in which you teach, it is suggested that you use your own community (in which you spent most of your childhood and adolescence) as an axis of comparison.

Studying local community newspapers can be a significant source in determining local community needs. Analysis of articles (front page, editorial, community-social, sports, entertainment, advertisement, and classified ads) with reference to need levels (physiological, safety, security, belonging-acceptance, esteem and status, self-actualization) can provide clues about introduction of needs-based instruction.

Getting acquainted in the community and interviewing local residents provides additional clues for instruction. Most residents are impressed by teachers who care enough to ask their opinion. The biggest payoffs can come from volunteer work in the community—in sum, becoming an integral part of the community in which you teach.

Additional information regarding needs of both your students and their community can often be gleaned from veteran teachers in your school. The school principal, because of the nature of his responsibilities, may well be the most "tuned in" person available with regard to community needs.

SUMMARY

In this chapter we have reviewed, in extreme brevity, some problems of the teacher who sets about making a change toward a psycho-social curriculum. For all the attention to these problems, the chapter is nevertheless a call to action, a call to accept the risks that confront those who respond to the call. We have suggested approaches that enhance the possibility of success and may reduce the risks. But the risks cannot be wholly evaded; they attend any move toward innovation. And we have not advocated surrender. We are deeply impressed by the fact that each succeeding class we teach brings greater numbers of students dedicated to such causes as racial and social equality, and the acceptance of the "community of man" concept. Perhaps this trend was inevitable. Yet success in fulfilling the basic survival needs of all seems very far off.

Lest youth be discouraged to the point of rejecting ideals which today seem at times so remote, the authors wish to conclude this portion of their own efforts to stimulate a psycho-social curriculum with the following quotation:

> But if civilization is to be coherent and confident it must be known in that civilization what its ideals are. There must exist in the form of clearly available ideas an understanding of what the fulfillment of the promise of that civilization might mean, an imaginative conception of the good at which it might, and, if it is to flourish, at which it must aim. That knowledge, though no one has it perfectly, and though relatively few have it at all, is the principle of all order and certainty in the life of that people. By it they can clarify the practical conduct of life in some measure, and add immeasurably to its dignity.

This statement is Walter Lippmann's; it was made in *A Preface to Morals* (pp. 322-323), published in 1929.

APPENDIX

Teaching About Controversial Issues

Controversy is the natural outgrowth of interaction. Our tendency to react negatively to the word and consequently our reluctance to deal with "controversial issues" in the classroom is a function of the process of enculturation. A culture which emphasizes cooperative effort must of necessity play down the notion of conflict. We argue that this ostrich-like posture denies the reality of our individual and collective existence.

The very notion of need assumes the desire for fulfillment. Fulfillment takes place in a finite time-space inhabited by many "others" who are also attempting to fulfill personal needs. The interaction which follows is conflict or controversy.

It may be the low-key conflict of self-discipline involved in the decision to act to fulfill a need. Or it may involve the relatively emotional conflict of childhood friendship relations. The evolution of awareness of controversy encompasses the day-to-day interaction of co-workers and neighbors.

Awareness of controversy and its consequences is heightened by focusing on contemporary events. We do a disservice to the child when we attempt to disguise evidence of conflict throughout his life-space. Traditionally, comments in social-studies texts have provided this con-

331

cern with more heat than light. We have attempted in the body of this text to confront the question at a personal level. However, focus on the individual tends to cover only directly observable conflicts. The papers included in the appendix seek to extend the child's understanding of conflict to extrapersonal and institutional relationships beyond the family. The controversial subjects are presented in specific learning packages by teachers focusing upon particular events which appeared to be related to the psycho-social needs of their youngsters. Potential users of such materials are admonished to use them only after critical analysis of their content and purpose.

The initial lessons on poverty, for example, are written from the perspective of a teacher working with socio-economically advantaged youngsters; their application in other settings could be ineffectual and perhaps even damaging to youngsters not as economically advantaged.

Further, their content often deals with current issues which may be seen differently with the passage of time; the rate of obsolescence of such teacher-prepared packages is usually quite rapid. While the authors realize that many of these lessons cannot be directly used in instruction, they do feel that the format of such lessons as well as the social significance of their content warrant their inclusion.

A SERIES OF INDIVIDUALIZED LEARNING PACKAGES ON POVERTY[1]

An Atlanta-area teacher had occasion to construct some individualized learning packages designed to elicit greater understanding of the concept of poverty among her children who come from middle and upper-middle income homes. It was her hope that these lessons would raise the level of empathy of her children for people not so economically advantaged. Her intention was not to construct lessons which might be seen as condescending or patronizing to the poor. They were used, instead, as the catalyst she needed to engage her students in reflection of a most serious social ill—the maldistribution of income and opportunity in our society. Any teacher who plans to build ILP's on the model of these should keep in mind that they are intended for children who are *not* poor; children who are poor might quite probably have negative reactions.

A DAY IN THE LIFE OF A POOR FAMILY
Objective
This is an ILP about the experiences of a boy or girl whose family happens to be poor. (The life of this boy or girl is not very different from

---

[1] These ILP's were prepared by Mrs. Mary Perkins, a graduate student at Georgia State University in 1971, whom the authors thank.

yours, in that he gets up, goes to school, comes home, and gets ready for another day.) You might think that he is just like you and does what you do, but there are some differences. When you have completed this ILP, you should be able to do the following:

1. Read one of the books below:

   Old Fashioned Girl, Alcott
   Little Women, Alcott
   Huckleberry Finn, Twain
   Oliver Twist, Dickens

2. Write a sketch about the children in the story. Be sure to include the following:

   a. The sleeping conditions described in the story
   b. The food they ate at their meals
   c. The clothes they wore
   d. The recreation they had
   e. Their feelings and attitudes—Were they hungry?

3. Write a sketch about yourself and include the same information listed in item 2, a-e.

4. Make comparative lists of the day's menus for you and for the children in the story.

5. Draw a picture of the house in which you live and the house in which the child in the story lived.

How to Complete this Objective

1. Look in the dictionary for the meaning of "self-esteem" and "respect."
2. Look in the card catalog for the following:

   Human needs
   Psychology
   Maslow

   You may find these names in encyclopedias.

RECOGNITION OF THE WORTH OF THE INDIVIDUAL

Objective

There are many ways to help the poor. In the nineteenth century, help for the poor was in the form of charity. To a sensitive person in need, charity is a bitter word. Today we have poverty programs and welfare programs. These programs attempt to recognize that each person, rich or poor, is an individual worthy of our attention. The poor are taught to help themselves. When you have completed this ILP, you should be able to do the following:

1. Define and discuss "charity."

2. Define and discuss "welfare."
3. Define "poverty programs." Tell what these programs hope to accomplish over and above providing necessary food and shelter.
4. Be able to tell how all the above are different from each other.
5. If you were poor, tell what program you would like to have and why.
6. Visit the Office of Economic Opportunity in your city. Tell what they are doing to help the poor in the inner city.

How to Complete this Objective

1. Look in the card catalog for the following:

   charity
   welfare
   poverty programs

   Also look in books and encyclopedias.
2. Visit the Office of Economic Opportunity.
3. Write to the Department of Health, Education and Welfare in Washington, D.C. Ask for pamphlets concerning their welfare and poverty programs.
4. Write to your State Welfare Department for any information.
5. Contact your church. Ask how they attempt to aid poor people.

PROTEST MUSIC

Objective

The popular songs of our country tell how the people feel about social evils. Songs are one way a person expresses how he feels. During the Depression there were many folk songs about the poor people. Many Americans were very poor; work was extremely difficult to find. Today, when poverty and its control are uppermost in the minds of the American people, we again hear many popular songs protesting poverty in a country as rich as ours. Other songs ally the middle-class American with the poor, and some songs upgrade the poor. When you have completed this ILP, you should be able to do the following:

1. Listen to the following popular songs on the radio or on records:

   a. Johnny Cash, "The Man Dressed in Black"
   b. Frankie Lane, "Poor People"

   Be able to tell the main ideas in these two songs—tell what the song writer is trying to say.
2. Make up a song about life as a poor person. Tell how you feel about poverty and the poor people. Be able to sing this song to the class.
3. Tell whether you agree with Johnny Cash's decision to wear black as long as there is poverty in this land. Give your reasons.

How to Complete this Objective

1. Listen to your local radio station to hear protest music. These are popular

tunes and you should hear them often. If not, send in your request to the local disc jockey and listen when they are played.

2. Consult with your English teacher to find out how to write a short song or limerick. She will help you with form and other technical matters.

3. Use any other source available, perhaps a friend's record.

CONTROLLING POVERTY: EMPLOYMENT

Objective

One of the chief causes of poverty is unemployment. When people are working they have money to live better. In the Great Depression of the 1930's, a large number of people were out of work—more than ever before. Decades later, unemployment is still a problem. (Today we have the largest number of unemployed in our country's history.) The government has attempted to take steps to overcome unemployment, so that poverty can be avoided or controlled. When you have completed this ILP, you should be able to do the following:

1. Report on Franklin D. Roosevelt's first attempts to help the unemployed. Be sure to include the WPA and the PWA, also the CCC.
2. Report on the Appalachia Project.
3. Report on the Anti-Poverty Program.
4. Report on President Nixon's plan to retain workers, especially in the aircraft industry.
5. Pretend that you are a Congressman. What poverty program would you recommend or support? Tell why.

How to Complete this Objective

1. Look in the library card catalog under the following:

Roosevelt, Franklin D.	CCC
New Deal	Appalachia
WPA	Poverty
PWA	Anti-Poverty

Look up these subjects in books and encyclopedias.

2. Read **Franklin Roosevelt: Man of Destiny,** by David Weingest.
3. Write to your Congressman and Senator. Ask them to send you their program to control poverty.
4. Write to a prominent black person whose reputation and activity has been concerned with poverty problems. An official of your state or city would be especially appropriate. Ask him how he feels about the poor black people, and what should be done to help them.
5. Use any other source that you might feel appropriate.

PEOPLE WHO TRIED TO HELP THE POOR—JANE ADDAMS

Objective

This is an ILP about a wealthy woman who dedicated her life to helping the poor. When Jane Addams saw how "the other half" lived, she made up her mind to help them. Miss Addams rented Hull House, which became a haven to her poverty-stricken neighbors. With a group of helpers, she tended children of working mothers, ran a kindergarten, taught immigrants to speak English, ran a soup kitchen, and in general tried to uplift the social conditions of the poor. When you have completed this ILP, you should be able to do the following:

1. Read **City Neighbors** by C. Ingram Jackson, or **Twenty Years at Hull House** by Jane Addams.
2. Give a short report about the book you selected.
3. Tell what Jane Addams did to help the poor. Be sure to include information about her brave humanitarian experiment with Hull House.
4. Pretend you are a working mother in 1889 and very poor. How important would a day-care center be for your children?
5. Compare the present Day Care Centers with those in the 1890's, or more particularly with Hull House.

How to Complete this Objective
1. In the library card catalog find the cards catalogued under:

Addams, Jane	**City Neighbors**
Hull House	Jackson, Claire
Slums	**Twenty Years at Hull House**
Tenements	

Also refer to above topics in the index of books and encyclopedias.
2. Contact a community Day Care Center. Find out how they take care of the children of working mothers. Find out how much they charge, their hours, and the like.
3. Interview a working mother who has a child in the day care center. Find out how she feels about this type of child care.

PEOPLE WHO TRIED TO HELP THE POOR: JACOB RIIS
Objective
This is an ILP about a newspaper reporter who was a crusader against poverty. An immigrant himself, he sympathized with others who were struggling against poverty. Riis's greatest victory was against tenement houses. He exposed the lack of sanitation and unsafe conditions. After 10 years, the city tore down the tenement houses and built parks. "The Bend has become decent and orderly because the sunshine was let in and shone upon the children who had at last won the right to play." When you have completed this objective, you should be able to do the following:

1. Know what a tenement house is. Illustrate by a picture. Do we still have tenements?
2. Be able to tell the class, or write a report, about Jacob Riis. Be sure to include the following information:

a.   When Jacob Riis lived.

b.   The part his background played in his life.

c.   His one-man crusade against the slums.

d.   His methods of fighting poverty.

e.   Mulberry Bend.

f.   His final victory.

3.   Read **How the Other Half Lives** by Jacob Riis.

4.   Pretend that you lived in Mulberry Bend in 1880. Tell what kind of house you would have lived in; how you would take care of your sanitary needs; and where you would play.

5.   Compare Mulberry Bend of the 1880's with the slums of the cities today. Note the similarities and the differences.

6.   Write a short essay on, "Why Children Need Fresh Air and Sunshine."

How to Complete this Objective

1.   In the library card catalog find cards catalogued under:

Riis, Jacob
How the Other Half Lives
Slums
Tenement Houses
Mulberry Bend

Also look for these subjects in the indexes of books, encyclopedias, and other reference books.

2.   Visit the poorer sections of the city near you.

PEOPLE WHO TRIED TO HELP THE POOR: MARTIN LUTHER KING, JR.

Objective

This is an ILP about a man who tried to help the black people overcome poverty by raising their wages. If wages are raised, people can live better and help themselves. Martin Luther King attempted to raise the wages of the garbage workers in Memphis, Tennessee, by supporting them in a strike against the city. It was while doing this that he was shot to death. When you have completed this objective you should be able to do the following:

1.   Write in your own words the story of Martin Luther King's fight against poverty. Be sure to include information about each of the following:

a.   His early work toward the acceptance of the black man by society.

b.   His real feelings about the poor black man.

c.   His work in trying to upgrade the living conditions of the poor blacks.

d.   The garbage strike in Memphis, Tennessee.

2.   Bring pictures to class of the garbage strike in Memphis.

3.   Bring a picture of Martin Luther King to class.

4. Listen to the recording of his famous speech, "I Had a Dream." Tell in your own words what you think Martin Luther King was trying to tell the American people.

5. Write to the Southern Christian Leadership Conference, 334 Auburn Avenue, NE, Atlanta, Georgia, 30303. Ask what the SCLC people consider specially important about Dr. King's work against poverty.

How to Complete this Objective

1. In the library card catalog, find cards catalogued under:

King, Martin Luther
Unions
Garbage

2. Write to the Martin Luther King Fund for Peace, Nonviolence, and Brotherhood, 234 Sunset Ave., N.W., Atlanta, Georgia 30314. Ask them to send you information about Dr. King's work against poverty.

3. Listen to a recording of "I Had a Dream."

4. Check back issues of magazines and newspapers for articles on Dr. King's death, April 5, 1968, and the events which preceded.

PEOPLE WHO TRIED TO HELP THE POOR: ROBERT F. KENNEDY
Objective

This is an ILP about a famous American who worked diligently to upgrade the living conditions of the Mexican-American people in California. Robert Kennedy actively tried to help the grapeworker's union. After his untimely death, his wife Ethel continued his efforts to better the living conditions of the grape workers. When you have completed this ILP, you should be able to do the following:

1. Write in your own words how Robert Kennedy tried to help the poor Mexican-American grapeworkers in California.

2. Tell what Ethel Kennedy is now doing to carry on the work of Robert Kennedy.

3. Pretend you are a grapeworker. Would you rather earn a very low wage and have the government support you partially, or would you rather make a decent wage and be self-supporting. Prepare a debate on this subject giving both sides of the issue.

How to Complete this Objective

1. In the library card catalog, look under the following names:

Kennedy, Robert F.   Chavez, César
Grape-workers   Kennedy, Ethel
Mexican-Americans

2. Look in past magazine issues, preferably **Newsweek, Life** or **Time,** for reports on Robert Kennedy's efforts to help these poor people.
3. Use whatever source is available. Perhaps your parents would remember.

POVERTY IS WIDESPREAD

Objective

Poverty is a problem not only in the United States, but in almost all the countries in the world. Wherever there are many people in a small area, poverty exists. Poverty is widespread in China, India, and Indonesia. In these countries there are more people than the land can accommodate. There are not enough jobs for the people in these overpopulated countries. When you have completed this ILP, you should be able to do the following:

1. Prepare a report about poverty in one country other than the United States. Be sure to include the following:

    a. The name of the country and where it is located.
    b. The population and the land area of the country.
    c. Aid the government is giving to the poor people there.
    d. The number of poor people increasing or decreasing.
    e. What you think can be done to help the poor.
    f. Pictures of the living conditions.

2. Pretend you are a poor person in India. Tell the class how you would spend your day, what food you would receive, and the type of dwelling you would live in. What kind of life would you lead? What kind of life would your children lead?
3. Make a report on the financial aid that the United States gives to the poor of other countries.

How to Complete this Objective

1. Look in the library card catalog and the indexes of books and encyclopedias for the following:

    a. India
    b. China
    c. Indonesia
    d. Central America

2. Look in issues of the National Geographic Magazine for pictures of these places.
3. Write to the Indian or Pakistani Embassies in Washington, D.C.
4. Write to your Congressman or Senator for information about United States aid to underdeveloped countries.
5. Talk to the Foreign Missions Committee of your church.
6. Use whatever sources are available.

A SERIES OF LESSONS CONCERNING VALUES— LIFE AND PROPERTY

The work that follows was prepared and conducted in 1970. The Detroit riots which are its base occurred in July, 1967.

LIFE AND PROPERTY[2]

A German magazine recently carried a picture story of the Detroit riots. One of the pictures showed a dead man lying in a store window covered with blood. The caption (translated) read: "A dead plunderer in the display window. He had just robbed the store along with another black. The store window dummy lies thrown upon the street. Then the police came. His companion fled with the loot. He paid with his life."

In the minds of many Americans, this picture would raise a question of right and wrong. There are at least two ways of looking at it.

I. Most Americans in the past have believed in what is called the sacred rights of property. It is wrong, they have said, for someone to steal something that does not belong to him, regardless of how poor he may be or how much he may need or want it. The law exists to protect the property owner, and it should do so at all cost. If the property owner catches someone stealing his property, he is in the right to kill that person if he so desires and should not be prosecuted for doing so.

II. Some Americans, on the other hand, have begun to believe that human life is more sacred than property. They point out that property (TV sets, clothing, etc.) can be replaced but that human life cannot. Anyway, they say, insurance companies repay the owners for stolen merchandise in many cases. If someone steals your TV set, they point out, there is a possibility that he can be apprehended and forced to repay you, but if you take his life, it is not within your power to give it back. Anyway, they insist, no material object is worth a human life.

A. Which of these two positions do you find yourself more in sympathy with? Explain. If you don't agree with either I or II what is your position?

B. Suppose you were to awaken some night and see a man stealing your TV set, or your parent's car, or something else you consider to be valuable to you. Supposing you have a loaded gun by your bedside and can shoot well, which of the following would you be most likely to do? (check one)

___ Kill the man?

___ Shoot the man in the legs to prevent his escaping?

___ Shoot in the air to frighten him into running away?

___ Call to him to stop, and if he doesn't, shoot him?

___ Call to him to stop, but not shoot at him?

---

[2] Prepared and taught by Earle Tomlinson, graduate student, Georgia State University, whom the authors thank.

___ Do nothing?

___ If none of the above, what would you do?

    C. Describe the way you think you would feel after doing whatever you checked above.

Assignment Number 1

The Value Conflict: The right to life vs. the right to property. Is one ever justified to take a human life to defend a property right?

Reasons for Choice of this Conflict: The students with whom I work are products of rural North Georgia. I surmised that there would be a tendency among them to protect property. (Practically all of their parents own their own homes. They may work in the city, but most of them raise poultry, pigs, or beef cattle on the side. Among these students are none who are from indigent homes.) Furthermore, the class is composed of six girls and twenty-three boys (eighth-graders, ranging in age from twelve to fifteen) and practically all of these boys are interested in hunting small game animals and deer, which means that most of them have and are able to shoot their own guns. This problem gestalt, therefore, would be quite relevant to them.

Teacher Aims: Realizing that all these students have watched on their TV sets as stores were looted during riots, that they have heard their parents and other adults wonder why the police permitted the looters to get away with breaking the law, and have probably come to conclusions about the morality of the situation themselves, the teacher felt that that they needed the opportunity to hear more than one point of view, to think about their choice of a value by bringing it home to them in a second problematical situation, and then giving them a chance to defend that choice before others who may not agree.

Procedure: The enclosed sheet was passed out to twenty-one of these eighth-grade students. They were told that they could complete the sheet during that (half hour) period or take it home overnight in order to think about it. The next morning the results were tabulated and written on the board. A class discussion followed.

Tabulation of Results

No. of Students Checking this Alternative	Alternative
0	Kill the man.
5	Shoot the man in the legs to prevent his escaping.
10	Shoot in the air to frighten him into running away.
1	Call to him to stop, and if he doesn't, shoot him.
2	Call to him to stop, but not shoot.
1	Do nothing.
2	If none of the above, what would you do?

The two who checked the last one above said such things as: "Call to him to stop and if he doesn't, shoot him in the legs," and "Watch which way he goes and call the police so they may set up a road block and capture him."

Only one person put down that he would be more in sympathy with position I. Nineteen said they would favor II, and one put down both I and II saying that it was wrong to steal, but it is also wrong to take a human life.

The answers to the question "How would you feel afterward?" ranged all the way from "I would not feel too bad about it if he was trying to steal from me" to "Scared" to "Bad, very bad."

Discussion Period

Teacher: As you can see from the tabulation on the board, practically all of you chose the first position as the one with which you were most in sympathy. However, there appear to be several different ways of thinking represented in our class. Would any of you care to discuss with the class the way you feel about it?

Kenneth (a highly intelligent student, editor of the school paper; he says he is a pacifist): I think the only way you can be justified to take someone's life is when he is threatening your life or someone else's.

Allene: I agree with Kenneth. No one is justified with killing except in self defense.

Kenneth: I may have to change that just a little. I think it's ridiculous the way the police stand and let people carry off TV sets and things during riots. It doesn't seem right to just stand and watch people steal.

Teacher: What would you advocate doing?

Kenneth: Shooting the people in the legs, I guess, in order to stop them.

Teacher: Do you think there might be a danger of innocent people getting shot if the police start shooting when there are so many people milling around? Look what happened at Kent State, for example.

Kenneth: Kent State was an entirely different situation. The students that got killed there had nothing at all to do with what was happening on campus to get the National Guard there. They weren't rioting.

[Silence]

Teacher: You see, this problem of rioting is new to our policemen in the United States. The Watts riot about five years ago caused many Americans to start thinking about the value of property and human life. Our society is becoming very complex, and we have to think through these problems for ourselves.

Mac: What about the policemen in England? They don't even carry guns.

Robert: Yes, but the citizens don't have guns either.

Teacher: What do you think about outlawing guns in America?

A Chorus: No!

Teacher: Well, you see, here in our community we feel that we need guns primarily for hunting, I suppose. But in cities, you can imagine that if everyone is permitted to have a gun it could present a very serious problem.

Kenny (first time to speak): Yeah, I think that is right. They all start killing each other.

Kenneth: Mr. Tomlinson, I plan to file for a CO when I register for the draft. Do you think they will ask me a question something like the one on this sheet?

Teacher: Quite possibly. They like to ask such questions as "Suppose you were to come home some day and an evident burglar was beating your mother up. If you had a gun would you shoot him or risk letting him kill your mother? You can't be sure whether he is armed."

Three or Four Students: I would shoot him.

Kenneth: I think I would try to sneak up on him first to hit him over the head with my gun.

Wanda: Are you a pacifist, Mr. Tomlinson?

Teacher: Well, I am not a pacifist to the extent that I cannot imagine a situation in which I may shoot someone. Some pacifists, you see, would not shoot a person even to protect their own lives. They would rather die than be guilty of harming someone. This is one extreme. Another extreme is the person who responds with violence to every situation that seems to threaten him in any way. Let me say that I am in sympathy with Position No. II on this sheet.

Wanda: I think I feel that way about it, too.

Teacher: Socrates once said that the unexamined life is not worth living. He meant that to live life to its fullest, we must know ourselves. We must understand the way we feel about things. It is discussions like this one that we have had this morning that help us to do that. We listen to what the other person says; we listen to his reasons for believing as he does, but then we make up our own minds as to what we think is right. I think Socrates would have approved of our class this morning.

Evaluation

I was rather surprised at the results appearing on the tabulation. I would have thought that at least half the class would have chosen position I. I allowed only about fifteen minutes for the discussion; I wish I had planned for more time. There were several doors opened during the discussion that may have led to a rewarding end (i.e., gun control laws, Kent State, pacifism, etc.). Perhaps the greatest value of this teaching strategy was its success as a method (I feel) of presenting values. I think it proved itself psychologically sound. It got the interest and participation of the students, it gave them an opportunity to choose a value from among alternatives, and gave them an opportunity to defend their value in public, further strengthening it.

TEACHING ABOUT CIVIL RIGHTS

The following individualized learning packages and other material grew out of the experience of a graduate student at Georgia State University in 1970 and 1971.

	Home	Church	School	News Media	Peers	Books	Personal Experiences	Unknown to Me
John F. Kennedy								
chocolate ice cream								
integration								
drugs								
Martin Luther King, Jr.								
N.A.A.C.P.								
sailfish								
Earl Warren								
Hank Aaron								
Little Rock Crisis								
Watts								
Lyndon B. Johnson								
James Meredith								
White Supremacy								
policemen								
Warren Burger								
Dwight Eisenhower								
Ralph David Abernathy								
hippies								
Ross Barnett								
Orval Faubus								
Ku Klux Klan								

The Evaluative Instrument. See the text for the rationale (particularly pp. 272–283).

SOME MAJOR ISSUES AND EVENTS IN THE
CIVIL RIGHTS MOVEMENT SINCE 1954[3]

The following unit deals with aspects of the Civil Rights Movement since 1954. The reasons for beginning at that point in time include my feeling that the decision of the Supreme Court at that time has had so many far-reaching effects on our country and has changed the life-style of many people.

I would hope that the following material and assignments could be handled by seventh-grade students, those with whom I have heretofore worked.

The reason for using the accompanying evaluation instrument before teaching the unit is twofold. First it would help determine what forces have been most influential in developing the child's concept of the terms listed. Knowing this might help one ascertain why a child feels the way he does about a particular term. The second purpose was to simply determine if the child had gained some knowledge about the terms prior to this learning experience.

Some terms not related to the Civil Rights Movement are purposely included.

Check the appropriate box to indicate the force which has most influenced your feelings about the items listed on the left.

General Objectives
A. To effect a clearer understanding of major issues and incidents involving civil rights since 1954.
B. To be able to empathize with those whose views are different from yours.
C. To encourage open discussion of problems with which you are confronted.
D. To bring about one's own definition of equality.
E. To gain a better understanding of the many societal problems reflected by this period.
F. To gain a greater faith in what our Constitution states.
G. To help students to effect an understanding by all citizens concerning the problems they face as a result of the movement for equality for all.
H. To gain a better understanding of the function of the Supreme Court of the United States.
I. To be able to take knowledge gained and apply it in the decision-making process.
J. To learn to read from many different sources and through divergent thinking come up with different solutions for problems faced.

Content, Procedures and Sources of Information
Some background information is assumed to have been covered in coursework earlier in the year (a review of some materials may be necessary).

---

[3] Prepared by Brenda Whitten, whom the authors thank. A few sentences dealing with this student's course work have been deleted.

An ILP—Public School Segregation Is Unconstitutional

On May 17, 1954, the United States Supreme Court declared that racial segregation in public schools is unconstitutional.

Objective

Supreme Court decisions affect all of us and we should have a clear understanding of why decisions are made as they are.

1. Why or under what conditions would a case reach the Supreme Court?
2. Why was **Brown vs. the Board of Education** the most important decision concerning equality in education during the twentieth century?
3. Why was segregation in a denial of the equal protection of the laws as guaranteed by the Fourteenth Amendment to the United States Constitution?
4. Consider all of the above questions as you assume the role of one of the justices and write a paper concerning what might have happened if the decision had been different.
   a. Which states were most directly involved?
   b. What were their reactions?

How to Complete the Objective

1. If possible, talk with a judge or perhaps interview an attorney and find out why a case moves to the highest court in the land.
2. Visit a court in session and compare what you experience with what you are able to learn about the U.S. Supreme Court through interviews and your readings.
3. Make use of all library facilities in your research.
4. Use **Reader's Guide to Periodical Literature.**
5. Compare information in American History textbooks.
6. Consider any resource people you may have in your community.
7. Consult Keesing's **Race Relations in the USA** 1954-1968.
8. Refer to the United States Constitution.

An ILP—The Little Rock Crisis, 1957-1959

May 31, 1955, the Supreme Court issued a unanimous opinion in which it directed states to make a prompt and reasonable start towards implementing its ruling that segregation was unconstitutional. What was the action taken by various states? (**Race Relations,** pp. 28-31)

Objective

The situation which happened in Little Rock, Arkansas, affected the actions which were taken by other southern states.

1. Make a chart showing in what order the states most directly involved carried out their task of desegregating the schools.
2. Discuss answers to the following questions concerning the Little Rock crisis.

    a.   Why did Governor Faubus take measures to prevent Negroes from entering Central High School?

    b.   What was the League of Central High School Mothers?

    c.   Why was the Arkansas National Guard summoned by Faubus?

    d.   How did Judge Davies of the Federal District Court intervene?

    e.   Discuss the different court rulings involved in the desegregation of Little Rock Schools.

    f.   What stand did President Eisenhower take?

3.   Write a paper concerning why it was necessary to go outside the state of Arkansas for help in settling this matter.

How to Complete the Objective

1.   Periodicals, 1957 on

    a.   **U.S. News and World Report.**

    b.   **Time.**

    c.   **Journal of Social Issues.**

2.   **Race Relations in the USA 1954-1968.**

3.   **Portrait of a Decade,** Anthony Lewis.

4.   All library facilities.

An ILP—Supreme Court Rulings
Objective

Supreme Court Rulings are so important that they affect all of us socially, economically, and politically. This ILP is intended to show the way the rulings affect how people live and how they relate to each other.

1.   How many justices are involved in Supreme Court rulings, and how is the Chief Justice different from the others in his duties?

2.   Who are the current justices serving in the Supreme Court?

3.   Why do some rulings have to be made by the Supreme Court?

4.   Show by diagram or some other illustration how cases move from the lowest court in our land to the highest, with some explanatory information included.

How to Complete the Objective

1.   Talk to a judge or an attorney.

2.   Make use of the librarian and all library facilities.

3.   Visit a local court in session and watch the proceedings.

4.   Obtain any helpful movies, slides, or other visual aids.

Some Factual Information for Teachers

Virginia's peaceful acceptance of token integration in 1959 was generally recognized as a turning point in the integration controversy, in view of Virginia's acknowledged position of leadership among the southern states, which had largely modeled their anti-integration tactics on Governor Almond's "massive resistance" program. (**Race Relations,** pp. 65-72) Racial desegregation in American schools proceeded slowly in 1959 and early 1960.

Lunch-counter demonstrations began in Greensboro, North Carolina, in February of 1960. They spread through all southern states. They had their first success in San Antonio, Texas, in March of 1960. Later, a biracial state advisory commission on race relations in his state was set up by Florida's Governor LeRoy Collins.

An ILP — Lunch-Counter Demonstrations
Objective

Is it morally fair to invite the public to shop in your store and then to bar certain segments of the population from eating in the facility provided by the same establishment?

1. Where and when were the demonstrations begun?
2. Where did they spread?
3. Where was their first success?
4. What were the views of Florida's Governor LeRoy Collins and what did he propose for his state?
5. What was the general outcome of attempts to integrate lunch counters in the South?
6. Write a paper concerning your feelings when you were refused participation in something you felt very strongly you should be a part of.

How to Complete the Objective

1. **Race Relations,** pp. 71-72.
2. Interview managers of larger and smaller concerns and compare their views on the matter.
3. Utilize **Reader's Guide to Periodical Literature,** February 1960 to end of year, for specific articles.
4. Interview a Negro who was involved in this particular desegregation process.

Some Factual Information for Teachers

In January, 1961, two Negroes were admitted to a formerly all-white University in Georgia, leaving Alabama, Mississippi, and South Carolina as the only states maintaining total segregation in their public schools and universities.

The Meredith Controversy. Justice Black of the United States Supreme Court on September 10, 1962, ordered that James Meredith must be admitted to the University of Mississippi. (1) Governor Ross Barnett ruled that all public schools and universities would operate under state officials and must obey laws passed by the state legislature. (2) Barnett personally turned Meredith away when he tried to enter the University. (3) On his fourth attempt at entry,

Meredith and two United States marshals were greeted by state police and a large mob. They abandoned attempts to register that day. (4) Barnett was found guilty of civil contempt when he failed to appear before the Appeals Court. (5) After several conversations with President Kennedy and Robert Kennedy, Barnett allowed Meredith to enter only after Kennedy ordered Federal armed forces to enforce the court's orders. (6) Mr. Meredith received his degree August 18, 1963, and the only other Negro student at Mississippi was expelled for carrying a revolver. He had done so, he said, for fear he might be murdered —Mississippi's educational system again became completely segregated.

Buses. On April 23, 1956, the United States Supreme Court ruled that racial segregation on buses running within a state is unconstitutional. Segregation on interstate buses had been declared unconstitutional in 1946.

Civil Rights Acts. (1) The 1957 Civil Rights Bill had 7 points and was signed in September by President Eisenhower. (**Race Relations,** pp. 108-109). (2) The 1960 Civil Rights Act, signed May 6 by President Eisenhower, strengthened the 1957 bill (**Race Relations,** p. 118). (3) The 1964 Civil Rights Act, John Kennedy's bill, was signed by Lyndon Johnson on July 2 (**Race Relations,** pp. 132-141). (4) The 1968 Civil Rights Act was passed April 10 and signed by President Johnson (**Race Relations,** pp. 209-211).

The Civil Rights Movement and Urban Riots, 1960-1965. (1) 1961, Freedom Riders. (2) June 12, 1963, murder of Medgar Evers. (3) June, 1964, murder of three civil-rights workers in Mississippi. (4) 1965, Selma-Montgomery demonstrations to get Negroes registered to vote, encouraged by Dr. Martin Luther King, Jr. Los Angeles riots in the Watts area. Message to Congress by President Johnson in March of 1965 to eliminate illegal barriers to the right to vote (**Race Relations,** pp. 186-193).

Names Connected with the Civil Rights Movement: Stokely Carmichael, Walter Reuther, Adam Clayton Powell, Roy Wilkins, Whitney Young, A. Philip Randolph.

Organizations Concerned with Civil Rights. Moderate: National Association for the Advancement of Colored People; National Urban League; Southern Christian Leadership Conference. Militant: Congress of Racial Equality; Student National Coordinating Committee (originally Student Nonviolent Coordinating Committee).

Death of Martin Luther King, Jr. Assassinated by James Earl Ray in Memphis, Tennessee, April 5, 1968. For circumstances, see **Race Relations,** pp. 262-271.

An ILP—School Busing

In a decision announced April 20, 1971, the United States Supreme Court declared state antibussing laws unconstitutional. The decision will probably have farther-reaching effects than the 1954 decision, and included these points:

1. Bussing outside of the neighborhood may be required.

2. Neighborhood schools must go if they maintain segregation.
3. Racial ratio is not required in every school, but is a starting point.
4. A small number of all-black schools may be permissible under certain circumstances.
5. Antibussing laws which obstruct desegregation of schools are unconstitutional.

Objective

Integration of all schools is here. Is bussing of students to effect this a necessary thing?

1. Which states are most effected?
2. Could bussing of students from one neighborhood to another be detrimental to the educational process?
3. What alternative suggestions would you make?
4. Redraw the attendance areas in your county area, in order that integration of schools might be made more realistic.
5. Write a paper which includes advantages and disadvantages to you of being bussed to a new area for schooling.

How to Complete the Objective

1. **US News and World Report,** May 3, 1971, pp. 12-14.
2. Other periodicals.
3. Obtain a map of your school system and the school attendance areas as they are presently set up.
4. Get population-studies information from the county in which you reside.

Role-Playing Exercise: Intergroup Relations

It was the beginning of a new school year. The State Courts had recently ruled all schools in your system would have to be integrated by the beginning of the school year and that all actions of discrimination must cease immediately.

As Sue started to leave for school her mother said, "Now remember, Sue —don't let Mrs. Benford put you by one of those niggers."

When Sue arrived at her new homeroom, she found her desk. Just as she sat down, Tom, one of two Negroes in her class, came in, sat down beside her and said, "Hello."

Assume the role of Sue. What would you now do? How would you react regarding the last thing your mother said to you?

BIBLIOGRAPHY

Blaustein, Albert P., and Robert L. Zangrando, eds. *Civil Rights and the American Negro.* New York: Washington Square Press, 1968.

Christine, Charles, and Dorothy Christine. "Four Simulation Games that Teach." *Grade Teacher*, October, 1967, pp. 109-120.

Dorsen, Norman. *Discrimination and Civil Rights.* Boston: Little, Brown and Company, 1969.

Grimes, Alan P. *Equality in America.* New York: Oxford University Press, 1964, pp. 41-88.

Keesing's Research Report. *Race Relations in the USA 1954-1968.* Charles Scribner's Sons, New York, 1970.

Lewis, Anthony. *Portrait of a Decade.* New York: Random House, 1962.

Lomax, Louis E. *The Negro Revolt.* New York: Harper & Row, 1962.

Nuspl, John J. "The Story of Tetonia." *Grade Teacher,* April, 1971, pp. 70-75.

Rogers, Virginia M., and Marcella L. Kysilka. "Simulation Games." *The Instructor,* March, 1970, pp. 94-99.

U.S. News and World Report. "Supreme Court Sets Rules for Bussing Students." May 3, 1971, pp. 12-14.

U.S. News and World Report. "A Far-Reaching School Decision in the Court's Own Words." May 3, 1971, pp. 40-42.

United States Constitution.

REFERENCES

Adler, Irving. *A New Look at Chemistry.* New York: The John Day Company, 1965.

Almy, Millie. *Young Children's Thinking.* New York: Teachers College Press, 1966.

Ashton-Warner, Sylvia. *Teacher.* New York: Simon and Schuster, 1963.

Association for Supervision and Curriculum Development. *Improving Educational Assessment: An Inventory of Measures of Affective Behavior.* Washington, D.C.: ASCD, 1969.

Axline, Virginia. *Dibs—In Search of Self.* Boston: Houghton Mifflin Company, 1964.

Bandy, Milon, director. *Economic Education: A Guide for New York Schools.* Oneonta, N.Y.: Center for Economic Education, State University of New York, 1970.

Beauvoir, Simone de. *The Ethics of Ambiguity.* New York: Philosophical Library, 1948. (Quoted in Gert Hellerick, "What Is Often Overlooked in Existentialist Situation Ethics," *Journal of Thought*, January, 1970)

Beeman, Paul. "Special Olympics . . . Cheers, Excitement." *The Atlanta Journal and Constitution*, May 30, 1971.

Berg, Harry D., ed. *Evaluation in Social Studies*, 35th Yearbook of the National Council for the Social Studies. Washington, D.C.: NCSS, 1965.

Bessell, Harold, and Uvaldo H. Palomares. *Methods in Human Development.* San Diego: Human Development Training Institute, 1967.

Bloom, Benjamin S., editor. *Taxonomy of Educational Objectives, Handbook I: Cognitive Domain.* New York: Longmans, Green, and Co., 1956.

Brameld, Theodore. "A Philosopher Looks at the Current Values and Changing

Needs of Youth." Paper presented at the ASSIST Center, Wayne County (Michigan) Intermediate School District, June 3, 1969.

Broek, Jan O. M. *Geography*. Columbus, Ohio: Charles E. Merrill Books, 1965.

Brown, George. *Human Teaching Is Human Learning*. New York: McGraw-Hill Book Company, 1970.

Brozen, Yale. *Exchange: Elementary School Economics*. Teacher's Materials, Industrial Relations Center, University of Chicago, 1968.

Bruner, Jerome S. "The Act of Discovery." *Harvard Educational Review*, vol. 31, 1961.

Bruner, Jerome S. *The Process of Education*. Quoted in Bruce Joyce, "Content for Elementary Social Studies." *Social Education*, 28:84, February, 1964.

Buros, Oscar K., ed. *The Seventh Mental Measurements Yearbook*. Highland Park, N.J.: The Gryphos Press, 1972.

Buros, Oscar K., ed. *The Sixth Mental Measurements Yearbook*. Highland Park, N.J.: The Gryphos Press, 1965.

Cain, Stanley A. "Human Ecology." *The Science Teacher*, March, 1967, pp. 13-17.

Carr, Edward Hallet. *What Is History?* New York: Alfred A. Knopf, 1962.

Christine, Charles, and Dorothy Christine. "Simulation Games that Teach." In Jonathon C. McLendon, William W. Joyce, and John R. Lee, eds., *Readings on Elementary Social Studies: Emerging Changes*. Boston: Allyn and Bacon, 1970.

Clark, Kenneth B., and M. P. Clark. "Racial Identification and Preference in Negro Children," in T. M. Newcomb and E. L. Hartley, eds., *Readings in Social Psychology*. New York: Henry Holt and Company, 1947.

Coles, Robert. "Profiles—Erik H. Erickson—II." *New Yorker*, November 14, 1970, pp. 59-138.

A Conceptual Framework for the Social Studies in Wisconsin Schools. Madison, Wisconsin: Department of Public Instruction, 1965.

Copeland, Miles. "The Strategy Left by Nasser: Blackmail the U.S. with Arab Oil." *Life*, October 9, 1967, pp. 34-37.

Coppedge, Walter R. "What the World Is Coming To." *Kappan*, October, 1970, pp. 75-78.

Cuban, Larry. "Black History, Negro History, and White Folk." *Saturday Review*, September 21, 1968.

Cuber, John F., Robert A. Harper, and William F. Kenkel. *Problems of American Society: Values in Conflict*, 3rd ed. New York: Holt, Rinehart and Winston, 1956.

Dewey, John. *Democracy in Education*. New York: Macmillan Company, 1916.

Dow, Peter, director. *Man: A Course of Study*. Washington: Curriculum Development Associates, 1971.

Dressler, David. *Sociology: The Study of Human Interaction*. New York: Alfred A. Knopf, 1969.

Dunfee, Maxine. "Evaluating Understandings, Attitudes, Skills, and Behaviors in Elementary School Social Studies," in Harry D. Berg, ed., *Evaluation in Social Studies*, 35th Yearbook of the National Council for the Social Studies. Washington, D.C.: NCSS, 1965.

Durkheim, Émile. *Education and Society*. New York: Free Press, 1956.

Durkin, Mary C., Alice Duvall, and Alice McMaster. *The Taba Social Studies Curriculum*. Menlo Park, California: Addison-Wesley Publishing Company, 1969. (A)

Durkin, Mary C., Alice Duvall, and Alice McMaster. *Grade Two—Communities Around Us*. The Taba Social Studies Curriculum. Reading, Massachusetts: Addison Wesley Publishing Company, 1969. (B)

Edwards, Allen S., and Dale P. Scannell. *Educational Psychology*. Scranton, Pa.: International Textbook Co., 1968.

Engh, Keith. "The Cruelest Trick-or-Treat Hoax." *Good Housekeeping*, October, 1970.

Environmental Studies. Boulder, Colorado: American Geological Institute, 1970.

Erikson, Erik H. *Childhood and Society*, 2nd ed. New York: W. W. Norton & Company, 1963.

Fantini, Mario, and Gerald Weinstein. *Toward Humanistic Education: A Curriculum of Affect*. New York: Praeger Publishers, 1970.

Faucett, Verna S., and colleagues. *Social Science Concepts in the Classroom*. Syracuse: Syracuse University Press, 1968.

Fenton Edwin. Address delivered at the First Regional Conference of the National Council for the Social Studies, Athens, Georgia, February 24, 1970.

Ferguson, Henry. *A Guide to Indian Books for Use in American Schools*. Thompson, Connecticut 06277: Inter-Culture Associates, 1968.

Fideler Company Textbook Series. *Teacher's Guide to Asia & Africa Social Studies Textbook*. Grand Rapids: 1969.

Fielder, William. "Two Styles of School Talk about Values." *Social Education*, January, 1967.

Follett Social Studies Program. Chicago: Follett Educational Corporation, 1969.

Fox, Robert, and Ronald Lippitt. *The Teacher's Role in Social Science Investigation*. Chicago: Science Research Associates, 1969.

Framework for the Social Studies in Wyoming Grades K-12. Cheyenne, Wyoming: State Department of Education, June, 1969.

Getzels, Jacob. "Cultural Values, Social Expectations and Individual Motives: Implications for the Classroom." Paper delivered at Georgia State University Conference on Expectation, Fall, 1970.

Ginot, Haim. *Between Parent and Child*. New York: Avon Books, 1969.

Goldmark, Bernice. *Social Studies: A Method of Inquiry*. Belmont, California: Wadsworth Publishing Company, 1968.

Gordon, Ira J., director. *How I See Myself* Test. Gainesville, Florida: Institute for the Development of Human Resources, School of Education, University of Florida, 1969.

Gross, Richard E., and Dwight W. Allen. "Problems and Practices in Social Studies Evaluation." *Social Education,* vol. 31 (April, 1967).

Gross, Richard E., and John U. Michaelis, directors. *Field Social Studies Program.* San Francisco: Field Educational Publications, 1970.

Hanna, Paul R., and John R. Lee. "Generalizations from the Social Sciences." *Social Studies in Elementary Schools,* 32nd yearbook of the National Council for Social Studies, a department of the NEA. Washington, D.C.: NCSS, 1962, pp. 62-89.

Havighurst, Robert J. *Human Development and Education.* New York: Longmans, Green & Co., 1953.

Hoffman, Alan J., and Janet Alleman. "Conceptual Framework for Developing Sociological Ideas Related to the Family." Unpublished manuscript, 1969.

Hoffman, Alan J., and John Mickelson. Paper prepared for Research for Better Schools, Inc., project SEARCH, L. Russo, Director, 1970.

Hogan, R. "Moral Development: An Assessment Approach." Ph.D. dissertation, University of California (Berkeley), 1967.

Inhelder, Barbel, and Jean Piaget. *The Growth of Logical Thinking from Childhood to Adolescence.* New York: Basic Books, 1958.

Investigating Man's World. Glenview, Illinois: Scott, Foresman and Company, 1970.

James, Linnie B., and Lamonte Carpe. *Geography for Today's Children.* New York: Appleton-Century-Crofts, 1965.

Jarolimek, John, and Phillip Bacon, co-directors. *A Behavioral Approach to the Teaching of Social Studies.* A monograph, Tri-University Project in Elementary Education, Social Studies-Social Science. Seattle: University of Washington, May, 1968.

Joyce, William W. *The Development and Grade Placement of Map and Globe Skills in the Elementary School Social Studies Program.* Unpublished Ph.D. dissertation. Evanston: Northwestern University, 1964.

King, Frederick M., Dorothy Kendall Bracken, and Margaret Sloan. *Concepts in Social Science.* Chicago: Laidlaw Brothers, 1968.

Kluckhohn, Clyde. *Mirror for Man.* New York: Fawcett Premier Books, 1965.

Kohlberg, Lawrence. "Development of Moral Character and Moral Ideology." In Martin Hoffman and Lois Hoffman, eds., *Review of Child Development Research,* vol. 1, New York, 1964.

Lee, Dorris M., and R. V. Allen. *Learning to Read through Experience.* New York: Appleton-Century-Crofts, 1963.

Lippitt, Ronald, Robert Fox, and Lucille Schaible. *Social Science Laboratory Units.* Chicago: Science Research Associates, 1969.

Lippmann, Walter. *A Preface to Morals.* New York: The Macmillan Company, 1929.

Lovell, Hugh. *Teacher's Guide to Economics K-6.* Salem, Oregon: Oregon Department of Education, Development Economic Education Program (DEEP), 1965.

McDonald, Frederick J., *Educational Psychology,* 2nd ed. Belmont, California: Wadsworth Publishing Company, 1965.

Mager, Robert. *Developing Attitude toward Learning.* Belmont, California: Fearon Publishing Co., 1968.

Mager, Robert F. *Preparing Instructional Objectives.* Palo Alto, California: Fearon Publishing Company, 1965.

Maier, Henry. *Three Theories of Child Development.* New York: Harper and Row, 1969.

Martin, Richard S., and Reuben B. Miller. *Economics and Its Significance.* Columbus, Ohio: Charles E. Merrill Books, 1965.

Meeks, Esther K., and Elizabeth Bagwell. *Families Live Together.* Chicago: Follett Publishing Company, 1969.

Murphy, Franklin D. "Yardsticks for a New Era." *Saturday Review,* November 21, 1970.

National Council for Social Studies. *Social Studies in Transition: Guidelines for Change.* Washington, D.C., 1965.

National Education Association, Educational Policies Commission. Report: "Moral and Spiritual Values in the Public Schools." Washington, D.C., 1951.

Ojeman, Ralph H. *A Teaching Program in Human Behavior and Mental Health.* Cleveland: Educational Research Council of America, 1959.

Preston, Ralph C., and Robert V. Duffy. *Primary Social Studies Test (Teacher's Manual).* Geneva, Ill.: Houghton Mifflin Company, 1967.

Rader, William D., director. *Exchange: Elementary School Economics.* Chicago: Teachers' Materials Industrial Relations Center, University of Chicago, 1968 (Yale Brozen, Economics Consultant).

Raths, Louis, Merrill Harmin, and Sidney B. Simon. *Values and Teaching.* Columbus, Ohio: Charles E. Merrill Publishing Co., 1966.

Rogers, Virginia M., and Marcella L. Kysilka. "Simulation Games . . . What and Why." *Instructor,* vol. 79, No. 7 (March, 1970).

Sanders, Norris M. "Changing Strategies of Instruction: Three Case Examples." Chapter 5 of *Social Studies Curriculum Development: Prospects and Problems,* 39th yearbook of the National Council for Social Studies, Dorothy McClure Fraser, ed. Washington, D.C.: NEA publication, 1969, pp. 139-173.

Sanders, Norris M. *Classroom Questions: What Kinds?* New York: Harper & Row, 1966.

Scott, Louise B. *Learning Time with Language Experiences for Young Children.* St. Louis: Webster-McGraw-Hill, 1968.

Scriven, Michael. "Student Values as Educational Objectives." Monograph. Social Sciences Education Consortium, Irving Morrissett, executive director. Boulder: University of Colorado, 1969.

Senesh, Lawrence. *Economics.* Social Science Education Consortium, Publication #105; Irving Morrissett, executive director. Lafayette, Indiana: Purdue University, 1968.

Senesh, Lawrence. *Our Working World*. Chicago: Science Research Associates, 1967.

A *Sequential Curriculum in Anthropology for Grades 1-7*. Anthropology Curriculum Project, University of Georgia. Athens, Georgia, 1969.

Shrodes, Caroline. "Bibliotherapy." *The Reading Teacher*, 9 (October, 1955), pp. 24-29.

Silberman, Charles. *Crisis in the Classroom*. New York: Random House, 1970.

Simpson, Elizabeth Léonie. *Democracy's Stepchildren*. San Francisco: Jossey-Bass, 1971.

The Social Sciences: Concepts and Values. Center for the Study of Instruction. San Francisco: Harcourt Brace Jovanovich, 1970.

Social Studies Framework for the Public Schools, Part III. Sacramento: California State Department of Education, State Curriculum Commission, June, 1962.

Stanford Achievement Test, Intermediate I Battery. New York: Harcourt Brace Jovanovich, 1965.

Sugarman, Daniel, and Rolaine Hochstein. *Seven Stories for Growth*. New York: Pitman Publishing Corporation, 1962.

Taba, Hilda. *Teacher's Handbook for Elementary Social Studies*, Introductory Edition. Palo Alto, California: Addison-Wesley Publishing Company, 1967.

Tanck, Marlin L. "Teaching Concepts, Generalizations, and Constructs." Chapter 5 of *Social Studies Curriculum Development: Prospects and Problems*, 39th yearbook of the National Council for Social Studies, Dorothy McClure Fraser, ed. Washington: NEA publication, 1969, pp. 99-138.

Thomas, R. Murry, and Dale L. Brubaker, eds. *Teaching Elementary Social Studies: Readings*. Belmont, California: Wadsworth Publishing Co., 1972.

Udall, Stewart. "*Ecological Balance*." Association for Childhood International, 1968.

Vander Zanden, James. *Sociology: A Systematic Approach*. New York: Ronald Press Co., 1970.

Van Dyke, Henry Thomas. *Youth and the Drug Problem*. Boston: Ginn and Company, 1970.

Wells, William. *A Becoming Curriculum*. Wayne, Michigan: ASSIST Center, Wayne County Independent School District, 1969.

Whitehead, Alfred North. *The Aims of Education and Other Essays*. New York: Macmillan Company, 1929.

Wilson, John, Norman Williams, and Barry Sugarman. *Introduction to Moral Education*. London: Penguin Books, 1967.

Wolk, Donald J., ed. *Drugs and Youth*. Washington, D.C.: NCSS, 1971.

Womack, James C. *Discovering the Structure of Social Studies*. New York: Benziger Brothers, 1966.

Zadrozny, John T. *Dictionary of Social Sciences*. Washington, D.C.: Public Affairs Press, 1959.

INDEX

Numbers in italic indicate pages on which complete references are listed.